STRETCHING THE HEAVENS

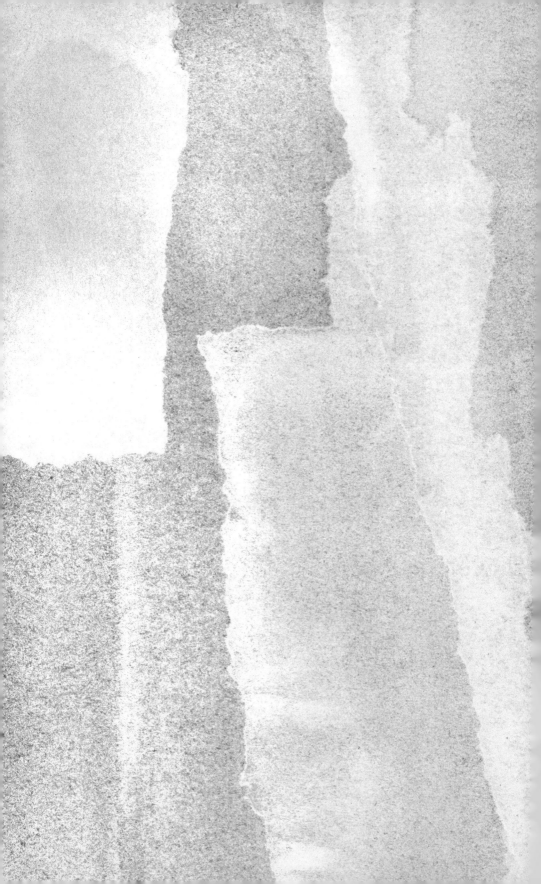

STRETCHING
THE HEAVENS

The Life of Eugene England

and the Crisis of Modern Mormonism

TERRYL L. GIVENS

THE UNIVERSITY OF NORTH CAROLINA PRESS | CHAPEL HILL

This book was published with the assistance of the
Anniversary Fund of the University of North Carolina Press.

Designed by April Leidig
Set in Whitman by Copperline Book Servces, Inc.
Manufactured in the United States of America

The University of North Carolina Press has been a
member of the Green Press Initiative since 2003.

Jacket photograph of Eugene England in 1985
courtesy Jennifer Georgia England.

Library of Congress Cataloging-in-Publication Data
Names: Givens, Terryl, author.
Title: Stretching the heavens : the life of Eugene England
and the crisis of modern Mormonism / Terryl Givens.
Description: Chapel Hill : The University of North Carolina
Press, 2021. | Includes bibliographical references and index.
Identifiers: LCCN 2021003504 | ISBN 9781469664330 (cloth ; alk. paper) |
ISBN 9781469664347 (ebook)
Subjects: LCSH: England, Eugene. | Mormons—Biography. | Mormon
Church—History—20th century. | LCGFT: Biographies.
Classification: LCC BX8695.E54 G58 2021 | DDC 289.3092 [B]—dc23
LC record available at https://lccn.loc.gov/2021003504

To Doug and Gail
fellow travelers

I don't know why I bother to defend myself with a single example,
seeing that it's the generally accepted privilege of theologians
to stretch the heavens . . . like tanners with a hide.
—Erasmus, *In Praise of Folly*

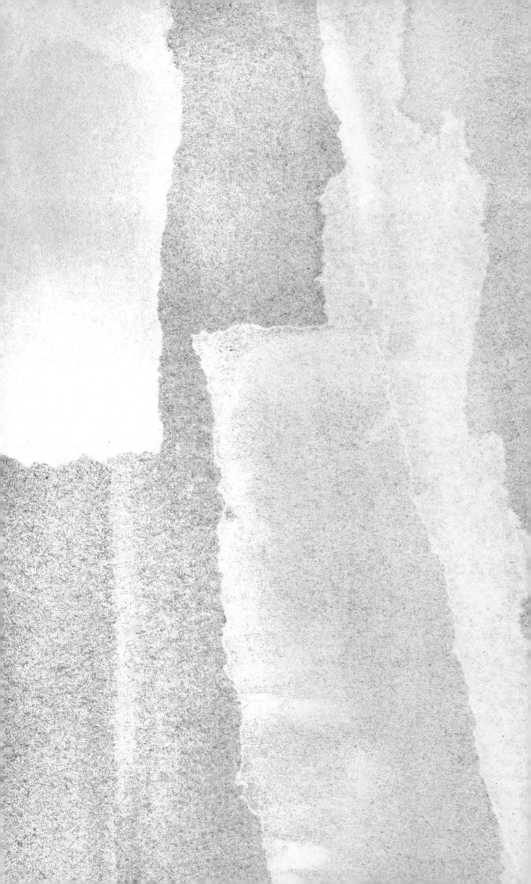

CONTENTS

Preface xiii

Introduction
A Polarizing Disciple 1

1
A Safe Valley 5

2
A Mountain in the Ocean:
Mission to Samoa 27

3
Stanford and Activism 39

4
Dialogue 63

5
A Mormon among the Lutherans 95

6
History, Hollywood, and
a Theologian Out of Season 109

7
Crossing Jordan:
Brigham Young University at Last 133

8

Heresy, Orthodoxy, and
the Perils of Provocation 149

9

England as Essayist 183

10

Fraying of the Fabric 199

11

J'accuse!
Beginning of the End 227

12

The Writing on the Wall 253

13

Legacy:
A Dangerous Discipleship 275

Notes 285

Index 323

FIGURES

The young Eugene England 11

The Downey, Idaho, farm boy 18

England in chemistry class 21

"Hello Dance" 23

Samoan missionaries 29

Newly commissioned Air Force lieutenant 40

Family at Stanford 92

Faribault, Minnesota, chapel 99

Provo, Utah, home 158

Assassination attempt on Pope John Paul II 177

Food for Poland rally 178

Study abroad group 249

England and Charlotte 251

Last day at BYU 259

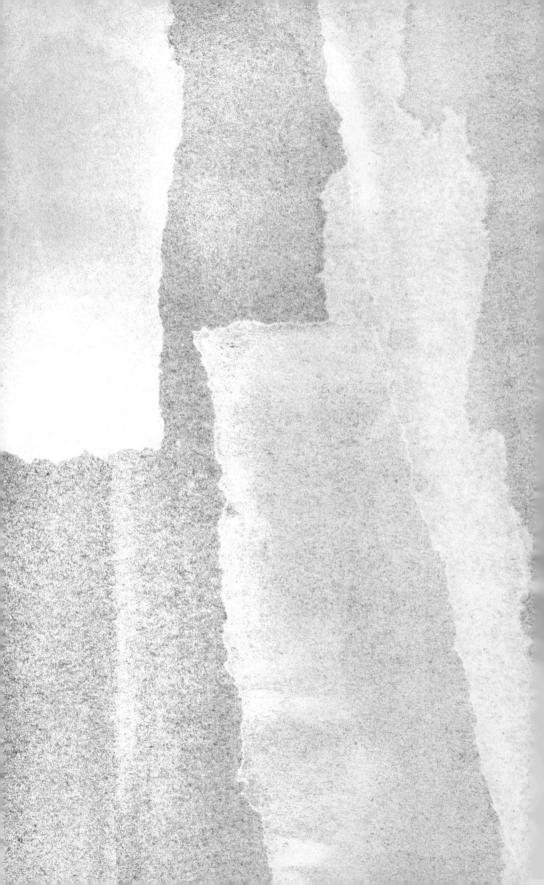

PREFACE

IN SEPTEMBER 2001, days before the attack on the World Trade Center, I was called as a bishop of a Latter-day Saint congregation in Richmond, Virginia. News came to me of the passing, three weeks earlier, of Eugene England, but I was consumed with my new calling and, along with the world, distracted by the devastation in New York. Even so, I felt the loss of England acutely. I had met him on few but memorable occasions over preceding years. I had known his work since my youth, had been influenced by his variety of thoughtful faith, and was flattered—as a young, untenured professor—by his interest in and support for my own work. I was therefore doubly saddened by the loss of a powerful voice in my religious tradition, and by the loss of a promising mentor and someone I would have cherished as a personal friend, I was sure.

A few years later, after I was established as a scholar and writer, his widow, Charlotte, contacted me, wanting to discuss a project she had in mind. The day is still vivid in my memory: it was spring, we sat in the backyard. The England home was legendary as the venue for informal soirees that had attracted over many years a lively circle of students, poets, and many of the leading lights of Latter-day Saint intellectual culture. The air seemed rife with a gathering of ghosts as we talked and sipped fresh lemonade. She explained that she would like me to undertake the biography of her late husband. I had several projects of my own, but most dissuasive to me was the generational divide. England had any number of contemporaries who knew him, loved him, and were more accomplished scholars than I. Anyone who knows Charlotte will understand how difficult it is to refuse her request—but I did, recommending more quali-fied candidates.

In April 2016, on a trip to Utah, word came to me that Charlotte was again soliciting my involvement in an England biography. A few tentative beginnings had been made by other scholars, but no finished product was on the horizon. With the distance of a decade, I had come to more fully appreciate not just the man and his legacy but also his place at the nexus of cultural conflicts and historic transformations within the church that deserved chronicling and elu-cidation. His life seemed emblematic not just of a personally fraught spiritual journey but also of a watershed in the collision of faithful discipleship and a secular onslaught that had its own particular coloring in the church of the later twentieth century. I learned that over 200 boxes of materials were now catalogued and available in the Eugene England collection at the University of Utah. In addition, Charlotte agreed to make available to me Gene's personal journals, mission diary, and extensive correspondence, files, clippings, and memorabilia not available in the archived collection. In addition, her son Mark shared dozens of hours of interviews he had conducted with England over a period of years. Dan Wotherspoon also generously shared extensive materials and recordings he had collected as a researcher doing his own biographical work. Although it took more than ten years, I am pleased that Charlotte's persistence was successful: England's story needed to be told, and I am grateful for all those who contributed their efforts and resources to make this book possible.

The Eugene England Papers were meticulously organized by his granddaughter Charlotte, who graciously oriented me to the archive. Copies of other documents are in the collection of Dan Wotherspoon (DW-C), whom I also thank for giving me access. Special thanks also to Jody England Hansen for help with photographs, and to my research assistants, Garrett Maxwell, Luke Lyman, and Calvin Burke, for tracking down numerous sources.

INTRODUCTION

A POLARIZING DISCIPLE

I knew again that I have no earthly city, no dwelling place. No country, no
church, no university, no journal, no movement, can ever be my home.
—England, "Finding Myself in the Sixties"

We need to grow up in our concept of salvation and consider how to learn from
experience to be adventuresome, self-correcting pilgrims in this great universe.
—England, journal entry, 10 January 1997

When I last saw Eugene England, he was in a wheelchair in the last stages
of a terrible death from brain cancer. He had been a vigorous, high-energy
sixty-eight, with a thick shock of brown hair that made him look two decades
younger. On this day, he was bald, emaciated, and weak. I remembered my
first encounter with him just a few years before. Young, untenured, I had been
invited by Gene to speak in a lecture series he initiated at Utah Valley University. After a painful exile from his beloved Brigham Young University, he had
secured a spot as writer in residence, and there created what some consider
the country's first Mormon studies program.[1] On this occasion, delivering my
remarks, I found the audience was not entirely receptive, and a sharply worded
question left me perilously mute: suddenly, I felt a gentle hand on my back. "I
believe," England interposed, "I believe Terryl answered that question in his
chapter on . . . ," then he slipped back to his seat leaving me to segue comfortably into a full response. That was the Gene England, known to thousands of
friends and colleagues and students as "the most Christ-like man I knew."

A different Gene England was known to many others. "This guy's a rene-
gade; he's off the reservation," was one student's initial impression. "There

was something dangerous about Gene."[2] A fellow teacher in the Church Educational System (CES) wrote to tell him, "I just want you to know that not everyone agrees with you and I'm one of them. You've been writing for twenty years as if you knew all the answers; maybe you should just be quiet for twenty years."[3]

Few figures in the modern Church of Jesus Christ of Latter-day Saints (LDS) left such a profound influence institutionally as well as personally—while being as divisive and variously appraised. He was the most conspicuous emblem of the liberal, intellectual wing of the church ("How do you manage to bear up so gracefully under being a symbol?" asked a friend).[4] He was the principal force behind the founding of Mormonism's most influential journal—still likely the most widely read unofficial organ in the church. He was the prime mover behind the founding of a self-conscious Mormon literature, as well as the larger field of Mormon studies—which now has a slew of programs and chairs in America and abroad. He founded the Association for Mormon Letters (AML), and was the church's most eloquent practitioner of the personal essay, a form he promoted as uniquely suited to a literary discipleship. Finally, by virtue of his propensity for finding himself in a conflicted public posture, England came to embody, in a painful and costly, agonistic way, the uneasy tension between conscience and authority. If it is a tension without resolution, that is a fact of existence that derives from a Latter-day Saints' unique reading of the Fall—a reading that England learned and lived to his own personal hurt.

The founding myth of monotheism positions the human at the intersection of competing cosmic forces of Good and Evil. God's injunction to remain true and faithful to his command, "Eat not of the forbidden tree," is countermanded by the cunning serpent, who incites Eve to disobedience and prideful rebellion. According to this, the first biblical etiology—an account of our present predicament and essential nature—a continual war is waged against and within us, enticing us to the Good or to the Evil that lies all around us to test, try, and assert dominion over us. Or so run 2,000 years of sermonizing on the story of "man's first disobedience, and the fruit of that forbidden Tree."[5]

The Church of Jesus Christ of Latter-day Saints' many theological innovations and nonconformities offer no more profound and consequential challenge to orthodoxy than its rewriting of the Eden narrative. In this reading, Adam and Eve are commanded to abstain from the fruit. *And* they are commanded to multiply, which procreative duty is dependent, in the Latter-day Saint version, on *eating* that very fruit they are forbidden to touch. The fruit is also explicitly associated, in the Genesis text, with beauty, goodness, and wisdom. Indeed, consequent to their ingestion of the fruit, God readily acknowledges that it has aided, not retarded, a godly ascent: They have "become as one of us," he observes.[6] Christian commentators early and late, reacting incredulously to those words, dismiss them out of hand. In saying he "has become as one of us . . . God was mocking Adam," explained the fourth-century theologian Ephrem the Syrian.[7] Hundreds of years later, the commentator on Genesis Andrew Willet agreed that the Lord "derides their folly," "speak[ing] ironically." Reformers Phillip Melanchton, Peter Vermigli, and Konrad Pellikan all employed the term *irony* as well to explain away the plain meaning of the text.[8] John Chrysostom went further and simply denies the accuracy of the passage, since it is obvious, he wrote, that "they did not become gods" *or* "receive the knowledge of good and evil."[9]

Latter-day Saints, by contrast, take the words literally, and as vindication that, when confronted with two competing Goods, Eve chose the greater. LDS scripture is unambiguous on this point, capturing Eve's rapture in the aftermath of the excruciating decision in a psalmic celebration: "And Eve, his wife, . . . was glad, saying: Were it not for our transgression we never should have had seed, and never should have known good and evil, and the joy of our redemption, and the eternal life which God giveth unto all the obedient."[10] Latter-day Saint apostle John A. Widtsoe gave the following theological explanation: "In life all must choose at times. Sometimes two possibilities are good; neither is evil. Usually however one is of greater import than the other. When in doubt each must choose that which concerns the good of others—the greater law—rather than that which chiefly benefits ourselves—the lesser law. That was the choice made in Eden."[11] Eugene England recognized this innovation on an old theme, which differentiated his tradition's theology of a fortunate fall from "any of the Judaic or Christian theologies or modern philosophies derived from it. . . . We must eat of the tree of knowledge of good and evil and thus inevitably sin and suffer and be suffered for to know the joy of redemption and growth."[12]

In some versions of Greek drama, a tragic situation arises not when Good comes into conflict with Evil but when the challenge to Good comes from another version of the Good with an equal claim upon us. In a crowded universe of ideal values claiming absolute preeminence, noble actors will inevitably encounter ethical values in violent opposition, "in a state of internecine warfare. It is like a house divided against itself, a contest between the family and the state, or one ideal against another, represented by a struggle between two people, or even within a single individual."[13]

Latter-day Saint Restoration theology posits just such a crisis as the founding mythos of human life on this mortal crucible called earth. The lesson is a sobering one—more fraught perhaps than a simple contest between demon and angel perched on opposite shoulders: the essence of the mortal probation, readers of Latter-day Saint scripture learn, will be a set of recurring scenarios in which the choice between competing Goods will try faith and rend hearts.

In the realm of Christian discipleship, unfolding within the framework of institutional forms, one particular version of this Greek tragedy has recurrently played out when an individual's moral imperatives collide with church teachings. Eugene England was nothing if not a devout Latter-day Saint, who never doubted the divine origins and mandate of the Church of Jesus Christ. And yet, a number of his ethical commitments brought him into frequent conflict with his church's leadership. England's religious dilemma was a conflict between two laudable values: in his case, loyalty to conscience and loyalty to an institution he believed was divinely led. This conflict was a delayed echo, with specifically Latter-day Saint dimensions, of the modernist crisis that had erupted in both Catholic and Protestant contexts at the century's beginning. As in the former cases, questions of authority and a growing historical consciousness were at the foreground—however, Latter-day Saint construction of both made the sixties and seventies, rather than the aughts and teens, the critical decades.

A Greek tragedy may be overblown as a template for England's life. He was, after all, a highly successful teacher and writer, a beloved husband, friend, and father, who died a painful and premature—though hardly ignominious—death. And he had a lasting impact for good on the tradition he so loved. Invoking such a dramatic template is an invitation to a more generous appraisal of both parties involved in certain classes of religious conflict, where equally laudable values, and not opposing moral poles, define the struggle.

1

A SAFE VALLEY

You may suffer a lot, but you live intensely. Your life may be among
the best things you have to offer and that story must be told.
—Richard Bushman to England, 18 March 1992

When people look back to the Church in the 70s and 80s,
they may well find you the dominant voice.
—Claudia Bushman to England, 1 November 1989

PIONEER BACKGROUNDS

I came from [a] rather cold, emotionally reserved, largely Anglo-Saxon
family background.—England, "No Cause, No Cause"

Gene England's father, George Eugene England, was born in 1904. He came
from Latter-day Saint stock, but he traced his line back to the Buchanan family,
who were awarded a massive land grant by the king of England that included
the island of Manhattan. The family story was that some or all of the estate
passed through the possession of President James Buchanan, who bequeathed
it to his posterity. George Sr. learned of the alleged bequest in 1933, the year
of Eugene's birth, and was told he would need to prove his connection to the
Buchanan family to inherit his share—over a quarter of a million dollars for
each descendent, by his reckoning ($5 million in 2020 dollars). The story had
the ring of more fantasy than fact, but George recorded it as faithful family history. "The hunt for descendants stopped when several attorneys for the family
died or mysteriously disappeared," he wrote, compounding the sensationalism.
"J. P. Morgan and others had a hand in that. They didn't want to give up their

hold on the properties in New York City." As a Latter-day Saint, however, some good came out of the united effort to prove the family connections: "Mother said that it accomplished one thing: everyone showed up on her doorstep with their genealogy done."[1]

The England family's Latter-day Saint roots ran deep. Thomas England was born in Somerset, England, in 1860. Converted to the Church of Jesus Christ, he emigrated to the States, pulled a handcart across the plains and settled in Plain City, Utah. There, his wife died soon after giving birth to George William. Thomas remarried, but George William never took to his new step-mother, though he stayed around long enough to support the family while Thomas returned to England as a missionary. When Thomas came home, George William set out to try working for his relatives in Moreland, a small town a few miles outside of Blackfoot in the Snake River Valley of southeast Idaho. He found a spot of land to work owned by the Abram Hatch family, who had a beautiful but frail daughter, Martha Jane. George and Martha fell in love and settled in the area. Eventually he found work on the Union Pacific Railroad with a bridge-building gang and raised his young family on a small farm he rented from his father. In 1904, George Eugene—father of Eugene England Jr.—was born.

George Eugene lived the hardscrabble life of an Idaho farm boy, tending animals, weeding crops, and watching his father carefully husband the precious irrigation water. Rights of access were a frequent cause of contention— George Eugene returned home one day to find a near tragic scene at the water gate: "I came home and found Mother and Dad down at the irrigation ditch. Dad's forehead was split and bleeding. He had gone over and turned on the water. [Mr. Bankhead] told him that it wasn't time for his turn yet, that he wasn't through. Dad said, 'Well, the time's up, so it's my turn now.' Bankhead swung a shovel at Dad. He threw his arms up and glanced part of the blow off, but it had cut a gash in his forehead. I could remember Mother weeping and holding on to dad, and making his way down to the house. . . . I had never seen anything so violent before in my life."[2] On good days, George Eugene would fish at the local pond for suckers and herring, using wire nooses at the end of poles, rather than fishhooks. He would pass on to Gene an abiding love of fishing. (One of his friends described his passion: "Typically I follow Gene on a stream. He always seems to be in the lead; he tends to vault over rock dams, ledges, and log jams. He's been this way all his life." He also remembered how Gene stalked fish like they were tigers, and emitted wild war whoops when he landed one.)[3]

When George Eugene was eleven, his father, George William, then homesteading 160 acres south of Pocatello, turned his hand to wheat farming. At first, he did so long range, but then he quit his job and, with young George at his side, he moved onto the homestead to work it in earnest. After a year, he traded his farm in Moreland for 80 more acres in Bannock Valley, and moved his family into a one-room shanty. These were years, George Eugene remembered, of "hard work and deprivation." Wild sage hens supplemented a meager diet, enriched on lucky occasions by their eggs. Meat was one pig killed yearly and portioned out as long as possible, supplemented with water gravy when milk was scarce. The nearest water was an irrigation ditch more than a mile distant. Winters were fierce enough that a wintry night blast could freeze horses where they stood—which happened to several mustangs in a herd his cowpoke uncles were trying to expand.

Such a life could easily be romanticized through the mists of memory, but George remembered most acutely the humiliation of it all. "When I was a young man, we were always poor and in debt and never had anything extra. I felt almost like the down-trodden, poor, white people that I saw in the south when I went on my mission in later years. I was embarrassed because I didn't have clothes that matched ordinary people's clothes. When I was in the seventh and eighth grades, I was wearing a pair of knee pants and long stockings which were completely out of style. I wore out the seat of the pants, and I had to go home from school."

It was a mode of life to build character. If it forged George's determination to make his humiliating poverty a distant memory, it also helps explain the ambitions he would harbor for his talented, but professionally stymied, son. The family next settled into a home in nearby Arimo, and George William continued his work for the railroad—now as a painter—and left the running of the farm to fifteen-year-old George. George Eugene's religious upbringing he described as a kind of casual Mormonism, and he found his father a severe and emotionally distant man. As a teen, young George found his avocation on the town softball team, which played on Sundays. Challenged by the bishop to quit the team so he could be ordained a priest, he made the decision to do so. (Young Latter-day Saint men are typically ordained priests—in a lay priesthood—in their midteens.) He dated that moment, 7 May 1922, as the day of his commitment to a life of gospel devotion. "It is right for us to commit ourselves and live up to those commitments," he said of his decision with plainspoken eloquence.[4]

Not least of the fruits of his faithfulness, he wrote, was his attendance at a stake conference where he met his future wife, Dora—though he didn't take much notice of her at the time. He'd been quite a ruckus-rouser to this point

in his life, but after his church commitment, the most trouble he got into was
when he and his friend tricked half a dozen younger long-haired classmates
into coming to a meeting, where they were held down one at a time to have
their hair clipped to what George and his coconspirators thought was a more
appropriate length. Later the victims returned the favor, tracking George and
his friend down and giving them reverse Mohawks. The feud escalated until
the school board had to intervene.

George didn't return to school in 1922 and decided he'd had enough of farming. His father told him that if he left home, he should not come back. That
wasn't particularly dissuasive to a boy who'd known nothing but grinding poverty, intermittent schooling, and backbreaking labor. He had prospects, he fig-
ured. "Dad didn't understand me," he later explained. "The Lord didn't put me
here to starve. He put me here, where there were opportunities to do things.
You can go out and do it if you will. I decided I was going to do it. So I got on
the train . . . and left home."[5] For Pocatello. He didn't comment on the irony
that the first job he acquired was the same one his father had held: painting
coaches for the railroad, laying on gold leaf and lettering for 29 cents an hour.

He labored hard, prospered at work, and lived a sober and devout life. Three
years later, recovering in surgery after a bout of appendicitis, he had a vision
of the Savior that left him more deeply rooted than ever in his faith. Feeling
undervalued two years into his four-year apprenticeship with the railroad, he
left for better pay and opportunity in Montana. There he was forced out of his
job when he wouldn't join the union, so he became a traveling salesman based
in Salt Lake City. The next year, he was offered a good wage to come back to
the railroad as foreman and realized he was at a critical juncture: twenty-two
and not even possessing a high school education. He decided to return home,
go back to school, get his diploma, and aim for something higher and better. He
financed the rest of his education by selling the pelts of badgers and muskrats
he trapped, and doing farm chores for his father while he finished two years
of schooling in one.

His religious commitments made and his educational plans proceeding
apace, George set his eyes on marriage. His thoughts turned to the comely
blonde he had met a few years back, sixteen-year-old Dora, daughter of one of
the wealthiest families in Downey, Idaho. (Gossip was that George acquired
his wealth by that marriage; the truth was rather different.) They courted over
the next several months. The fall of 1928, a year after graduation, found George
again in the hospital recovering from minor surgery. And once again, he had
a visionary experience. "The Savior appeared to me, glorified in white. He
assured me that I was accepted in spite of my youthful transgressions, and

that I would be blessed in serving him. It was the same in every detail to the experience I had had four years before, with one great exception: Dora Rose Hartvigsen was at the side of the Savior, and he presented her to me as a gift from him."[6]

But first he needed more financial security. With his father, he started a paint contracting business that ran successfully for a few years. Dora's father offered him money to invest, but he declined the offer. No sooner had he saved enough money for college than his bishop called him to serve an evangelizing mission. George asked Dora's father for permission to marry, presented her with a ring, then left to serve in the Southern States mission from December 1929 until February 1932. While he was serving, Dora graduated from the Utah State Agricultural College. George returned with $75 left to his name and resumed painting and farm labor while Dora taught school. By October they figured they had saved and waited long enough, so they traveled to Logan, Utah, to be married in the Latter-day Saint temple and for George to start at Utah State.

In Logan, with George studying, painting, and doing custodial work, Dora became pregnant. In the afterglow of a successful mission, a happy marriage to his patient bride, and preparing for a more prosperous future than he had yet known, George was overjoyed. "I was impressed to promise the Lord that if he would bless us with a son, I would dedicate him for the work of the kingdom. I would see that he wanted not for material things of the world if he would accept. I read in the Old Testament about Hannah promising the Lord that if He would give her a son, she would dedicate him to the Lord. Samuel, who became a great prophet, inspired me to make such a promise."[7] On 22 July 1933, in the little white-painted cinderblock hospital in Logan, Utah, the anxiously desired blessing came: Dora delivered a beautiful baby boy. They called him George Eugene England Jr.

That summer of 1933 was the Great Depression's worst. George worked as a carpenter, bridge builder, and painter—anything he could do to keep food on the table. Still, his small family suffered less than most of their countrymen. George's brother remembered a traveling insurance salesman from back East telling him, "'You people out here in the West don't know what a depression is. You have plenty of food. You might not have money, but you had plenty of food and you traded with the stores, produce for clothes and all that kind of stuff.' That's what Dad did. Instead of taking money for his paint jobs he'd get grain and hay to feed our cow. . . . Then he'd take the grain down to the mill and they'd make cereal out of it and flour. . . . So we really didn't have the depression. . . . We ate well."[8]

The first Sunday of September, the day of young Eugene's baby blessing, Dora's parents drove the sixty miles from Downey, Idaho, in their gray model A. They brought with them a jar of boiled cream, some garden greens, and a sack of potatoes. In that evening's worship service, after the administration of the sacrament (the eucharist), Jacob Larson (J. L.) Hartvigsen, George Eugene, and three men of the bishopric held the infant before the congregation, while George gave him a blessing for a long and righteous life and formally bestowed his name, George Eugene England Jr. Most of his life he would be called Gene Jr. by his parents and sister, "Little Gene" by his mother's family, and "Slifus," a Norwegian nickname, by his granddad.

After graduation in 1936, George Sr. moved to a small house in McCammon, Idaho, where he taught shop and general science at the local school. It adjoined a large pond next to the railroad tracks. Dora read to her son for hours. She covered the front room floor with a linoleum sheet and let Gene play with a toy cannon that ignited wooden matches and shot them through the air. One day he shot a swan from the back porch.

The next year, in a move that would foreshadow his own son's career, George Sr. took a position with the Church Educational System to teach seminary in Downey, twenty miles south. Seminary, a daily hour of LDS gospel instruction during regular school hours, had been a program of the church for over twenty years. A replacement was needed for an instructor whose views had been deemed too unorthodox by the leadership. (The instructor had been teaching that Christ was a great teacher but not divine. He alleged that he had been persuaded by the writings of Obert Clark Tanner, an enormously influential figure in the Latter-day Saint community. Tanner, author of a popular Sunday school manual, was himself quite liberal, but he never explicitly denied the divinity of Christ.) George signed on and taught for three years.

The home in which Gene spent his earliest years was a ramshackle cottage owned by Dora's father, the hot-tempered Norwegian they called J. L. George had to shore up the floors with supports and reroof it to make it habitable. George remembered little Gene, not yet four years old, bringing him his lunch. By spring, George had saved enough to begin transforming the cottage into a real home—with an indoor bath among other improvements. George worked for J. L. during farming season and taught school at other times. The hope was that George's work investment would lead eventually to his inheritance of the farm.

About this time, Gene had a prophecy pronounced upon his head by Bryant S. Hinckley, father of the future church president Gordon B. Hinckley. Bryant was known as a kind of inspired phrenologist—a "pretty good predictor

Eugene England at three or four years old.
(Courtesy Charlotte England)

on people's heads." Gene had come through a traumatic birth process "looking like an upside-down ice cream cone," with a deep sharp ridge through the middle of his head. J. L. thought the abnormality deserved a reading, and took him to Bryant. The old man did a careful examination from crown to brow, then pronounced his verdict: "I pity the parents who have to raise this boy."[9]

The next summer, George dug out a basement by hand to add a furnace room and bedroom. They soon needed it, for in 1938, Gene's sister, Ann Christine, was born. George and Dora had always hoped for a large family, but a childhood fall had injured Dora's uterus, and their doctor was surprised at her two successful pregnancies and told them any more were unlikely. For the next seven years, Gene was a farm boy, and he reminisced fondly about this time:

> I grew up in a safe valley. The years five through twelve, when we are most sensuously attached to the landscape and when, I think, the foundations of identity are firmly laid, I lived in gardens and wheatfields. They

had been claimed a generation before from desert knolls and sagebrush flats but were now constantly fruitful, watered by canals or sufficient rain for dryland grains and surrounded by low mountains that were protective, inviting, never fearful. We hiked into the mountains for deer and trout to supplement our meat, eaten sparingly from the pigs butchered each fall, or sometimes we rode out to look for horses that had strayed and, once a year, on the Sabbath nearest the 24th of July, with all the Sunday School, we went in cars to have classes out of doors and eat a picnic together and explore those safe canyons of Cherry Creek or Nine Mile that brought us our water.[10]

Downey was "a prototypical Mormon village," in England's view, settled a few decades after the Saints entered the region by pioneers who moved north from Utah's Cache Valley. "The ideal place to make saints," Brigham Young said of such towns, though England could only say that this held true in the case of his best friend, Bert Wilson. Wilson remembered Downey as an isolated oasis, its "thinly populated streets," hung in wintertime with meager strings of lights that whipped back and forth on blustery nights.[11]

This first year in Downey was the time when Gene, called Eugene the first dozen years of his life, met the boy who would become his closest lifelong friend. They started first grade together in the fall of 1939, in the brand-new Downey Elementary schoolhouse. Showing the precipitous nature that characterized his entire life, Gene no sooner met Bert Wilson than he invited him to his seventh birthday party. Happy to be asked, Bert appeared on schedule with his gift. Unfortunately, the party was more aspiration than actual event; Dora was unprepared, Bert was unexpected, and Gene was delighted, since once the boys were together, mothers were easily convinced to approve an impromptu sleepover.

Well into the night, camped in the front yard, Gene rose and began sprinting in circles, to Bert's amazement. Gene explained that he was unsettled by the stars, by thoughts of infinity, and the disturbing possibility that the universe might not have existed. Why did anything exist? The precocious spiritual vertigo would trouble him well into his adulthood.

Sleepovers notwithstanding, it was a few years before Bert broke into Gene's secret society of friends—who called themselves the DD Daggers, complete with club insignia and arm tattoos (ink pen only; after all, they were Mormon boys). Gang regalia for these "sons of Tarzan" was shorts, no shirts, and hunting knives they carried through the orchards and barns of Downey.

With Bert, Gene hiked the Downey hills, shooting at jackrabbits with sling shots, exploring ancient car bodies in an abandoned junkyard, playing cowboys and Indians and ending up at nearby Downatta, with its hot springs and pools, for a swim. Like most farm boys, they got into their share of scrapes. Clifton Jolley, who only knew Gene later in life, once envied Bert his childhood friendship with England. Bert replied, "No, it was awful! Gene didn't tell you about shooting the county commissioner's goose, did he? We went out shooting, and one of us killed the goose. I screamed out, 'Oh no! We've killed the commissioner's goose!' I threw up and he was hysterical."[12]

Being as intellectually gifted as Bert and Gene were, their boredom at school probably got them into more than their share of trouble. Bert remembered one grading cycle when he scored an A in every subject except for the C in "deportment." Gene's was likewise nearly perfect. All A's, except for the D in deportment. One school friend saw all the marks of Gene's future conflicts in their earliest form: Gene and Bert were constantly getting themselves into trouble, he remembered. They'd act up or engage in secret mischief, but they always were found out. The only difference between them, Bert reminisced, was that Gene always seemed to be surprised when the chickens came home to roost. He never thought through the consequences.[13] "How could he have been so naive?" wondered Ed Geary. "Just a little calculation about self-interest would have avoided the trouble. But a calculating Gene England would not have been Gene England."[14] Such naivete would plague him throughout his life, even as the stakes grew higher. "In [his] enduring innocence," Bert would later write, Gene "did not always have eyes to see or ears to hear."[15]

As Bert remembered, Gene tormented their poor teacher, Miss Gilbert, and after school hours he "pulled the legs off a sizable number of the water skippers in the canal behind his house."[16] At the same time, his actions were never marked by malice or real rebellion. The one time he used foul language on the school grounds, it was apparent to the embarrassed bystanders that Gene was oblivious of what his crude language meant. Gene read comic books and listened to the radio and played childhood pranks. At recess he played marbles with the other boys (both ringers and ligers). But he was also growing into a thoughtful and studious young man. Downey was a small farming community, leagues away from any city lights. Nights were crisp and clear, and in the summer, he and Bert would frequently throw a sleeping bag down outside and gaze at the stars. On moonless nights, the Milky Way was vibrant with stars, and Gene's conversation would turn somber and speculative.

By 1940, Gene's father was ready to move from sharecropping to ownership—and a violent confrontation provided the catalyst. Gene remembered awakening to the sound of loud voices in the kitchen. J. L. held a chair over his head, ready to bring it down on his son-in-law. "Go ahead and hit me," George was urging, with Dora in between, trying to stave off a broken head. They had been arguing about management of the farm. George was doing most of the work, the undisciplined J. L. running around in his truck and planting his wheat fields too late for the crop to ripen by harvest time. A horse J. L. was managing had just tipped a drill and broken a tongue, which George attributed to his poor horsemanship. J. L. let loose a string of expletives as he waved the chair. George ordered him out of the house, dissolved the partnership, and headed for Pocatello, where he found work as a painter for a new government housing project. A repentant J. L. begged George to return and he did, but on the condition that J. L. let him buy the farm outright, using funds saved from his teaching job.

George was a skilled farmer and immediately set out to enlarge his holdings. He took over payments on a foreclosed neighboring farm and added 440 acres, for a total of over 1,100. He smoothed out ravines and gullies, consolidated his plots, and vastly increased the farm's efficiency, using new dry-farming methods he'd picked up as a student at Utah State. These included planting new strains of wheat and leaving stubble to rot rather than burn, thus enhancing soil quality. By the time Gene was eight, he was working full summer days alongside his father. George Sr. operated the twenty-four-foot rod weeder, with a revolving arm that ran beneath the soil, clearing out weeds and smoothing the surface. Gene sat on the back, cushioned with a brown corduroy pillow, ready to jump off and clear the mechanism whenever it clogged with rubble. George Sr. borrowed money for a $2,000 grain elevator and storage bin on the railroad line, so he could hold and sell when prices were good. J. L. doubted this risk-taking, but wartime conditions raised the price of wheat—a lot— and the government abolished allotments, freeing up more land for commercial farming. As a consequence, the price rose in those years from an average of 52 cents a bushel to $1.50 and even $3.00. In just two years, the farm was paid off.[17]

These were also the years when Gene England's spiritual foundations were firmly laid. The first religious experience to which he would refer, and one that established an unshakeable faith in church leadership, occurred early in his childhood. At a stake conference, the apostle and future church president Harold B. Lee was speaking. George Sr. and Dora were near the front of the chapel with Gene and Ann, and Lee was discussing the days leading up to Christ's return. Dora was particularly moved, as Lee spoke of "how horrible they would be, especially for mothers with babies and young children." Lee "looked up into the heavens and he started praying for them," she recalled. "I could feel the spirit of the Holy Ghost settle over the whole congregation as if we could see angels. It was just a feeling that was beautiful and warm and I . . . wasn't the only one that felt it. Many did, and Eugene Jr. asked, 'Mother, what happened?' Then he turned to his Dad and said, 'What happened?'" Decades later, England would recall the episode in conversation with his son, Mark.[18] It was his first sensation of a porous veil separating this world from transcendent agencies and realities.

His mother's influence on his spiritual formation was deep. Dora was a woman of faith. Struck down in the flu pandemic of 1918, her miraculous recovery was attributed to priesthood ministrations, and she was convinced she'd had other dramatic recoveries from illness, similarly attended by priesthood blessings. The largest presence in Gene's life, however, was doubtless his father. And the most pivotal moment in laying his religious foundation seems to be, as he recollected, a farmer's simple prayer he overheard a few years later.

> One June morning when I was about eight, my father took me out into the young wheat on our lower 320-acre field and knelt and asked God to bless and protect the crop. I stood looking into my father's fiercely intent face as he knelt there. He grasped the wheat stalks in both hands and pledged again, as I had heard him in family prayers, to give all the crop, beyond our bare needs, to the Lord to use as he would, and he claimed protection from drought and hail and wind. Beside and in me I felt something more real than the wheat or the ground or the sun, something warm like the sun but warm inside my head and chest and bones, something like us but strange, thrilling, fearful, but safe. I first knew that experience as a frightening but awe-inspiring encounter with pure Being, but over time I have interpreted it in Mormon Christian terms. I have come to understand it as an assurance of Christ's approval of my father's consecration and thus a call to unconditional, universal mercy and generosity on my part, a feeling of responsibility that has never left me. It has become the sure ground of my beliefs and the touchstone by which I test all values.[19]

In William Wordsworth's autobiographical poem, the poet describes the foundational event in his particular poetic sensibility and Weltanschauung. One evening, having stolen a boat for a pleasure ride as young lad, a towering peak "upreared its head" from behind distant cliffs, as if in titanic pursuit. The further he rows, the larger the "grim shape" looms; the terrifying specter of the night, "it seemed, with purpose of its own and measured motion like a living thing, strode after me."[20] His conclusion shapes his life ever after: the physical and the moral universes operate in concert and sublime harmony. His act of "stealth and troubled pleasure" disturbed more than the glassy surface of a lake.

England, as a scholar of Romanticism, likely knew those verses. As he matured, the rudest awakening of his life would be the recognition that, as the philosopher Max Scheler wrote, the tragic nature of our universe centers on the precisely opposite state of affairs: the blind indifference of a material, terrestrial sphere to the moral worth of its inhabitants and their actions.[21] In his youth, however, England's perceptions were exactly aligned with Wordsworth's. "My earliest feelings about religion," he called these impressions. "I was quite young. Six or seven probably. I just remember having a very kind of profound conviction that the universe worked morally. If you went against it you suffered the consequences. And they did seem natural consequences." This was "a very strong feeling . . . confirmed by incident after incident."[22]

Gene's religious sensibility came to be focused on that personal God with whom he was convinced his father was communing in the wheat field. "My religion began with feelings. It was only later that they were confirmed with intellectual experience."[23] As a mature writer, Gene would return to that wheat field epiphany, rendering it poetically and extending his analysis of its significance:

> We drove from town just as the sun
> Squinted down left fork into our eyes.
> We stopped the truck and crossed the swale
> To the highest ridge on the lower field:
>
> The stalks still green, the heads just formed,
> Beards now turning silver-tan,
> Still and moist in the windless dawn,
> Closing calmly as we walked the rows.
>
> Plucking random heads, we counted and chewed
> The milky kernels. And then he knelt,
> Still grasping the wheat in fierce repose.
> I stood and watched his face. He said,
>
> "Thou art the Prince who holds my heart
> And gives my body power to make.
> The fruit is thine: this wheat, this boy;
> Protect the yield that we may live!"

And fear thrilled me on that hushed ground,
So that I grew beyond the wheat
And watched my father take his hold
On what endures behind the veil.[24]

"Later in reflecting on it I felt that it was akin to what I recognized as the spirit of the Savior. I don't think I was aware enough then to make that kind of indication that I was feeling that what my father was doing was right, consecrating his work and his profits to the Lord. That was a very moving and memorable experience that I've never forgot and it was a touch stone for the rest of my life. That feeling became the way I would measure everything—if it was in tune with that feeling. That was my way of testing if it was true, or connected with the Savior."[25]

Land and crops weren't the only things George Sr. consecrated. More than once, he told the story of the vow, Hannah-like, he had made before Gene's birth. "I prayed you into this world, my son. I wanted a son so bad, and when it looked like we would lose you, I pled with the Lord. I consecrated you to the Lord and promised you would never have to slave in the dirt like I did. I told the Lord I would work my fingers to the bone . . . if you could live and be a teacher and writer for the church."[26] Such consecration, a mingling of such sacrifice and expectation, would be an indelible burden that goes far to explain both the direction of Gene's aspirations and the trauma of his disappointments.

A year before the war's end George had paid off his farm. Gene was now eleven and running the elevator and hauling wheat as needed. He was supposed to run the machinery to convey the wheat up to the silo as it was dumped by a hauler. But he soon learned the pit would hold two loads of wheat. He could therefore run the auger and conveyer belts every other load. Gene remembered using the time in between to read books like *Kidnapped* and *The Black Arrow*.[27] His friends recalled, perhaps more typically, that the time between cycles was employed in terrific battles with Bert and the other boys in their gang using home-fashioned rubber guns that fired strips of inner tubes cut for the purpose. The elevator and machinery were the perfect setting, providing plenty of cover for stealth warfare. Sometimes they would venture as far as an abandoned flour mill on the other side of the tracks, for a new setting. On other occasions the boys would show their bravado by climbing the exterior of the four-story bins, using the metal support bands for footholds. On less adventuresome days Gene found time to spend at Bert's on the piano, practicing the theme from *The Third Man* (he never progressed much beyond that tune). Winters they would skate on the local canals. When he was old enough to

England the Downey, Idaho, farm boy.
(Courtesy Charlotte England)

drive, Gene became the worker trucking in the wheat from the farm, and Bert took over elevator duties.

One year (1940 or 1944), the apostle Spencer W. Kimball spoke in the Downey Stake, and changed the course of George Sr.'s life. Speaking movingly about his love for the "Lamanites" (a Book of Mormon designation the Saints applied to Native Americans), and the need for contributions to fund those who wanted to serve as missionaries, he profoundly touched George's heart. Under Dora's urging, he committed a considerable $80 monthly gift, the beginning of a lifelong investment in the church missionary program that would grow exponentially over the decades. By 1994, the interest on a $5 million bequest he had given the church was supporting over 1,500 missionaries a year—some 17,000 all told.[28] Such consecration, which blossomed amid very modest circumstances and only deepened with his growing resources, characterized a type of discipleship that Gene would both admire and inherit.

George Sr. also helped purchase chapels, provided education and job training for indigent members, and aided members going through difficult times. More than once, his and Dora's generosity left them short of funds themselves. "We give all our money away instead of using it for ourselves a little," complained Dora on one occasion. "Only one or two of our men, who owe for land, have paid, so we have been rather broke all summer."[29] (Years later, George Sr. and Dora also turned over immensely valuable Salt Lake property to Gene and Charlotte, but following his parents' pattern, they just deeded it over to the church, as they did with subsequent holdings they derived from his parents' corporation.)[30] In spite of his father's wealth and philanthropy, Gene showed no great interest in his father's business ventures; George Sr. frequently invested and traded on Gene's behalf, but Gene disposed of his assets so openhandedly that when he and his wife finally built their own home in Provo in 1976, they were happy to accept George Sr.'s offer of assistance ("It cost us over $30,000," the elder Eugene recorded).[31] George and Dora would also help Gene and his young family with housing and a car in their Palo Alto years.[32]

By 1945, the farm was thriving, George had bought out J. L.'s share, and he and Dora now decided on a major life change. Dora wanted Gene to have what she thought were the benefits of a city upbringing, and George saw business prospects. "It was a better opportunity for our children in school," explained Dora, "and we knew they were bright. We knew Eugene was very bright because when he was in grade school in Downey they would use him in plays. The high school would use him if they needed a young boy" because "he knew everybody's parts."[33] So they purchased a home on Redondo Avenue in Salt Lake City and moved in with twelve-year-old Gene and seven-year-old Ann. Gene entered Irving Junior High School. George would continue to run the farm in Downey for the next six years, with Gene helping out in the summer.

Gene continued to watch his father's consecration to the church. The church apostle John Widtsoe appointed George to supervise regional relief efforts for the European Saints after World War II. Soon he was overseeing the shipment of half a ton of goods every week. Gene would organize his own relief effort for suffering Poles, thirty-five years later. Though they lived selflessly and modestly, the family continued to prosper. Dora had excellent investment instincts, and she and George began a series of real estate purchases. One indulgence was a thirteen-and-a-half-foot fishing boat. Gene and his father would not always see eye to eye, but no difference would ever impede their fishing partnership.

At the junior high school, Gene quickly found a new circle of friends: Like Bert, they would be close throughout life. Gary Christensen (Chris), John Gary Maxwell (Max), and Floyd Astin. What bound them together was a shared love and healthy competitiveness in their academic pursuits. (Chris became a Rhodes scholar, Max an MD, and Floyd an attorney.) "Extraordinary friends," he called them, considering their influence on him to be profound during his formative years. They were friends "with whom I could share, really a lot, everything, physically and intellectually and spiritually. . . . We all went to firesides together, and talked, in very advanced ways, about spiritual matters for people that young. We learned about, not about world events really, but about literature, relationships, about the gospel, in very serious ways."[34] Those firesides, he later reminisced, were where he "first came to love the gospel intellectually."[35] Most days, the four friends walked together to the school that was just northwest of the Sugar House Prison (relocated to Draper in 1951). They went down the small Parley's Canyon creek that coursed westward through the Allen Park Aviary on Thirteenth East, through the southern edge of the campus of Westminster College, and then into the fringe of the business section of Sugar House.

One day, Gene was absent along with Chris and Floyd. In chemistry class that day, Max signed the roll for his absent friends. He also did the homework assignments for all three and turned them in with forged signatures. When the identically executed work was returned, Gene alone received an A. No question could remain in his friends' minds as to who the teacher's pet was. Gene didn't play on any sports team, but with his friends he was a keen tennis player, touch football player, and fast-moving, scrappy guard on the basketball court, as one friend described him. Summers Gene was still spending in Downey working on the farm, growing increasingly certain this was not the future he wanted. Floyd sometimes worked in the field alongside him.

In high school, most all the Latter-day Saint students enrolled in seminary, but Gene's participation was particularly intense. On Sunday evenings, they often had guest speakers. One frequent visitor was Adam Mickey Duncan, a civil rights activist concerned about the plight of African Americans in Utah. Many evenings ran overtime, as Duncan and England's circle of friends participated in discussions about the tension between their faith and the status of their Black brothers and sisters, who were at that time still denied priesthood and temple privileges in the LDS church (dating back to an 1852 ban that would be lifted in 1978). Max felt it was in these intense, intimate, and safe

High school yearbook photo of England in chemistry class.
(Courtesy Charlotte England)

circles that England first learned to probe for resolution of difficult issues between faith and conscience. But for now, orthodoxy still held him in its grasp.

England would remember that "more and more in my teenage years I fell in
love with the theology. . . . The ideas were not only consistent with each other
but consistent with what we are learning about human nature. When psychol-
ogy was telling us about human needs and how the gospel actually meets the
need for humans to be creative and to experience self-actualization, I found
that just really convincing and true to my own experience."[36]

His faith, shared by his close pals, kept him out of serious trouble—in ways
that could be humorous. Cruising State Street in a car one afternoon, they
picked up three attractive girls looking for a ride. Floyd remembered that,
"feeling a little frisky ourselves, we picked them up." With no real room in the
sedan, and no seatbelt laws, the obvious solution appealed to all concerned:

"The girls sat on our laps. After a few blocks, the girls were more frisky than we wanted to be, and they began to move in on us in a very amorous way. We were getting far more than we bargained for, and being frightened, we let them out of the car as soon as possible."[37]

When graduation came, the foursome celebrated with a freestyle ascent up the face of Mount Olympus, foolhardy and hair-raising for the unprepared amateurs. But they made it safely to the summit, before deciding to take the walking path back down. Then, days later and minus Chris, they embarked on a road trip through the Pacific Northwest along Highway 1, sleeping on beaches and vineyards, eating bakery bread and pilfered grapes, and feeling on the way home the afterglow of a shared rite of passage. Passing through Las Vegas, they wanted to try out a casino. Not surprisingly, the security guards did not recognize their new adult status, so obvious to and deeply felt by them, and they were turned away.

The next fall Gene enrolled at the University of Utah—and so did Max, both soon pledging the same fraternity. Initiation involved the typical male, scatological hazing: sliding naked and blindfolded across a detergent-drenched floor singing tunes and the like. They did their brothers the benefit of raising the fraternity's grade point average, but, finding no benefit to themselves, both dropped out soon after pledging. In those university years, the spiritual paths of the four began to diverge.

SNOW ANGELS AND THE "EAST HIGH DRAG"

> Charlotte was the first girl I kissed. The only girl I kissed. She was a freshman
> and I was a sophomore in College. I was eighteen or nineteen.
> —England, interview with Mark England

The friendship of Gene and Floyd Astin, one of his fellow DD Daggers, had continued throughout high school. Floyd was dating Charlotte Hawkins, a beautiful brunette with wide blue eyes, a healthy sense of humor, and spunk. Only Gene had a car, so he often found himself chauffeuring the other couple on their dates. "I found I could talk and joke, even share my woman troubles very easily with Charlotte. She was frank and witty and always sincere," he recalled.[38] Fortunately for Gene, Charlotte's mother, fearing her daughter's relationship with Floyd was moving into marriage territory, persuaded the couple to break up.

After graduation in 1951, Gene and Floyd moved on to the University of Utah, completing a successful freshman year. That summer, Gene's thoughts

University of Utah yearbook photo of England with
Charlotte on their first date at the "Hello Dance," 1952.
(Courtesy Charlotte England)

returned to the now-unattached Charlotte. The next September, with Charlotte entering the university, he invited her to the "Hello Dance." Charlotte
was surprised to hear his voice on the telephone. He had always been one part
of the other couple in their double-dating—and she hadn't expected to be the
object of his attentions. "Flabbergasted" at the invitation, she hardly knew how
to respond, and replied with nervous levity. Reflecting on her odd behavior
afterward, he almost cancelled the date. But he did not.[39]

They arrived early, casually dressed, and promptly occupied the dance floor.
Other arriving couples were attired in more fancy swag, and Charlotte, now
uncomfortable, wanted to leave. Gene convinced her to stay, and they soon lost
their insecurities, swept up as they were in a private world they were already
forming. They were both skilled in the "East High Drag," a modified foxtrot,
and the photographer on site knew a blooming romance when he saw one.
Their nondescript clothing notwithstanding, he snapped a photo of the charismatic couple, which appeared in the yearbook months later. The courtship
was officially on.[40]

Over that fall and winter, they attended all the dances they could fit in, some
in prime venues like the Saltair, Salt Lake's "Coney Island," or the Lagoon, a

concert hot spot headlined by the likes of George Gershwin, Nat King Cole, and Rosemary Clooney. They watched low-brow movies like *Samson and Delilah* and art films such as *The Seventh Seal*. Afterward, they would park in front of her house before saying goodnight. If the lingering was suspiciously prolonged, Mrs. Hawkins would turn on the porch light to signal Charlotte it was time to come in.

Those winter evenings when it was too cold to venture out, they would spend on the sofa in the Hawkins's front room, reading Pogo comics and laughing themselves silly. One night they drove up to a nearby golf course for a quiet walk across snow-covered fields that soon transformed into a running snowball fight. An exhausted Charlotte collapsed in laughter, and made a snow angel where she lay. She then jumped up, and moved over, to make another so that the arched wings just touched. She repeated the process twice more, "until she had a row of four angels, each perfectly symmetrical and all joined together, like children's paper dolls," Gene would recall decades later. "Her face was shining above her plaid coat, and I knew I would marry her."[41]

The engagement would not take place for almost a year. Part of the delay was England's need to finance a ring. He worked as an aide at the veteran's mental hospital for a full year to save the thousand dollars for a full carat. Then, too, like many a suitor, he passed through a period of second-guessing his decision. He found the push he needed from his family dentist. Responding impatiently to Gene's doubts, he told the young man, "Listen, she will be booting you up the golden stairs all the way." It was then he realized that in terms of things he really valued, "in moral qualities and fundamental intelligence she was startling. So I got over that period of doubt." By September he was ready to act. His plans were to take an evening hike up the majestic Mount Timpanogos and propose at the summit. He carried the ring the entire way but couldn't find his moment. That next Sunday, 17 September, they went to an early morning broadcast of the Tabernacle Choir. After the music, they went for a walk around the Salt Lake Temple. Charlotte recalled what happened next: "We were walking around and he said if we stand right here we can see the sun coming up over the temple ground wall. So we were standing there and it was just peeking up, and all of a sudden it just, you know—you know how it is when it first comes over and it's just this bright, bright light—and he held my hand and he just slipped a ring on. I looked at that and the sun and everything and all these men I dated flashed through my mind. Well that's what happened at that time, and so I was engaged."[42] Gene realized afterward that he never actually asked her to marry him. "I just assumed she would."[43]

As he made plans for his future, his spiritual and intellectual paths were taking shape as well. The greatest influence on Gene's life at this time was one of the revered spiritual mentors of midcentury Mormonism, Lowell Bennion, who had published the first English-language study of sociologist Max Weber. Bennion had also founded the Latter-day Saint Institute of Religion, adjacent to the University of Utah, the year after England's birth (it was only the church's fourth institute, a program offering non-credit LDS religious classes). He also founded the state's first food bank and homeless shelter, as well as the Teton Valley Boys Ranch. In a church that tended toward insularity and dogma, Bennion was an open-armed humanitarian and a practical Christian.

Bennion fed Gene's disdain for materialism in all its forms, adding to his growing sense that his own father was too consumed with his business pursuits—in spite of his generous commitments. It was under Bennion's influence, too, that Gene experienced a kind of spiritual awakening, and the first stirrings of discontent with the church's doctrinal status quo on one topic in particular. As he remembered it, the class was being led by Bennion in 1953. Gene's marriage, graduation, and mission were all in the future.

> A student asked why, if God is no respecter of persons, as the scriptures and common sense clearly indicate, a difference existed in God's church between blacks and all others. I immediately answered, as I had been taught all my life, 'Well, God is also a God of justice, and since blacks were not valiant in the preexistence, they are cursed with the consequences.' In the discussion following my remark, Brother Bennion . . . simply asked me how I knew blacks had not been valiant. When I had no answer but tradition, he gently suggested that the God revealed in Christ would surely let blacks know what they had done wrong and how they could repent, rather than merely punishing them—and since God had done no such thing, it seemed better to believe that blacks had been, and were, no different spiritually from the rest of us.

It is impossible to exaggerate the impact of this experience in shaping Gene's future career as a writer, thinker, and interrogator of church teachings. He concluded, "As I thought about this, . . . I came to realize . . . that many of my beliefs . . . were based on flimsy and unexamined evidence."[44]

Bennion's writings, England came to appreciate, showed the dangers presented by Latter-day Saint theology in its present state; lacking a tradition of systematic theology, Latter-day Saints had "a tendency to 'pulverize' the gospel, to analyze and defend and explain it in small chunks that may have no logical connection and may, in fact, contradict each other." Bennion's thought pointed in the direction of possibilities unrealized: "the coherent moral and spiritual force available in Mormon thought."[45] Bennion was no theologian or systematic thinker—but his common-sense approach to lived religion instilled in England the passion to translate church doctrines into a more organic, coherent framework for discipleship. The point deserves emphasis, because it holds the key to England's own vocation as he would come to conceive it.

Gene was ready to move ahead with marriage to Charlotte, but deciding the timing of the wedding was complicated. The Korean conflict, which had put a temporary halt to missionary work, ended that summer of 1953. Now a mission felt possible and even obligatory. George Sr. advised Gene to counsel with the apostle Spencer Kimball, so influential in the senior England's life. Kimball, to Gene's surprise, said marriage was the "chief mission" in life, and having found one's eternal companion, that should be one's highest priority. So he and Charlotte planned an immediate wedding but assumed that Gene would serve nonetheless. "I had told the Bishop that I would be ready to go and they were beginning to allow one [missionary] from each ward and I was top of the list."[46] They proceeded with their wedding, which took place three days before Christmas.

It was a modest affair, with family, friends, and relatives. Afterward, closed roads prevented their planned excursion to Sun Valley, so they honeymooned in Las Vegas instead. Probably not the best choice, as it turned out. They were expelled from a casino (they looked underage), Charlotte didn't get any of Buddy Hackett's off-color jokes (he opened for Nat King Cole), and she commented to Gene that so many women in the audience looked too young for their husbands (they weren't wives, he explained).[47] In March 1954, his bishop arranged a mission interview with LeGrand Richards; Charlotte attended in her supporting role, the interview transpired without a hitch, and they went home to await the call. Charlotte expected she would wait out Gene's mission with her parents. Alternately, newly married wives were sometimes called on six-month missions while they waited for their spouse, and they considered that too might be a possibility. A few weeks later, with no plans yet in place, the mission call arrived.

2

A MOUNTAIN IN THE OCEAN

MISSION TO SAMOA

Here we are on a mountain in the ocean—
trying to bring God to these people.
—Charlotte England, mission journal

Few moments in a Latter-day Saint's life can equal the anticipation with which a mission call is opened. Young men and women can be assigned to Mongolia; the island of Palau in Micronesia; the Republic of the Congo; Omaha, Nebraska; or one of over 400 other missions dispersed through six continents. In 1954, sixty countries hosted LDS missionaries, with Fiji and South Korea added to the mix the year England departed. And so the prospective missionary opened his call with no inkling of where he would spend the next two and a half years. His field of labor, he read excitedly, was to be Samoa. But that was not the biggest surprise; his companion was. Completely unexpectedly, Charlotte was called to serve alongside her husband of a few weeks.

One can only imagine the thrill to both of them. Instead of facing painful years of separation and loneliness, they would embark together for the South Pacific as virtual newlyweds on the adventure of a lifetime. They rushed to the University of Utah library, to look at maps of Samoa. They read Margaret Mead's *Coming of Age in Samoa*. They studied a crude, simplified grammar written by a returned missionary. And they tried to focus on coursework, as they finished the winter quarter at the university. May they spent packing and preparing for their June departure. They sold their car, an Oldsmobile, to finance most of the mission costs, which would run $70 per month for the two of them.

Calling newlyweds to serve together was unusual but not unprecedented. Church records show that for reasons unknown, the practice was limited to those serving island missions. In addition to others called to Samoa, couples were called to New Zealand, Hawaii, and Japan in the decades preceding the England's assignment.[1] No Language Training Center existed in the 1950s, so they spent a mere week in the Salt Lake Mission Home, receiving instruction and training. On 9 June, they were set apart for their missions by the apostle and future church president Harold B. Lee and departed late that evening from the old Union Pacific Station. The platform was crowded with well-wishers, some from their ward, most from Charlotte's side of the family. She cried, as Gene tried awkwardly to comfort her. On board, other missionaries played their ukuleles and sang, and the newlyweds joined in. It was Charlotte's first time on a train—and at a one-hour stopover in Ogden, she reacted to "a very poor area of town" as if that were her first exposure to want. "Someday if I ever can I want to help these people," she wrote in her journal even as she was en route to a place where she would offer a different kind of sustenance to the inhabitants.[2]

First, however, they had another stopover in San Francisco to obtain their visas. Her brother, George Hawkins, and his wife, LaRue, met them, along with sundry relatives, and together they dined at the Woman's Athletic Club. Gene passed the next morning fishing (only catching baby sand and leopard sharks). After the predictable bureaucratic obstacles, they received their documents and reembarked, this time for Hawaii. After several days steaming on a mostly quiet ocean, they arrived on Oahu, where they spent a day touring the island, visiting Pearl Harbor, the Latter-day Saint temple, and scenic vistas. Stopping over at Fiji on 22 June for ten days, they found the church branch weak and rudderless ("too many Wesleyan ideas" and "no real organized meetings"). They encountered a number of British expats, who left a bad taste in Gene's mouth. They had "a mass inferiority complex" and resented "their new position as a 3rd rate country" in the postwar world, he wrote. Most galling of all to Gene was their callous condescension toward native peoples.

England's first mission impressions also revealed the shock of novelty as felt by a twenty-year-old Idaho farm boy. "Surrounded by water, and strange, strange people." And those were just the fellow passengers—not inhabitants of a foreign realm! But Gene and Charlotte were breaking the mold in some of their fellow passengers' eyes: "On the boat they had dances and played games and the first time Gene and I went out and danced we really got the looks from the missionaries. Then somebody said, 'you know missionaries can't dance.'

The young newlyweds arriving for mission service in Samoa, 1954.
(Courtesy Charlotte England)

I didn't think that applied to us because we were, well, a couple. . . . So we didn't dance anymore."[3]

Most of the other missionaries on board were assigned to other missions, and they departed the group singly and in pairs as the ship made its way across the Pacific. In Fiji they bid farewell to the last of their traveling companions. "Each time we say goodbye, I feel further and further away from home," wrote Charlotte in her journal. "Leaving Brent [Eager, a high school friend] was the hardest," Gene noted in his. Finally, after a rough two-day passage on the 5,000-ton *Matua*, their three-week journey was over. At 6:30 A.M. on the morning of 2 July, they caught their first sight of Samoa.

The missionary couple arrived to find a population of 100,000 Samoans dispersed among three main islands and affiliated with three main religious groups: In addition to Latter-day Saints, most Samoans belonged to either the interdenominational London Missionary Society or the Roman Catholic Church. Like many Westerners, the Englands had imbibed the stereotypes expressed by Margaret Mead: the Samoans were an Edenically simple and promiscuous people.[4] Gene and Charlotte found themselves in a scattered mission consisting of a modest number of single young men, about fifty-five "elders" (male missionaries) along with fifteen "sister" missionaries. A married couple was a novelty, England remembered. Even before disembarking, they were greeted by the white-suited mission president, Howard Stone, and then dispatched immediately to Vaiola ("Living Water"), on the largest island, Savai'i. A small launch delivered them (along with a load of hogs and a nose-less Samoan) to their first area of labor, to the accompaniment of flying fish and dolphins.

Upon arrival, they found themselves facing a massive—and unsmiling—Samoan police official, backed by two uniformed subordinates. The official addressed them harshly and confiscated the papers they timorously produced. The two missionaries (elders in the Saints' vernacular) escorting the Englands whispered that a trip to the police station looked inevitable. As the crisis climaxed, the official, along with the elders, burst into laughter, pleased at having duped the green missionaries. He then confessed that he was himself a Latter-day Saint and invited the couple to his home. There he regaled the Englands with stories of his own past (Samoan royalty, but exiled to this post because of his Mormon faith), his favorite Latter-day Saint tenets (the eternal human soul, the "fall" as a planned ascent toward divinity), and his own contributions (he had translated into Samoan the Pearl of Great Price, the church's fourth book of scripture). He also disabused them of any confidence in Margaret Mead's depictions of Samoan culture. She "didn't learn the language and therefore wasn't trusted, and was, in fact, fed outrageous stories . . . that ended up as sober facts in her book."[5]

In a gesture that captured perfectly the collaborative, companionate ideal of their marriage, Gene and Charlotte shared a mission journal, he writing on the left side and she always on the right. "Not lonely or homesick—just rather dazed," Gene had written in his first diary entry (13 June 1954). Charlotte, ever the aesthetically attuned, wrote that this new world was fast becoming "beautiful and . . . not so strange: mango and breadfruit trees and coconut palms and taro patches and banana and taamu plantations and now and then a native hut" (11 July). Their initial work in Samoa was not evangelization but education. Leaving the coast, they rode by horseback into the tropical interior. Assigned there to the church school, Charlotte taught nine fifteen- and sixteen-year-olds, while Gene taught a larger group of younger teens. With no particular training to do so, the young couple found themselves teaching religion, arithmetic, reading, English grammar, and spelling, in addition to health and physical education from 8:00 A.M. to 3:00 P.M. daily. Saturdays they traveled by horseback to the coast to visit members in a more pastoral capacity. Gene's friendship with Fitisemanu, the pranking police official, blossomed. Charlotte was befriended by the branch president's wife, A'iga, who spent long evenings coaching her in Samoan as she held the American's hand affectionately in her own, though it was swollen grotesquely with elephantiasis.

On 22 July, Gene turned twenty-one. "No present, no oven to bake a birthday cake," noted Charlotte sadly. Gene celebrated by climbing a hill in the neighborhood where he spent time "composing," then returned to a dinner of canned goods and donuts. An earlier birthday celebration for the mission president's wife had featured taro, palusami (corned beef, onions, and coconut cream wrapped in taro leaves), niu, roast pig, fish, and tapioca. Missionaries today are confined in their reading to a few church-approved titles. It's unlikely that given such strictures, Gene's insatiable appetite would have been curbed. In their absence, he maintained a steady diet of titles, including Robert Wilder's *Ride the Tiger*, John Steinbeck's *East of Eden*, and Epictetus. Charlotte wrote of falling asleep to the cadence of Robert Frost's poetry read by her husband, never commenting on the incongruity of listening to descriptions of New England farm life in the shade of coconut palms and amid the cries of Samoan flying foxes and singing bulbuls.

Not all the life-forms were welcome. The first evening in a new village, Charlotte stepped into the shower and turned on the spigot. Instantly, the water forced hordes of roaches out of the drain—and up Charlotte's legs. Gene rushed in in response to her screams and scattered the roaches. Later that evening, she entered the kitchen with a kerosene lamp. The light immediately sent more hordes of roaches scurrying across the floor. Once again screams, pandemonium, and soon Gene was rushing back and forth beating at them furiously with his slippers, as she yelled and pointed. From outside, it appeared that Gene was attacking Charlotte, as the blows and repeated cries continued. Alarmed villagers, feeling they must intervene, knocked at the door, only leaving when assured that she had not been the target of the violence. But first, Charlotte took the opportunity to introduce themselves as the new missionaries.[6]

The misadventures continued, with Gene exhibiting more zeal than sense. Charlotte spotted a rat of alarming size on the refuse heap outside. Gene grabbed a machete and launched into action. He managed to land a lethal blow, only to have two more emerge. They circled round the house, with Gene in hot pursuit, waving the machete wildly. One swing inadvertently sliced through a hornet nest. They swarmed and stung his hand, Gene panicked and slapped at them with the weapon still in his hand, hacking deeply through his own skin. He bore the scar, and the story, to the end of his days.[7] Evenings, Gene would read and Charlotte would "scratch out a few notes" on her violin.

Sometimes she would sketch the local children and women. Other evenings, they would teach the gospel to interested Samoans at "cottage meetings."

England's response to Samoan culture was in key regards the opposite of Margaret Mead's. He deplored what he saw as the spiritual detritus of colonialism and racism, and was devastated when he saw its persistence among his peers. He determined to avoid such tendencies in spite of the severe temptations toward racism and classism as well as garden-variety cultural snobbery.[8]

At the same time, England's sympathies for the "colonized" Samoans did not translate into cultural relativism. Working with and ministering to the people in a pastoral capacity, he was immersed in their lives, their practices, and, he emphasized, the fruits of their cultural norms and personal choices. As a consequence, after his initial disillusionment with Western chauvinist lenses, "I really became convinced . . . that there are things that hurt people . . . such as infidelity." As a consequence, "I moved back towards the sense of . . . absolutism, in the sense of 'there are universal principles—across cultures.'"[9]

Mission life was challenging. The couple were frustrated with "petty jealousies and egotism" that fractured the Saints' community on the islands. The language was beautiful to listen to, but their proficiency was slow in coming. Missionaries had grown weary of embedded cultural traditions that impeded their work and grew apathetic. Worse yet, noted both Englands, the Western missionaries serving with them had grown coarse and treated the Samoans like servants. "Everything seems wrong here," a despondent Gene wrote in his journal. "It doesn't even seem like the church." Even the mission president seemed infected by a kind of listlessness, Gene lamented. Gene and Charlotte's relationship prospered as they found in each other steadfast hopefulness and solidarity in the face of pervasive inertia. "The stars are like a field of daisies," Charlotte recorded in her journal. "Makes me feel very close to Gene and God. May they both always be at my side." ("I don't see any beauty today but Charlotte," reads his entry in the same period.) After one particular explosion by other missionaries, he noted, "It all converged; Charlotte cried with me in the dark and was sorry she was here. Please, God, don't let her be hurt and changed by these things she should never see." They worked long hours, teaching school, early morning seminary, preparing lessons, visiting members, serving in the local congregation, teaching classes there too, organizing special programs at church and school, instructing the children in music. Monday evenings they taught a gospel class, Wednesday and Friday evenings they instructed the teachers. Other nights were given to the women's and the youth's church meetings.

Through it all, young Charlotte (she was twenty) frequently noted her exhaustion but persevered. The school was chaotic and lacking records. They had 30 students to start with and hoped for 150. The rain was remorseless, and the wet climate wrought havoc on her violin. Her legs broke out in rashes from the hordes of mosquitos. Inadequate outhouses, outdoor saltwater baths, and the grousing of other missionaries wore at her spirits. Gene, for his part, was restless and handicapped by his failure to master Samoan. He worked hard to clean and improve their long-neglected living quarters, and repair the church houses. He built a chicken coop. But he wished he could cry sometimes, he complained. They both plugged away at their school assignments, improvising on the fly. Charlotte felt she had aged ten years in the first month, not discerning any measurable impact that their teaching was having on students unused to discipline or rigorous schoolwork. "A very disheartening, discouraging, disillusioning day," reads one entry. Much of their work was retraining the Samoan teachers they supervised. Teaching Sunday school classes at church, they were shocked at how little the gospel had taken root among the members. With little medical care available in the area, the residents called on Gene and Charlotte "in droves" for minor first aid—mostly boil lancing, patching minor injuries, and the like, with occasional maiming from machete cuts.

Gradually, their teaching bore fruit; though he might not have known it yet, Gene had found his vocation. By their third month, Gene could sense "the groping, the growing, the molding—the stir of beauty in good, untaught minds." They responded to his unflagging efforts to awaken their curiosity with "wonder-cupped faces and shining eyes of recognition or joy of newness." About the same period, Gene begins to marvel in his journal at how his experience of reading scripture and poetry alike (from Robert Frost to the Rubaiyat of Omar Khayyam) was suddenly richer, more meaningful. Observing so much human need around him, spiritual and emotional, and the inadequacy of any human response by his coworkers, sharpened his focus on the inner life—of himself and those he served. One sees throughout his entries a spirit fine-tuning itself to the vibrations of the human heart.

Meanwhile, Charlotte's steadfast patience and evident devotion to her students evoked growing receptivity on their part. "More encouraged than last week," she wrote. "I seemed to touch their hearts for a change," she wrote a few days later. "If I could just teach them love, kindness, and gentleness—I would be happy." Their labors only heightened the contrast with the more experienced—and more cynical—elders, whom Gene was by now dismissing angrily (to his journal) as "depraved. . . . No spirituality, no diligence, no godliness." Such venting was always followed by self-reproach for his lack of charity toward his fellow laborers ("I am worse for hating them"). Charlotte silently mourned the elders' failure to be good role models. "God must weep to see ministers of his gospel treating it—and me—like they do." Another source of division between the couple and the other missionaries was just that—they were a couple. Enforced celibacy for two or more years was a hard enough ask of twenty-something-year-old men. It didn't help that they worked alongside a young married pair literally on their honeymoon, who had the audacity to hold hands in public, as one elder rebuked them.

Samoan culture sometimes fed the worst American stereotypes. One morning, Charlotte wrote, "I thought I heard blows and looked up to see a brute about 180 pounds beating up a girl who looked about 20 something and tiny. Gene and Elder Hanks ran out to stop him and almost had a bush knife for doing it." At the same time, mission practices did nothing to combat the worst stereotypes of Westerners. A mission-sponsored Gold and Green Ball drew 1,000 people, many of them local, Western bigwigs the mission president wanted to impress. All comers were seated by sister missionaries: "the white people on the first two rows and all the Samoans seated behind them." One of the more perceptive elders noted that the entire affair "set us back at least six months in our relations with the Samoans." Other barriers to cultural harmony were more systemic: One of the lessons Gene taught in school was "all about the curse of the Lamanites"—that is, God's supposed blighting the Native Americans and Polynesians with dark skin, in Latter-day Saint understanding. Gene would later become one of the most acute critics of the church's teachings about race; for now, he could only fume, "hating the hundreds of missionaries who have come here, had a good time, lived off the fat of the land, done their 'job,' and not taught these people anything important."

Through it all, Gene and Charlotte never ceased marveling at the island sunrises and sunsets, the flora and fauna. They couldn't expel the ten-inch lizard that shared quarters with them, but at least he kept the moth population down, hunting them on the ceiling overhead. Cultural barriers frequently added to their failures. The LDS islanders were supposed to provide them with food, but the couple was supplied irregularly, and frequently made do with a limited variety of canned goods. "We're doing something wrong," Charlotte inferred from their social isolation, "and nobody will tell us what." Gene wrote in a similar vein, "The resentment of everyone," that is, missionaries and Samoans alike, "is showing on us."

At one point, Gene was so exasperated that he wrote a letter of complaint to an admired General Authority, Marion D. Hanks (Gene had been a student in Hanks's Institute of Religion class at the University of Utah). With acute insight, Hanks helped England to understand that part of the problem was doubtless the ill grace with which he condemned the shortcomings of his contemporaries and predecessors. Gene's moral indignation earned him a stinging rebuke, not for being wrong but for being judgmental. He called Hanks's response "the most helpful letter I have received from another human being in my life, he taught me to see the danger of riding off by myself on a white horse, to realize that just as one must not only be sincere but also right, so one must not only be right but also effective, and it wasn't very effective to go around self-righteously condemning my fellow missionaries."[10] The lesson was one that England would attempt to learn, time and again—with varying degrees of success. But the seeds of his future conflict with institutional authority appear clearly. He recognized an unseemly desire in himself "to be the great deliverer of the gospel from all its misunderstanding and unappreciative hangers-on." The church needed agents with "uncompromising desire for truth and reality and hatred of success." He wanted to be that person—"badly."

One convert baptism—in a fairyland setting—was a moment of sublime beauty in the midst of largely disappointed hopes:

> I led Sholly [he had just started using this name for Charlotte] on horseback along a muddy trail with elders Hanks and Martin and President Kalosi Pe'a. It was Saturday afternoon with a hint of rain. We saw a bat hanging in a tree (as big as a cat) passing Tapu 'ele 'ele in the evening quiet; houses circling a grass malai, swallows swirling and swooping in groups. Got off horses and walked a little way and down into a steep ravine. It was something from Walt Disney or at least the dreams of youth—a large pool surrounded on three sides by 50-foot rock walls with dropping vines and the jungle at the top, except in one place where the waterfall comes over when it rains. . . . We stood on the rock ledges and had our short service. Then they waded out and Elder Hanks baptized her and then she swam out and bathed. A girl threw her a lemon from the bank for her hair. We went home in the early dark.

Six months into their missions, they were reassigned to the Sauniatu District. Christmas saw them separated for the first time in their marriage; he began to work with other elders, while she lived and worked with sister missionaries. In February of the new year they were reunited. Their charge at this time was not educational but pastoral. Vailuutai Branch was struggling, and they were tasked with building it up—through both evangelizing and ministering to members. And minister they did, giving instruction and encouragement relentlessly but without significant progress. In July 1955 they transferred to another village, Moto'otua, with a similar charge, in addition to hosting two branch primaries (children's Sunday school–type weekly meetings). Finally somewhat competent in Samoan, they felt at least one barrier disappear. As elsewhere, they were surprised at how poor the members' understanding of Restoration teachings and principles was. ("Tried to teach them how to pray," he noted after one primary lesson, "but their devotion to the Lord's prayer seems unbreakable.") Attendance at church meetings was always erratic and familiarity with basic history of the church and its tenets spotty, so they emphasized basic Christian values with a smattering of LDS doctrine. In the fall of 1955, they became circuit riders of sorts, rotating from village to village monthly.

Pursuant to Spencer Kimball's earlier admonitions, they made no effort to postpone the beginnings of a family. Charlotte became pregnant but miscarried. She became pregnant again, with a due date of March 1956. Remote from modern medical facilities, they felt anxious as the pregnancy approached term. Gene worried his wife "would have to cut the cord with a can lid," but eight months along, the mission president transferred them to Hawaii. Charlotte worked in the office while Gene assisted the district president. Marion D. Hanks, passing through, visited and gave Charlotte a blessing. The baby came weeks late after a seventy-two-hour labor that left Charlotte exhausted and bed-ridden for a few weeks. Shortly thereafter, Elder Harold B. Lee came for a conference, greeted the missionaries he had set apart, and held baby Katherine. Counseling with Gene, he recommended that the mother and child return stateside, while Gene finish out his mission faithfully. Charlotte and child flew home where, surrounded by family, she recuperated.

Gene made no journal entries for weeks on either side of the birth—then picked up a few weeks later, dutifully but sporadically recording his mission labors. Hitting the two-year mark, he now saw his past twenty-four months through the lens of a stronger mission populated by more obedient elders and more devout members; "Fantastic, dream years," he wrote in his journal, unconscious of irony. But his handwriting betrayed a young man bereft of his Sholly. His entries become hasty, illegible, fragmented. One other significant change is conspicuous. His entries are markedly less about himself and other missionaries; it's as if his newly acquired fatherhood has deepened his capacity for empathy, reflection, and other-orientation: "Roger, emotionally sick from need for love, consistence, a home—lying on bed staring through tunnels of eyes," reads one entry. Another speaks of "Bruce, rebellious, hurt.

Father too blindly strict—beats . . . Why can't we know with children so much depends—so much opportunity lost—so much greatness lost in youth." Or yet another, "Fine meeting with mother and four children. Nicholas a brilliant, sensitive, lonely child, but all very good. 'Where did God come from?,' Nicholas asked."

And then, as if the work eclipsed his record-keeping, and with Sholly no longer there to share the pages of his journal—his record ends. Almost nine months after Katherine's birth and Charlotte's departure, on 22 December 1956, Gene completed his mission service and arrived home to daughter and waiting wife. It was their third anniversary.

3

STANFORD AND ACTIVISM

When he was able to meet personally with his critics, he most often was
able to achieve, if not complete peace, then at least an armistice. But there
were times, even when he tried to downplay his brilliance, that he was just
too smart for his critics. I told him more than once that when dealing with
ecclesiastical leaders he should let them win every now and then.
—Kenneth Godfrey, in a note to Charlotte, August 2001

Before embarking for Samoa, Gene had been settled into a mathematics major.
He had achieved most of the required hours—but his experiences in Samoa
had reoriented his interests. "Being on a mission and working with people and
getting interested in how people thought and in their cultures made me realize an interest I had long had was really my primary interest: literature and
writing."[1] It was the human subject, and the human interactions, that together
clinched the deal for him in his new choice. On his mission, he said, he "experienced what human needs are and how genuinely joy-producing it can be to
experience love and service and self-fulfillment and creativity. I had seen that
in Samoa in myself and other people."[2] The writing may have been on the wall
from as long ago as his first year at the University of Utah, actually. In 1951,
he had presented himself to the university newspaper staff and volunteered
to write for the sports section. An editor recalls, "Unfortunately, that didn't
last for more than a couple of articles because the typical sports fan couldn't
understand what Gene was writing about. Too many words longer than four
letters. . . . Gene wisely moved on to other literary efforts."[3] Following his
mission, he found more success as editor of the university literary magazine,
The Pen.[4]

England now finished the Reserve Officers Training Corps (ROTC) program
he had begun in 1952, completed his English requirements, and graduated in

Charlotte pinning bars on newly commissioned Lieutenant
Eugene England, 1958. (Courtesy Charlotte England)

June 1958, six months after Charlotte gave birth to their second daughter.
ROTC was a reasonable choice for a few reasons. The Universal Military Training and Service Act of 1951, passed to meet the demands of the Korean War,
was still in force. Almost 150,000 men were inducted in 1958;[5] in that era
between the Korean and Vietnam wars, many young men opted for the perks
of an ROTC commission (especially educational expenses) over the risk of
being drafted. Besides, Gene remembered, "I was still a somewhat sentimental
patriot—willing to serve in Vietnam if I had been sent."[6] His disillusionment
with the war and American motives was still three years in his future.

Commissioned a second lieutenant in the Air Force, he was committed for
a three-year stint and assigned to study meteorology for a year at the Massachusetts Institute of Technology. (Color blindness precluded any flying assignment.) They headed east in August, rigging the old Dodge to hold two baby
beds, for eight-month-old Jody and two-and-a-half-year-old Katherine. Once

arrived in Cambridge, they quickly found housing in nearby Waltham with
the help of local Latter-day Saints: a typical nineteenth-century frame house,
tall, painted red, and a bit drafty. Gene would commute in their old, gray, two-
door Dodge. The temperamental car didn't work in rainy weather; he hitched
rides on those days. The house had plenty of room for the young family, even
with the twelve-year-old foster child, Francine, who soon became part of their
household. It was an intense program, but Gene managed to squeeze in some
literature courses on the side. Studying William Faulkner with Carvel Collins
(largely responsible for bringing Faulkner public acclaim) was too good an
opportunity to miss. Of course, as one friend recalled, he had to "cut class at
MIT and come down to Harvard and to the English classes" taught by Collins
and others.[7] Housing was expensive, the stipend miniscule (about $3,000 that
year), so entertainment was limited to excursions to the beach and farmers
markets with Sholly and the kids.

Immediately upon arriving, the Englands had begun serving in a local girls'
camp. One day, Charlotte was helping in the kitchen while watching a pair of
girls nearby. A camp leader told her they were in need of a foster home, and
that any arrangement would be better than their present situation. Gene was a
student, Charlotte had one young girl, an infant, and was expecting her third
child. But she agreed to take in Francine. She would be the first of a multitude
of informally adopted souls who would become part of the England family for
periods ranging from days to months. The child remained with them for almost a year until, overcome with longing for her birth family, she was returned
to relatives.

After a year at MIT, Gene was stationed at George Air Force Base in Victorville, California, as an Air Force weatherman. They spent two years there
(summer 1959–summer 1961). Gene excelled at his job. It was inevitable that
with his expansive love and gospel commitments, he would be drawn to teaching in the Church Educational System, and when an opportunity to teach early
morning seminary to church students arose, he jumped at the chance, also
teaching a youth group on Tuesday evenings. A friend stationed there with
him recalled one memorable forecast Gene made. Dangerously high winds at
7:45 A.M. the next morning, Gene predicted. The sun came up on a clear and
serenely calm Mojave Desert, and the wing director of operations questioned
the forecast. England wasn't there to defend himself—he was teaching seminary, so the planes launched at 7:30. The high winds hit at 7:47, grounding
flights, and the young lieutenant had more credibility thereafter.[8]

While serving in Victorville, an LDS F-104 pilot was killed in a midair collision with another starfighter. Upon learning of the tragedy, Gene rushed to

comfort the pilot's wife and children—and was asked to give the sermon at the Air Force memorial services. He fasted and prayed for three days while providing comfort and preparing his remarks for a man he had barely met. This would be typical of his life of compassionate generosity.[9]

The second summer there Jennifer was born but suffered distressingly ill health. Charlotte's motherly intuitions overcame the doctors' stubborn skepticism, and Jennifer was diagnosed with severe birth defects—the result of a diaphragmatic hernia—that usually ends in the infant's death during gestation or in reparative surgery. The happy outcome in this case, however, was an entirely successful operation. Gene now completed his two relatively uneventful years in the Air Force. Knowing that his future lay in academia, not the military, he returned to the University of Utah, where he worked and took a semester of graduate courses in English. He taught English and was activities director during the 1961–62 school year, while making plans for doctoral study.

In the 1960s, the "largest amount of money given for graduate work by any single foundation" was the prestigious Danforth Fellowship.[10] The foundation targeted students pursuing a career in college teaching and covered tuition, fees, and living expenses. In 1962, Gene was one of 120 recipients of the award and entered Stanford University to study with Wallace Stegner, who would become America's premier Western writer. At the time, Stegner exuded a frustration bordering on bitterness, born of the sentiment that his brand of writing was out of sync with the amorality and experimentalism prevalent in his period's literature. He also described Western writers as rootless, lacking "a present and living society that is truly ours and that contains the materials of a deep commitment. . . . Instead we must live in exile."[11] Gene didn't share his sense of alienation, finding himself fully invested in his Latter-day Saint community, and embraced by it. And yet, the beginnings of a lifelong rupture with the dominant LDS culture soon erupted.

VIETNAM AND LDS PATRIOTISM

The subject of Vietnam seems to be leading me toward my first serious disagreement with you. . . . Such an effort seems to violate American and Mormon concepts of a just war.—England to Marion D. Hanks, 23 November 1967

The Church of Jesus Christ of Latter-day Saints has the distinction of being the religious group most systematically persecuted by state and federal governments in America's history. And yet, ironically, from the twentieth century on the Saints have generally been seen as among the nation's most patriotic citizens. At the beginning of the last century, apostle Anthony W. Ivins explained the church's position regarding armed service at a General Conference: "We do not hasten into war, because we do not believe in it; we believe it to be unnecessary; but, nevertheless, if it shall come, we believe it to be our duty to defend those principles of liberty and right and equality which were established by the Father."[12] The 1960s witnessed some of the most divisive issues in America's political history—and the Vietnam War was at the forefront. In one typical expression from church leadership, as the war in Southeast Asia raged, the influential Ezra Taft Benson criticized in a General Conference those who "would prefer . . . surrender to the communists" to "nuclear war."[13] True to form, rank and file Latter-day Saints were overwhelmingly supportive of the nation's involvement in Vietnam. In 1968, Elder Boyd K. Packer, a World War II veteran and assistant to the Twelve, told the worldwide church that when a nation "calls the manhood of the Church into the armed service of any country to which they owe allegiance, their highest civic duty requires that they meet that call," and he criticized those who were "repudiating their citizenship responsibilities . . . on moral grounds."[14]

On this issue, Gene England broke decisively and vocally with his coreligionists. As he recalled the process by which his dissent unfolded,

I had believed, with a certainty that was complete and religious, that the U.S. Constitution had been inspired by God, that our government therefore was essentially Christian, devoted to goodness and truth, and directed by God in its purposes and actions. In particular, I had believed our presidents were sincere and truthful. On 4 August 1964, our government announced that North Vietnamese gunboats had twice attacked an American destroyer in the Gulf of Tonkin, and that consequently we had bombed Hanoi and were greatly increasing our buildup of American troops. At the Stanford library, I had been reading reports and analyses in periodicals from around the world—not just American sources—of what was happening in Vietnam. I had become increasingly uneasy about our policies and now became convinced (as was later admitted) that our government was lying about the Tonkin Gulf Incident—and suddenly my whole world shifted. For me, being convinced that a president had lied and that our government was willing to deceive us and kill people far away, in my name and using my taxes—for what seemed more and more an unworthy and unjust cause—was a life-changing experience.[15]

One of his first decisions at Stanford was to join the Graduate Student Coordinating Council, Stanford's version of the Free Speech Movement that had developed at Berkeley just across the Bay. The group published a newsletter and organized antiwar rallies (along with working to pass local fair-housing laws). Charles Petty was a student at Stanford in the mid-1960s. Enrolling in a Christian ethics class as an undergraduate, he was surprised to find one other Latter-day Saint in the class—Gene, who was auditing the course as a graduate student that year of 1963–64. Gene was also meeting weekly with freshmen he invited to his home to discuss religion and literature. Petty and his wife became fast friends with the Englands and found rare allies in each other politically. "He was vocal in his opposition to the Vietnam War, which put him at odds with his ward," remembered Kathleen Petty. "People thought he was a radical."[16]

In every prior American war, the First Presidency of the Church had publicly acknowledged every individual members' right to petition for conscientious objector status. Support for the Vietnam War came from the highest channels, and in this conflict the church did not publish information in the church newspaper, as they had previously, for individuals seeking a religious exemption. Petty had returned to Stanford from mission service in Germany to find controversy over the war had heated up considerably. Like England, he rejected the grounds for American involvement, and being of draft age he petitioned for conscientious objector status. He was one of few Latter-day Saints to take that route. Henry Eyring, Petty's bishop, signed off on his request, attesting to his sincerity while declining to support his decision. England, however, was entirely sympathetic to Petty's petition. Meanwhile, a second Latter-day Saint student, knowing of England's antiwar stance, also asked England's support in filing his conscientious objector status, which was also granted. That boy's parents blamed England for the student's decision, and complained bitterly to church leaders. The father told Gene, "I will see that you never get a job teaching for the Church," and he sent a letter to the head of the CES.[17] England received his first of many letters, warning him against rocking the boat as a church educator. England didn't heed the caution—and a pattern was established that would be repeated countless times.

He began applying to teach institute (college-level classes for LDS students, but without university credit) at this time, but without success. In 1966, he received a reply from a director of the program that captured his fraught position: He was well regarded for both his faith and his intellect, but he was quick to reveal his unorthodox views to all comers. "Even though it seems that every time we get into a real discussion on some phase of the Gospel, we end up on opposite poles, I want you to know that I have a great deal of respect for your ability, and know that when you put your hand in service to the Lord you will bring about much good," George Pace wrote.[18] No openings were available, but he would keep England in mind for future spots.

England had not questioned church doctrine or authority, but he had challenged a Mormon cultural commandment: Do not act in defiance of prevailing church norms of thought and behavior. In the founding days of the church, Joseph Smith had bridled at orthodoxy tests, proclaiming in one case that "I never thought it was right to call up a man and try him because he erred in doctrine. . . . I want the liberty of believing as I please. It feels so good not to be trammeled."[19] England's iconoclasm erupted in a Latter-day Saint environment worlds removed from that of Joseph Smith. The intellectual adventurousness of pre-1930s Mormonism had met with institutional hostility in that decade, and a new climate had prevailed ever since. The 1960s would see the most profound clash of competing paradigms—Smithian legacy and institutional retrenchment—the church had known, and England would be at the very forefront. Only by setting the stage can England's place in LDS cultural history be understood, with repercussions still playing out.

THE LATTER-DAY SAINT INTELLECTUAL LEGACY

At last a Latter-day Saint [who] really says something! [He] take[s] us out
of our intellectual flatland and finds us room to turn around in, breathe
deeply, and do some exploring.—Hugh Nibley, preface to England's
Why the Church is as True as the Gospel

Joseph Smith's commitment to the life of the mind, personally and institutionally, was absolute. He studied German and Hebrew, and tried to master ancient Egyptian hieroglyphics. He organized a School of the Prophets, where his peers were enjoined to "become acquainted with all good books, and with languages, tongues, and people" (Doctrine and Covenants [D&C] 88:79, 90:16). He founded a museum, library, and university in Nauvoo, Illinois. "Intelligence is the great object of our holy religion," he declared. And intelligence, he continued, "is the result of education, and education can only be obtained by living in compact society. . . . One of the principal objects then, of our coming together, is to obtain the advantages of education; and in order to do this, compact society is absolutely necessary."[20]

The Latter-day Saint embrace of intellectual formation was rooted in a very particular conception of salvational progress, one that saw in present processes patterns of things pertaining to worlds past and future alike. Smith was much influenced by the philosopher Thomas Dick, whom he quoted approvingly. In his most popular work, Dick had written that "the principles of mathematics, . . . the truths of natural philosophy, astronomy, geography, mechanics, and similar sciences, will be recognized, and form the basis of reasoning and action, so long as we are sentient beings and have a relation to the material system of the universe."[21] As Brigham Young translated this extrapolation of the schoolroom into the eternities, "[When] 'the elements . . . melt with fervent heat[,]' the Lord Almighty will send forth his angels, who are well instructed in chemistry, and they will separate the elements and make new combinations thereof."[22] Consequently, in Orson Pratt's salute to education, "the study of science is the study of something eternal. If we study astronomy, we study the works of God. If we study chemistry, geology, optics, or any other branch of science, every new truth we come to the understanding of is eternal; it is a part of the great system of universal truth. It is truth that exists throughout universal nature; and God is the dispenser of all truth—scientific, religious, and political."[23] (Latter-day Saints also envisioned, unofficially, a formal educational program in the premortal realm: Mosiah Hancock, in vision, saw innumerable spirits, "arranged in classes," where "they were taught in the arts and sciences, and everything necessary to make the heart happy. The teachers . . . received the instruction they imparted from certain notable ones, who in turn got their directions from the Father and the Son. . . . I also saw Joseph, Brigham, and many others engaged in this work of education.")[24]

The church's first generation yielded a bumper crop of both autodidacts, like Orson Hyde and the Pratt brothers Parley and Orson, and the well-trained, like Oberlin graduate Lorenzo Snow. Parley Pratt was the closest the church had to a systematizer of Latter-day Saint doctrine, while Orson was the most highly regarded speculative theologian of the new faith (frequently reined in by the authoritarian Brigham Young, who himself authored a fair number of theological innovations, later discarded). Their recurrent clashes brought into sharp relief the irreconcilability at the heart of the faith tradition's central paradox: personal autonomy and intellectual freedom contending against prophetic authority and institutional power.

The Utah Saints continued to foster a rich intellectual culture, founding a Polysophical Society, the Universal Scientific Society, a Wasatch Literary Association, and assorted "literary societies for reading and debate"—in addition to a university.[25] As one evidence of Latter-day Saint social progressivism, when the University of Deseret reopened in 1868 after a hiatus of some years, women comprised almost 50 percent of the class.[26] (At this time, women nationwide received less than 15 percent of bachelor's degrees awarded; all told, only 0.7 percent of American women eighteen to twenty-one years of age were attending college in 1870.)[27]

In this same era, B. H. Roberts reminisced, he had belonged to the Young Men's Club of Centerville, Utah. This remarkable, independent group of boys paid the then hefty initiation fee of $2.50 (and 50 cents monthly), "all of which was turned into books." The group existed expressly "to encourage reading and meet . . . at stated period—usually once a week—and to retell the stories of their reading." They amassed "a rather considerable library" and even raised enough funds to build their own public hall.[28]

In 1870, Brigham Young ratcheted up the level of institutional support by establishing a series of Latter-day Saint academies (tuition-supported high schools), throughout the Mormon West. Three years after his death, there were some two dozen academies from Canada to Mexico. That year, according to the 1880 census, Utah's literacy rate (ages 10 and above) was 95 percent, when in the country as a whole it was 87 percent, placing it ahead of thirty-four states and territories.[29] To manage the church's growing educational system, a board of education was organized in 1888.

As with most Christian denominations, the rise of Darwinism in the late nineteenth century virtually demanded either accommodation or denunciation by church leadership. Because they steadfastly resisted the liberalizing typical of mainline Protestantism, one might have anticipated the latter of the two responses—wholesale rejection. In fact, the Latter-day Saint church is in this regard an inconsistent story, exhibiting a mixture of both fundamentalism and radicalism, orthodox opinions and unexpected openness, as the case study of evolution illustrates. Traditional Christian belief regarding creation was rooted in three tenets: God created the earth out of nothingness (ex nihilo creation), the process lasted six literal days, and all of this transpired about 6,000 years ago. Latter-day Saint teaching, however, did not align itself behind any of those three articles of faith.

Latter-day Saints reject creation ex nihilo outright. Smith taught as early as 1833 that "the elements are eternal," incapable of creation or destruction (D&C 93:3). As for six days of creation, the Book of Abraham produced by Smith equated those days with sequential "times" (4:5–31). Finally, Smith's views of the age of the earth were more consistent with modern science than those of contemporary Christians. Writing to William Smith, W. W. Phelps reported Smith as understanding that "eternity, agreeably to the records found in the catacombs of Egypt, has been going on in this system (not this world) almost two thousand five hundred and fifty five millions of years [2.5 billion years]:

and to know at the same time, that deists, geologists and others are trying to prove that matter must have existed hundreds of thousands of years."[30]

Within a few decades, however, two developments ignited controversy in the church's premier educational institution, Brigham Young University, challenging the optimistic assessment of Orson Pratt that "the study of science is the study of something eternal. . . . Every new truth we come to the understanding of is eternal; it is a part of the great system of universal truth."[31] Higher criticism was making inroads in American biblical scholarship even as debates over Darwinian evolution gained steam nationally. In response to the first, the church's General Board of Education in 1908 prohibited the use of "any text book of the New or Old Testament written by a non-member of our church."[32] The next year, the First Presidency issued a statement that effectively condemned human evolution, calling the idea one of the "theories of men."[33] In 1911, three Brigham Young University professors were summoned to a hearing: Ralph Chamberlin, a biologist who was introducing his students to evolutionary theory, and Joseph and Henry Peterson, teaching modernist approaches to biblical studies. After a day-long hearing, the professors were judged to be endorsing evolution "as a demonstrated law," treating the Bible "as a collection of myths," and in general, undermining the faith of students.[34] Their dismissal was recommended to and accepted by the BYU Board of Trustees.

The cultural shift this development suggested was by no means monolithic or without countervailing currents. In many ways, that decade and the one just ahead heralded a particularly propitious climate for intellectualism in the church. James E. Talmage (1862–1933) was a geologist who had studied at Lehigh, Johns Hopkins, and Wesleyan (and was the first Latter-day Saint, in 1896, to receive a doctorate). He gained an international reputation, was made a fellow of several elite learned societies (including the Royal Society of Edinburgh), comfortably embraced post-Darwinian science, led the University of Utah as president, and was ordained an apostle in 1911. His publication of two seminal works of Latter-day Saint theology (*Articles of Faith* [1899] and *Jesus the Christ* [1915]) were the only major theological works to be commissioned and approved by the hierarchy.

About this same time, two other scientists who would become apostles received their doctorates: John A. Widtsoe and Joseph F. Merrill. At the exact moment BYU was trying to segregate gospel instruction from secular learning, Widtsoe was moving in the opposite direction, with titles like *Joseph Smith as Scientist* (1903–4, 1908), *Science and the Gospel* (1908–9), and *Rational Theology* (1915). Clearly, the church's consensus about the merits of worldly learning was fracturing. A turning point occurred in the 1930s with a bold but disastrous experiment. BYU professor Sidney Sperry had gone east to obtain a degree in divinity studies, enrolling at the University of Chicago in 1925. Meanwhile, Church Education Commissioner Adam S. Bennion, in spite of suspicion and resistance from some in the leadership, was encouraging CES teachers to study cutting-edge historical and literary approaches to biblical scholarship. (Bennion, like every other commissioner and superintendent of education in the 1920s and 1930s, held a PhD.)[35] He organized a rigorous seminar for seminary teachers to "enrich and integrate the[ir] intellectual and theological thinking," and then, impressed with Sperry's training, he selected three teachers to follow in Sperry's path, even subsidizing their study.[36] Russel B. Swensen, George S. Tanner, and Daryl Chase were the first of several Latter-day Saint teachers who pursued divinity studies at the University of Chicago Divinity School in that generation. They would be followed by T. Edgar Lyon, Carl J. Furr, Heber C. Snell, Vernon Larsen, Wesley P. Lloyd, Therald N. Jensen, and Anthony S. Cannon. At the same time, Merrill was bringing Edgar Goodspeed and other prominent biblical scholars to the BYU campus to teach summer sessions for seminary teachers.

At the same moment, more powerful figures were moving in the opposite direction. Permission to publish the brilliant autodidact B. H. Roberts's *The Truth, the Way, the Life*, the first attempt at a monumental synthesis of Latter-day Saint theology, had stalled in a committee of five apostles in 1930. One reason was Joseph Fielding Smith, a powerful voice suspicious of "dangers lurking in modern thought."[37] Four months later, Smith publicly and forcefully "denounce[d] as absolutely false the opinions of some that this earth was peopled with a race before Adam," and condemned current efforts at a synthesis of science and the gospel.[38] His remarks would later be counterbalanced by a Talmage speech insisting on the harmony of true science and true gospel understanding, "The Earth and Man," which was, according to some sources, published by the church.[39] But the shift in the winds had begun.

As these developments unfolded, the balance in the quorum shifted dramatically. In 1933, both B. H. Roberts and James Talmage, the church's two leading intellectuals, died. The same year, J. Reuben Clark was called to the First Presidency. Clark was a staunch defender of orthodoxy who, in Armand Mauss's opinion, "had a more profound impact on the Church than any other First Presidency appointment since Jedediah M. Grant's during the 'Reformation' in 1854."[40] In the fading generation, the church's most erudite scholars had been called upon not just to expound doctrine but to produce numerous church teaching manuals. Talmage's *Great Apostasy* (1910) was originally designed as a manual for the Young Women's auxiliary, and his *Jesus the Christ* was the official Melchizedek Priesthood manual in 1916. Roberts had produced a highly influential, five-volume *Seventies Course in Theology* which was used in that quorum for the years 1907–11; the Young Men's Mutual Improvement Association published a three-year manual based on his study of the Book of Mormon, *New Witness for God* (1903–6). John Widtsoe's *Science and the Gospel* was the Young Men's Mutual Improvement Association Manual of 1908–9. His *Joseph Smith as Scientist* (1908) was adopted for that program in 1920–21, and he also produced for that organization the tellingly titled manuals *How Science Contributes to Religion* (1927) and (the coauthored) *Heroes of Science* (1926–27). Widtsoe's *Rational Theology* (1915) was used as a Melchizedek Priesthood manual. Clearly, the church valued these men of science and gave them a powerful role in shaping the attitudes of church members, and youth especially, toward science and the gospel. Now, official attitudes toward a vigorous intellectual culture reversed course.

The coup de main came in August 1938. With the permission of President Heber J. Grant, J. Reuben Clark delivered an address to the church's seminary and institute teachers that laid down the law unambiguously, with repercussions that would persist even beyond Eugene England's life and career. In "The Charted Course of the Church in Education," Clark articulated a vision that became the official statement of guidelines and underlying philosophy informing the worldwide network of Latter-day Saint educators. It is unlikely that any address of the twentieth century did more to shape and constrain the church's intellectual culture for coming generations. (Only in 2016 did a senior apostle reformulate the philosophical underpinnings of CES culture.)[41] First, Clark declared CES objectives: "These students (to put the matter shortly) are prepared to understand and to believe that there is a natural world and there is a spiritual world; that the things of the natural world will not explain the things of the spiritual world; that the things of the spiritual world cannot be understood or comprehended by the things of the natural world; that you cannot rationalize the things of the spirit." Further emphasizing a dichotomy between spirit and reason, church and world, he warned church educators,

> You are not to teach the philosophies of the world, ancient or modern, pagan or Christian, for this is the field of the public schools. Your sole field is the Gospel. . . . We pay taxes to support those state institutions whose function and work it is to teach the arts, the sciences, literature, history, the languages, and so on through the whole secular curriculum. These institutions are to do this work. But we use the tithes of the

Church to carry on the Church school system, and these are impressed with a holy trust. The Church seminaries and institutes are to teach the Gospel.[42]

The impact of this address, which came to hold quasi-canonical status, a kind of code of Hammurabi for church educators, cannot be overstated. The strains of reconciling Zion and the world, spirit and matter, the sacred and the mundane, had proven too much. There would be no more paid sabbaticals to the Chicago Divinity School for church employees, and conversely, no more invitations for their faculty to come and instruct CES employees at BYU. Two years later, the increasingly influential Clark would direct Commissioner of Education Franklin West that teachers "should carefully refrain from saying anything that will raise doubt or question in the student's mind about the gospel. . . . Every fact, every argument, every reason that can be found must be used to support church doctrines—the gospel—not to question them."[43]

Most Latter-day Saints with a commitment to the life of the mind mourn the passing of an intellectual golden age of the church—and understandably so. However, it is imperative to recognize that the church leadership had good reason to fear the secular détente was not working to the membership's advantage. Those leaders concerned about the rising tide of secularism and its impact on their youth found statistical evidence to validate their worst fears. Surveys conducted in the mid-1930s of church youth, as well as of BYU students and alumni in particular, revealed a number of worrisome facts: One study showed that of rural young Latter-day Saints, only half were regular churchgoers or paid tithing, and fully a third were not observing the Word of Wisdom (the church's health code). BYU students and alumni reported only slightly higher levels of faithfulness. Among BYU students, 14 percent questioned whether the Latter-day Saint church was more divine than other Christian churches, 20 percent doubted that church authorities received revelation or that God answered prayers through divine intervention, and nearly two-thirds doubted the church's teaching of an actual Satan. Perhaps more disturbing to leaders, only 42 percent felt their faith in the church increased while at the church university.[44] A generation after the shift in CES philosophy and practice, according to a 1973 follow-up poll, orthodoxy at BYU had increased by over 25 points overall.[45]

Outside affirmation of the new course came as well. The author of one of the most comprehensive studies to date of American teenagers and religion writes that "Mormons generally have high expectations of their youth [and] invest a lot in educating them. . . . These investments pay off in producing Mormon teenagers who are, by sociological measures at least, more religiously serious and articulate than most other religious teenagers in the U.S." Equally heartening, this increased religiosity does not seem to have come at a cost to Latter-day Saint commitment to a vigorous academic life. "Mormon teenagers fared best when it comes to avoiding risky behavior and doing well in school," the study concluded.[46] In the 1940s and 1950s, meanwhile, the cultural war was still playing out, with some lamentable casualties. Foremost in this number was Lowell Bennion, the most influential figure in Eugene England's life.

LOWELL BENNION, MENTOR AND MARTYR

That crucial change in me was not imposed from outside by authority, it was educated, educed, led out of me by Brother Bennion . . . the best practical philosopher the LDS Church has produced in the twentieth century.
—England, "The Achievement of Lowell Bennion"

Lowell Bennion was perhaps the most beloved lay Latter-day Saint of his era. However, if his life was an inspiration and prod to England, it should also have been a warning. He was, as Sterling McMurrin aptly put it, the closest thing Mormonism had to its own saint.[47] Scholar, humanitarian, and teacher, Bennion had won such confidence from the leadership that President David O. McKay personally asked him to address the church in a world conference (the priesthood session) in 1958—an opportunity almost exclusively reserved for sitting world authorities of the church. He had precisely the influence and trust that England coveted all his life. Even so, the admiration in which Bennion was held by senior leadership did not save him in the end from the rising tides of change that would derail his career before completely engulfing England.

In 1953, the Church Educational System had come under the control of Ernest Wilkinson, archconservative president of Brigham Young University and administrator-chancellor of the Unified Church School System, a title that replaced that of church commissioner (for his tenure alone). One sign of the period's increasing hostility to science was the dismissal of his predecessor in the commissioner's office, Franklin West. West was much beloved by his teachers for the freedom of thought he promoted; in his view, he was released because "there was a little feeling because I was a scientist, that I couldn't be an honest-to-goodness sound believer in the church's theology."[48] Wilkinson's next ambition was to replace church Institutes of Religion with church junior colleges, though he failed to persuade the leadership, alarmed at the costs projected. He was particularly ill-disposed toward the University of Utah institute.

His second year running the CES, in 1954, Wilkinson directed his subordinates to maintain a file of those institute's teachers "who have critical attitudes." Bennion's name went on the list. Bennion didn't improve his standing by publicly challenging apostle Mark E. Peterson's defense of the Negro Doctrine, as it was called, in a 24 August CES convention.[49] The second morning of the conference, apostle Joseph Fielding Smith spoke for two hours on his book *Man: His Origin and Destiny*, a polemical onslaught against modern science, Darwinian evolution, and contemporary geological understanding. Bennion rose to politely and diplomatically plead for a pedagogical approach that did not pit science against religion. One of Bennion's like-minded (and also blacklisted) colleagues, George Boyd, followed up with another question, prescient in its theological pertinence: Doesn't dogma require "a unanimous decision?" Otherwise, how are we to know, in the face of competing pronouncements, "what is authoritative—coming from the past?" Smith was brooking no compromise or middle ground, however. Bennion was called in the next day to meet with Smith and Peterson, who merely reasserted the claim that they were speaking authoritative doctrine.

Bennion and a third blacklister, Ed Lyon, met with LDS church president David O. McKay. It was no secret that McKay, along with apostle James Talmage (and Henry Eyring), emphatically disagreed with Smith's fundamentalist reading of church doctrine. The institute teachers received McKay's private moral support but raised Wilkinson's hackles for requesting the meeting in the first place. The situation is powerfully revealing of another tragic trade-off in Latter-day Saint culture, a trade-off responsible for creating the catastrophic collisions that would militate against England as they were now working against Bennion.

The problem is best appreciated by contrasting the leadership structure of the Latter-day Saint church with that of Catholicism, another highly hierarchical institution. The Roman Catholic Church has over a hundred cardinals widely dispersed throughout the world, and over 5,000 bishops, who together with the pope constitute the magisterium, or teaching authority of the church. Their Latter-day Saint counterpart is a group of only fifteen men: the prophet, his two counselors, and a quorum of twelve apostles. They meet weekly and work in constant proximity and interaction. Harmony and solidarity are indispensable in these conditions and, as a consequence, collegiality and mutual courtesy become paramount considerations in the church's governance. This is not a simple matter of politics or pragmatism. With such a concentration of power and authority in a small, perennially visible, compact body, dissention and disagreement could have damaging consequences for a membership born and bred to believe in a divinely led church. Hence the striking explanation for sacrificing personal preferences and convictions to harmony, which Hugh B. Brown expressed to England shortly before his death: "I think all my brethren in the quorum are wrong in this decision," he said referring to their persistence in defending the policy of denying Blacks the priesthood in the 1960s. But "I would do nothing to destroy the unity of that quorum on which your and my salvation depends."[50]

It is crucial to understand both the historical as well as the theological premises that make such concessions logically and spiritually coherent in Latter-day Saint thought. In the first place, the Saints are a people who coalesced at a time of widespread persecution and soul-challenging hardship. Only passionate intragroup loyalty assured their survival and prosperity in the Utah wilderness. England loved to repeat one episode of the church's past that best encapsulates the devotion of his people to each other. As his student Dian Monson relates, "I remember how admiringly he would tell the story of Levi Savage, a member of the Martin Handcart Company and one of the few to challenge the decision by company leaders, among them an apostle, to embark on the trek across the plains at such a late season in the year. After voicing his strenuous objection to the decision and realizing his objection would go unheeded, Savage told fellow company members: 'Seeing you are to go forward, I will go with you, will help you all I can, will work with you, will rest with you, will suffer with you, and if necessary, I will die with you.'"[51] The ending of the story is a part of Mormonism's cultural canon: Almost 150 Saints starved and froze to death when winter overtook the company, as Savage foretold it would. England knew—and practiced—the same principle of costly loyalty.

In the second place, in Latter-day Saint understanding, council consensus is not a substitute for divine revelation; council consensus *is* the particular form that revelation is believed to take. The Church of Jesus Christ began with all spiritual authority vested in the person of Joseph Smith, largely as a function of his charismatic gifts. In 1831, as he worked through the gospel of Matthew in his retranslation, the sixteenth chapter registered profoundly and manifestly on his religious thinking. Keys, or the formal delegation of authority from God to his representative, operating within formal priesthood offices, gave further definition and emphasis to that authority. But by 1835, as Richard Bushman notes of Smith's subsequent restructuring of the leadership, "Smith not only shifted the responsibility for revelation from himself to his councils, he moved the locus of revelation from the individual prophet to the church's administrative bureaucracy."[52] A few days after calling the first quorum of twelve latter-day apostles, Smith counseled them to carefully record quorum decisions, as being on a par with "the great and glorious manifestations" made to Smith's presidency, with a view to publication as a matter of "covenant or doctrine." As Bushman has noted, "The implication was that decisions in council were to be of equal authority with revelations to the prophet."[53] In other words, consensus on the part of keys-holding leadership was not just the equivalent of revelation, it was to be understood as the form revelation took in a council-led church.

This consensus-driven practice, rooted in Latter-day Saint theological understanding, has costly consequences. Change and innovation are frequently thwarted until total consensus is reached; and when maverick individuals break ranks, they may be silently tolerated rather than disciplined or repudiated. A prominent case in point was the crossfire in which Bennion and his colleagues found themselves in their resistance to the antiscientific pronouncements of a faction in the leadership. For instance, in 1958 Joseph Fielding Smith's similarly inclined son-in-law and Seventy (one day to become an apostle), Bruce R. McConkie, published the most influential compendium in Latter-day Saint history: *Mormon Doctrine*. Two apostles assigned to review the book for church president David O. McKay recommended over 1,000 corrections, and McKay suspended its republication "even in a corrected form."[54] Nevertheless, after making some changes, McConkie republished his book in 1966, and the church's publisher marketed the immensely influential title all the way until 2010. Official objections notwithstanding, church publications have quoted from the book prolifically in lesson manuals and teaching materials.

The book's enduring success, in spite of its contested authority and accuracy, is perhaps a testament to the human proclivity for neatly packaged dogma. The cost of the cultural taboo against disharmony was in this case substantial. The leadership permitted (and institutionally endorsed through its publication arm) a book claiming to be church dogma, even though the leadership had adjudged the book to have over a thousand doctrinal errors. In addition, McConkie's personal hostility to science and secular learning generally had such conspicuous if implicit institutional endorsement that it plagues the church to this day. His views and those of some of his colleagues were amicably ignored rather than authoritatively condemned. The ground was riven between opposing camps, and with the leadership favoring harmony over faction, and the most outspoken leaders on the fundamentalist end of the scale, the more liberal-minded thinkers and writers were on borrowed time. McKay's tenure would end with his death in 1970, but the gentle leader had already shown his reluctance to curb the more dogmatic of his colleagues.

When Wilkinson learned that the McKay meeting had actually been arranged by supervisor Joy Dunyon, Dunyon was summarily fired. Boyd was transferred out of state. McKay hesitated to intervene in the CES but made his support for Bennion's approach known to Wilkinson, which preserved Bennion's job. Bennion was also a great favorite of Hugh B. Brown, another voice of moderation in the quorum. By 1962, however, Bennion was being forced out of the institute. He had again suffered attacks for his heresy (a colleague complained to Joseph Fielding Smith that Bennion was "teaching false doctrine"),[55] and he was given a choice of reduced teaching, a leave of absence, or a transfer to BYU. One explanation given him was his criticism of exploitative missionary practices under Henry D. Moyle ("kiddie-dipping" in the waters of baptism children too young to know what was happening, which was transpiring on a large scale in some Latin American missions).

William Berrett, director of seminary and institutes, was given the unpleasant task of delivering the news to the institute's most beloved teacher, the man who had built the program from scratch. Berrett was philosophical about his own role in Bennion's dismissal: "Everybody who works for the church knows that he has many bosses. . . . I don't suppose anybody could teach as freely as Lowell taught without having some opposition."[56] When apostle Brown learned of the firing, he decried the step but felt he could do nothing. President McKay was likewise blindsided but also declined to intervene. In precise foreshadowing of England's later career, Bennion tried to get to the root of the reasons for his dismissal, requesting a meeting with Wilkinson. After patently specious explanations, Wilkinson went to the real factor: Bennion's failure to support the church's "Negro question" and criticism of Moyle's missionary methods. Wilkinson confided in a confidential memo that he was almost equally distressed that Bennion "practically refused to keep rolls and had practically no methods of grading his students" (this in a church-sponsored class designed for spiritual formation).

In another foreshadowing of England's plight, and in a tragic revelation of questionably weighted considerations so often at work in the church, Wilkinson freely acknowledged that Bennion "has had a great influence for good on the lives of thousands of students." With doubtful sincerity, the administrator added that they would be "most happy" to have Bennion on BYU's faculty of religion.[57] Bennion opted to take an associate dean position at the University of Utah instead. As would be the case with England's ouster three decades later, the official announcement was that the teacher had "resigned." And as with

England, Bennion did not publicly dispute the announcement's accuracy. One gauge of Bennion's popularity, and the extent of public fury at his dismissal, came in Wilkinson's failed run for the U.S. Senate two years later. Wilkinson believed he knew one reason for his loss: "By direction of the Board of Education, I removed Lowell Bennion as Director of the Institute at the University of Utah. . . . Many rumors erupted in Salt Lake County as to the reason for his dismissal and this hurt me in that county."[58]

In his last recorded communication with Wilkinson, Bennion asked for a more honest explanation for his ouster. "Would you care to tell me more specifically why I was released," he wrote in August 1962, "and by whom . . . in order to pass on the truth to those who inquire[?]"[59] No reply was forthcoming.

MORMONISM AND RACE

He denieth none that come unto him, black and white.—2 Nephi 26:33

One of the key contributions that Gene England made to his faith tradition— at his cost—was to illuminate the chasm between Latter-day Saint theology and Latter-day Saint culture, and it was in the realm of politics that this fissure emerged most starkly. Historically, the Republican Party had not been a welcoming home to Latter-day Saints. In fact, the party's founding 1856 platform pledged to oppose "those twin relics of barbarism—Polygamy and Slavery."[60] Largely in response to the sexual revolution of the 1960s, church members increasingly aligned themselves with the political party that claimed the mantle of "family values." That meant that the Republican Party was suddenly home to a majority of Saints. (At present both Latter-day Saint scripture and official pronouncements emphasize sexual morality as a—if not the—paramount moral concern. Sexual sin is "most abominable above all sins save it be the shedding of innocent blood.")[61] The Republican opposition to abortion further galvanized the Saints' loyalty in contrast to the Democratic Party's unstinting support of abortion access. These two developments only added to the momentum of the migration of Latter-day Saints toward the Republican Party, until at the present day they are the most Republican-leaning of any religious group in America, at 70 percent.[62]

Predictably, perhaps, Saints developed a tendency to conflate conservative political positions in general with Restoration gospel truth. England persistently picked that identification apart, arguing that far too many American values associated with conservatives were in fact antithetical to the gospel. As he said to a student reporter, "The values we've upheld as Americans are values of racism and sexism and materialism, anti-environmentalism, militarism."[63] He was doubtless correct that when occasional critiques of those values associated with the Right came from the church prophet, it ruffled fewer feathers (as when President Ezra Taft Benson condemned the worship of wealth, or President Spencer W. Kimball declared, "We are a warlike people . . . perverting the Savior's teaching[s]").[64] Such few pronouncements aside, only scattered prominent voices have emerged from within the tradition to point out the Democratic Party's closer alignment with other values that should be of fundamental concern to Latter-day Saints, including economic and racial equality, receptivity to immigrants, and antimilitarism.

For England, the church leadership's support for the Vietnam War was a conspicuous example of dissonance. Equally distressing, in his view, was widespread Latter-day Saint indifference to racial injustice. England's dissent from patriotic support of the war went against the grain of cultural Mormonism, but doctrinal orthodoxy was never at stake. No church doctrine required assent to what growing numbers would see as an unjust war, and Latter-day Saint scriptures could be invoked to justify pacifism as readily as to vindicate armed intervention ("renounce war and proclaim peace," reads D&C 98:16). Racial politics was decidedly more fraught with danger, for the simple reason that the church had in 1852 instituted an official policy denying the priesthood to Black members, and consistently reaffirmed the ban. This institutional form of racism, then, could not be easily dismissed as cultural practice; it was codified in official policy. Of course, lacking scriptural support, the practice *was* susceptible to criticism as a product of cultural formation; that tentative recognition was slow in coming, and England played a significant and little-known role in the awakening.

As Lowell Bennion had learned, to question such a policy in the 1960s— though not out of harmony with liberal American society of the day—could only be seen by church leaders as dangerous dissent. The background to the racial ban is known in outline. In the early 1850s, under circumstances not fully elaborated in the historical record, Brigham Young declared that members of African descent were not eligible for ordination to the otherwise universal male priesthood; and neither they nor women of African descent could participate in temple rituals, necessary in Latter-day Saint belief for progress into the highest, or celestial, realm of heaven. Young made no specific claim of revelation to support his prohibition. It seems to have been rather a perfect storm of inherited Christian beliefs, a recovered book of scripture, and a unique Latter-day Saint story of human origins that made the doctrine almost inevitable. Christian precedent for reading the Biblical curses of Cain and Ham as applying to Blacks was commonplace; a "translation" of Smith, "The Book of Abraham," referred to a "lineage" that disqualified Pharaoh from holding the priesthood. (The reference is now read as pertaining to rights of the firstborn, but the words were easily construed to reinforce a racial prohibition.) Finally, the belief in human premortal existence provided a speculative space for positing prebirth events as a rational basis for punishing select individuals. And so beginning with early apologists and continuing into the 1960s, some Latter-day Saint writers imputed to Blacks, in their premortal condition, a stance of neutrality or passivity in the great war in heaven, leading to their disqualification for priesthood blessings.

Like most Saints of his generation, the young England initially found those explanations sufficient warrant for the practice, and for refuting charges that the ban was racism pure and simple. The turning point came, as we saw, in an institute class he attended in 1953. His teacher, Bennion, challenged his unreflective statement that there was a good theological rationale for the racial ban. The seeds had actually been planted even earlier, by a Sunday school teacher with firsthand experience of apartheid. "Mickey Duncan came back from a mission in South Africa and taught our Sunday school class and he had very liberal and advanced ideas that he shared with us about blacks and the priesthood, about theology. He talked freely, complex theology, agency. He would have members of the class actually prepare little presentations. So we got, by the time I was 14, 15, 16 years, thinking, reading source books. [James E.] Talmage, Joseph Fielding Smith and others. And then we would talk about that. In fact for about two years we had liked that so much, we arranged to have him teach a weekly fireside to us."[65] Duncan was not afraid to unsettle the assumptions of those who had experienced very little racial diversity in their culture—let alone racial tensions.

The charismatic Bennion added intellectual heft and his own spiritual magnetism to the incubating dissent. By 1968, a growing number of Saints were raising questions. In politically progressive Palo Alto, the intellectually restless England was increasingly willing to challenge the status quo. Further inspiring him was his experience in Samoa, where he saw the colonialist condescension toward a people he loved, and where, for a time, he himself felt the sting of being a racial minority. "I'm beginning to know how a negro feels in America all the time," he recorded at one low point. The comparison was an exaggeration, but the experience sharpened his sensitivity to racial division. England was not yet a church institute instructor (that came in 1967 or 1968),[66] but as he already interacted with many Latter-day Saint students, he felt particularly conflicted. He had the burden of building faith among students while believing the church's unofficial support for a distant war and its very official support for a discriminatory policy were morally wrong.

What set England apart from most dissidents in religious history is that his objective was neither protest nor necessarily reform. He wanted to find a way—for himself and his students—to follow the disciple's path, but within the bounds of the institutional church. "I particularly remember the concern about the Viet Nam War that enveloped the campus, but was hardly mentioned at Church," remembered one friend and student. "Gene's concern with the issue of blacks holding the priesthood made an even greater impression on me as a young adult. . . . Gene was the one adult representing the church in our lives who cared about the same issues that we as students were facing. His concern bridged the gap between our faith community and our everyday community, teaching us that the gospel was relevant at all times and places."[67]

Johnson, in the 1964 election, was the first Democrat to win England's vote. Of course, Johnson went on to win in the largest landslide since the election of 1820, and the great exodus of Latter-day Saints from the Democratic Party was still one election away. One scholar notes that "the 1960s would be liberalism's last hurrah in Utah for more than half a century." This was because "the Democratic coalition, forged in economic crisis" of preceding decades, came in this era to embrace social and moral positions that alienated large numbers of voters, reawakening "submerged religious identities."[68] Among those alienated numbers whose religious identities came into political play were most Latter-day Saints, who deserted the Democratic Party, seen as increasingly hostile to "family values."

England would later vote for Ronald Reagan—twice. Only at BYU could a Reagan supporter be marginalized as a dangerous progressive. Johnson's support for the Civil Rights Act was doubtless a factor in England's support in the 1964 election. And even though Johnson was not exactly a peace candidate, he was closer to that label than Barry Goldwater. England was reacting more and more negatively to the anticommunist rhetoric of the Cold War. He made his choice on that basis, though he came to believe that Johnson's administration was "genuinely evil in terms of having no moral position at all."[69] In the heated Palo Alto political environment, England persisted in his vocal opposition to the war, writing and participating in demonstrations.[70] However, it wasn't his peace activism that led to his earliest conflict with church authorities—it was civil rights. Specifically, a member of the local high council (twelve men with advisory roles to the stake president) owned extensive properties and allegedly practiced flagrant racial discrimination. England became a community activist aligned against him. That set the stage—but his real misstep was to use the church directory and mail every member his own statement of support for a ballot initiative addressing the problem. "I didn't see it as a political matter," he explained by way of justification, but one, as mandated by the gospel, "based on our own scriptures."[71] The stake leadership was less sanguine on the question and chastised him for using church directories in a partisan campaign. That was the first time he incurred church censure, but it was local and low key. He progressed rapidly.

England's use of a church directory, like his prior run-in with the father of a conscientious objector, most likely had not put him on the radar of the higher church leadership. That was about to change. England had known Marion D. Hanks when the latter was himself an institute teacher at the University of Utah. Gene and Charlotte had taken Book of Mormon classes from him, and the experience rooted his faith deeply in that LDS scripture.[72] He had corresponded with Hanks as a missionary, receiving that gentle rebuke for his judgmentalism of other missionaries. He continued the correspondence when Hanks became president of the British Mission in 1962. He sent Hanks some of his poetry (which Hanks judged "great"), along with a query about these two issues that troubled him. In response to his frustrations, Hanks counseled: "As to the 'abysses'—try to circle them. . . . I am not suggesting that you close your eyes or your mind. . . . I am just suggesting that your highest happiness will be found lifting and deepening and broadening and loving, and not standing on the edge making strange noises or asking questions that any fool can ask while others with maybe fewer answers are inside doing the work." He continued, justifying the general dearth of social justice warriors and liberal pronouncements from the leadership: "As to the silence of the brethren on some of these matters, the program of respect and loyalty which the Church engenders in its leaders is at the cost of the contentment of most. Nobody likes to shut up when he feels he ought to be saying something, but in the long run there seems to be little virtue or gain in sporadic and personal outbursts."[73]

England responded full of hurt, defensiveness, and frustration. "Your letter disturbed me, especially when it seemed to carry the tone of one on the inside speaking to one on the 'edge,' or to the Gene that is still a wild-eyed adolescent idealist or a naively crusading Samoan missionary. I'm not those things. . . . I'm not on the edge or mucking around in abysses. . . . It distresses me that I haven't made these things sufficiently clear to you." He then played the integrity card while flattering his critic: "If I have questions and recognize abysses . . . they are questions and abysses that the moral exactness of Christ himself and his prophets and your own teachings and example encourage me to face." Then, with dubious persuasive force, he insisted that "whatever you may think . . . I am no longer prone to outbursts."[74] Ever patient and forgiving, the genial Hanks responded with a consoling note. To which England then replied, "You've reduced me to tears. . . . Thank you, Duff, for your love."[75]

4

DIALOGUE

My faith in [Christ] encourages me to enter into dialogue.
—England, "The Possibility of Dialogue"

England had arrived in Palo Alto in 1962, already convinced that "the two greatest problems America faces [are] South east Asia and the ghetto."[1] As a fervent Latter-day Saint Christian, he translated those concerns to the LDS policies that most occupied his religious life: the church's uncritical support of the Vietnam War, and its scripturally unfounded, racially based priesthood ban.

England was by temperament an optimist. Latter-day Saint theology fed that optimism. A religion that denied original sin and inherent depravity, asserted the literal parenthood of God (as a Heavenly Father and Mother), and espoused the eventual deification of virtually all human beings could not help but shape its theologically informed disciples into hopeful, positive Zion-builders. This buoyant disposition and perspective are indispensable to understanding England's life and modus operandi. One word more than any other characterizes his aspirational energies to build consensus and cooperation: *dialogue*. Soon after his arrival at Stanford, an idea took shape in his mind for a journal devoted to open and honest engagement with tough questions, with all views presented in a faith-building context devoid of dogmatism. Other Latter-day Saints had been laying the groundwork for his project for decades.

As conservatism and retrenchment replaced the intellectual heyday of Mormonism's 1930s and 1940s, a group of prominent intellectuals including Lowell Bennion, T. Edgar Lyon, George T. Boyd, William Mulder, and Sterling McMurrin, part of a group who called themselves "the Swearing Elders," began to meet and discuss Latter-day Saint topics with a critical—in some cases jaundiced—eye. They floated among themselves the project of a

journal devoted to a scholarly examination of things Mormon, unhindered by
church oversight. England knew many in the group besides his mentor Bennion, and likely heard of such discussions.[2]

Returning home from his mission, as his inclinations turned toward literature, theology, and humanistic inquiry generally, he found himself increasingly
impatient with the limited scope of church publications, which were didactic
and devoid of intellectual content. Some of this was youthful idealism. As he
recalled, "I was so young and didn't know very much about what the Church
was doing. I was critical of Church publications . . . because I didn't find them
very meaningful." He wished for a journal that combined "open consideration
of our faith" with a mature "literary expression."[3] The decisive factor in what
he was about to propose, however, was his experience in the ministry of the
CES. "I saw young people in the Church with great talent and ability having a
real struggle relating their educational experience to the Church experience,
and falling off to one side or the other. . . . I saw students overawed by their
educational experience, finding their religious background wanting in comparison, or their religious leaders and heroes small in comparison. . . . I began to
see that there needed to be a journal that could somehow bridge that chasm."[4]

In 1959, the church's university had launched *BYU Studies*. At first, England
thought that journal might address the need he had diagnosed. "We were very
thrilled with the first issue, and then disappointed when subsequent issues
didn't fulfill the promise." It became apparent that its official hosting institution imposed too many strictures. "What was needed was an independent
journal."[5] Indeed, there was substance behind England's suspicions. Historian
Leonard Arrington published an article in the first issue of *BYU Studies* on the
Latter-day Saint Word of Wisdom, the health code prohibiting tobacco and
alcohol. His thesis that the code's strict enforcement in early Utah was more
financial than spiritual in motivation raised hackles with administrators, and
the university suspended the journal's publication for a year. The lesson was
learned and controversial subjects were henceforth avoided.

At the time that *BYU Studies* launched, Gene was still an undergraduate at
the University of Utah. He met a fellow student, Gene Kovalenko, and they
hit it off immediately. Kovalenko remembered that even at that age, "there
was just a presence, a man that I needed to know." They soon felt the desire to
expand their energizing conversations to a larger circle, so they invited three
others to join what they named the Dialogue Group. It was a kind of informal
debating club but marked by a tone that was a hallmark of England, and de-
noted by the group's name. Kovalenko explained: "Gene was my most severe
critic. . . . But I never for a second believed or felt that he was antagonistic or

rejecting. He just didn't agree, and he was clear about it. But there was always a sense of brotherhood and caring. So that was what I remember especially and value the most, was that challenge. That loving challenge. I don't think he had an unkind bone in his body. I've never seen him angry. I never saw him upset."[6] Mary Bradford remembers that in those undergraduate days at the University of Utah, in 1957, she and the Englands were having lunch on the lawn. "Charlotte had brought homemade bread. Gene and Carl Keller—who went to school with us—were talking about starting a journal. We said, 'The *Improvement Era* [the church's official magazine] is okay but there's no room for everybody to publish. We need another way to publish what we want to do.'"[7]

Eight years later, galvanized by his social conscience, disappointed in the *BYU Studies* failure to challenge orthodox history in even the most innocuous of ways, and surrounded by like-minded budding intellectuals, the time was ripe. England had been excelling at both his studies and his early poetry efforts, winning Stanford's Stegner Creative Writing Fellowship in Poetry. But he was a swirling nexus of energy, and his progress toward his degree was slow. Activism, friendships, raising a family, teaching institute, poetry writing, and essay writing (more political than academic) all absorbed his time. Then, at a moment when all his energies should have been devoted to his dissertation, he—joined by like-minded friends—conceived the project that would become the greatest obsession of his life, and the bane of his relationship to his faith tradition.

Five founders met in the early summer of 1965. In addition to England there were Wes Johnson, professor of African history at Stanford; Joseph Jeppson, professor of history at the College of San Matteo; Paul Salisbury, a Salt Lake City architect; and Frances Menlove, a psychologist. Committed to the venture, they sent out a prospectus to gauge the potential audience, announcing that "many men need some medium in which to consider their historical and religious heritage in relation to contemporary experience and learning. Some are excited about the dialogue this encounter provides and the good fruit it bears in their lives. Others find themselves alone in their experience and cut off from such a dialogue—and too often feel forced to choose between their heritage and the larger world. We are now preparing to publish a journal designed to meet the needs of both these groups."[8]

Response to the proposal was sufficiently enthusiastic to energize the group, and they immediately proceeded to publication plans. Their agenda was emphatically and explicitly centrist or, more accurately, pluralistic: "We were very serious about this," England said. "*Dialogue* was not and would not be a liberal journal nor a conservative journal nor any particular 'kind' of journal."[9] In fact, as he expressed his ambition, "my main theme" was "to deconstruct the polarity of 'conservative' and 'liberal.'"[10] Or as the self-description indicated, "*Dialogue: A Journal of Mormon Thought* is an independent national quarterly established to express Mormon culture and examine the relevance of religion in secular life. It is edited by Mormons who wish to bring their faith into dialogue with human experience as a whole and to foster artistic and scholarly achievement based on their cultural heritage. The journal encourages a variety of viewpoints."

The timing of the journal's launch appeared at first propitious. Leonard Arrington had just organized the Mormon History Association (MHA) as an independent forum for Latter-day Saint scholarship. The group had planned to immediately launch its own journal, *Latter-day Saint History*, but learned of the imminent publication of *Dialogue*. So instead a motion was made and carried that the group's scholars would submit historical pieces to the newly formed *Dialogue*,[11] and a special issue sponsored by the MHA was slated for Fall 1966.

Even before the first issue appeared, the *New York Times* got wind of the effort and found it noteworthy enough to devote an article to it in December 1965.[12] The publication editor, Paul Salisbury, could hardly have given an interview better calculated to alarm the church leadership. "It is difficult to hold nonconformist views within the church and prosper in Utah," he said, explaining the largely non-Utah composition of the editorial board. Then adopting a preemptive defensive posture, he told the reporter that "we are active members of the church; *however* we seek to give voice to a growing intellectual community to open the door to a variety of viewpoints impossible to express in existing Church journals" (my emphasis). Deliberately or not, the ill-considered "however" did the opposition's work for them. His phrasing had explicitly set two clauses—and two propositions—in opposition. Faithful devotion to the church was in tension with intellectual voices. Not only rhetorical effect was at stake; if Salisbury had said, "we are active, believing, faithful members of the church, *therefore* we want to enhance the intellectual conversation in the church," he would have avoided a stance of confrontation *and* he would have better reflected the view of England and Joseph Smith and Brigham Young alike, that intelligent engagement with doctrinal matters was of the essence of true discipleship. As England later phrased his alternative to the J. Reuben Clark model of church education: "I wanted to help young Mormon students . . . be true to both revelation and reason, to what they had grown up believing and what they were learning from the best higher education."[13]

Salisbury waved more red flags when he announced that the first issue would explicitly challenge positions of "the church" and "Mormon leaders" rather than criticize the culture or expand a church-wide conversation. In tones easily construed as patronizing, he said, "We will of course be concerned with the church stand" on pending right-to-work legislation, "the stand of the church against pacifism in the Vietnam war, and the position taken by Mormon leaders in relationship to Negroes."

Finally, Salisbury made the infelicitous comparison of *Dialogue* with the Catholic monthly *Ramparts*. That magazine's impassioned opposition to the Vietnam War might have passed without great concern. However, it also published the diaries of Che Guevara (introduced by Fidel Castro) and Eldridge Cleaver. The same year Salisbury invoked *Ramparts* as a model, the Central Intelligence Agency launched an investigation of that journal's suspected Soviet ties.

The *Times* article was a public relations fiasco and was probably read by every senior leader of the church. It goes further than impute a general anti-intellectualism to explain *Dialogue*'s immediately manifest resistance. These first impressions were never erased from the minds of most leaders. England protested to a friend that the press coverage was unfair and misleading: "The *Times* stringer in Salt Lake apparently was able to draw our man, Paul [Salisbury], out a bit, add a few misattributions, and a misleading tone and completely misrepresent us. It seems now that the *Times* man caught Paul when Paul was just a bit miffed over the run-around the Salt Lake papers had been giving him for over a week. All of them, including the *Church News*, unwilling to do a straight news story on us for reasons that sound suspiciously like plain fear of anything that even remotely might be controversial."[14]

Attempting some damage control, England quickly fired off a letter to the First Presidency in order to correct "some misleading and untrue information which has been circulated with regard to *Dialogue*, both by individuals and by news media—and that you may know that the brochure we sent you previously is the only information officially released by us at this time to describe our policies and plans. We are making every effort to see that there is no misleading amplification of this information before our first issue can exhibit on its own merits our fulfillment of the purpose expressed in the brochure."[15]

He followed up days later (late December 1965) with a trip to Utah, meeting personally with apostles Hugh B. Brown and Gordon B. Hinckley. In response to concerns expressed by Hinckley, England tried to address the perennial concern in LDS leadership circles that members would be misled by unauthorized voices: "I can't emphasize too strongly that *Dialogue* is *not* a theological journal or anything remotely like one; when we talk about *a* journal of Mormon thought, we are not talking about *the* Mormon position on any doctrine, but the thinking of individual Mormons about the whole range of their academic, cultural, and professional concerns, as their heritage and beliefs influence their thinking and decisions in these areas. . . . I hope you will look carefully at our first issue . . . and judge *Dialogue* by the merits and potentialities of the actual work in that issue."[16]

Even as he penned those words, the first issue was coming off the press in late March and sent to the initial subscriber base, a healthy 1,300 readers. In addition, the board sent copies to every General Authority of the church, repeating the board's insistence that the journal did not "speak for Mormonism or attempt . . . to compete in any way with the official organs of spokesmen of the Church." The board members expressed their faith that "*Dialogue* can help hold many of our young people close to the Gospel and will introduce Mormonism in a positive way to many who have not been reached by other means."[17]

In the background, other developments of seismic importance had taken shape between the launches of *BYU Studies* and of *Dialogue*. And these were hugely inauspicious for the new journal. In the General Conference of 1961, the apostle Harold B. Lee announced an initiative he had orchestrated under the direction of President David O. McKay. He described a felt need for "more co-ordination and correlation between the activities and programs of the various priesthood quorums and auxiliary organizations and the educational system of the Church."[18] Another way of framing the objective was not just to avoid redundancy and inconsistencies of effort but also to centralize the supervision and control of "the auxiliaries of the Church" that some members were seeing as "far more effective and powerful . . . than were the Priesthood quorums."[19]

The premiere example of this fact was the women's Relief Society. Through much of the church's history, the society had operated with a fair degree of autonomy. In the nineteenth century, it supported a number of women who went east to obtain medical training. Latter-day Saint women had soon launched a grain storage program, began an ambitious silkworm industry, and in 1872 inaugurated their own journal, the *Woman's Exponent*, unabashedly feminist in its orientation. Leonard Arrington declared the journal "the first 'permanent' woman's magazine west of the Mississippi and second in the nation after the Boston *Woman's Journal*."[20] Founded as a semiprivate venture, the magazine eventually became the official organ of the church's Relief Society and would run until 1914, replaced by the *Relief Society Magazine* the next year. The society was founded by women and functioned with a fair degree of autonomy at the local level.

Such examples of independent initiative faded under the purview of the new

"all-Church coordinating council"—better known as the "Priesthood Correlation Program"—announced by Lee. One early casualty of the new council was
the *Relief Society Magazine*, shuttered along with other semi-independent publications. The specific language accompanying the 1961 announcement helps
to explain how the rise of independent publications like *Dialogue* (and *BYU
Studies*), while fulfilling a new and critical need for independent expression,
at the same time posed a direct challenge to the spirit of these official efforts
to render church teaching and messaging more uniform: "The function of the
all-Church coordinating council is to formulate policy which will govern the
planning, the writing, co-ordination, and implementation of the entire Church
curriculum." This move was intended to ensure the teaching "of the gospel in a
more efficient and effective way in harmony with the instructions of the First
Presidency." Even more portentous of the looming tensions was the concluding
explanation for the initiative: "I construe [these developments] to be a consolidation of the forces of the Lord under the direction of the prophet, just as an
army, in order to meet a superior force of the enemy in numbers, the forces of
our opposition to the forces of evil must be consolidated in order to give them
the most effective possible defense. We are in a program of defense."[21]

The consequences of these programs and rhetoric for England's journal
were therefore predictable, and opposition to the magazine emerged from a
number of quarters, shutting down conservative participation and support.
Kenneth Godfrey, for instance, was a young, credentialed, and accomplished
historian whom Gene asked to serve on the editorial board. Flattered to be in
such elite company (four future college presidents, a Bancroft Award winner,
university deans, and a future apostle also agreed to serve, he noted),[22] he
immediately accepted. *Time* magazine and the *New York Times* contributed to
the heady atmosphere with their coverage, and *Christian Century* sent a letter of congratulations. Godfrey was employed by the church's seminaries and
institute program, however, and his overseers were not pleased. Alma Burton,
his supervisor as well as stake president, was "almost entirely negative" in his
response. William E. Berrett, the president of the Church Educational System,
summoned Godfrey and chastised him for not seeking prior approval before
accepting the position. Then learning that Burton was making noises, Godfrey
visited with him again, to be told that if he maintained his connection with
Dialogue he "would never become a general authority." Godfrey insisted such
a warning was a nonstarter; nevertheless, he called England and resigned his
position.[23] Even so, he contributed an essay on the German theologian Dietrich
Bonhoeffer a few months later.

Ironically, in the months after the inaugural issue of *Dialogue*, England himself approached Berrett about a teaching spot. When he responded to England in late 1966, he said, "Personally I have been very pleased with *Dialogue* and your general attitude as editor." Nevertheless, he hedged, the looming "problem" was "whether your editing *Dialogue* would cause any of the Board of Education to feel to refuse approval of your appointment."[24] For the time being, his appointment was put on hold.

When Richard Sonne, England's stake president, learned of the *Dialogue* board's plans to publish an analysis of the recently recovered Egyptian papyri associated with the Book of Abraham, he threatened to call a member of the First Presidency. (Given the highly controversial status of Smith's "translation" of those papyri that were mostly destroyed in the prior century, recovery of these fragments was a momentous and potentially explosive development for the church). England, never one to pursue his agenda in secret, contacted President N. Eldon Tanner himself, who "approved of having respectable Egyptologists translate the fragments and expressed his own faith that in the long run faith would trump doubt. Abraham and Joseph Smith, he was certain, would be vindicated."[25] Tanner asked England to wait until the church published the fragments in the *Improvement Era*, and England complied. (As it turned out, the church acceded to Hugh Nibley's request to publish them in *BYU Studies*, since the church magazines were so slow in moving.)[26]

Dialogue was England's attempt to effect a reconciliation that the Clark manifesto had effectively precluded. For those attuned to the language of both, the collision was inescapable. Clark's talk had explicitly declared that "the things of the natural world will not explain the things of the spiritual world; that the things of the spiritual world cannot be understood or comprehended by the things of the natural world." England, by contrast, held that "my Mormon faith affirms the world as good. . . . [Christ] insists that my words and actions be integrated with each other and relevant to that world—that they not just speak to it but really make the connection. . . . We must be willing to consider that anything we believe or base our lives upon may be a partial truth—at best seen . . . 'through a glass darkly'—or even may be dead wrong."[27]

S. Dilworth Young, a presiding Seventy in the church, hurried off a handwritten letter to England upon reading those words, which he considered tantamount to apostasy. "Since I open myself to the possibility that [Joseph Smith] was 'dead wrong,' I'm willing to bet that my faith will fly out the windows and I shall cease to believe the story at all." Then he warned, "If the Brethren will read that . . . sentence they are going to feel that the magazine is what they feared."[28] A few voices rose in *Dialogue's* defense, including those of Marion D. Hanks, Paul Dunn, and Hugh B. Brown. Brown related to England that Ernest

Wilkinson, president of BYU until 1971, came to the board of trustees suggesting that *Dialogue* be banned from campus distribution. Brown silenced the president with his wry observation that "there were things by people in this room that probably should be banned as well."[29]

The effort to welcome engagement between the world of science and scholarship, on the one hand, and Latter-day Saint tenets, on the other, was one reason why *Dialogue* was doomed to controversy and resistance in that historical moment. At the same time, the Clark suspicion of academia also explains the intense hunger and yearning for a more energetic synthesis of intellect and faith that made the journal's endurance possible in the face of institutional resistance. Another obstacle to the journal's wider acceptance was a general misunderstanding about the role of vigorous discussion in a church predicated on "direct revelation" from God, not committees or magisteria, as the source of truth and doctrine. Elder Boyd K. Packer drew troubling conclusions from this very premise. In Packer's message to the All Church Coordinating Council Meeting, he read part of a letter from a church intellectual who wrote, "My concern is that the Brethren are contending with the church's own scholars. . . . In the Catholic Church, the great scholars' efforts were used *by* the Church to refine and strengthen the doctrine (St. Augustine, Thomas Aquinas, for example). In our Church, the scholars are put down, even banished."

Packer's response was to state that the writer "needs to understand that the doctrines of the gospel are revealed through the Spirit to prophets, not through the intellect to scholars."[30] In other words, "What has Athens to do with Jerusalem?" That was the message many in the church were still hearing and promulgating, even though—as the Catholic Church has long recognized—the priestly vocation and the theologian's vocation are not in competition. This canard had earlier been corrected by Heber J. Grant, but sadly he did so in a private and not a public setting. In 1945, a church magazine urged upon its readers the maxim that "when our leaders speak, the thinking has been done."[31] Many Saints are familiar with that expression; few are aware that when church president George Albert Smith learned of it, he immediately and indignantly repudiated the statement. "Even to imply that members of the Church are not to do their own thinking," he wrote, "is grossly to misrepresent the true ideal of the Church."[32]

A third obstacle *Dialogue* had to overcome was found in the cultural ramifications of a cooperative ideal. In their history of economic and social practice, Saints had few equals in their communitarian success. Unity and harmony characterize the people to an unusual degree. Theologically, unity and harmony are the very essence of spiritual aspiration. After all, "the Lord called his people Zion because they were of one heart and one mind," records a Latter-day Saint scripture (Moses 7:18). The downside was an illegitimate inference from this fact that colored so much of the public resistance to England: "Must we measure the value of all discussions and teachings by whether 'the Spirit' is present, defined narrowly as a feeling of complete agreement and peace?"[33]

A final reason for resistance to a journal like *Dialogue* arises from Latter-day Saint discourse that is replete with language of a gospel fullness restored. Hence, directs one scripture, "Ye are not sent forth to be taught, but to teach the children of men" (D&C 43:15). In context, that was appropriate counsel directed at missionaries in particular, but the sentiment pervaded church culture to an alarming degree. Not a great recipe for dialogue. Some described Gene's teaching style as "Questions to Gospel Answers."[34] It was said with affection but hinted at a subversive approach that did not sit well with the orthodox mainstream.

It is no wonder, then, that powerful opposition from some in the church's headquarters quickly materialized. And some potential supporters, correctly anticipating the direction and intensity of such headwinds, declined to be involved at all. Henry Eyring, future apostle, was one who balked. England describes a conversation he had with Eyring, who was a bishop at Stanford at the same time England was there. He had asked Eyring if he was interested in contributing to the journal, and Eyring told England that he thought the purpose of *Dialogue* was good and it was needed, but that he could have nothing to do with it because there was a risk it could disturb some of the General Authorities, whom he loved. He offered moral support but decided to remain aloof. He could hardly be blamed, given the similar concerns that England's own mother, Dora, expressed at the time. "Eugene Jr. is the managing editor of a new quarterly. . . . We worry about this kind of thing getting out of hand and ruining his chances to be of use to the Church."[35] Initially England could not understand Eyring's conflicted response to *Dialogue*, but he said he came to understand it better over time.

Predictably, perhaps, a natural bifurcation precisely opposite to the founders' intentions emerged; the more orthodox scholars sent submissions to *BYU Studies*, and the heterodox to *Dialogue*. The journal's first issue was nonthreatening enough. England wrote a hopeful essay on "The Possibility of Dialogue." In it, he staked out a kind of discipleship with a paradoxical formulation, one that was more addressed to the intellectually pretentious than the philistine multitudes. Defending not just intellectualism but also—at the opposite end of the questing spectrum—a simple faith beyond the reach of self-questioning, he urged that we must "respect certitude as well as doubt." Powerful cultural crosscurrents alone can make sense of this entirely atypical counsel. The seemingly ironic plea is also one of the most distinctive dimensions of England's curious variety of discipleship.

This is not a standard Christian formulation. Christianity generally invokes faith as that which operates in the absence of knowledge, of certainty. *Certainty*, however, is a term that frequently appears in the pronouncements of Joseph Smith, often in a doctrinally prominent position. In the "Lectures on Faith" which he employed in teaching the elders in Kirtland, Ohio, it is affirmed that from earliest times faith has been a prelude to sure knowledge: "The inquiry and diligent search of the ancient saints to seek after and obtain a knowledge of the glory of God . . . [was rooted in] the credence they gave to the testimony of their fathers. . . . The inquiry frequently terminated, indeed always terminated when rightly pursued, in the most glorious discoveries and eternal certainty."[36] Such certainty, Smith believed, may be temporally late in coming, but is logically the starting point of true religion. "It is the first principle of the gospel," he wrote, "to know for a certainty the character of God, and to know that we may converse with him as one man converses with another."[37] It is easy to see why Smith's own conviction about a personal encounter with a conversing deity would ground his sense of epistemological certainty. However, he clearly saw his own experience as a prototype to which others could—and should—aspire.

Few Latter-day Saints talk of having experienced visions or visitations. But the rhetoric of certainty and fullness are still distinguishing features of Latter-day Saint religious culture. This is most evident in the church's "fast and testimony meetings," usually held the first Sunday of each month. In this worship service, members rise spontaneously to "bear testimony" to gospel truths as they feel moved upon by the Spirit, in a manner roughly similar to the conduct of Quaker services. The details and degree of eloquence vary tremendously, but the template seldom does: Some variation of "I *know* Christ lives," "I *know* Joseph Smith was a prophet of God," and "I *know* the church is true" constitutes the core of the message. So central to church practice is this affirmation of absolute certainty about saving truths that it indelibly alters the very nature of religious conversion.[38]

This cultural anomaly explains Dilworth Young's incomprehension at England's entirely reasonable proposition that disciples needed to be open to the possibility of error in the church or its teachings. England's audience here is principally fellow intellectuals, the highly educated, the scholars and academics, whose training and dispositions tend more toward epistemological caution than bold professions of certainty. Almost prophetically, however, England anticipated the faith crises in the Church of Jesus Christ of Latter-day Saints of the early twenty-first century. Rodney Stark had predicted in 1984 that Mormonism was en route to becoming the first new world religion since Islam. A generation later, the seemingly unstoppable growth trends had stalled.

As "nones" became the fastest-growing category in American faith affiliation in the present era, the Latter-day Saint faith experienced its own wrenching confrontation with rising generations more prone than any of their predecessors to question, interrogate, and doubt the historical and doctrinal foundations of the church. England had insisted in that first *Dialogue* issue that it was launched "for the express purpose of helping young LDS students . . . build and preserve their testimonies." His initiative was a concrete exemplification of not "looking upon doubt as a sin—or as a virtue—but [seeing] it as a condition, a condition that can be productive."[39] Such an honesty, he readily acknowledged, "will not save us; but it can bring us joy and new vision and help us toward that dialogue with our deepest selves and with our God which can save us."[40] But few at that time were listening. Only decades later did senior apostles such as Russell Ballard, Jeffrey Holland, and Dieter Uchtdorf publicly speak compassionately and nurturingly about the need to accommodate those like the man in the gospel of Mark, who pleaded, "Lord I believe; help thou mine unbelief."[41]

The 1970s and 1980s, however, were not decades when such indulgence of the fragile in faith was common. For the general church membership, it has long been doubt, the reluctance to profess certain knowledge of the Restoration's claims, that has warranted suspicion. England recognized that this culture of certainty had distorted Restoration teachings. He insisted that, on the one hand, it was true that scripture declares "to some it is given . . . to know" gospel verities (D&C 46:13). Intellectuals must trust and respect those who claim spiritual knowledge, one of whom was England himself. As he continued his essay, "I have been able, in all my proving, to discover and to continue to hold some things fast as certainties—faith in the divinity of Christ and in the saving power of His teachings and atonement, faith in the divine mission of His Church and His modern prophets. . . . Yet I have found that my very specific faith does not cut me off from this rich complexity, but actually intensifies and informs with meaning my involvement in it."

On the other hand, the same scripture that affirmed religious certainty as a gift of the spirit acknowledges that "to others it is given to believe." England, going against the cultural current of the church of his day, understood this to mean that room had to be found in the religious community for legitimate expressions of doubt. Ironically, he found himself in the besieged position of having to defend the very principle of faith itself. As he elaborated a few years later,

"The increase in questioning, even in skepticism, since the Enlightenment, . . . some see as evidence of Satan's battle against the Restoration. But, on balance, I believe that such skepticism has been positive: it has certainly undermined false religion and bad faith. . . . If skepticism is properly understood and used it can reinforce the need for both religion and faith. . . . Skepticism, in the perspective I am searching for here, the questing, questioning approach of heart and mind, leads directly back toward the balance of humility and fearlessness we find only in truth *faith*."[42]

This may be the most portentous instance of England's Cassandra-like prescience that could have had immeasurable impact for the good of the wider church if his concerns had been more widely recognized and legitimized earlier. By and large the church laity and leadership alike made little room for doubt in Latter-day Saint culture, pleas like England's notwithstanding. By the early twenty-first century, the church was experiencing the largest exodus of believers since the Kirtland era (crises in 1837–38 shrank the church membership by a third). The General Social Survey that examined Latter-day Saint retention rates through 2016 indicated that those for Generation X dropped to 62.5 percent, with the drop for millennials even more pronounced: only 46 percent of those born after 1981. In other words, among those who identified as Latter-day Saints as teenagers, fewer than half still claim that identity as adults.[43] Whether the attrition amounts to hemorrhaging and whether the prevalence of disaffection amounts to a crisis are still matters of debate. What is beyond question is the extent to which doubt has, in most quarters of the church at least, finally begun a process of decriminalization. Many factors are at play in the shifting environment of Latter-day Saint faith, but a simplified account would point to professionalization of the church's history, the resulting revisionism of foundational narratives, and the acknowledgement of the complexity of key concepts such as translation, revelation, and prophetic reliability. In a culture that essentially criminalized doubt, thousands of members found themselves faced with limiting black and white options, to affirm or reject. With no room to embrace complexity and fallibility and a messy past, they chose rejection. Only recently have apostolic voices extended the church's arms to embrace those unable to articulate honestly a template of religious certainty.

Other essays in the inaugural issue of *Dialogue* enacted the first stages of England's visionary experiment. An article by Leonard Arrington surveyed the progress and maturing of Latter-day Saint historiography, honestly apprising achievements and deficiencies. R. A. Christmas subjected the *Autobiography of Parley P. Pratt*, a nineteenth-century church apostle, to a literary critique, and concluded that it was a work "of real power," and urged fellow Saints to seek out similar gems—"to find them, study them, and criticize them honestly."[44] However, it is also possible to detect in this first issue the seeds of an edgier provocation. Frances Menlove wrote a piece on honesty, praising institutional Catholicism's example of "self-examination and house-cleaning," while drawing attention in the Latter-day Saint tradition to a widespread tendency toward "inauthenticity and sham." She addressed liberal shortcomings, but those were easily construed as cover for her pointed critique of religious conservatives: "In his desire to preserve and protect he may become indiscriminate and fail to make important distinctions between historical accidents and timeless truths. . . . Behind the mask of fanatical preservation may be the real fear that the truth of the Church is too fragile to tamper with."[45]

The relevance of this critique to the institutional decision, a year earlier, to shut down *BYU Studies* in response to a frank examination of the Word of Wisdom's history is not likely to have been lost on readers. "The Mormon Church," Menlove continued with a broad brush, "in all its manifestations, both historical and contemporary, is an intermingling of the human as well as the divine." This was in fact the premise of what would shortly be called "the New Mormon History," which would have its own disappointing trajectory. Challenging orthodox construals of prophetic direction and inspired leadership was tricky enough without the tonal deafness that would be the bane of England's own future. Admonishments about "the responsibility of the Church" and pronouncements of what "the Church must" and must not do might have passed unnoticed in a Congregationalist church (where Menlove would later minister). The Saints, however, had never aspired to be anything other than theocratic in their governance. Perhaps in no other tradition were the fatal consequences of steadying the ark so frequently invoked as a morality tale directed to the laity as they were in the Church of Jesus Christ. Menlove's was precisely the kind of rank-and-file advising that generations of leaders had inveighed against.

Conscious of the immediate tendency of the journal to attract voices from the Left, England tried hard to recruit General Authorities of the church as contributors, but with little success. Hugh B. Brown allowed a sermon to be published—but he was already known to be a rare instance of a "liberal" leader, so the tacit endorsement was of limited help. Other early issues, by their boldness in addressing the most controversial aspects of Latter-day Saint history and doctrine, aspired to replace Clark's alarm about the mingling of Athens and Jerusalem with a hopefulness in the fruits of a greater freedom to "prove all things." Such hopefulness was evident in those who believed, as England did in the case of the Egyptian papyri, that "competent scholars working with an authentic ancient text would over time come to some consensus that would only enlarge the pool of human knowledge"—and vindicate Latter-day Saint claims. If they did not, then such "truths" were not a legitimate part of the gospel. As Henry Eyring's father had famously and reassuringly stated, "In this Church you don't have to believe anything that isn't true."[46]

The naively optimistic England insisted that anxiety could only be a product of hostility to the intellectual enterprise itself, usually denoting testimonies too fragile to constitute real faith. And so England forged ahead, in an early issue, with a project that called into question the very foundations of Latter-day Saint origins. At almost the same time that the Joseph Smith papyri, believed by most Saints to have perished in a Chicago fire, were recovered, the Reverend Wesley P. Walters completed a manuscript titled "New Light on Mormon Origins from the Palmyra Revival."[47] In it, he claimed to have demonstrated that Joseph Smith's narrative of revivalism in 1820 was inconsistent with the history of his area of residence. The absence of revivals in that area in that period would suggest that the story of the First Vision, the foundational event behind the Church of Jesus Christ's restoration, is fanciful invention or at least inaccurate history. Walters submitted his research to England for publication in the fledgling journal—the first of many critical tests of the journal's claims that it would both be academically rigorous and promote faith.

England circulated the essay to some scholars at BYU, where it created no little consternation. Perfectly exemplifying England's philosophy that provocation could be painful but productive, the gesture turned out to be unsettling but salutary in the long run. As Godfrey described the lesson, "For too long Latter-day Saint historians had ignored libraries in the east preferring to do their research using the holdings found in the archives of the Church. With the approval of general church officers, a committee was formed and several professors and graduate students were sent to New York and other states to scour libraries and other depositories looking for documents that had some association with what historian Richard L. Bushman later called 'Joseph Smith and the Beginnings of Mormonism.'" The findings greatly enlarged historians' understanding of the religious environment out of which the First Vision emerged. England decided to publish the essay—along with scholarly responses—in a 1969 Dialogue roundtable titled "The Question of the Palmyra Revival." The resultant essays "were among the first that focused readers' attention on what could be learned when historians used primary sources long neglected or newly discovered."[48] Godfrey believes that the fruitful consequences of England's faith-filled daring continue to reverberate. "Those Brigham Young University professors and their students who gleaned America's libraries created a virtual wave of faith-filled articles, monographs, and books over the next four decades, which in 2008 culminated in the publication of the first volume of the *Joseph Smith Papers*. . . . In a real sense, the roots of the Joseph Smith Papers project go as deep as those first issues raised by Walters. To its credit, *Dialogue* was willing to publish his controversial article."[49]

Many readers—and the leadership especially—saw such critical expression as subversive of faith and inconsistent with institutional loyalty. "What surprised me," England said as the scope of the challenge became apparent, "was that somehow just the very idea of an open forum was taken by many in the Church to be a liberal idea, which seems to me really a misuse of the term. . . . We have tried to direct our editorial effort towards making the balance—the mix—really work. . . . Well over three-fourths of our editorial effort has gone towards getting what would be classified as more conservative articles. They're harder to get [because] the conservatives have tended to see just the idea of the journal and the journal itself as 'liberal' and therefore dangerous."[50]

For the liberals, however, the new journal was intellectual catnip. An overwhelmingly conservative member base meant a relatively limited readership. But it also meant an absence of competition for the liberal voices that did exist—and from the minority left-of-center membership submissions poured in. In the early years, England noted the impressive acceptance rate of a mere 5 percent.[51] And the readership responded enthusiastically. The journal began with the healthy base of 1,500 subscriptions. The successful first issue generated a surge to 2,500.[52] These were impressive numbers for an unofficial journal of a minor religious tradition. (They would be impressive for many academic journals!)

The second issue was a careful blend of nonthreatening scholarship, interfaith engagement, and quiet celebration of what others were labeling the social gospel. A survey of "Mormonism and the Arts" was followed by a foray into the intersection of Mormonism and political theory and another essay that examined church doctrine against Paul Tillich's theology. A book by Sterling McMurrin, philosopher, John F. Kennedy's commissioner of education, and lapsed Latter-day Saint, had been subjected to a roundtable in the first issue. McMurrin was a controversial figure, whose excommunication had been urged by Joseph Fielding Smith in the 1950s. President David O. McKay had reassured McMurrin, however, that "if they put you on trial for excommunication,

I will be there as the first witness in your behalf. . . . You just think and believe as you please."[53] (McMurrin was never summoned to a church court.)

To publish a roundtable of McMurrin's work on Latter-day Saint theology had been a modest invitation to controversy. Giving McMurrin his own voice in the second issue, we hear a stand-in for England's own. Assessing the contemporary state of theological reflection in the church, McMurrin laments that "Mormon liberalism . . . showed some life in the thirties, [but] never quite made the grade. The liberals talked a great deal, but they had no courage of decision or action. . . . They are still around, but in influence they have been displaced by a breed of noisy and deceptive irrationalists who give the appearance of orthodoxy while denying its spirit."[54] This was precisely England's belief, though he declined to express it so baldly. Like McMurrin, he believed that Mormonism was in its essence the most liberal of religious theologies ("Mormonism is fundamentalism turned against itself," McMurrin wrote).[55] And that those who thought themselves the most vociferous defenders of orthodoxy were in reality breaking faith with Smith's universalist, eclectic, and antidogmatic tendencies. England also passionately held, as McMurrin did more sanguinely, that "Mormonism has far more intellectual strength than is commonly supposed, even by most Mormons," with an obscured heritage of intellectual "adventure, vitality, and creativity."[56]

The piece by Karl Keller, however, was the kind of writing least likely to find a comfortable home in any other Latter-day Saint publication. "Every Soul has Its South" was a personal essay in which Keller (identified, significantly, as a branch president) described his summerlong experience "fighting Jim Crow and Mister Charlie and Uncle Tom with voter registration and literacy schools in a rural area of southwest Tennessee." In the face of intense opposition and suspicion on the part of his branch members, he joined the effort "because I was frankly worried . . . worried in fact that I should somehow while propagating and preaching the Kingdom of God miss it, miss it altogether."[57] His brief but moving account was enlisted to England's overarching thesis: that the call to be civically, publicly, engaged with "the least of these" was not a task separate and apart from the life of Latter-day Saint discipleship. As Keller experienced, "I returned with greater identification with the moral self which I know as a Mormon that I must . . . become."[58]

Subsequent issues ramped up the challenges to the cultural and theological status quos of the church. The third was devoted to a critique of Latter-day Saint historiography, with hard-hitting references to the neglected "ugly strain of violence in early Mormon history," hard to reconstruct because "no one can be sure what has been concealed."[59] The pervasive attitude governing access to historical materials "needs to be defined and criticized." In what became the central demand by historians for a new approach to Latter-day Saint historiography, P. A. M. Taylor articulated the reigning paradigm as one that saw all records of past events as attesting to a providential history, not "raw material for independent research into mundane phenomena."[60] Davis Bitton leveled a devastating account of "Anti-intellectualism in Mormon History." The original remit to engage in real dialogue and not simple critique found a rare expression in James Allen's "Response" to Bitton's piece. More frequent than actual debates, however, was the expression of perspectives seldom—or never—heard in other Latter-day Saint publications. Theologically, *Dialogue* broke new ground with one of England's own essays that would become a principal, enduring source of tension in his relationship with church leaders. "That They Might Not Suffer: The Gift of Atonement" challenged traditional LDS readings of the atonement as a kind of penal substitution, making empathy rather than justice the occasion of Jesus Christ's suffering.

England did not postpone for long direct engagement with his two political preoccupations: war and race. The journal published a roundtable discussion of the Vietnam War in its second year,[61] along with articles on "The Blasphemy of Indifference" (regarding race relations and modern warfare) and "A Voice against the War."[62] The journal tackled the racial question through a series of historical treatments and revisionist essays.[63] The civil rights movement, George Romney's political prominence, and McMurrin's public criticisms had all focused attention on the controversial racial priesthood prohibition, and Latter-day Saint scholars began to investigate the doctrinal and historical foundations for the practice.

Meanwhile, *Dialogue* incurred the wrath of several influential figures when it published a letter from Secretary of the Interior Steward Udall in 1967. A political liberal, he lambasted the church for banning African Americans from the priesthood, calling it "a belief and practice that denies the oneness of mankind." He correctly pointed to Joseph Smith's progressive views on race and the fact that Blacks were "accepted . . . into full fellowship" by early Latter-day Saints. "We Mormons," he insisted, "violate the rights and dignity of our Negro brothers, and for this we bear a measure of guilt." "Surely that day has come," he urged, to give Blacks "full fellowship."[64] Coming from a figure of national standing, the letter was an embarrassing, public reproach. Udall by this point in his life had drifted away from his Latter-day Saint faith, but the platform he assumed as a lonely insider condemning the racist policy of a monolithic, intransigent institution was good politics, and he was doubtless sincere. "What a sad irony," he observed in the essay released to the press, "that a once outcast people, tempered for nearly a century in the fires of persecution, are one of the last to remove a burden from the most persecuted people ever to live on this continent."[65] Udall then released his letter to the press. The fallout for England was immediate.

Arthur Haycock had been England's mission president in Hawaii, and was soon to be called as personal secretary to Joseph Fielding Smith upon the latter's succession to the church presidency. He wrote with fatherly disappointment and stern reproof: "Your magazine has fallen into the trap and has been used as an instrument by Secretary Udall . . . to embarrass . . . the Church. . . . Your magazine has done the Church a great disservice."[66] England defended both the decision to publish the letter and the journal itself. "We could see no reason to discriminate against Udall because of his prominence and the publicity that might evoke." As for the journal itself, he proudly asserted ample "evidence that *Dialogue* is fulfilling its purpose of enhancing the testimony of young people in the Church. . . . Just today I received a letter from a member of a Stake Presidency telling me of young people he knew whose reading of it had renewed their testimonies and kept them in the Church; he did not know of a single case, even by hearsay, of someone whose faith had been injured by what they had read."[67] That testimonial would be echoed countless times in correspondence England received.

In spite of his rejection of Haycock's criticisms, England was concerned enough that just a few days later he wrote to First Presidency member N. Eldon Tanner. He explained his reasons for publishing the letter, adding to his earlier defense the fact, as he now astutely observed, that suppressing the letter would have incurred worse publicity than publishing it. He then made personal affirmations of faithfulness, almost desperately. "I love the Lord and his gospel and want only to serve him and help build his Kingdom. I . . . try to live responsive to your counsel (and that of other brethren) concerning the things that I do."[68] President Tanner replied with a brief note, polite but guarded, neither condemning nor exonerating England. "I realize that you have real problems in determining what should and should not appear in *Dialogue*. . . . My only counsel to you is that you continue to try and guard and protect the name of the Church."[69]

Meanwhile, England was continuing to seek an appointment as institute instructor in Palo Alto. In 1968 Berrett assented, giving England a half-time contract. The appointment came with a warning: "You are a young man of promise, and I am very anxious that you do not do anything to hinder your service to the Church in any way. . . . In the light of certain criticisms that have arisen in the Palo Alto area, I wish that you would keep in close touch with President Sonne."[70]

Berrett's gesture was risky, and it soon backfired. The preceding January, Marion Hanks had visited Palo Alto. On that occasion, both Vietnam and the racial priesthood ban came up in his conversations with England. In the former case, Hanks was the wrong person for England to talk to in hopes of finding a sympathetic ear. Hanks was the church's serviceman's coordinator, and served extensively in that area of Southeast Asia. England remembered that "he opposed quite strongly my views on Vietnam."[71]

At the very moment of his letter from Berrett, England organized a "day of concern" for Latter-day Saint students in the summer of 1968, and even convinced C. Terry Warner, a philosophy professor from BYU, to come down and address the student group. Knowing the issue was divisive and that many students were themselves caught between the church and conscience, the leadership sent Neal Maxwell, recently called as a regional representative, to both observe and participate.[72] England's antiwar stance had been noticed.

Shortly after Hanks's departure from Palo Alto, England was teaching his institute class on "LDS Theology and Current Issues," when the discussion returned to Vietnam and the racial priesthood ban—most likely he was the one to raise the topics. England made no secret of his deep anguish over a policy he clearly believed was not inspired and wanted his students to engage the issue—with faithfulness, perhaps, but sharing in his discomfort as well. In England's retelling, he "made several comments about [Hanks] in class that I didn't think were critical but this person did. She was a close friend of his and reported it to him and he wrote me a letter."[73] It turned out that reports came to Hanks from more than one source. "Two other persons, both male," Hanks later reported to England, "resented what was said in class."[74]

Hanks found England's reported remarks to be disloyal and offensive, to both him and the church president, David O. McKay, and they discussed the episode in Hanks's Salt Lake office that summer. England apologized but, as was his wont, needed further assurance after the meeting that he had, in fact, been forgiven. In his insecurity, he feared that in spite of Hanks's gracious demeanor, "a breach still existed between us." England wrote a plaintive letter to him on 5 September 1968, in which he conveyed both his regret about his "lack of wisdom and foresight in stimulating a discussion that could be so seriously misunderstood." At the same time, he revealed his continuing tone deafness to his own voice. "It's only been as I have thought things through over this month that I've realized how serious the effect of that class discussion was and how deeply sorry I am about it. . . . As it gradually became apparent to me in your office that I had genuinely offended you and that there was evident reason for you to think I had trespassed both on your special calling and your friendship, I was mainly stunned." He pleads for forgiveness four times in the space of one and a half pages. At the same time, England sounds the theme that forms the backbone of his spiritually tempestuous journey. How, he asks, can a Latter-day Saint "be completely dedicated to the authority of the church and its prophetic leadership without abdicating his own agency and moral responsibility?"[75]

Hanks replied with a brief, restrained letter. Of the class experience, in which he apparently felt his own integrity as an official in the church had been questioned, he wrote, "I will confess that the experience involved was the most surprising to me of any that I have encountered." He then assured England he was not one to remember slights and had not written the young scholar off. He did, however, express a veiled caution: "You must occasionally assess the honest truth about yourself. . . . You are not an ordinary man and you cannot move by ordinary standards of consideration and responsibility."[76]

Five days later, however, the dam broke. In a follow-up missive, Hanks erupted in fury at England. "I really don't trust you enough to write this letter," he began, "or trust your judgment, but I will have to take one more chance on that." Hanks had just received a call from "the most beautiful soul I have ever known on earth," the one whom England believed was the complainant to Hanks, and who had consequently been made "the object of some terrorism on the part of her neighbors instigated by you." Still wounded by the conflict with Hanks, and frustrated that a student had complained to a leader rather than confront England directly, England had in a delayed reaction blasted his anonymous critics in a classroom tirade, challenging them to approach him directly rather than over his head when they were offended by his words. In response, students loyal to England had exhibited their anger at the female student assumed to be the Deep Throat of the institute cohort, leaving her isolated and "castigated mercilessly." "I don't give a damn what you can do to me," fumed Hanks in language seldom heard since J. Golden Kimball's tirades, "but I do resent very vigorously what you have now done." In blasting England for his "little performance" that elicited the mob action against the young woman, he questioned whether the institute teacher was creating an "England cult." After expressing his "disgust" and "resentment" at the whole affair, he ended with an ironic plea: "*Please* do *not* now proceed to *correct* this latest adventure."[77]

England, of course, could not refrain from doing exactly that. He apologized to the young woman, and wrote to the apostle. He tried to deflect Hanks's uncompromising indictment of his actions and intentions, yet he was far from his own best advocate. He admitted to chastising the class for the "many occasions during the past year" when students had felt it necessary to protest England's teaching to "the Bishop and the Stake President and even General Authorities." He ended with a desperate, "Am I just plain untrustworthy? . . . Please help me."[78] Hanks relented, and handwrote a two-sentence reply, urging England to disregard the latest reprimand, and to reread the earlier letter—the one that urged him to "assess the honest truth about yourself."[79]

Months later, he is writing to Hanks again (with whom, even in the midst of earlier tensions, he had felt a "special kinship of soul"),[80] concerned about the cultural tensions perhaps felt more acutely in the Palo Alto area of the church than anywhere else. "The students I work with at Stanford and Berkeley have become enamored of social radicalism and found . . . the Church deficient in solving the problems they feel so acutely." He references a talk given by President Harold B. Lee as having given the unfortunate (and inaccurate, England wants to believe) impression among area young people of a liberal persuasion that "their political views" represent "animosity toward the Church."[81]

No reply to this query is extant; at this point or shortly thereafter, Hanks ceased to respond to England's letters. England continues to write, opining in one of his letters to Hanks that "the break seemed to come with that letter of mine nearly three years ago which you didn't answer. Although it greatly needed one (because of the confused anguish which prompted it), it probably didn't deserve an answer, because as I remember it was full of the untampered passion of my convictions about the Vietnam War. . . . The passions have cooled now, though the convictions have not much changed."[82]

England came to believe that Hanks had forgiven him for, as he told his son, during the years to follow and through his term at St. Olaf in Minnesota, "At least a couple of times a year we would visit Elder Hanks. He really was the one we were closest to." However, it is unlikely that he ever regained the full trust and confidence of Hanks. In the early Palo Alto years, he remembered, their visits were "a kind of therapy session for him. . . . I would stagger out and say let me go back to the trenches because he would talk in the most frank and brutal way about the other general authorities." If Hanks was indeed trusting and unguarded in those face-to-face meetings, such intimate sharing was not a part of their later exchanges.[83]

Meanwhile, the frequency of England's vocal—and controversial—moralizing disturbed the stake president, Richard Sonne. He didn't want England's contract to teach institute renewed for 1969, nor did England's supervisor. Only after England gave assurances that he would refrain—in the classroom—from promoting his own views regarding the war and the church's racial ban was he rehired. He would complete his contract with no further incidents.

That didn't mean he wouldn't give full expression to his concerns through other means. As editor at *Dialogue*, he kept the pressure up. In 1969, *Dialogue* published Lester Bush's review of an academic study of the church's prohibition against Blacks in the priesthood: Stephen Taggart's *Mormonism's Negro Policy: Social and Historical Origins*. The reviewer's thesis was that "the present Mormon Negro policy is a 'historical anachronism'—an unfortunate and embarrassing survival of a once expedient institutional practice."[84] Bush's review was devastating to the church's official narrative surrounding the ban. A First Presidency statement of 15 December 1969 affirmed the long-standing view that, based on the principle of "continuous revelation," "Joseph Smith . . . taught that Negroes, while spirit children of a common Father . . . were not yet to receive the priesthood, for reasons which we believe are known to God."[85]

Taggart adopted this position uncritically: "Joseph Smith," Taggart wrote, "upon obtaining a 'clear impression of the explosiveness of the slavery issue' . . . reached the decision to exclude Negroes from the priesthood." Bush's review essay noted that no reliable contemporary evidence supports this view. With this revelation, Bush was laying an explosive charge under the theological rationale for the controversial and historically distressing exclusion of Blacks from the priesthood. In a further blow to such foundations, he quotes from a reported 1954 conversation in which President David O. McKay was heard to say "there is not now and there never has been a doctrine in the church that the Negroes are under a divine curse. . . . Withholding the priesthood from the Negro . . . is a practice, not a doctrine, and the practice will someday be changed."[86] In sum, Bush concludes, the historical record is entirely devoid of any claim present or past to found the priesthood ban on "a specific revelation."

England gave the Brethren advance warning about the article—even forwarding a prepublication copy. He then called Hugh B. Brown, who was at this time first counselor to McKay, to discuss its pending publication. Brown was an anomaly among the Brethren—a Democrat and more inclined to favor intellectual freedom than his colleagues. England loved quoting his wry remark to a BYU audience: "We are not so much concerned with whether your thoughts are orthodox or heterodox as we are that you shall have thoughts."[87] England would never find a more congenial listener at church headquarters. Initially unsure about the article, Brown subsequently advised against publication in a meeting with editor Paul Salisbury. (Whether his change of heart was too late to stop publication or the board proceeded in spite of his counsel is unclear.) Personally, Brown found Bush's piece "a very good manuscript," but "many of the Brethren were upset" about it, and publication would further damage *Dialogue*'s standing with them. "Upset" may have been an understatement. Alvin

Dyer, another counselor in the Presidency of the church, found it "abominable" and "full of error from start to finish," though he failed to transmit to Brown any of the examples he promised to specify. Joseph Fielding Smith, president of the Quorum of the Twelve, and Harold B. Lee, second in seniority after Smith, were both adamant that the ban was doctrine, not policy, McKay's statement notwithstanding. At this juncture, as a very public gesture of support for the beleaguered journal (and its editor), Brown gave permission for the journal to publish a talk he had recently delivered at BYU.[88]

The controversies surrounding the prohibition on Blacks in the priesthood came to a head four years later in 1973 when Lester Bush prepared a comprehensive overview of the priesthood policy that, in his opinion, "virtually undermined the entire traditional case for the inspired origins of Mormon teachings" on the subject. His work was historic and paradigm-shattering, landing like a thunderbolt. Bush traced the ban's background, finding not revelatory direction but culturally inherited mythologies and simple prejudice. He then submitted his manuscript to the apostle Boyd K. Packer for review.[89] Having met personally with Packer, Bush would later insist that "there was no suggestion of 'don't publish it,'" and scholars in the church's Historical Department praised the manuscript. When the article went to press as the centerpiece of a special *Dialogue* issue devoted to the race issue, fault lines became more pronounced and momentum for change grew.[90] Little known is the fact that Bush credited England with urging him to write the article: "It's been nearly four years since . . . your suggestion that I develop a more detailed history of the Negro doctrine," he wrote England when the article came out.[91] Ironically, Bush indicated to England that he had "shied away from some of the more sensitive implications of the history because of the uneasiness which seemed sure to develop in response." Subsequent events showed he had been more than sufficiently explicit to catalyze historic change.

The fractures occasioned by Bush's discoveries revealed in stark detail the difficulties even Latter-day Saint leadership found in balancing institutional loyalty with historical forthrightness. Packer may have accepted the virtue of intellectual honesty in this case, but other individuals—expecting resistance from headquarters—opposed the revisionism on that account. Robert Rees, as editor of *Dialogue*, was warned by a BYU administrator not to publish the Bush article even though Rees "had checked the material carefully, had it reviewed by two general authorities, and arranged for three responses and thought it was responsible publishing." "If not, I hope I can be forgiven," he said. "No, the Brethren won't forgive you," the administrator predicted. Rees responded, "Then that disturbs me more than the blacks and priesthood issue." Marion

Hanks, listening to Rees's account, chimed in, with the uncompromising rectitude that typified his life, "and well it should."[92]

Some of the records Bush had relied upon were recalled from public access in the BYU library, there was talk of the magazine having passed a "Rubicon" in the leadership's eyes, and rumors swirled of angered General Authorities and planned retaliation. In fact, the article proved a history-making catalyst. A General Authority later assured Bush that the scholarship he published on the subject had "started to foment the pot" that would eventually prompt the leadership to reconsider the policy.[93] Spencer Kimball, who spearheaded the revocation of the ban in 1978, "had studied [Bush's article] carefully and marked it up extensively."[94]

England not only engaged this most controversial of issues at the editorial level; he also chimed in as a writer. His general strategy for dealing with difference might have been dialogue, but his intention was provocation, not common ground. Here, the contrast with his predecessor Lowell Bennion is instructive. One of Bennion's students noted in reference to the priesthood ban that Bennion "dealt with the dilemma mainly by loving black people and keeping up a dialogue with black leaders." Avoiding "public confrontation," he "took the high road of patient emphasis on New Testament morality."[95] Even Bennion's detractors could acknowledge that his dissent from church policy was private, limited to personal interaction in conversation or the classroom. The danger he represented was local and his motives hard to malign: God will forgive us "if [we] err on the side of mercy," he said in persuading McKay to approve a marriage involving dubious lineage.[96] England, in contrast, went public, and he hit hard. In a church that had experienced decades of persecution and misrepresentation, England was openly showing disloyalty; at least, that was how his rhetoric struck leaders. His criticism went beyond a challenge to the policy and made the explicit charge of egregious racism. And the examples he excavated were enough to make the most steadfast defender of the church uncomfortable.

His first published criticism of the ban came in 1973, in the same issue as the Bush article, "Mormonism's Negro Doctrine: An Historical Overview." He titled the essay, poignantly, "The Mormon Cross."[97] England begins his powerful meditation by rehearsing the (unconsummated) sacrifice of Isaac by Abraham. The ban is, he argues, a comparable instance of being asked to do something that violates sacred norms of behavior and respect for human life and dignity. While many Latter-day Saints were at this time continuing to propound theological rationales for the practice, England frankly confessed that "apart from my own sins and failings, this is, in its way, the heaviest cross

I have to bear."[98] Though by today's standard, that was an example of tone-deafness—"*Your* cross?!"—his depiction of a Latter-day Saint teaching as a cross was revolutionary enough in its context.

His dilemma is the archetypal instance of the vocation of tortured disciple-ship that Saints trace to the Garden of Eden: not a contest between Good and Evil but between two competing and incompatible Goods. For Eve, the choice was between a commanded abstinence from the Tree of Knowledge and a command to multiply; between the safety of Eden and the enticement of a fruit—and an existence—that was good, beautiful, and wisdom-bestowing. For England, it was between moral sense and institutional commitment: "The policy of denying blacks the priesthood is rationally untenable from a number of perspectives—historical, theological, ethical, social, psychological, in fact from all perspectives but one—ecclesiastical authority. But for me that perspective outweighs all the others because I am convinced that ecclesiasti-cally the Church is doing what the Lord has directed."[99] That is a remarkable statement by contrast with the more liberal Saints, who dismissed the ban as culturally conditioned racism pure and simple.

While condemning most ex post facto rationalizations for the practice as damaging and self-serving, he proposes his own: The ban is an instance of a lower law given to a people of privileged race who are not yet prepared to ac-cept all persons into full and equal Christian fellowship. The ban may be del-eterious to those proscribed—the Black race—he argues, but it reflects poorly only upon those whose spiritual immaturity made such a ban necessary for the establishment and early growth of the church.

In the course of his article, he makes an important and prescient contribu-tion to the groundwork for the ban's revocation. He describes an interview with President of the Quorum Joseph Fielding Smith, the principal proponent of the theory that premortal unworthiness accounted for the priesthood ban. Following his visit with Smith, he relates a remarkable exchange and change of heart. England asked,

> Must [I] believe in the pre-existence doctrine to have good standing in the Church? His answer was, "Yes, because that is the teaching of the scrip-tures." I asked President Smith if he would show me the teaching in the scriptures (with some trepidation, because I was convinced that if anyone in the world could show me he could). He read over with me the mod-ern scriptural sources and then, after some reflection, said something to me that fully revealed the formidable integrity which characterized his whole life: "No, you do not have to believe that Negroes are denied

the priesthood because of the pre-existence. I have always assumed that because it was what I was taught, and it made sense, but you don't have to [believe in that theory] to be in good standing because it is not definitely stated in the scriptures. And I have received no revelation on the matter."

That report would strike many as implausible; Smith was the second-ranking authority in the church and the most doctrinally influential man of his generation. A prolific author and renowned scriptorian, it strains belief that only at England's impromptu prodding he would recognize the astonishing fact of an absence of scriptural support for the most controversial and contested doctrine of the day. In fact, Smith had said in print, decades earlier, that "we know of no scripture, ancient or modern, that declares that at the time of the rebellion in heaven that one- third of the hosts of heaven remained neutral."[100] And yet England insisted in print, twice, on this account of Smith's surprised discovery.[101]

Confidently inferring from this circumstance that no impediment outside the membership's own limited generosity of spirit need indefinitely prolong the ban, England asked his audience, "What can we do? We can get ready for living the higher law, first by working to root out racism in ourselves through getting to know blacks and something of black aspirations and culture. And we can help get Americans ready, black and white, by working honestly and vigorously to overcome the burden of our racist past."[102] What elevated his plea beyond clichéd liberal moralizing was the premise he had convincingly argued: The most plausible source of the ban was human weakness, not divine foreordination, and that put the solution within reach of a membership prepared to make progress against racist presuppositions.

His essay itself may not have moved the leadership to reconsider. Nonetheless, the Bush essay written and published at his instigation apparently did. And if England's story is accurate that he prompted Joseph Fielding Smith to a recognition—or recollection—that no scriptural support for the ban existed, then his influence on the ban's revocation was indeed considerable. For, in 1978, the ban was indeed lifted. And in 2013, official pronouncements on the priesthood ban were interpreted by some as intimating that the ban was rooted in a racist past rather than revealed doctrine: "The Church was established in 1830, during an era of great racial division in the United States. At the time, many people of African descent lived in slavery, and racial distinctions and prejudice were not just common but customary among white Americans. Those realities, though unfamiliar and disturbing today, influenced all aspects of people's lives, including their religion."[103]

THE PINK ISSUE

The enormous positive effects of being taught priesthood responsibilities and
Christ-like behavior are countered by false but popular theological notions that
we continue to teach or countenance in the Church or at BYU—because
they allow Mormon men to think they are superior to their wives.
—England to Gordon B. Hinckley, 25 September 1989

Dialogue made history of another kind when the editors led another groundbreaking initiative. In June 1970, Laurel Thatcher Ulrich invited a few Latter-
day Saint friends to her "ordinary looking, gambrel-roofed house" in Newton,
Massachusetts, to discuss the burgeoning women's movement. Present were
some of the most important emerging—or soon to emerge—female voices in
Mormonism. Ulrich herself was at that time a mother of young children—
a Pulitzer, a MacArthur "Genius Grant," and tenure at Harvard were years
away. Claudia Bushman was in a PhD program and would go on to be a prominent historian at Columbia and elsewhere. Judith Dushku was another future
scholar active in the discussion. The group had recently published an impressive guidebook to Boston, and ideas and projects soon percolated in new directions. "Our basements were full of wheat and our station wagons full of children," Ulrich recalled, but aware of the young *Dialogue* journal, they conceived
the ambitious idea of editing a special issue on feminism. Weeks later, England
was visiting the Bushman home, where she presented him with the proposal.
"Gene certainly took a chance on us," Ulrich remembered. "I think we were
all surprised at how easily he accepted our offer."[104] But even so, their issue reflected no monolithic feminist model: aspiring lawyers and stay-at-home mothers of twelve children were both represented, "radicals without children and
mothers without jobs," with the majority "somewhere in between."

The issue arrived just before Christmas 1971. If England still held to his
fantasies about avoiding the liberal label, the female editors of the special issue
realized full well that they were in revolutionary mode. "We experienced the
usual queasiness about countering the brethren," Ulrich wrote, and "that
worry eventually led some of our sisters to withdraw their support for the
issue." The issue was a historic—and influential—revelation, one that revealed
the fissures in Latter-day Saint culture and eased the transition into a more
embracing church by resurrecting precedents from a remarkably feminist Mormon past. While Leonard Arrington's history department was recuperating
the heritage of the faith's nineteenth-century women doctors and politicians,

the *Dialogue* issue made those stories relevant and powerful guideposts for the present. As Thatcher recalled,

> In a year when Relief Society lessons, conference talks and Church News editorials routinely condemned working women, we proudly published on the back cover of our pink *Dialogue* this quotation from Brigham Young: "We believe that women are useful, not only to sweep houses, wash dishes, make beds, and raise babies, but they should stand behind the counter, study law or physic, or become good bookkeepers and be able to do the business in any counting house, and all this to enlarge their sphere of usefulness for the benefit of society at large. In following these things they but answer the design of their creation."

The editors of *Dialogue* could do little to arrest its leftward trajectory. Five years into the experiment, England lamented that the journal was tilting away from his ideal: "I don't think we've been very successful in avoiding the liberal image," he said.[105] The journal's content was being shaped not so much by "design as by the reality of what we have received or had to deal with" in submitted material. He hoped by that point to have the beginnings of a base from which "we can more directly move toward . . . testimony-oriented expression."[106] That dream never materialized.

For England, the personal toll of his association with the journal was continual. Initially it was largely the high demands on his time and energy, the strain of sustaining the journal financially, and the personal attacks and rumors that circulated. "Vicious rumors," he called them, which questioned his motives, his loyalty to the church, and even alleged family strife and imminent divorce in his and other founders' marriages.[107] Still working on his dissertation at Stanford, England served as first counselor to Bishop Hank Taylor. When time came for a new bishop (Taylor was called to the stake presidency in 1966), Taylor let England know he would not be his replacement—and that his role in *Dialogue* was the reason. This was the first time that England's marginalization really struck home, along with the knowledge that he would be both misunderstood and denied leadership opportunities as the cost of his commitment to the journal. It was also a rude awakening from his naive, simple faith. Until then, he had been confident that "the Lord directed things and he inspired people to call them and that was it." Henceforth, the realities of how the human factor intruded into the chain of inspiration and revelation were painfully evident.[108]

England's great passion for sociability took ambitious expression in Palo Alto, giving him welcome distraction. Along with a close-knit group of other

England's family while at Stanford, ca. 1965.
(Courtesy Charlotte England)

young families, he and Charlotte lived a kind of ad hoc communalism. As Charlotte remembered, they "went on picnics, movies, played tennis and capture the flag, took trips to the beach, explored Monterrey, visited the Martinelli factory, walked down Cannery Row buying fish at the wharf then barbecuing it at our campsite in the woods. We visited the Nestle chocolate factory, anticipating free samples, only to find we paid for our own at the counter (big disappointment), got the children out of bed at midnight to see how they processed Brussel sprouts for freezing where they didn't give samples either (no disappointment there). We ate dinners at each other's homes, traded baby-sitting, shared cheerios in church and liked being in each other's company."[109]

Their close kinship led to a plan; the group would pool resources and purchase several acres for a shared compound. Jack Zenger recalls that Gene was the principal mover behind the scheme.[110] They found their Shangri-La in 160 acres of redwood forest in the Santa Cruz mountains. The parcel had a river, small waterfalls, lush ferns, and towering trees. The sixteen families came up with $110,000 and bought the land, which they named Bearmont. With time, the men of the group constructed a lodge; more impressive (at least to the children) was the mammoth tree house that Charlotte supervised, eventually including three levels. With time, the Englands and the other fifteen families would scatter to the four corners of the earth; the beauty of Bearmont, the associations it cemented and the memories it spawned, were sufficient to forestall the inevitable for several decades: It remained a retreat for a second and third generation until the group sold the property years after Gene's passing.

5

A MORMON AMONG THE LUTHERANS

I did find at St. Olaf, compared to Stanford or California State University,
much greater freedom—from legal and professional as well as
social pressure—to be forthright about my convictions.
—England, "Great Books or True Religion?"

By 1969, England had been at Stanford for seven years. He had an MA to show
for his time served, but his other projects—*Dialogue* most of all—consumed
so much energy that progress on his dissertation (on the obscure American
poet Frederick Goddard Tuckerman) was slow. "It seems like a heavy cloud
that hangs over your head," observed one concerned friend.[1] England had been
teaching for a few years at nearby California State, Hayward, but it was not a
viable career path.[2] In his life and in his writing, he was subverting facile cat-
egorization. England was of course aware of the irony of his position as a committed Latter-day Saint student radical at Stanford. "I saw more and more how
relative are the terms liberal and conservative. I found I could change from
one to the other simply by walking across Stanford Avenue from the university
to the Institute building. On campus, among graduate students and antiwar
and civil rights activists, I was that strange, non-smoking, short-haired, family-
raising conservative; at the Institute, I was that strange liberal who renounced
war and worried about fair-housing and free speech."[3]

Even in his radicalism, however, he put dialogue first. While teaching at Cal
State Haywood, students shut down the campus at the time of the Cambodian
crisis (in 1970). Knowing of England's antiwar stance ("I certainly didn't hold
back from talking about it" in class), they asked him to address a rally. To their
surprise, he declined, telling them universities were the only institution in
American society still capable of change and transformative power, and to
shut down the most meaningful public forum for the exchange of ideas was

simply wrong.[4] In 1969, he had published "The Quest for Authentic Faculty Power."[5] While he applauded student activism and demands for a greater voice in university governance, he challenged contemporary definitions of power, and defended the university as "the most humane institution in our society." Borrowing from a Latter-day Saint definition of righteous power ("by long-suffering, by gentleness and meekness, and by love unfeigned"; D&C 121:41), he pleaded for "authentic power": "the power to redeem," not to coerce.

The article's combination of humanistic concern, spiritual values, and eleva-tion of pedagogy over careerism resonated with the president of St. Olaf, a Lu-theran college in Northfield, Minnesota.[6] The next year, that positive impres-sion and a fortuitous connection (a graduate school friend was on their search committee) led to an unexpected job offer. Not yet even fully credentialed, England was asked to come as dean of academic affairs. He was ambivalent "about the wisdom of moving into full time administration this early in my teaching career," but he was inspired by the mission and spirit of the campus. In a tactic that he would repeat time and again, he counseled with President Harold B. Lee and Neal Maxwell before accepting.[7] It was a curious move. He had corresponded with Maxwell, but the two men were not close. And it is doubtful he had had much if any contact with the church president. He seems to have been motivated, as he would be throughout his life, by a genuine desire to be of maximum service to the church, on the one hand, and to find personal affirmation from men of authority and influence, on the other. With a $1,000 advance to help with moving expenses, he resigned his full-time appointment at Hayward and that summer loaded his family into the car for a cross-country trip.[8] His academic career appeared to be up and running for real.

The England family—Gene, Charlotte, Kathy, Jody, Mark, Jennifer, Becky, and Jane, with a two-month-old puppy and "a heavily tranquilized cat"—arrived in Northfield in the fall of 1970, pulling a U-Haul behind them. "A bit like crossing the plains in reverse," Gene told the small congregation of Saints meeting weekly above Joe's Bar. Only months into his new position, he was invited to give a "chapel talk" in March 1971. His daring title was "Are Mormons Christian?" It was a courageous gesture because evangelicals had long answered that question in the emphatic negative. Increasingly, Catholics and mainline Protestants—including Presbyterians and Methodists in addi-tion to Southern Baptists—were making official statements to that effect.[9] En-gland was now at a Lutheran college where, by his own account, at least two of his colleagues were telling their students that England's religious tradition was not Christian. And he was untenured. Yet he confronted the prejudices directly and diplomatically. He framed his talk as a rejection of the theological (Is Mormonism Christian?) in favor of the religious (Am I, a Mormon, also Christian?). With this maneuver, he demonstrated his propensity for unity over disharmony. For by rendering the question into one of universal Christian discipleship, he downplayed Latter-day Saint distinctives and exceptionalism, established a core kinship between Lutherans and Latter-day Saints, and gave voice to his own abiding faith in Christ at the heart of his own discipleship.

England would insist for years afterward that his evangelism cost him his job at the Lutheran school, and perhaps it did (no paper trail for such a reading exists). Indeed, his remarks unabashedly portrayed the Church of Jesus Christ as not only Christian but also more in line with "the Hebrew and early Christian vision of the soul" than other Christians, and as more vigorously resisting the "general retreat in liberal Protestantism from literal acceptance of Christ as the divine Savior." However, it is just as likely that his version of Christianity was not too Mormon but too liberal for the faculty there (and as it would later be at BYU). The litmus test of true Christianity, he opined, was consistency with three New Testament themes: regard for the marginalized, antimaterialism, and a compassion most perfectly manifest in pacifism. (He employed for illustration a Book of Mormon story in which an embattled people made a covenant with God "that rather than shed the blood of their brethren they would give up their own lives"—Alma 24:18.) Mormonism was not in actual fact distinctive in its exemplification of those dicta; this was England's version of the social gospel that he wanted to equate with the church, and that he defended before his Lutheran peers.[10]

His third criterion—compassion manifest as antimilitarism—was risky in both this era and this particular moment at St. Olaf. In March 1970, the Vietnam War was at its height. And at St. Olaf the faculty had just voted, after contentious debate, to retain the ROTC program at the college. England chided his colleagues that "in the faculty meeting in which the final decision was made the terms God and Christ and Gospel were mentioned only in the opening prayer."[11]

One new colleague responded to his remarks, saying that while England had convinced him that "it is entirely possible for a Mormon to be a Christian," he would not extend that courtesy to "the Mormon Church" as a whole.[12] Another colleague, in a formal administrative evaluation a few months later, noted how he had come to "appreciate the incredible differences between the Mormon and the Lutheran faiths," and praised "the type of living confession which Dean England used to back up what he was saying."[13] Significantly in light of what was to follow, he added his ambiguous observation that the counseling England engaged in as a dean was religiously informed but "not dogmatic proselytizing in the pejorative sense of the word."

BRANCH PRESIDENT

> I suddenly entered an entirely different world, one that tested me severely
> and taught me much about what "religion" is. . . . I was pushed to the
> limits of my faith by my sense of responsibility to my branch.
> —England, "Why the Church Is As True As the Gospel"

England had at the time of his campus lecture plenty of others to minister to on a regular basis. Days after arriving, England had been called to preside as the "branch president" of the small congregation of Saints. Charlotte recalled how the first day they "drove about 30 miles south to Faribault and it was up the stairs, over Joe's Bar and there was this little group of people, maybe eight or ten, and we thought, 'What have we gotten into?' We came in from this intellectual, energetic world, and we went in and this older couple, they were running it and trying to hold it together."[14] Months later, he located a lovely old schoolhouse in which the Baptists had been meeting in southeast Faribault. He purchased the building for $11,000. The Saints retrieved pews "from a little congregational church that was going out and was selling the pulpit and the railings and the benches and we got it carpeted and it had a basement where we had classes. [It was] just a very small place and [we] just turned it into a little church and it was great."[15]

England's leadership style, not surprisingly, was iconoclastic. A Latter-day Saint congregation's most important executive, always a male, is the "executive secretary." Gene gave the position to the retiring branch president's wife. "They said, 'Well she's a woman.' And he said, 'I don't care. She knows the people and the area better than anyone around and her name is Frances and they don't know that she's a woman.' So she stayed on."[16]

Charlotte was immediately cast in a supporting role that demanded more of her than she was initially prepared for. Newly appointed by Gene to run the woman's organization, she received a call from the mission president's wife, who asked her "to dress the body of a woman who had died in the Oddfellow's home there. The mission president called from Minneapolis when he found out we had moved there and said, 'I'd like you to take that.' I said, 'Are you kidding? First of all, dead bodies are so scary to me.' I said, 'Just. . . . I can't . . . You've got to call in somebody else.' He said, 'There is nobody else.'"[17]

Faribault Chapel, Minnesota, where England presided as branch president, 1970–75.
(Courtesy Charlotte England)

Charlotte's comment about the transition from the intellectual intensity of
Palo Alto to the blue-collar realities of life in the rural Midwest signaled more
than a cultural adjustment. It became Gene England's baptism into his lifelong commitment to bridge the divide between abstract theology and simple
Christian service. He later referred to "the conviction I had gained as a Branch
President that the Church—and its truth—are centered in the experience of
service and intimate involvement with other human lives and needs."[18]

Happy to have their own chapel, forty-nine members assembled for their
first worship service on Easter Sunday, 11 April 1971. Charlotte played a violin
solo, Gene preached and pronounced a blessing on the congregation, and they
held a ceremony on the lawn afterward, planting two lilac bushes as symbols
of the church setting down roots in their new abode.[19] Soon they were hosting
firesides, pioneer treks, and old-fashioned box socials (as in the musical *Okla-
homa*), where baskets were auctioned off to the highest bidder, who shared the
lunch with the sister (or young lady) who had prepared it. Funds went to missionaries in the field ($47 to Elder Greg Reece in 1972) or to finance a branch
vegetable garden. Produce from the garden went to the neediest in their midst,
with the remainder shared among the rest.

As branch president, "I was in charge of twenty families scattered over seventy-five miles, ranging from Utah-born, hard-core 'inactives' with devastating marital problems to bright-eyed converts with no jobs or with a drunken father who beat them. Of the seventy or so members I got to know, at most four or five were ones I would ever have chosen for friends when I was at Stanford—and with whom I could have easily shared my most impassioned political and religious concerns and views, the ones that had so exercised me before."[20]

The congregation grew steadily, baptizing children and new members in the Mississippi River near Hastings, and in a small stream near the England's home in Northfield. By the time of England's departure less than five years later, the branch had doubled to a hundred members. He was remembered as a great scholar who spoke the gospel message "in simple language that everyone could understand."[21] Christine Carlicci remembered being a new convert to the church and living fifty miles from Minneapolis, unaware of a closer branch. "I recall saying a little prayer that someone would find me out in the sticks, and shortly thereafter, Gene called me on the phone! Somehow, he knew about me and came out to meet with me one dark Sunday evening. . . . The Holy Ghost whispered to Gene that I needed to be located and he sought me out. My adventure in the Gospel was jump started by a faithful and obedient man."[22] Two years after his call, England was driving the 1,200 miles to Salt Lake City, his car full of young members of the branch (among their number converts from St. Olaf), en route to attend the church's October General Conference.[23]

The circle of intellectual sparring partners was smaller, but he again formed lifelong friends, including Frank and Jean Odd. One night near midnight, he and Charlotte banged on their door, loaded everyone in their Chevy, and drove three miles south of town to see a large field "twinkling with a firmament of fireflies."[24] While in Minnesota, he maintained his correspondence with church leaders in Salt Lake City. His correspondence with Maxwell in particular may have been a simple product of his sense that his real work in future years would be in the Church Educational System—either at Brigham Young University or in the seminary and institute program. No person was more pivotal in this domain than Maxwell, the commissioner of church education since 1970. In a letter that is an astonishing blend of graciousness and social ineptitude, England wrote to congratulate Maxwell on his new posting. At the same time, the not-yet-minted PhD offered some uninvited advice: Commenting on a recent article by Maxwell, he noted that "I sometimes have trouble with your syntax when it gets a little mannered."[25] What makes his impudence the more remarkable is that Maxwell's prose was some of the most eloquently wrought of any church official of his era—occasional overalliteration notwithstanding.

The cringe-worthy lack of judgment displayed by a junior professor presuming to correct a gifted church commissioner is an immensely telling sign of England's greatest and most self-destructive weakness: an inability to assess accurately his own tone and reception when interacting with church officials. (He almost repeated the error when, years later, he listened to a member ask the Seventy Jeffrey Holland a question, and wrote, "The question was better than the answer, and I was tempted to later tell Jeff that, but controlled myself.")[26]

Maxwell, a man who came increasingly to be revered for his meekness and humility, gamely replied: "Help me understand your message about my 'syntax' when it gets a little mannered. I value your editorial judgment, so don't hesitate to elaborate when you have the time. I must go on learning and growing before the laws of nature make that too difficult."[27] In light of future events, England might have been better served by a touch of indignation than by encouragement.

The next year he sent another letter to Maxwell, again offering unsolicited advice. He confessed to misgivings about not "sticking to [his own] stewardship" and sensed he probably should "give [his] energies to [his] own responsibilities and let you worry about yours," but he rationalized this offer of counsel by invoking his interests as a parent and educator. To the new commissioner, he proffered advice about church school admission standards, seminar and institute staffing, and the possibility of satellite campuses to expand BYU enrollments.[28] The ever-gracious Maxwell responded genially, even indicating that he had shared England's suggestions with some of his colleagues and BYU president Dallin Oaks.[29] At this time, England's contributions, even unsolicited, carried enough weight to merit appreciative consideration. Joseph Christensen, associate commissioner for seminaries and institutes, who had been copied on the letter, responded even more promptly with an invitation to discuss England's suggestions.[30] Over the years, England's correspondence with Maxwell continued, with frequent expressions of appreciation and respect on both sides. Maxwell encouraged England in his work at St. Olaf, lauding his "impact" and "contributions."[31] In another letter he expressed "thanks for your quiet Christian service and dedication."[32]

Meanwhile, life at St. Olaf passed peaceably enough. By his third year in administration, however, England was feeling dissatisfied. In addition to the burdens of ministering to a small branch, his tendency to disperse his energies in so many directions along with his extensive administrative responsibilities were impeding his ability to finish his dissertation. In October 1971, he had received an ominous warning from the graduate program at Stanford. They had extended his candidacy time frame already and warned him that "unless [he]

showed genuine progress on the thesis there would seem to be no adequate reason for extending the limit of [his] candidacy again."[33] (He managed to eke out
a few more extensions and would finally complete his work at the end of 1973.)

Yearning for the life of a teacher-scholar, he sent out a query letter to the
department chair at BYU, Marshall Craig, but there were no openings.[34] At
the same time he wrote BYU president Oaks of his intention, expressing the
hope that Oaks would not look "with disfavor" on his application. He had recently hosted Oaks when the latter came to Northfield to speak at a conference on "The Church College and the Law." The response from Oaks was not
overwhelming. "If there is a position and if you are nominated for it, you can
be sure I will not oppose your filling it."[35] It may have been simple understatement, or it might have reflected a guarded neutrality toward a candidate already suspect in some quarters.

In January 1973, approaching forty, England continued to feel the call of the
classroom and knew he was destined for a life as an administrator unless he
changed track. At considerable risk, he resigned the deanship and took a position in St. Olaf's experimental Paracollege, a highly individuated curriculum
for motivated students (it ceased its separate existence in 2000). His teaching
would commence that fall, but the conditions of his switch from administration to faculty were never made clear. A letter from the vice president's office
designated him a replacement for a colleague on leave, giving him a one-year
contract "open to renewal."[36] In accepting the new position, England indicated
his understanding that his tenure clock now began.[37] He expressed to others
some concern that the move would make his future at St. Olaf "questionable,"
but he was so "anxious to get back to front line teaching" that he would take
the risk. He also turned down an offer to be a dean of students at the University
of Utah for the same reason.[38] His resignation was not just risky but financially
devastating. He took a pay cut from the then-generous $19,500 administrative
salary to under $12,000 as an assistant professor.[39]

England's work in the dean's office had been admired by many. Academic
Dean Lloyd Svendsbye himself was most impressed with England's personal
qualities. "I have seldom met a person with the high humane standards and
concerns which you express to everyone," he wrote him. "I have marveled at
the way in which you have given of yourself to support and undergird someone
in our community who is reaching out to you for help. . . . All of us are going
to appreciate the gentle way in which you remind us daily by your example
that life is lived most fully when it is lived selflessly in the service of others."[40]
The chair of philosophy gave him kudos for his influence in returning the
college to a healthier concern for "the religious and moral dimensions of life

and learning."[41] Others, however, were less enthusiastic about his work and continuing presence on the faculty. His appointment to the Paracollege, with a home in the English department, was a "one year period only" contract, but England presumed it would be annually renewed. When he came up for renewal in early 1974, England did receive notice of his reappointment, but he was jolted to learn that "this is a terminal appointment."[42] The department apparently resented the vice president's imposition of a faculty member upon their department without their input and wanted to look elsewhere for a permanent faculty member.[43] Always the optimist, England believed that he could still finagle another reappointment or, failing that, he would formally apply for at least one position he knew was coming open in the college.

Gradually, however, the writing on the wall became clear to England. He would find no future among the Lutherans. He would later allege that his failure to be renewed at St. Olaf was decided after some students showed interest (and some were actually baptized) in the Latter-day Saint faith.[44] It is hard to corroborate such a rationale, though it sounds reasonable enough, especially in light of England's success in the classroom of the undergraduate teaching college. One of his evaluators at St. Olaf noted that his student evaluations were considerably higher than both the college and departmental norm, placing him in the top 10 percent for the majority of items surveyed.[45]

However, even England admitted that less sinister considerations were at work. In early 1974 he wrote again to BYU, this time to Dean of Humanities Bruce Clark, inquiring about a position. (Always with an eye toward affecting the intellectual culture of the church, he also rather boldly requested a meeting "to discuss the future of the humanities at BYU.") His prospects at St. Olaf were dim, he indicated, "because the English Department, which is at this point all male, is taking affirmative action to bring women on to the staff . . . and there is only one tenurable slot apparently available in the next ten years."[46] To a colleague at St. Olaf, he later gave yet another explanation, which he found credible but lamentable: "The reason the department is willing to give me is that I'm just not as good as they can get in the present market. . . . And what they mean by 'good' seems to be measured strictly in academic terms, without any reference to the goals and nature of St Olaf . . . let alone spiritual goals of this place."[47]

Still sensing the probability of at least some religious factor in play, he queried the president of St. Olaf about subtle discrimination. President Sidney Rand responded that after conferring with the dean and department chair, he "believe[d] there is no 'hidden agenda'" involved in the decision. Rand then pointed out that by removing himself from the administrative track, England had effectively imposed himself on the English department without their input in the hiring decision (a rather disingenuous charge, since the decision was hardly England's to make without administrative complicity). Women and minorities were a higher priority for them, Rand added more credibly.[48] England recognized the reasonableness of the explanation, acknowledging to another correspondent that he was resented as "a former administrator" even as he insisted that the reasons were "partly religious."[49] Not yet willing to abandon the fight, England followed up with a second letter to the president, pointing out (1) his impressive publication and teaching record and (2) the presence of other white males on the department's candidate list.[50] Rand replied that he had informed the department he would only consider a woman or minority a tenurable candidate. The matter was closed.[51] Except that it wasn't. England now wrote a three-page letter challenging Rand's arguments—a desperate move that elicited a third reply from the patient president. He reminded England that his 1974 contract had clearly stipulated it was "a terminal contract." There was no room left to maneuver.[52]

From that point on, the religious factor dominated England's narrative. He may well have been right. As he told a student interviewer, he had "published, as well as written and edited, more than the whole department put together" (which was probably true; one book, three articles, two reviews, eight essays, an edited journal and a collection of personal essays).[53] As he wrote a friend the same day of Rand's definitive veto, "So it looks like St Olaf and the U of Utah won't have me because I'm too Mormon, and BYU won't have me because I'm not Mormon enough."[54] (One cannot help but be reminded here of Erasmus's similar complaint: His reformist views made him "a pariah among conservative Catholics," while his restraint made him "an outcast among the Lutherans.")[55] England's age, too, was a factor he knew. "Other places won't have me in this market because they can get young hotshots . . . at a cheaper price." England was almost forty-two.

His alienation from both the secular and orthodox worlds was no figment of his imagination. The church's suspicion of his work for *Dialogue* would soon flare into professional roadblocks. And he was under fire from liberals for being too loyal to the church. Karl Keller had been his close friend, but when England criticized an antiwar piece he submitted to the journal, Keller erupted in fury. "I resent the vile tone of *your* criticisms of my piece," he began. "I was never aware that one's voice was supposed to imitate the vague, simpering, theosophical tone of *your* pieces." Then more to the point: "The American public supported each move into the war, especially the conservative element in the nation. That's *you* Gene, and the Church, and all the others in the country who are so nationalistic, Bible-drunk, and God-ass-kissing that you can't see past your own devils. . . . In one marginal note you call me blasphemous . . . . Did you still think the Church was above criticism? The Church is just as capable of enormities as any other faction." Then, in what was doubtless the most stinging rebuke, Keller insisted: "Why do you complain? I think I learned all this from you!"[56]

About this same time, England wrote to Neal Maxwell, commissioner of education, about a spot at BYU. Maxwell was not optimistic, citing enrollment caps, frozen faculty numbers, and a "buyers' market" generally. He encouraged England to look elsewhere.[57] In March 1974, he wrote Marion Hanks, exuding optimism about his book on a virtually unknown poet (Frederick Goddard Tuckerman) that would "cause (as soon as my book is published, hopefully this year) a major reassessment of American literature."[58] Even so, he feared, given the contemporary emphasis on minority hiring, "my chances of getting tenure when I come up for it in a few years are nil in this all white male, highly tenured department."[59] England asked for an hour or two of Maxwell's time to counsel about career decisions.

England had earlier inquired again of BYU president Dallin Oaks about employment at BYU, acknowledging certain "concerns." Oaks responded that those had been resolved even prior to a meeting England had with the trustees, and that he would be treated "routinely, just as we handle any appointment matter." But at the same time Oaks repeated that there was "no vacancy at the moment."[60] However, shortly thereafter England learned from other sources that the situation had changed, and he submitted his application in the fall of 1974. He wrote to Hugh B. Brown in January, seeking his support.

Brown was the apostle in whom England could most reasonably expect to find a sympathetic ear. He had spoken out in defense of *Dialogue* and permitted them to publish a sermon of his; he had expressed solidarity with England on the priesthood ban; and he was a rare liberal in a conservative church and quorum. However, he had suffered a humiliating rebuff in 1970, when Joseph Fielding Smith became the new church president. For the first time in the modern church, a new president declined to retain a counselor in the new presidency (Brown had been a counselor to McKay). Brown returned to his place in the Quorum of the Twelve apostles. Now, in 1975, England asked him, "If you feel it would be helpful you may want to speak on my behalf." It is unknown if he championed England's application.

While he waited anxiously for word, days after writing Brown England received formal notice from St. Olaf that he would not be considered for a permanent position. "The screening committee . . . have given preference to other candidates," the English chair informed him.[61] Early in the new year, Oaks called England to break the news personally that he had been turned down for a BYU position. Subsequently England wrote to Oaks, alarmed at rumors that had reached him that his denial of employment was being used (by Dean Bruce Clark for one) "to warn subordinates and others that the Brethren are cracking down and they had best disassociate themselves from *Dialogue* or face various unnamed dangers. . . . If there is any chance that I might, as you suggested, eventually find a place at BYU . . . then my case must be if anything minimized and certainly not blown up into the threat of a purge."[62] Bruce Clark, the dean of humanities, wrote to express his disappointment, assuring England that both Oaks and Vice President Robert Thomas had been in his court.[63] Higher forces were at work, his friend Mary Bradford tried to console him. She described the environment at BYU as "oppressive and we agreed that the Lord is probably protecting me from that place in letting his servants keep me away."[64]

As is typical at BYU (and with most employers), no reason was given for the rejection of England's application. England, however, must have known that his church loyalty—or at least, his deference to church orthodoxy—was the heart of the problem. Here, with his first church rebuff, we find the signs of a curious bewilderment on England's part that would persist in his letters until the very hour of his death. "For the first time," he wrote to Oaks, "I've had to feel directly what it means to want to serve with all my heart [and] to have the service rejected, apparently because of some past action or present unworthiness, and yet to have no apparent way to repent."[65]

England knew full well that his association with *Dialogue* had given the leadership heartburn. In fact, weeks after writing to Oaks, he met with Elder Packer to plumb the reasons behind his application's failure. In an April meeting, the apostle told him point blank that his association with *Dialogue* was the reason.[66] In addition, England knew his very vocal political positions were far outside the Latter-day Saint mainstream, and that he had already had to repair relationships with offended leaders like the beloved and influential Marion D. Hanks. Still, England was consumed by his dream of a Latter-day Saint republic of letters, in which faithful dissent from the party line would be seen as loyal provocation; he wanted to hope that his love for the gospel and the institution that framed it would cover a multitude of sins; and he acted on the belief that his unwillingness to question the integrity or good faith of the Brethren would be reciprocated. He wrote to Packer after their meeting that it "reconfirmed my assurance that the Lord's will is being done and that He has not rejected me but is chastening me in ways . . . which may yet make me more able to serve

Him well."[67] One cannot fully fathom the heart of the man or the tragedy of his life, if one does not see his tragic flaw as a persistent, willful, naivete.

Meanwhile, knowing his employment checks would soon stop, he had been exploring a range of unlikely options. He was sending out applications, some a bit of a stretch (like the one for a journalism position at Weber State, where he actually made it to the final three candidates).[68] He also tried the University of Denver and Carlton and Amherst. Closer to home he queried Utah State in Logan, but they had no openings either. He conceived the idea of launching a Joseph Smith University in Carthage, Illinois, proposing to purchase a Catholic school that was for sale. He even called George Romney to offer him the presidency of his pipe dream. ("I'm too old for new projects," the elder statesman replied.)[69] Desperation led to other far-fetched schemes. He wrote to a maker of cedar homes, and proposed that he be given materials "for a slightly modified Nile model home from your River Series; we will build it between the two largest cities in Utah (Salt Lake City and Ogden) and use it in some agreed upon manner as a model home and sell homes for you there."[70] Another application went to a position as president of the Experiment in International Living in Vermont. Days later, he was surprised by an invitation to give an honors keynote address at BYU and turned his attention back to academic possibilities. Even as he defended *Dialogue*, he couldn't suppress the growing panic felt by the head of a growing household (six children) about to face unemployment with no prospects in view. "I still don't know how I am going to feed my family next year."[71]

Years later, England learned more details surrounding his 1975 application. In a conversation with Bob Rees, who would be similarly blocked in 1991, Marion D. Hanks described a contentious 1975 board of trustees meeting where it was reported that "someone in another group had raised an objection" to England's hiring. To this Hanks responded that "such objections by people not present should not be considered." Elder Howard W. Hunter rather undiplomatically reminded Hanks he was not a member of "that other group," likely referring to the apostolic quorum. Hanks held firm. "But I am of this group, where I am to speak as honestly and forthrightly as I can." The disagreement turned heated. Hanks failed to win the point and resigned from the board in frustration.[72]

6

HISTORY, HOLLYWOOD, AND
A THEOLOGIAN OUT OF SEASON

*What I'm really doing is trying to chart a new course for myself, because
I span these two periods—I have been part of the growing pains and mistakes
of the recent past, of improperly resolved loyalties and defensiveness and uncertain
role in the Kingdom, but I have also had some experiences, especially these past few
years, including a reacquaintance with the pioneer intellectual tradition, that are
changing me and make me want to be part of what I hope for your generation
to define and exemplify—the new Latter-day Saint intellectual life.*
—England, "Great Books or True Religion?"

Shortly before his March meeting with Packer in the spring of 1975, England
wrote to Church Historian Leonard Arrington, asking if Arrington could find
a spot for him. "I have about ten books and over thirty essays definitely in mind
that I think I could do, perhaps as well or better than anyone right now, and
that would contribute significantly to the building of the kingdom." He offered
some examples: "Intellectual Heroes of the Restoration," a volume of intellectual history, a biography of Joseph Smith, and a "critical study of Mormon
literature."[1]

He did not conceal the extent of both his financial and emotional crisis: "I
don't presently have a job lined up for next year and the prospects are dim, I
will definitely need all the financial assistance you can possibly give me." He
then confided, "Despite all the ebullience displayed above, I'm rather low right
now from some recent blows to my sense of self. . . . A letter about prospects for
doing some work with and for you next year might help." Arrington responded
a few weeks later offering hope that gathered force like an auctioneer as he
gauged both England's talent and his needs. He proposed a $1,000 fellowship

at first, then thought he could swing $2,000. "Perhaps even $2,500 for the period September 1, 1975 to August 1, 1976. . . . If they bless us with a good budget and all goes well in clearing your name, we might even be able to go as high as $4,000 or $5,000."[2]

That was all England needed to hear. With those funds he was perhaps half-way to a sustainable income. On May 18, 1975, England performed his last act as president of the Faribault branch, dedicating a new chapel for the congregation he had loved and served so fervently.[3] About this time, he heard from Joe Christensen, an associate commissioner under Maxwell in the Church Educational System, that he could teach institute classes part time in Ogden and Salt Lake City. That summer, he loaded up his family and drove to Kaysville, Utah. His mother wrote in her journal with relief, "Eugene Jr. and family have decided to move to Kaysville, Utah. They are here in Salt Lake, now for a week before Conference, to look for a place to build. He has a chance to teach in the English Department at Weber State College [that did not pan out]. They like small towns and small college life, so that is what they are looking for." For three months, they lived in a family-owned cabin before purchasing a home in Kaysville—"an old one on Main Street—close to the schools and the church."[4]

No good deed goes unpunished, as Arrington learned weeks after hiring England. As he recorded in his diary, "Neal Maxwell telephoned me to warn me that one certain brother in the Twelve was a little upset about him offering Eugene England half time employment with the Institute and with us offering him 'employment' in the Historical Department. He was fearful that this would cause Gene to turn down offers for permanent employment that might come to him. . . . Eugene should not be discouraged from accepting full time employment outside the Church and its educational system. He left no references who it was, but I thought it might be Elder [Boyd K.] Packer or Elder [Mark E.] Petersen."[5] England believed that Packer, warming to England after their conversations, had secured his employment with the CES.[6] Arrington assumed, with good reason, that the apostle whom England thought had secured his employment was likely the one opposing it. England's misreading of the situation was typical of him. The man who could work wonders with a Shakespeare text was a terrible interpreter in social interactions with those in power.

Summer found England settled into work at the Historical Department under Arrington. An unusual opportunity arose when Heber Wolsey, head of church public relations, heard that Philip Yordan was planning a movie on Brigham Young. Yordan was a prolific, Academy Award–winning Hollywood producer and screenwriter, with several high-profile films to his credit, including most famously *King of Kings* and *El Cid* (both 1961). In more recent years he had turned to science fiction and war movies like *Day of the Triffids* (1963) and *Battle of the Bulge* (1965). The latter would be his last significant work, and his many future productions ranged from forgettable to awful—with titles like *Marilyn Alive and behind Bars* (1992) and *Too Bad about Jack* (1994). In 1975, however, his star had not yet begun its abrupt waning; his interests had at that point returned to religion and he had chosen Brigham Young as his subject. It had been thirty-five years since the Darryl Zanuck production of that name with Tyrone Power, and Yordan hoped to win church approval and cooperation for his remake. The church public relations department, ever on the lookout for missionary opportunities, thought the project a promising prospect.

Wolsey put Yordan in touch with the Historical Department, and Arrington assigned England to assist historian Ronald Esplin with preparing background material in support of Yordan's project. By mid-August 1975, England had completed the first "task paper," called "Brigham Young in England," together with ten proposed scenes. England was delighted to be working on what could prove to be a high-profile production, and a "tremendous missionary tool" in the bargain. Yordan liked England's initial drafts and went to Salt Lake City for a meeting with those involved in the project. The next month, Arrington reviewed England's work and was enthusiastic. He suggested that regardless of the movie's future, a half-dozen or so essays like the few he had done could be published as a collection. England heard through the grapevine that Arrington was even considering taking him on board to assist in the writing of the major Brigham Young biography that he was himself planning. (England went on to draft some of the chapters, and Knopf would publish the book in 1985 as *Brigham Young: American Moses*.)

England was finally in a good place emotionally. He confided in his journal that the previous year had "brought the most severe spiritual crisis of my life."[7] (That entry, dated 12 August 1975, was the first in a journal England would only keep sporadically over the next quarter century; a dismal record for one so passionate about the value of journal-keeping in the pioneer past.) The pain of dismissal from St. Olaf, his first real position, and the loss of his position as president of the small Faribault Branch, the most spiritually fulfilling calling he had yet known, were compounded by rejection of his application at both the University of Utah and Brigham Young University. He now read those setbacks as painful prompts to a career reorientation: historian and biographer of the church's founding luminaries. Perhaps one day after work on Young, he confided in his journal, he might produce "a biography of Joseph, the man for me and my heart."[8] "Perhaps this is what the Lord has been chastening me towards."[9]

At the same time, England could not imagine giving up his teaching opportunities. Discussing his future at the Historical Department, which still needed more funding than the department had available, he told Arrington he wasn't looking for a full-time staff position, "but only about $6000 a year to supplement my Institute work and a desk someplace where I could work unmolested." They conceived a plan whereby England's father donated a valuable piece of land to the church, with a portion of the proceeds going to Leonard Arrington's Mormon History Trust Fund. The happy outcome was that Arrington "is willing on the basis of this development to guarantee me $6000 a year for the next two years, which with my teaching should keep us alive."[10]

England continued working on Yordan's film treatment for several months, with the producer making several trips to confer with Arrington, England, and others involved in the project. By the spring of 1976, Yordan was impressed enough with England and what he saw as the abundant and underutilized talent and resources in Utah that he invited England to join him in forming a production company to make movies in Utah. England was desperate—or dreamy-eyed—enough to seriously consider it, even soliciting advice from some of the apostles. Packer and Haight, perhaps seeing an avenue whereby England could pursue his talents independently of the Church Educational System and at a happy remove (for all parties) from their supervision, encouraged the venture. Gordon B. Hinckley, however, advised caution and suggested England await the outcome of the Brigham Young project. Hinckley's advice was perceptive. Yordan's studio plans came to naught, and the movie—released in 1977—was entirely lackluster.

During his second summer at the Historical Department, England was enjoying a fishing trip on Bear Lake with his father and his friend Andy Hansen. Fishing was the greatest diversionary passion of his life. Returning home, England napped in the back of the Jeep while Hansen drove. Midevening, Hansen fell asleep and crossed the median, colliding head on with an oncoming car. "When I came up out of unconsciousness," England recalled, "I had my hands on my father's head and could feel his hair and blood. I couldn't hear the words I was saying, but I felt them from the blessing part of me, the deepest part, before consciousness. Dad was more conscious than I was but more hurt. I gradually began to see the ground, the fir trees, then the cars just down from us. There was a blue Austin impaled at a slight angle onto the front of the Jeep. All of the Jeep's doors were sprung open, and the freezer of huge fish was splashed across the highway. I kept my hands on Dad's head and began to hear his moaning, then felt pain emerging in my own chest and struggled to breathe."[11]

Eugene Sr., who had been seated in the front, had suffered a broken jaw and facial bones, several broken and cracked ribs, a crushed spleen, and a crushed aorta that was bleeding. Gene fared almost as badly, with three fractured ribs and a collapsed lung.

In the hospital and awake, Gene again administered a priesthood blessing to his critically injured father, who described the ordinance: "He talked to and reasoned with the Lord as though He was present. The whole terrible experience seems to me to be worth hearing my son plead with the Lord to spare my life. He felt that if the Lord didn't sanction it and bless me that I would surely die."[12] Both survived, and the accident may have been the prompt England needed to move on. Both of his positions were still part-time, and he wasn't pursuing the career he had planned and hoped for. The same month of his accident, August, he wrote to Jeffrey Holland, who had just replaced Maxwell as commissioner of education (Maxwell was now on the First Quorum of the Seventy, one step down from an apostleship). Even with an advocate, however, the path ahead was far from clear.

In addition to the cloud of suspicion still engendered by his role at the helm of *Dialogue*, England learned that two of his essays had deepened the sense among the Brethren that he was a dangerous thinker. The first, "That They Might Not Suffer," was his 1966 venture into atonement theology. The second, "The Mormon Cross," published two years earlier, prior to leaving St. Olaf, launched a series of provocations assailing racial policy and attitudes in the church. Each was at the heart of tragic narratives that unfolded over a period of years and arose from peculiarities of Mormonism's relationship to theology.

THEOLOGY IN A PROPHETIC CHURCH

The theologian's calling and task are from the Church, and so his responsibility is to the Church, the God who has entrusted the most sublime truths about himself to fishermen and tentmakers, and to their successors down to this day. Theology exists to serve the Church, so the theologian must answer not only to evidence and argument, but to those divinely empowered to teach the truths of the faith authoritatively.
—Catholic writer Bruce Marshall, "The Theologian's Ecclesial Vocation"

In 1975, England had a conversation about the project of a Latter-day Saint intellectual history with James Allen, assistant church historian. Allen urged caution; "he expressed his concern, apparently shared by his colleagues, that the Church leadership is not ready to encourage those kinds of things."[13]

Although in the academy the lines that separate doctrine from intellectual history may be clearly defined, in the Latter-day Saint church, they are frequently confused, as are the terms *doctrine* and *theology*. Consequently, the theological enterprise has not fared well. Even as brilliant an intellectual as Sterling McMurrin confounded the categories: "The worst thing that could happen to any theology is now happening to the theology of the Mormons—by the default of the prophets it has been appropriated by the academics."[14]

Doctrine, a New Testament term, means teaching or instruction, and in religious studies carries the meaning of an *authoritative* teaching or instruction. *Theology*, in contrast, is "God-study" or "God-discourse." It represents human attempts to articulate the implications, grounds, rationality, or ramifications of religious propositions. When Joseph Smith first established his School of the Prophets for the instruction of the church's elders, he sanctioned a set of lectures that were called "Lectures on Theology." In one of those lectures that he delivered in Kirtland, Ohio, he approved a contemporary definition of *theology*, with one crucial modification. Joseph Smith's older contemporary Charles Buck had called it "that science which treats of the being and attributes of God, His relations to us, the dispensations of His providence, His will with respect to our actions, and His purposes with respect to our end." Smith defined it as that "*revealed* science." And with that change, he set in motion a confusion—or conflation—that persists in Latter-day Saint culture to the present. Theology outside of church circles, by implication, would be a fruitless enterprise predicated on erroneous foundations. John Taylor, Brigham Young's successor, referred to sectarian theology as "the greatest tomfoolery in the world."[15]

With the 1890 manifesto ending polygamy, the status of an important component in the church's doctrinal system was suddenly thrown in doubt; emphases shifted from the relational to the personal, from the other-worldly to the proximate, even while, as part of the church's quest for Americanization, consolidation and elucidation of the basics rather than the expansion and speculation of prior generations became the rule. As a consequence, with a few important exceptions, a growing distinction appears in the Latter-day Saint consciousness between "doctrine" as true, inspired, and authoritative teachings, on the one hand, and theology as the purely human pronouncements associated with an apostate Christendom, on the other. Theology, in this later view, is what happens when revelation fails.

The shift reflects a diminishing excitement about the unbounded range of Smith's vision. (A loss of "adventure, vitality, and creativity," in Sterling McMurrin's words.)[16] Parley Pratt, for example, reveled in the way Smith ruptured traditional Christian categories of thought: "What a glorious field of intelligence now lies before us, yet but partially explored. What a boundless expanse for contemplation and reflection now opens to our astonished vision. What an intellectual banquet spreads itself invitingly to our appetite, calling into lively exercise every power and faculty of the mind, and giving full scope to all the great and ennobling passions of the soul."[17]

The contrast is stark with Taylor's successor Wilford Woodruff, who was a long way removed from the heady visions of Joseph Smith and speculations of Young. In response to the controversies over Young's Adam-God theology, Woodruff urged commonality and unanimity of belief: "I want to say this to all Israel: Cease troubling yourselves about who God is; who Adam is, who Christ is, who Jehovah is. For heaven's sake, let these things alone. Why trouble yourselves about these things? . . . God is God. Christ is Christ. The Holy Ghost is the Holy Ghost. That should be enough for you and me to know. If we want to know any more, wait till we get where God is in person. I say this because we are troubled every little while with inquiries from elders anxious to know who God is, who Christ is, and who Adam is. I say to the elders of Israel, stop this."[18]

The church did commission apostle James Talmage to produce an official theology—which was an exposition of the church's entirely schematic and unrepresentative creed, the *Articles of Faith* (published with the same title in 1899) and an official Christology (*Jesus the Christ* [1915]). By 1930, B. H. Roberts was finishing his masterwork, an ambitious, systematic theology of Restoration doctrine called *The Truth, the Way, the Life* (first published posthumously in 1994). It was killed by a reading committee of the leadership, however, largely at the instigation of Joseph Fielding Smith, who objected to what he saw as Roberts's compromises with scientific theory. Smith wrote his own three-volume compendium, *Doctrines of Salvation* (1954), which was more declarative than expository. This was also the case with the most influential LDS treatise of the twentieth century, his son-in-law Bruce R. McConkie's *Mormon Doctrine* (1958), discussed above. It was, the author said, "the first major attempt to digest, explain, and analyze all of the important doctrines of the kingdom. . . . . the first extensive compendium of the whole gospel—the first attempt to publish an encyclopedic commentary covering the whole field of revealed religion."[19]

For almost half a century, McConkie's *Mormon Doctrine* had an influence and authority unparalleled by any other volume in the history of the church. Its simple, declarative title, its apostolic authorship, its alphabetical compendium format, its omnipresence in church lesson manuals and materials, effectively made it canonical. McConkie and Boyd K. Packer, less prolific as an author but as magisterial—and influential—in his pulpit pronouncements, were the dominant voices of those three decades when England was active as a writer and teacher. McConkie's work claimed to cover "the whole field of revealed religion"; Packer's emphatic defense of the apostolic prerogative to declare doctrine and defend the church from error earned him the sobriquet "the watchman on the tower."[20] Against the background of those two dominant figures, speculative theology could hardly be understood in any terms other than Taylor's "tomfoolery." It was a waste of intellectual energy at best, a dangerous allure to heresy or apostasy at worst.

Eugene England was a Latter-day Saint theologian born out of season. By the 1970s and 1980s, Mormon theology had become a virtual oxymoron. England recognized the crucial distinctions between doctrine and theology. Doctrine was authoritative, and it was dogmatic, absolute and divorced from historical and cultural considerations. As England described one influential church Seventy, "He believes that traditional male formulations of ideas, if by prophets, simply cannot be affected by cultural context." The result, he wrote, was a drive for what he called "CD-Rom theology," compilations of "ideas by the Brethren and the scriptures, with absolutely no regard to context, rationality, or even consistency."[21] England, by contrast, saw theology as a handmaid to doctrine, not a competitor. His principal model in this regard was the same B. H. Roberts who was the last great practitioner of Mormon theology. He quoted Roberts's charge, which he took personally to heart as his "inspiration and guide." In 1906, Roberts had written,

> I believe "Mormonism" affords opportunity . . . for thoughtful disciples who will not be content with merely repeating some of its truths, but will develop its truths, and enlarge it by that development. . . . The work of the expounder has scarcely begun. The Prophet planted by teaching the germ truths of the great dispensation of the fullness of times. . . . The disciples of "Mormonism," growing discontented with the necessarily primitive methods which have hitherto prevailed in sustaining the doctrine, will yet take profounder and broader views of the great doctrines committed to the Church; and, departing from mere repetition, will cast them in new formulas; cooperating in the works of the Spirit, until they help to give to the truths received a more forceful expression, and carry it beyond the earlier and cruder stages of development.[22]

With Roberts as his inspiration, England declared that while he did not "presume to chart the Church's course or to create new doctrine," he did "wish to consider . . . the great 'germ truths'" of Mormonism "and to venture new formulations, what might become more forceful expressions, that could help us, in our changing times."[23]

This self-conception explains the deep anguish at the heart of England's experience. He saw himself as at the furthest possible remove from the vocation of church dissident. Quite the contrary—he saw himself as a provocateur, perhaps, but never a dissident. ("I always saw myself as an apologist for the church," he said shortly before he died.) England's perspective is best illuminated in a 1994 journal entry, as he sensed the hopelessness of his ideals, confronted with the onslaught of his church's culture of harmonious acquiescence. His reading of John Harris's essay "Risk and Terror" proved an epiphany,[24] allowing him to give expression to a theological understanding perhaps too subtle to have made inroads in the Utah culture of his day. Harris had suggested in his essay that "God's job, like that of all teachers and parents, is to work himself out of a job."[25]

It is unlikely that such a view can be found anywhere in the orthodox Christian tradition after Augustine. Augustine believed "'our true good is free slavery'—slavery to God"—a "radical departure" from the moral "autonomy of the human soul" taught by Clement and others in the first four Christian centuries.[26] England was trying to take Mormon culture back to its—and Christianity's—earliest theological roots. Smith had famously taught the most radical version of theosis in Christian history—boldly proclaiming the human potential to be fully divine. "You have got to learn how to make yourselves Gods," he preached shortly before his death, "the same as all Gods have done—by going from a small capacity to a great capacity, from a small degree to another, from grace to grace, until the resurrection of the dead, from exaltation to exaltation—till you are able to sit in everlasting burnings and everlasting power and glory as those who have gone before, sit enthroned."[27] "As God now is . . . man may become," in Lorenzo Snow's paraphrase.[28] For generations of churchmen, humankind's very existence was conceived as contingent, utterly dependent on God's sustaining power. For Brigham Young, by contrast, God's own purposes envision the gradual emancipation of the human from divine dependence. "They are organized to be just as independent as any being in eternity . . . [we are] calculated to be as independent as the Gods, in the end. . . . [but] I do not expect to see the day when I am perfectly independent, until I am crowned in the celestial kingdom of my Father, and made as independent as my Father in heaven." "This is the place where every man commences to acquire the germ of the independence that is enjoyed in the heavens," he said on another occasion.[29]

Here we find a number of incongruences with Christian orthodoxy: the eternal, noncontingent nature of the human soul; the aspiration to literal divinization; and the limits of grace in any salvational scheme. For if humans are to metamorphose into gods and goddesses in their own right, it is through a(n immensely long) process of adaptation to and conformity with the same laws that God abides and that sustain him in his perfect holiness. Smith taught that we must replicate the process by which Christ attained to his status ("whatever constitutes the salvation of one, will constitute the salvation of every creature which will be saved: . . . the prototype [of] the saved being . . . is Christ.")[30] Christ attained, through perfect obedience, to perfect holiness, and we must follow the same path ("if they do not they cannot be like him"). In other words, contra the whole Protestant heritage, with its foundation in *sola gratia* (salvation by grace alone) and the doctrine of imputed righteousness, Latter-day Saints proclaim that "with all eternity before them for the exercise of every power with which the Creator endowed them, spiritual, mental and physical," they can be "perfected by experience and obedience to eternal law, and ready to act in the harmony with celestial intelligences."[31]

In light of Latter-day Saint conceptions of humans as literal offspring of God, with a destiny of full divinity, Martin Luther's dictum that "we are justified by God's judgment though wholly a sinner" is utterly defeatist and negates the transformative power of Christ's atonement. England understood this perfectly: "I have thought for some time that the old and usually fruitless argument about whether we are saved by faith or by works is resolved by seeing salvation as a condition of being, gradually brought about through a combination of God's gifts and our response to them that changes us—not a mere reward for works or irresistible infusion of grace."[32]

Little like this boldness of spirit, however, was evident in the conformist culture against which England was pitted. Rather, he found "the emphasis is on surrendering our will to an absolute God, learning to 'live by the Spirit,' which seems to mean cultivating a pious dependence on what 'feels' right, following the Brethren in every detail, even anticipating their desires, because they are absolutely pure representatives of that absolute God. All this seems absolutely contrary to the unique Mormon idea of earth as a school where we learn, by guidance surely, but ultimately by our own choice and experience, *how* the universe works and how to be like God as creative agents within that universe." And although his complaint may sound shockingly unorthodox, it was a reflection of a uniquely Latter-day Saint Christian viewpoint: Lamenting the prevailing doctrinal climate, he opined, "It's almost as if eternal life will consist of eternal dependence on God."[33] Where was the "'stretching the envelope' in our journey toward godhood," he wondered. This version of ontological autonomy did not in any way contravene the willed interdependence, the eternal relationality, that England saw as central to Restoration conceptions of humankind's place in a web of belonging here and hereafter, vertical as well as horizontal.

Years later, he returned forcefully to this theme, conversing with his son: "I don't think we are here on this earth to simply learn how to get guidance. If that were so it seems to me that we could have stayed with God. Obviously, we had to get into a situation where we weren't going by direct guidance but had to exercise our judgement and our agency a great deal in order to learn how to live in this universe. So I become more and more convinced that that is why we are here. At crucial points getting a sense that divinity exists and cares about us is very important, but that continual guidance is counterproductive, it doesn't teach us how to be Gods." Even more provocatively, he summarized, "I think being in contact with God constantly is moving towards the devil's plan" (a reference to Latter-day Saint belief that Lucifer's strategy is to destroy human agency).

Hence, in England's view, even petitionary prayer, asking for guidance in all things, can be theologically ill-founded. "When I was in the bishopric at Stanford, I found myself constantly counseling young latter-day saints who were just going through hell over whether they should go to Harvard or to Yale and I remember thinking one day well God probably doesn't care whether you got to Harvard or to Yale. That is why you are not getting an answer. It doesn't matter. Probably one will be better for you than the other but it will be because you make it better."[34]

Part of the problem, as England recognized, was that the Saints were at that moment moving "radically towards traditional Christian theology," with Calvinist overtones.[35] He would have been dismayed had he lived another few decades to see Latter-day Saint authors moving even further away from core doctrine, making a concerted effort to convince evangelicals that Latter-day Saints, too, embraced a theology of *sola gratia*, or something close to it, with a flurry of books touting salvation by grace. England was on the right side of his church's theological history, but at the wrong moment in the church's institutional history. For at the moment England writes, influential Saints were in a revisionist mode, unknown to themselves. They were Protestantizing Mormonism, shifting to a grace-centered discourse. If anything, England underestimated the enduring as well as accelerating overlap of Calvinist preconceptions and Latter-day Saint religious culture.

Joseph Smith's self-described restorationism did not eliminate all traces of that Protestant background, and remnants of the old vocabulary and formulae infiltrated even Smith's vocabulary (such as the triad of divine omniscience, omnipotence, and omnipresence).[36] Nonetheless, the distance of the Latter-day Saint God and doctrine of salvation from Protestant conceptions is immense, and unambiguous. Mid-twentieth-century Mormonism sacrificed much of its theological radicalism in order to better assimilate into the American (and traditional Christian) mainstream. In yet one more in an endless stream of tragic ironies, England was in this case the legitimate conservative, fighting for a Latter-day Saint theological understanding truer to its sources. He captures the problem in stark terms in explaining LDS obliviousness to the radical power and beauty of what he would call "the Weeping God of Mormonism."

> Highly respected and prolific Gospel scholars and general authorities . . . have encouraged a rather negative, pessimistic [so-called] neo-orthodoxy in Mormonism generally and especially in the semi-official Mormon theology taught in the LDS Church Education System, particularly in the BYU religion department. O. Kendall White has documented these changes most fully, and Thomas Alexander has given the best historical consideration to what he calls "the reconstruction of Mormon doctrine" away from its original radical adventuresomeness, as part of the twentieth-century accommodation to American culture.[37]

Some influential voices—especially those with fundamentalist backgrounds and sympathies—applauded these developments. England singled out Robert L. Millett, later the dean of BYU's Religious Education college, who praised these newfound emphases on an absolute God, human sinfulness, and salvation by grace. Millett considered them a "retrenchment and a refinement" of early Restoration thought. So too did BYU professor Stephen Robinson, who, in attempting a bridge-building publication with evangelicals, ended up "sounding more Evangelical than Mormon" on crucial issues like inerrancy and sufficiency of the biblical canon, salvation by grace alone, the "substitutionary" atonement, and—most important—the nature of God. England with good reason saw these new emphases as Protestant incursions, not found in Joseph Smith's teachings.

The doctrinal foundation of Protestantism is the Reformers' view that the critical New Testament word *dikaioun* [verbal form of the noun "righteous"] "means 'to *pronounce* righteous,'" whereas the prior, Catholic view was that it signified "to *make* righteous."[38] What is at stake is whether salvation is bestowed when we are *considered* righteous before God's eyes by virtue of Christ's righteousness, or whether a growing conformity to Christ's moral example, facilitated by his grace, *transforms* us into sanctified individuals. Smith explicitly repudiated the Protestant conception of salvation by grace, defining the Restoration in clear opposition to a pronounced or "imputed righteousness:" Only "that which is governed by law is also preserved by law and perfected and sanctified by the same. That which breaketh a law, and abideth not by law . . . , *cannot be sanctified by . . . mercy,*" i.e., *by grace* (D&C 88:34–35; my emphasis). The same dismissal of Protestant grace is evident in the Book of Mormon's recurrent rejection of the doctrine that we can be saved "in our sins," which is effectively the case with Luther and the whole tradition of grace as imputed righteousness, wherein we are "always wholly a sinner." In that conception, we are saved through Christ's righteousness. He stands in as surrogate before the judging eye of God for our own always insufficient righteousness. ("We are justified by God's judgment though wholly a sinner," in Luther's language.)[39] Or as the Thirty-Nine Articles, the basis of most Protestant groups state, "We are *accounted* righteous before God, only for the merit of our Lord and Saviour Jesus Christ by Faith" (Article 11; my emphasis).

James Talmage, writing before these new trends in Latter-day Saint religious language, pronounced this version of justification through imputed grace not just wrong but "a pernicious doctrine."[40] It makes God an arbitrary sovereign, consigns man to irremediable sinfulness, and denies the inherent divinity of a mankind "whole from the foundation of the world" (Moses 6:54). God's grace is real, but in Smith's understanding it emerged at the premortal council when Christ offered to sacrifice himself to make human resurrection universal and human exaltation possible. Grace cannot bestow salvation because salvation is neither a gift won nor a reward earned. It is a condition attained when sanctified individuals become the kind of persons, in the kinds of relationships, that constitute the divine nature.

These theological perspectives of England would be years in developing. And they would culminate in his finest piece of theological explication: his posthumously published "Weeping God of Mormonism." Here he followed his theological instincts to a recognition of perhaps Joseph Smith's most prescient contribution to religious thought. Latter-day Saints worship an emphatically passible deity, that is, a God the Father fully capable of being moved by human suffering. Although the Old Testament describes a God who is alternately angry, jealous, or mollified, Catholic theologians since Augustine had insisted that such emotional permutations were figurative and the creedal formulations of the Protestant world universally affirmed faith in a God "without body, parts, *or passions.*" It was only "toward the end of the nineteenth century [that] a sea change began to occur within Christian theology such that at present many, if not most, Christian theologians hold as axiomatic that God is passible, that He does undergo emotional changes of states, and so can suffer."[41] England appears to have been the first to recognize the novelty of Smith's contribution in historical context and the uniqueness of its place in a religious canon.

In his paper, England focused on "a concept of God" that he labeled "the essential foundation of all Mormon theology, one that makes our theology radically different from most others," even as he noted that "it is also a concept which many Mormons, like the younger Enoch, still have not understood or quite accepted." The claim is powerfully illustrated by the remarkable text Smith produced in 1830, wherein the ancient prophet Enoch is caught up into heaven. There, in this account typical of the ascension narrative genre, Enoch is witness to a baffling spectacle. The God of all creation is weeping. Three times the stunned prophet asks how such a display of emotional vulnerability can even be possible in a God who is "from all eternity to all eternity." The answer, he learns, is simple but poignant. God is weeping over the pain and misery of his children. "Wherefore should not the heavens weep, seeing these shall suffer?" (Moses 7:29, 37).

A God who weeps over human misery (and does so in actual corporeal form!) is the most economical and irrefutable argument conceivable for the church's placement far outside the historical Christian tradition with which many of England's contemporaries were pleading affinity. God's distress at the predicament humans have brought upon themselves clearly evidences a disappointment, a regret, at the course of events—which can only mean they are not consistent with his will. We are here at almost the farthest remove imaginable from the God of Augustine and John Calvin, for whom in the latter case "everything is governed by God's hand,"[42] from who is saved to where and when earthquakes hit. The Latter-day Saint God, by contrast, does not orchestrate human behavior, choice, and events to comport perfectly with his will. He participates in rather than transcends the ebb and flow of human history, human tragedy, and human grief. Sterling McMurrin, like England, recognized that "Mormon theological writing and sermonizing are more often than not replete with the vocabulary of absolutism. But, like it or not, the Mormon theologian must sooner or later return to the finitistic conception of God upon which both his technical theology and his theological myths are founded."[43] England unabashedly embraced a finitistic God the Father, physically embodied and susceptible to vicarious suffering. He found in that conception his faith tradition's greatest strength, rather than weakness.

This was perhaps England's finest essay—and it was uncharacteristically free of explicitly controversial claims. If he had begun his theological forays with that essay, his church career might have unfolded very differently. And yet, we see a direct connection between his last theological essay, on the Weeping God, and his very first, an exploration of the meaning of atonement. They are inherently fruit of the same theological seed: a conception of God as possessed of a tragic but redemptive capacity for infinite empathy. This empathy became the focus of England's most theologically ambitious essay, based on a 1966 sermon he delivered and published in the third issue of *Dialogue* as "That They Might Not Suffer: The Gift of Atonement."

"THAT THEY MIGHT NOT SUFFER": GRAPPLING WITH ATONEMENT

My most important [mission] experience was seeing how the atonement works. . . .
Lowell Bennion had taught that the atonement is not something that pays for our
repentance, it . . . actually gives us the power to repent in the first place. . . .
It was a very powerful lesson to me about how the atonement works
and it's probably led to my major contribution doctrinally.
—England, undated interview with son Mark

England's earliest provocations that set him at odds with the Latter-day Saint community were his antiwar stance and the pressure he brought to bear on the priesthood ban, in his own teaching and writing and in the coverage he gave the policy in *Dialogue*. The McConkie rebuke of his talk on the progressive nature of God (see below) would be the most widely publicized of his doctrinal conflicts with the Brethren. His theory of atonement, however, was the theological work that most persistently damaged his standing with the leadership. Over his long series of conflicts with the Brethren, England repeatedly asked for specifics to their criticisms. Yet when focal points of unease with England's writings were forthcoming, even the clearest signals did not always register with him—or if they did he chose to ignore them. Nowhere was this in greater evidence than with the doctrinal issue more important to Latter-day Saints than any other: the atonement of Jesus Christ.

Atonement in Christian Thought

The centrality in Latter-day Saint theology of Christ's self-sacrifice is captured in the words of Joseph Smith, that Jesus "died, was buried, and rose again the third day, and ascended up into heaven; and all other things are only appendages to these."[44] LDS belief about the meaning of Christ's atoning death overlaps to some degree with Christian atonement theology, though it is much closer to Catholic than Protestant versions. Latter-day Saints begin with the entirely atypical premise that God intended that Adam and Eve "should Eat & fall,"[45] to launch a painful but necessary immersion in a world of educative suffering. Sin is therefore an inevitable and important part of humankind's moral education. At the same time, sin—the willing choice to violate moral law—alienates humans from God and produces a spiral that leads humans further and further away from him and his influence. This process of self-damnation, and the impossibility of self-elevation from sin and death, makes some kind of intervention by a higher power necessary. Yet that intervention must occur without destroying human agency. In other words, human freedom to choose—*which entails the freedom to bear the consequences of those choices*—must not be nullified by an outside Savior. Jesus Christ mediates the collision of these two principles—God's loving mercy and human freedom—by bearing the painful consequences of human choices, and empowering those humans to choose afresh. This process of repentance, rechoosing, and continually self-correcting and reorienting one's life continues until one finds oneself in harmony with God and the eternal laws that undergird the universe. Salvation in Restoration thought is therefore not a gift God can bequeath or endow, or a gift an individual can earn. It is a mode of joyful existence in full harmony with eternal law and the divine nature alike. The atonement, Christ's undeserved and impossible-to-merit gift, is what creates, in the Book of Mormon's words, "the conditions of repentance" (Helaman 14:11) on which the ascent toward exaltation depends.

The sticking point of atonement theology, for a number of contemporary theologians and some Latter-day Saint writers including England, are the echoes of a crude "satisfaction" model of atonement that developed in the Middle Ages. This replaced the even earlier varieties of Ransom Theory, in which Christ ransoms himself to Satan, who holds sinning mankind captive. Under St. Anselm (1033–1109), an infinite offense against a perfect God and His honor required the satisfaction of an infinite payment. As he wrote, "To sin is to fail to render to God His due. What is due to God? Righteousness, or rectitude of will. He who fails to render this honor to God, robs God of that which belongs to Him and dishonors God. . . . And what is satisfaction? . . . More than what was taken away must be rendered back."[46] Only Christ, as human, could share in the debt, and only Christ, as God, could pay that infinite penalty. Thus only Christ as man-God could accomplish atonement. Christ dies in our place to satisfy God the Father's offended honor. The Reformers, especially Calvin, reformulated the theory to emphasize the violation of law rather than of honor, and the consequent need for a penal substitution, rather than satisfaction. God punishes Christ rather than humankind.

Such distinctions, however, are largely academic. In virtually all versions of atonement theology, satisfaction of either debt or honor or justice is just retributive vengeance by another name. From the early Christian centuries, an actual entity, Satan, or medieval conceptions of the sovereign's honor, or a reified universal, Justice, demanded a payment be made for sin. The philosopher Friedrich Nietzsche's analysis seems accurate: Christians have largely imagined that the infliction of punishment provides some kind of pleasure that cancels out the pain of the offense (which is what retributive justice really presupposes); Christ's suffering provides the satisfaction necessary to zero out the sum total of a human offense, resulting in a state of equilibrium.[47]

These ideas are jarring to modern sensibilities; in fact, it is largely the "embarrassment among Christians" of seeing Christ's sacrifice in terms of Pauline metaphors about ransom, scapegoats, debts, and martyrs, writes one theologian, that has prompted a range of new atonement theology.[48] Substitutionary atonement ideas were upsetting to some of Anselm's contemporaries as well. The theologian Pierre Abélard (of Héloïse and Abélard fame), protested: "Indeed, how cruel and perverse it seems that [God] should require the blood of the innocent as the price of anything, or that it should in any way please Him that an innocent person should be slain—still less that God should hold the death of His Son in such acceptance that by it He should be reconciled with the whole world."[49]

As an alternative, Abélard proposed "that Christ died for the sake of love, providing a model of self-sacrificial passion for humankind. Salvation entailed imitating Christ in his love for others, the love that God revealed in Jesus's death for his friends. As Christ had done, we also do."[50] His idea came to be known as "moral influence" theory. In this version, "Christ's self-sacrifice is *personally and subjectively* efficacious, calling forth our response to his whole death-culminating ministry of service to mankind." It had the virtue, wrote one theologian, of being "the first . . . doctrine of the atonement . . . which had nothing unintelligible, arbitrary, illogical, or immoral about it."[51] Although it had little impact at the time, it found popularity among liberal Protestants in the nineteenth and twentieth centuries.

The closest thing to a uniquely Latter-day Saint theology of atonement was developed in the early twentieth century by B. H. Roberts, who attempted to reconcile scripture with a less retributive take on God's justice.[52] The significance of Roberts's thought is in his reinterpretation of penal substitution theory through the lens (consistent with both Smithian and Book of Mormon theology) of moral agency. He thus recasts the language of justice, punishment, and retribution into an emphasis on choice, consequence, and human freedom. In Book of Mormon language, a clear differentiation of alternatives, the ability to choose them, and the stability and expectation of their unfolding in consequence of such deliberate human choice undergird the cosmic order over which God presides and serves as guarantor. Without a framework of law that reflects these oppositional realities, choice would be uninformed, consequences random, and agency void. As Alma asks, "How could [man] sin if there was no law? How could there be a law save there was a punishment?" (Alma 42:17). Or as church president Russell M. Nelson points out (as did Dallin Oaks in discussing abortion), true agency requires that after we freely make choices we be "tied to the consequences of those choices."[53] The emphasis on choices "freely" made comports with the church's noninclusion of rape and incest victims in the prohibition on abortion. LDS scripture, like Paul, is emphatic in employing substitutionary language, with the caveat that Christ appears in those scriptures to be maintaining and assuring the continuing operations of moral agency, and that agency requires the continuity between choice and consequence: "The one [person] raised to happiness according to his desires of happiness, or good according to his desires of good; and the other to evil according to his desires of evil; for as he has desired to do evil all the day long even so shall he have his reward of evil when the night cometh" (Alma 41:5).

Roberts's theory was little read and had no impact on Latter-day Saint thinking. As a result, Saints have by and large embraced the language and metaphors of penal substitution. In a particularly influential discourse, Boyd K. Packer emphasized "justice, the eternal law of justice, will be the measure against which we settle [our] account." At some point, in his analogy, our "creditor" will "appear . . . and demand . . . payment in full" for our misdeeds. Consequently, "Justice demands that [we] pay the contract or suffer the penalty." Fortunately, Jesus will "pay the debt . . . and free the debtor."[54] In a later talk he reiterated these themes: Christ paid "the penalty for all mankind for the sum total of all wickedness and depravity; for brutality, immorality, perversion, and corruption; for addiction; for the killings and torture and terror—for all of it that ever had been or all that ever would be enacted upon this earth."[55]

Revising Abélard

England believed substitutionary interpretations had two shortcomings. First, they ignored the scriptural attestations that depicted Christ's suffering as involving solidarity with human pain rather than—or in addition to—penalty for human sins. One critical Book of Mormon passage, for example, emphasized that Christ "will take upon him their infirmities, that his bowels may be filled with mercy, according to the flesh, that he may know according to the flesh how to succor his people according to their infirmities" (Alma 7:12). Neither sin nor substitution is indicated in those words. Nor is substitution or sin invoked in a second description of his atonement: "He suffereth the pains of all men, yea, the pains of every living creature, both men, women, and children, who belong to the family of Adam" (2 Nephi 9:21). Both these verses emphasize empathic suffering *with* humankind, rather than a penal substitution in humankind's *place*.

Second, England felt metaphysical readings of the atonement denuded it of its immediacy, relevance, and practical efficacy. "In too much Christian theology, as well as folk religion, the Atonement has remained an event remote from the common life of man, somehow involving Adam and God and mysterious supernatural realms," including "strange metaphysical structures such as absolute justice . . . but having nothing very clear to do with redeeming the daily round of studying differential equations and commuting to work and waking up in the night in the deep loneliness and pain of our regret." And Latter-day Saint thought in this regard, he hints, is not the solution but is often complicit in the theological failure. "Mormons are certainly not immune." This gentle rebuke becomes the prelude to a drastic revisionism in Restoration Christianity's core doctrine. For at this point England utterly denies atonement's rootedness in some transcendent legal framework that demands ransom or punishment or satisfaction—or the upholding of some divine order predicated on choice and consequence. "Christ's mission was not to straighten out some metaphysical warp in the universe that Adam's taking of the fruit had created. The effects of the Atonement were not metaphysical but moral and spiritual." In other words, England is invoking the perspective of Abélard (whom he mentions by name) as a view more congenial to Latter-day Saint conceptions of the divine and of salvation.

Accordingly, England shifts the theological weight of sin. Rather than emphasize sin as an offense against God and his sovereignty, he diagnosed sin as principally a matter of alienation—from God and from self. The guilt and shame resulting from sin, not the moral failing itself, was for him the principal defect in need of remedy. In this regard, he seems to have been unique among Latter-day Saints in teasing out the implications of Elihu's unsettling query to Job: "If thou sinnest, what doest thou against him? Or if thy transgressions be multiplied, what doest thou unto him?" (Job 35:6). According to this vision, God's primary preoccupation would not be with his own wounded majesty but with human suffering: "We find ourselves cut off from *ourselves*. . . . We act contrary to our image of ourselves and break our deepest integrity. . . . We also suffer the inner estrangement of guilt—that supreme human suffering which gives us our images of hell." Hence, Christ does not suffer to satisfy Justice but *our* sense of justice (man "feels that every action must bear its consequences; . . . the demands of justice that Amulek is talking about, which must be overpowered, are from *man's own sense of justice*, not some abstract eternal principle"). His unconditional love "has the power to release man from the barrier of his own guilt."

This is an atonement theology at the furthest remove from Calvinist preconceptions. "We are inescapably moral by nature," he writes. That is why the principal challenge atonement addresses is not that it makes God's forgiveness of human sin possible. God has forgiven us before the deed is even done. The problem atonement must resolve is how we can forgive ourselves and repair our integrity, our faithfulness to our true nature, so that we may once again "let our confidence wax strong in his presence through the feeling that our lives are in harmony with his will." Thus, in a reversal of more common interpretations, "We do not repent in order that God will forgive us and atone for our sins, but rather God atones for our sins . . . in order that we might repent and thus bring to its conclusion the process of forgiveness." In other words, "*the . . . atonement actually gives us the power to repent in the first place*." It does not do this by any divine calculus of repayment, compensatory suffering, or righting of the scales of justice. In England's elegant prose, the mystery of atonement is no mystery; in a process shorn of metaphysics, we find ourselves face-to-face with the supreme instance of unconditional sacrifice, "the shock of eternal love expressed in Gethsemane." And we are transformed by that recognition.

This is, of course, Abélard's moral influence theory of atonement. The purpose of Christ's sacrifice was to transform us, catalyzing our sorrow, repentance, and reconciliation with God. How did this compare with Latter-day Saint teachings? Certainly LDS scripture emphasizes the impact of the atonement as an incomparable instance of sheer, selfless love. As with theologies of the "moral influence" type, B. H. Roberts also suggested that the atonement's efficacy on individuals was due in part to its exemplary power as a "love-manifestation." "Shall this suffering for others have no benefitting effect upon those others for whom the suffering is endured?" he asked. Roberts finds its exemplary purpose was "to demonstrate, first of all, God-love for man, by a sacrifice that tasks God that man might be saved; and second, to inspire man-love for God, by the demonstration that God first loved man, and how deeply God loves him; and third, to teach man-love for man."[56]

Indeed, the Book of Mormon does refer to Christ's sacrifice as a powerful catalyst to "draw" men to Christ (2 Nephi 27:14). And England's focus on alienation is certainly true to the etymology of atonement (at-one-ment), translated by John Wycliffe as "reconciling." From the perspective of Latter-day Saint orthodoxy, however, two problems exist with England's theological revisionism. First is the language of substitution in LDS (and biblical) scripture that England neglected to address. As one example, Book of Mormon prophet Alma declares that repentance "could not come unto men except there were a punishment, which also was eternal as the life of the soul should be" (Alma 42:16). As another, Lehi teaches that "he offereth himself a sacrifice for sin, to answer the ends of the law" (2 Nephi 2:7). The Book of Mormon elsewhere refers to the "demands of justice," and the Doctrine and Covenants explicitly declares that Christ suffers in our stead if we repent (D&C 19). Some kind of substitution seems clearly implied. Had England offered his interpretation as a supplement to or tempering of substitutionary atonement rather than a whole-sale replacement, he probably would have raised no hackles.

Second, and more difficult to overcome, is the fact that in the version pro-pounded by England (and similar influence theories), atonement is a power-ful, inspiring, sublime catalyst to salvation; but this model does not establish a convincing rationale for its utter, unqualified, absolute indispensability to human salvation. A stupendous display of sacrificial love does not adequately differentiate Christ's "infinite" atonement from other historical or conceivable human parallels. Clearly, most in the world do not experience "the shock of eternal love," and many find their way to self-acceptance and inner peace with-out knowledge of either Christ or his atonement. In other words, relegating the atonement to an emotionally powerful catalyst to transformation may be more Pelagian than Christian (a useful but not universally necessary catalyst). Like the reputed theology of the early Christian Pelagius,[57] England seemed to be suggesting that in principle, one who did not need "the shock of eternal love" could find his own way to repentance and salvation.

Given England's challenge to such a cardinal doctrine, his decision to pub-lish the essay in an early issue of *Dialogue*—the third—was risky at best and easily read by his detractors as the provocation they were waiting for. After the horse was out of the barn, England wrote to a person of influence whose appro-bation he would increasingly court in the years ahead—Neal A. Maxwell, then serving as a vice president at the University of Utah. England sent the essay and asked for his reactions. Maxwell's response was gentle but unequivocal: "I am not satisfied about how well grounded your view is, but, more importantly that the view is entirely true."[58] What should have been even more alarming—one of the church's most powerful voices, and the one who's opinion and influence would effect England's eventual downfall, seconded Maxwell's judgment. So-licited for his opinion as well, apostle Boyd K. Packer "strongly opposed" his interpretation.[59] More than once, England compounded his own difficulties by soliciting and then disregarding counsel from the highest levels. In actual fact, his reactions demonstrated that he was seeking affirmation, not guidance. When Elder Holland notified England in the summer of 1976 that he still carried "a couple of extra bags," it is more than likely that his stubbornness, as well as his particular theological transgressions, was what Holland meant.

In the years following the essay's publication, criticism from Maxwell and Packer notwithstanding, England promulgated his atonement theory unabashedly. Two decades later, and only four years after its republication, another person of high consequence would become personally involved in the fireworks his theological foray provoked. In 1988, Milton Wille, an engineering professor and a member of England's congregation, was so alarmed by his perceived heresies expounded in Sunday school class that he complained to the stake president, Merrill Bateman. Bateman and the local bishop (Roman Andrus) directed Wille to meet directly with England about his concerns. This must have been extremely gratifying to England; one of his most consistent complaints about Latter-day Saint culture was the tendency, manifest by rank and file but tacitly condoned from on high, to run to the leadership with every allegation of impropriety or criticism rather than abide by the New Testament counsel to resolve offenses in face-to-face encounters, person-to-person. The two met as directed, and Wille provided a detailed report of the meeting he had with England, which he described as "friendly and cordial."

The main source of Wille's alarm was England's heterodoxy on the subject of Christ's atonement. He had described in his original complaint, and repeated in his report, what disturbed him most: "He categorically rejects the idea of any principle of heavenly, eternal, or God-related justice or even mercy in terms of meanings espoused by the Church. Rather, he sees Christ's role as simply a motivator. . . . The issue of justice he sees as strictly a mortal-human problem. We demand justice of others as well as of ourselves. . . . Our understandings of gospel principles heighten our guilt feeling or, in other words, our demanding justice of ourselves. Christ loves the sinner unconditionally." And the atonement's efficacy comes through "the emotional impact of the recognition of that unconditional love." It was an accurate summation of the principles expounded in the essay.

At this point in the meeting, and incomprehensibly, England defended his position by appealing for implicit General Authority support. "He related that he had sent copies of a statement of his views on the atonement to the Brethren for their consideration. He indicated that only Elder Boyd K. Packer responded to his request and strongly opposed Brother England's doctrines on the atonement. He further indicated that he considered the lack of responses from the other Brethren, and particularly President Hinckley and Elder Maxwell, as indicating that they didn't feel strong objections."[60] The reply was both disingenuous and mistaken, for Maxwell had indeed, as we have seen, responded unambiguously to England's essay. Perhaps in the intervening two decades that rebuff slipped England's mind. At the same time, to disregard Packer's objections as "only" one voice was hardly credible in the context of Packer's official position as acting president of the Quorum of the Twelve and his unofficial position as the most authoritative doctrinal voice in the church in that decade—especially on the subject of atonement. England's theology of atonement, in other words, had been explicitly rejected by two of the most influential and respected apostles of the modern era and ignored by the rest.

To establish the accuracy of his account, Wille wrote that England "agreed that what I had written to you [i.e., the above description which had been sent in Wille's original complaint and which he now read to England] was basically correct"; he copied England on this second communication to ensure his accuracy. No record of Bateman's response is known. However, he would not forget the episode, unfortunately for England.

As was his practice, in the absence of explicit prohibition and regardless of clear condemnations, England persisted in promulgating his heterodoxy: "I teach the Atonement in every class because I find it explored in all great literature and because the mercy it embodies is the only answer to the imitative violence which is our greatest human plague. I teach *King Lear* as Shakespeare's answer to the question he poses in *Hamlet* and elsewhere—how can we learn to deal with offenses, even violence, in ways other than in the escalating, self-defeating cycles of revenge? Shakespeare clearly wants us to think of Cordelia as a Christ figure (she says, 'It is my father's business that I go about.')"[61] In the United Kingdom in 1992, England was still teaching his version of atonement theology: "I gave the lesson in High Priests Quorum, . . . focusing on the Atonement as a way not so much to get forgiveness *after* repentance as a source of power and means to give us sufficient faith to repent and forgive ourselves."[62] England even took Cordelia's words of forgiveness, "No cause, No cause," as the title of his valedictory to his department prior to resigning under pressure years later.

England loved Shakespeare's plays—*King Lear* in particular—because he thought they taught the ineffable power of Christ's atonement better than any sermon. "Shakespeare," he wrote, "had faith that the dramatist can lead souls to repentance if he is willing, like Cordelia . . . to risk all." And so he saw the ending of this most devastating of all tragedies as no tragedy.

Shakespeare, in denying us the ending in justice that we yearn for, takes us into a realm where pity (and grace) can exist. He asks us to believe that a love which transcends mere justice is worth any sacrifice, worth dying for, and the only thing that really continues living. Cordelia's "life" is indeed, as Lear affirms, the "chance which does redeem all sorrows," and I believe that life is, in fact, given to Lear. If we deny that, I think we deny Cordelia and the truth of what she, at great cost, taught Lear. Lear's final vision should be ours: He calls us—"Look at her, look, her lips, / Look there, look there!"—to see clearly and retain as our focus the being and the drama, spoken by those lips, that led from "Nothing" to "No cause, no cause" and redeemed him.[63]

7

CROSSING JORDAN

BRIGHAM YOUNG UNIVERSITY AT LAST

You have a much greater amount here of what is the most important
academic freedom, in my opinion, the freedom to express and discuss
openly your positive religious and moral views and convictions
rather than merely your negative ones or your criticism.
—England to Phi Kappa Phi students, 1974

England's query to Holland in the summer of 1976 was not his first effort to
revive the possibility of a BYU career. A few months earlier, he had been in the
Church Administration Building where the apostles and other senior church
officials had their offices. His visit was prompted by a disturbing report he
received from his CES superior Joe Christensen in mid-March 1976. "Joe Christensen . . . called me in out of the blue [and] informed me that 'a number' of
General Authorities had commented to him about my articles in [recent] issues
of *Dialogue*." The problem, he was told, was not content but his association, as a
church employee, with the magazine. England was astute enough to recognize
that of course content was the issue. "The Mormon Cross" was not named
explicitly, but it was the edgiest of his recent output. He had also published his
"Letter to a College Student" (late 1973) in which he blasted Latter-day Saints'
"spiritual imperialism" and "various forms of fanaticism, racism, militarism,
[and] authoritarianism."[1]

In 1974, in response to the invitation to address the BYU honor society Phi
Kappa Phi, he had delivered (then published) the talk, "Great Books or True
Religion? Defining the Mormon Scholar," a spirited defense of faithful intellec-
tualism. Most of the essay was safe enough, but as an example of a more daring

scholarship, he had raised the alarming possibility (first posited by B. H. Roberts) of "a new and more naturalistic understanding of the manner in which Joseph Smith may have used divine instruments—the Urim and Thummim, etc.—in translating the Book of Mormon."[2] He also called upon the church to "affirm . . . where we can . . . such things as the women's liberation movement." He then became more combative: "As one measure of our failure [that of his generation and the one preceding], I ask you to name those thinkers and writers who are now willing and able to appear in all four of our periodicals for expression of ideas, *Exponent II, Dialogue: A Journal of Mormon Thought, BYU Studies,* and *The Ensign.*"

England had misjudged his position once again; those first two were exactly the wrong standards to which the leadership wanted young Saints to aspire. England could not have thrown more combustible material on the fires already burning had he wanted, as he learned immediately after Christensen's report. Disturbed by what Christensen told him, he made a visit to Elder Robert Hales, who told him—to his dismay—that "he had been sent back to Boston in November to ask Claudia Bushman to resign as editor of *Exponent II.*"[3] (She did; "one of the great trials of her life.")[4] This was a new development that reshaped the landscape. The Brethren were now acting to position efforts like England's as inconsistent with faithful membership.

Learning this, England went immediately to see Elder Packer. "There the roof fell in: it seems that again I had failed to anticipate counsel because he had expected (though never saying anything about it) that after our interview last spring about not being accepted for BYU because of *Dialogue* I would have no more to do with it."[5] This is one of those moments where England's obliviousness to clear and loud signals is hard to fathom. Of course Packer would have expected England's resignation, since he had in fact been utterly explicit about his *Dialogue* connection as an impediment to his hiring at that meeting in March 1975. In fact, Packer had at that time told England he needed to do a better job of "sensing counsel," and then proceeded to lay out his criticisms of *Dialogue.*[6] According to a secondhand account, Packer at one point pulled a bookmarked issue off his shelf, and pointed to a poem. "That is the problem I have with *Dialogue,* he said. The poem, no great piece of art, was entitled 'Prophet' and referred to Joseph, the 'Stout, paunched, hook-nosed mystic . . . who gimped his way from fourteen on' after he 'Dreamed God the Father, [and] the Savior Son.'"[7]

Dialogue was by now seven years in distribution, and the poem clearly typified, rather than inaugurated, a mode of journalism that did not shrink from frank and even undignified ways of depicting Latter-day Saint icons and events. Oblivious to the import of what Packer was telling him on that occasion, England wrote a postmeeting letter in which he defended his resistance to prior counsel on the subject of the magazine, and then, incredibly, proceeded to compare his journal to a university and relate that "after prayerful consideration," he was convinced "I could not work to make things better . . . by shutting down the journal."[8] Packer made one more attempt to get his message across to a stubborn listener: Almost a year after the meeting, he sent England a copy of his 1 February 1976 address, "Arts and the Spirit of the Lord."[9]

And so now, in his office with England just weeks later, and so that there could be no mistaking his position, Packer read aloud to England "long sections" from that recent talk on art and artists, a hard-hitting piece in which he observed that "people who are very gifted, it would seem, tend to be temperamental," adding, in the words of a senior apostle, "more temper than mental." His next words were an unstinting reprimand to the man sitting before him: "Few have captured the spirit of the gospel of Jesus Christ and the restoration of it in music, in art, in literature. They have not, therefore, even though they were gifted, made a lasting contribution to the onrolling of the Church and kingdom of God in the dispensation of the fulness of times. They have therefore missed doing what they might have done, and they have missed being what they might have become. I am reminded of the statement 'There are many who struggle and climb and finally reach the top of the ladder, only to find that it is leaning against the wrong wall.'"[10]

The rebuke was unmistakable—and England felt the sting. In the apostle's view, "I was missing the Lord's way of using my artistic talents to serve him," he later recorded. And then Packer said with direct reference to *Dialogue*, using the emphatic and sacred language of prophetic authority: "As the Lord liveth, let it alone. It will not prosper and you will not with it!!" The warning, he added, extended in fact to any independent publication, including *Exponent II* and *Sunstone*. Then Packer focused his concerns more specifically on England's character: "He seemed to say that I was too ambitious for position or recognition in the Kingdom—that until I could truly say to the Lord that I was content to serve in the last rank of foot soldiers and struggle through the mud and tears of this world . . . I would be out of tune."

Afterward, in the privacy of his journal, England lashed out bitterly and perhaps unfairly at what he saw as Packer's—he may have meant the institutional church's—skewed appraisal of character. "He seemed to condemn my condemnation of the sycophants and toadies who buck for General Authority or serve as lackeys in Church bureaus. . . . Men . . . who seemed to me at times to be willing to sacrifice integrity to maintain their position or good graces of those over them, are really the humble ones" and "I was the arrogant and ambitious one."[11]

And here we arrive at the heart and core of England's dilemma. For though he saw himself as anything but a toady or a lackey, increasingly owning his role as symbol of Latter-day Saint intellectual independence and fidelity to higher principle, he recognized that one could only serve as that symbol and effect positive change if one remained loyally *within* the institution that he loved too much to either leave or leave alone. And incapable in his mind of differentiating his loyalty to Christ from his loyalty to what he was convinced was Christ's church, he proceeded to do precisely what he had so roundly condemned. He submitted to Packer's counsel in order to remain in—or in his case, move closer to—the Brethren's "good graces." He resigned his position with *Dialogue*. It is hard to say if the blow was softened or magnified by his recognition that, in essential ways, the experiment was proving a failure. Months before, some graduate students at the University of California at Berkeley and the Graduate Theological Union launched *Sunstone*, another independent Latter-day Saint journal. England wrote a revealing letter, appearing in *Sunstone*'s inaugural issue, admitting disappointment in his own journal's failure to succor "those who face special problems in developing their faith" and cautioning the new periodical's board to "put your loyalty to his work of saving souls above everything, above your own prestige and ambitions, your academic standards."[12] England's implicit foreboding was justified; the new journal not only continued but extended *Dialogue*'s edgy journalism—including thoughtful appraisals of Mormon art, culture, and history—but increasingly publishing unabashedly strident attacks on orthodoxy and defending dissident perspectives.

After the sacrificial offering of his *Dialogue* affiliation, he proceeded the very next day to test the waters of his standing with the apostles. He first stopped in the office of newly called apostle David Haight, who had been England's stake president in California—and "the only G[eneral] A[uthority] who has sought me out to praise one of my articles in *Dialogue*," he noted sadly. Haight pointed out that Packer had originally been England's defender in the quorum, until he had "my articles in *Dialogue* thrown up to him."[13] If England perceived in those words the roots of Packer's irritation at having wasted his capital and injured his own reputation for discernment by a misplaced faith in England's character, he showed no sign of it. England left Haight's office and went straight to Packer's, who proceeded to ask him what his connection to the magazine was now. "Nothing," he responded. How had the editors reacted?, the apostle queried. "With understanding, support, and silence," England said.

Having now spent the better part of two days seeking assurances of the Brethren's "good graces," he returned to report the events to Charlotte. Her response had more than a hint of rebuke. "She asked why I keep seeking to know what the General Authorities think. Good question," England confided to his journal.[14] It was more than a good question. It was the key to England's psychological makeup. His friend Lavina Anderson had asked him months earlier how he bore up so gracefully under the pressure of being "a symbol." He responded that he had faith he was trusted by the Lord, which was the key to his keeping proper perspective.[15] Clearly, his faith was less than constant.

Eugene England Sr. had recorded in his personal history his conviction that "parents can pretty well set the course of their children's lives if they will drill into their characters the ideals they should have."[16] It is abundantly evident that England felt a great chasm between the ideals his parents had in mind for him and his failure to achieve them. He grew up hearing repeatedly the story that he had been consecrated to the work of the Lord. His friends thought it obvious that England Sr. wanted a General Authority son, and "Gene labored his whole life over guilt for not fulfilling his father's ambition for him."[17] Toward the end of his life, a therapist assigned England to recapture his earliest childhood memories. Tellingly, his first two involved the trauma of disappointing his father. The first one involved an early bladder accident. "I have wet myself I feel uncomfortable but not because of the wetness. My parents are there, with some friends who have come to visit, and they are embarrassed. I feel disapproved of: a trouble to my parents." His second memory focuses even more narrowly on his father. "I am in a boxing ring, in a school. My father teaches there and has arranged for me to have a boxing match with the son of another teacher. I can feel the heavy, big, dark red gloves on me and look down to see them. I have been hit in the face and am crying. I think my father is embarrassed because I am crying. I can see that the other boy is not crying and feel that his father is proud of him."[18]

"*His* father is proud of him." More than sixty years after the fact, the sting is still right at the surface of recall. George Sr. made no secret of the fact that Gene's career choice was also a source of lasting disappointment. As George Sr. noted many years later in his personal history, "George Eugene England, Jr. was blessed with a brilliant mind. . . . He had the opportunity to be a great scientist. Henry Eyring[19] couldn't entice him, so he called me to try to get me to persuade him, but I wouldn't."[20] England recognized that his career choice was a long-lasting source of disappointment to his parents. Decades later, the son remarked of the father, "He still brings up that call from Eyring, and his chagrin that [I] turned away from business and science alike."[21] A close friend who could be brutally frank with him recognized the albatross of his father's expectations in his life that could erupt in his writing. She rejected an essay at a time when she was editing *Dialogue*, writing him that it "seems to unload on me, the reader, your own personal quarrels with your parents and Utah, along with a load of collective guilt."[22]

Another factor was powerfully at work as well, in judging England's success or failure in life. Latter-day Saint culture can be as susceptible to class distinctions and the trappings of status as any other; however, to wealth and power the culture adds an emphasis on ecclesiastical standing that transcends all other forms, at least for males. It is doubtful that any other Christian tradition incorporates that unique blend of lay ministry and corporate-like progression through a hierarchy of ranks that are a function of priesthood calling. Status inevitably inheres in ordination as a bishop or setting apart as stake president, but General Authority status confers worldwide prestige and authority.

England's aged mother, Dora, mentioned in passing to her grandson Mark and without comment that "when people come here to visit us, and we have had quite a few visitors, they always tell us about which child is bishop and which child is in a stake presidency."[23] Dora's mention of such a fact is not just a window into a Latter-day Saint foible; it signals an unspoken lament of both parents: Gene was neither. His father, by contrast, had been president of the North Central States Mission (1954–57), counselor in the Salt Lake Temple presidency, and president of the London Temple (1964–66). He served on the Church Genealogical Committee and was a sealer in the Salt Lake Temple for twenty-three years. That England saw his own failure to achieve high church office as a personal deficiency is evident in a number of statements that take the same form. In a typical version, one can hear the note of disappointment: "The stake president approached me and said [with reference to *Dialogue*], 'What you are planning looks very good, but if you do it, you will never hold [a] high position in the Church.' He was right."[24]

When England prepared to pass the *Dialogue* torch to a new editor in 1975, he spoke of its cost: "losing a real scholarly career in English literature, perhaps my opportunity to be a poet, and any kind of normal, to say nothing about ambitious, church career." Then he added with doubtful conviction, "quite likely blessings rather than losses."[25] When George Sr. died in 1996, England remarked at his funeral, with a depth of pathos few may have recognized, that

shortly before passing, his father told him, "You're a good man." Then England
said, "Dad, I especially need to know who I am right now in my life. I'll remember I'm your son, and that I'm a good man."[26]

But if Charlotte had raised any doubts in England's mind about either the
propriety or necessity of continually seeking the church's blessing, he quickly
discarded them. Less than a week later, he was back at the Church Administration Building, once again making the rounds. First he visited the apostle
Gordon B. Hinckley, for advice on the film company project. Then he found
Robert D. Hales, an assistant to the Quorum who would himself be ordained
an apostle in 1994. Hales expressed some of his own frustrations with what
England called "the bureaucratic jungle of Church headquarters." On a more
positive note, Hales was confident "that things can open up—citing the recent
Ensign issue on 'Women and the Church,' which took six months to pull off and
is only a beginning but which he is planning to follow through on next year
with what he thinks will be the best things ever done anywhere on women."[27]
Turning to personal advice, Hales counseled England to regain a "power base,"
suggesting BYU as the best place to do that. "Be careful, bide your time, and
get on the faculty there," he urged, assuring England he would "help when he
can, but he can't right now."[28]

England kept at work conscientiously in the Church History Department.
In January of the new year, 1977, he was called as bishop. The next month his
mother noted in her journal that David B. Haight, England's stake president
in Palo Alto and now an apostle, sent word that he had had a good visit with
her son. Dora wrote of her hope that he would help secure a spot at BYU for
Gene.[29] All the pieces were certainly falling into place. His calling as bishop
assured him that he was in good standing with the church leadership—
since they approved all bishop appointments. One more event had transpired
to create the critical mass necessary to prompt England's reapplication to BYU.
In 1975, Assistant Church Historian James Allen had given a talk that England
attended in which he spoke "about the need for a Mormon literary history."
That prospect of a Mormon literary history, and of a more vibrant, ongoing
tradition, would become a guiding obsession in England's life and career. Here
he would find his scholarly vocation: the excavation and expansion of a latent
Mormon literary tradition originating in the pioneer past. He had resigned his
position with *Dialogue*, he had hints of Haight's support, and Jeffrey Holland
was the new commissioner of education. It was time to set his sights on BYU
once again.

England, as was his wont, decided to approach Holland in person before beginning a formal application. "So one day while I was there working in the church office building (that was in the spring of 1977) I just went to [Holland] and said, well look you and I know that this is simply a political decision and decisions change. How about going back to that point and telling me you want me. He did and he said OK."[30] This time, England's application was approved—and years later he told his family he was still at a loss to explain what had changed behind the scenes.[31] In fact, he knew precisely what had changed: he was no longer officially affiliated with *Dialogue*. In any event, thrilled to at long last have the position he craved, he began classes that summer. The timing was, in some ways, the worst possible moment for a person of England's disposition and record to be embarking on an academic career at the church's flagship school. Church Historian Leonard Arrington gave a particularly tragic assessment of the state of Latter-day Saint intellectual culture that summer of England's hire—and it included bad news for England of which the professor was not even aware. The church historian confided in his journal, "We seem to be going through a period of anti-intellectualism. . . . [People such as] Lowell Bennion, Gene England, despite his devotion to the Church and the Gospel, his sincerity, and his desire to please, is not permitted to publish. . . . Just because he was a founding editor of *Dialogue*."

England was far from alone.

Carol Lynn Pearson was put on the blacklist because she gave a talk four years ago which was mildly favorable to ERA [the Equal Rights Amendment]. Through prayers and tears she finally got Elder [Boyd K.] Packer to make an exception for her and she may now continue to publish in Church magazines. But for a period she was on the blacklist. Jim Allen is now on a blacklist because of his *Story of the Latter-day Saints*, although he doesn't know it yet, and it would break his heart if I told him. I am on a kind of blacklist. The *Church News* has been told not to review *Building the City of God*, and not to publish any of my books without specific clearance by the Quorum of the Twelve. Scott Kenney is on a blacklist because he is publishing *Sunstone*. Claudia Bushman is on a blacklist because of *Exponent II*. And so on. . . . It is now necessary for Mormon intellectuals to publish under pseudonyms. I will not reveal here the pseudonyms being used, but there are several who use them, and thus far they are "getting away with it." It reminds one of the Susa Young Gates, Emmeline B. Wells, Orson F. Whitney and other personalities at the turn of the century who used them and "got away with it."[32]

The context for these upheavals was "The New Mormon History," a characterization of the more professional turn in Latter-day Saint history writing led by Leonard Arrington, the first academically trained church historian in the Latter-day Saint tradition. What scholars deemed "professional," however, was judged by some in the leadership as secular and faithless. Ezra Taft Benson addressed the concern head-on at BYU. In an address to the students in 1976, he had lamented that in "our own Church history . . . the emphasis is to underplay revelation and God's intervention in significant events, and to inordinately humanize the prophets of God so that their human frailties become more evident than their spiritual qualities."[33]

The issue gained steam months later at the time of England's BYU appointment. In mid-1977, University of Utah student Richard S. Marshall submitted a senior paper in his honors history class titled "The New Mormon History." As Gary Bergera notes, "His interviews with LDS historians, some of whom disputed the quotations, gave the impression that they thought a more secular approach to LDS history was needed." Arrington called the paper a "land mine" that had "exploded." Colleague Davis Bitton agreed that the "misquotation[s]" made it seem that the Church History Division was in league with "fundamentalists and apostates." Unfortunately for England, the church Board of Education took note of the fact that he was among those quoted.[34]

Friends of England, seeing down the road more clearly than he, tried to caution the idealist about the perils of his new employment. Richard Bushman, England's contemporary and the most eminent Latter-day Saint historian, had written Gene at the time of his first application to BYU, revealing both prescience and a keen understanding of his friend: "You are a severe critic of your environment, Gene. I am not sure but that the anguish of being at BYU would outweigh the rewards. It is not the ideal Christian community you envision. . . . You may require more of your associates than they can give. At BYU it might be difficult not to spend your energies trying to straighten out the church university rather than preaching the gospel to the world." And then he added bluntly, "Frankly, I think that we are most likely to keep on course when we focus on our primary mission."[35]

Initially, at least, England was laser-focused on his mission. His Stanford PhD in American literature, combined with his hands-on experience sifting through the abundant archives in the church Historical Department, gave him the tools and the motivation to pursue a nineteenth-century mandate recently renewed by President Spencer Kimball and yet to find fruitful implementation: the staking out of a Latter-day Saint literary tradition.

ASSOCIATION OF MORMON LETTERS

Gene England was for Mormon belles lettres what his friend and contemporary
Leonard J. Arrington was for Mormon history. . . . Future anthologies will call this
era of Mormon letters, "The Age of England."—Richard Cracroft, "Eugene England
and the Rise and Progress of Mormon Letters"

You have been the patron saint, the dean, and the protector of Mormon writers
for a long while now.—Richard Bushman to England, 5 August 1992

There he sits across the room, arms outstretched across the empty chairs beside
him, brown tweed jacket betokening the professor he is, listening intently to lofty
pronouncements about moral criticism, deconstruction, and the strengths, and
flaws, of Mormon letters. I remember him from yesteryear, tousle-haired, sun freck-
led, stretched along the canal bank behind his home, captivated by waterskippers
tracing lines across the still, reflective water. We are grown old now—we young men
of long ago. Now we sit, stiff and cramped, on hard-backed chairs, speaking with
learned phrases about meaning in literature—and life. Then we felt; now we reason.
Then we experienced; now we dissect—literature and life.
—Notes scribbled on an envelope by Bert Wilson at a
meeting of the Association for Mormon Letters

The Latter-day Saints had launched a determined effort to establish their own
literary tradition in the late nineteenth century. In 1888, following a long era
of suspicion toward literary fiction, Orson Whitney, Latter-day Saint apostle
and man of letters, delivered a declaration. Just as Ralph Waldo Emerson had
called for American artists' "day of dependence, our long apprenticeship to the
learning of other lands, [to draw] to a close," and chided Americans for listening "too long to the courtly muses of Europe,"[36] so also was Whitney's appeal
both chastisement and challenge. Insisting that "culture is the duty of man,"
he transformed the church's long-standing ambivalence toward literature into
unqualified endorsement, urging this people to "do the works of Abraham."
With Victorian extravagance, he invoked the day "when Zion, no longer the
foot, but as the head, the glorious front of the world's civilization, would arise
and shine 'the joy of the whole earth,' when, side by side with pure Religion,
would flourish Art and Science, her fair daughters; when music, poetry, painting, sculpture, oratory and . . . drama, rays of light from the same central
sun, . . . would throw their white radiance full and direct upon the mirror-like
glory of her towers."

"What has all this to do with literature?" Whitney asked. "It is by means of literature that much of this great work will have to be accomplished." The literary tradition he hoped to foster he called a "home literature," and it was to follow the familiar cultural pattern of establishing both continuity and difference, of affirming Mormonism's credentials as a culturally literate community even as it asserted its transcendent peculiarity:

> It is from the warp and woof of all learning, so far as we are able to master it and make it ours, that the fabric of our literature must be woven. . . . [But] above all things, we must be original. The Holy Ghost is the genius of "Mormon" literature. . . . No pouring of new wine into old bottles. No patterning after the dead forms of antiquity. Our literature must live and breathe for itself. Our mission is diverse from all others; our literature must also be. . . . In God's name and by his help we will build up a literature whose top shall touch heaven.[37]

Whitney's summons to greatness came not just in the midst of Latter-day Saint cultural mediocrity but during a low-water mark in American letters as well—at least as gauged by consumer appetite. The American market in the three previous decades had been dominated by the works of British and American masters. Nathaniel Hawthorne, George Eliot, William Thackeray, Walt Whitman, Anthony Trollope, Charles Dickens, and Robert Louis Stevenson had all been best-selling authors in the period from 1850 to the mid-1880s. The year of Whitney's address, however, the four best-selling novelists were Hall Caine (*The Deemster*), Marie Corelli (*A Romance of Two Worlds*), A. C. Gunter (*Mr. Barnes of New York*), and Mrs. Humphry Ward (*Robert Elsmere*).[38] Perhaps Whitney thought 1888 would be a propitious year for Latter-day Saint authors to shine in a rather undistinguished field.

Whitney's hope was that Mormon authors would produce a literature that explicitly espoused LDS values while achieving aesthetic greatness. The response to his appeal, seconded by other leaders, was an outpouring of literature, primarily through church-sponsored periodicals but also in longer works of fiction. Whitney's summons to artistic excellence was the most prominent expression of the "home literature" movement, but the initiative had actually been under way for some time. In 1879, a Utah editor remarked that "the exercises of writing essays, and publishing manuscript papers, have been quite generally adopted throughout the Territory, and have already resulted in the development of considerable literary talent among the members."[39] To further this endeavor, the editor announced the inauguration of a church magazine called the *Contributor*, designed to "foster and encourage the literary talent of their members . . . that it might say to every young man and every young lady among our people, having literary tastes and ability, *Write*."

In addition to the *Contributor*, the *Woman's Exponent* was a ready vehicle for meeting the challenge. Latter-day Saint women found expression through essays, autobiography, and poetry. Susa Young Gates would found the *Young Woman's Journal* in 1889. In 1915 the *Relief Society Magazine* premiered, and one of its departments for more than half a century was "Art and Literature." Original fiction and poetry were published, and regular literature lessons trained readers in critical reading and appreciation. Most of the resultant literary production, sadly, was didactic and mediocre.

The seeds of a renewed orientation were latent in James Allen's remarks when he made a case for a greater valuation of nonliterary genres like diaries and letters. Motivated by Allen and immersed in nineteenth-century sources, England did impressive work bringing to light a number of remarkable first-person accounts by nineteenth-century Saints. One such figure, Joseph Millett, is now famous in Latter-day Saint culture for a journal entry that England featured in a 1975 article on one of the era's many unsung heroes:

> One of my children came in, said that Brother Newton Hall's folks were out of bread. Had none that day. I put . . . our flour in sack to send up to Brother Hall's. Just then Brother Hall came in. Says I, "Brother Hall, how are you out for flour?" "Brother Millett, we have none." "Well, Brother Hall, there is some in that sack. I have divided and was going to send it to you. Your children told mine that you were out." Brother Hall began to cry. Said he had tried others. Could not get any. Went to the cedars and prayed to the Lord and the Lord told him to go to Joseph Millett. "Well, Brother Hall, you needn't bring this back if the Lord sent you for it. You don't owe me for it." You can't tell how good it made me feel to know that the Lord knew that there was such a person as Joseph Millett.[40]

Meanwhile, other scholars were thinking along similar lines. In 1974, Richard Cracroft and Neal Lambert published their anthology of Mormon literature, *A Believing People*.[41] A third scholar, Ed Geary, had contributed significantly to the effort. As an undergraduate, he had discovered the writings of the gifted Virginia Sorensen on the library shelves, and was overwhelmed by the first fiction that spoke directly to his western Latter-day Saint experience. Scanning the nearby shelves, he discovered dozens of well-written regional novels by Latter-day Saint authors, published nationally during the 1930s and 1940s. By then almost entirely forgotten, several of these authors had been prominent on a national stage. Most notable in these efforts were *Children of*

God (1939) by Vardis Fisher, *The Giant Joshua* (1941) by Maurine Whipple, and *A Little Lower than the Angels* (1942) by Virginia Sorensen.[42] With these three novels, Latter-day Saints had proved themselves capable of serious engagement with Mormonism as a literary theme.

Just as England was joining the faculty, Geary published two essays about these largely forgotten novelists, whom he dubbed "Mormondom's Lost generation." England credited these essays with helping him "see how Sorensen and [Maureen] Whipple provided a particularly Mormon response to the West."[43] The Cracroft and Lambert collection attempted to make "a beginning in identifying [the LDS] cultural heritage" that evolved from the production of new scripture like the Book of Mormon and from subsequent literary works of human rather than heavenly inspiration and origin. Their anthology brought together a rich array of journal writing, biography, and history, as well as samples of Latter-day Saint poetry and fiction—and represented a compelling case for an amorphous but distinctive tradition. The works of the Saints ranged, in their words, from Panglossian simplemindedness to the dignified and profound, but all "strikingly at odds with the humanistic existentialism of modern literary fashion."[44] It was an important step that significantly moved forward the question, Is there a Mormon (literary) art?

Reading the collection, England believed the way forward was to focus on genres particularly conformable to a Latter-day Saint religious sensibility and culture. He came to feel, as he later wrote in "Mormon Literature: Progress and Prospects," that "our history of close self-examination in journals and testimony-bearing provide[s] resources that have mainly been realized in great sermons and various forms of autobiography but increasingly find expression in powerful and informal essays."[45] As he later amplified his views, "I became convinced that the Mormon heritage shows to best advantage in various forms of personal witness to faith and experience, genres in which the truth of actual living, of quite direct confession, is at least as important as aesthetic or metaphorical truth, such as diaries, letters, sermons, lyric poetry, autobiography, and increasingly the personal essay."[46]

Immersion in the new journal had given England a powerful forum to implement his literary values. "As editor of *Dialogue*, I studied early Mormon letters and diaries and journals and published personal essays and sermons. I became increasingly uneasy about the adequacy of formalist criteria (that is, those mainly concerned with aesthetic qualities—structure, style, texture, etc.) to account for the experiences of my students and myself with literature that powerfully affected us despite its obvious lack of traditional types of formal aesthetic perfection."[47] In 1975, church president Spencer W. Kimball renewed Whitney's powerful call to cultural arms. At the centennial celebration of BYU's founding, he presented his vision for "The Second Century of Brigham Young University," anticipating and encouraging an "educational Everest." He cited Charles H. Malik, former president of the UN General Assembly, who had voiced a fervent hope that "one day a great university will arise somewhere . . . I hope in America . . . to which Christ will return in His full glory and power, a university which will, in the promotion of scientific, intellectual, and artistic excellence, surpass by far even the best secular universities of the present, but which will at the same time enable Christ to bless it and act and feel perfectly at home in it." Then Kimball added, "Surely BYU can help to respond to that call!" and zoomed in on the arts in particular: "We cannot give in to the ways of the world with regard to the realm of art. President [Marion G.] Romney brought to our attention not long ago a quotation in which Brigham Young said that 'there is no music in hell.' Our art must be the kind that edifies man, that takes into account his immortal nature, and that prepares us for heaven, not hell."[48]

Ongoing conversations in the Historical Department brought other scholars interested in the Saints' literary heritage to the fore and led to concrete plans. In 1976, England's colleague Maureen Ursenbach Beecher convened eight or ten people for a discussion about the prospects for a more authentic Mormon literary tradition. It was England who suggested a formal organization. Thus was born the Association for Mormon Letters (AML). The organization would serve as a catalyst and focal point for some of England's most important academic work.

Arriving at BYU in 1977, England was now in the optimum position to bring to more tangible fruition these renewed aspirations for a praiseworthy Mormon literature. He immediately began teaching the Mormon literature class that Richard Cracroft and Neal Lambert had pioneered a few years earlier. In 1979, he was invited by BYU's Redd Center for Western Studies to give a lecture, "Mormon Literature: An Historical Appreciation," for which his work in the Historical Department had well-equipped him.[49] Virtually overnight, he was the leading light in this burgeoning new field.

Scholars don't blink at the category of Jewish literature (Franz Kafka, Isaac Bashevis Singer, Saul Bellow, and hundreds of others come to mind), or Catholic authors (Flannery O'Connor, Graham Greene, G. K. Chesterton, and Walker Percy, for example). But no one would think to designate a group of writers as constituting "Episcopalian fiction" or "Jehovah's Witness literature." The question is, where do Latter-day Saints fit on that continuum? Not all sociologists agree with Thomas O'Dea's assessment, in the *Harvard Encyclopedia of Ethnic Groups*, that Latter-day Saints constitute "the clearest example to be found in our national history . . . of a native and indigenously developed ethnic minority."[50] But Sydney Ahlstrom's befuddlement speaks volumes: "One cannot even be sure if the object of our consideration is a sect, a mystery cult, a new religion, a church, a people, a nation, or an American subculture."[51]

England harbored no misgivings: the Saints comprised a distinct people, with a distinct culture, and their literature deserved recognition as a distinctive literary field.

> If I taught at a predominantly Black college, I would want (in fact, as a literature teacher I would feel responsible) to know and whenever possible teach James Baldwin and Ton[i] Morrison, or if at a predominantly Jewish college, Saul Bellow and Chaim Potok, or if at a Catholic college, Graham Greene and Flannery O'Connor. You may laugh at these comparisons, but for instance, in his use of grotesques to teach mercy towards 'the least of these,' and in his focus on the difficult process of salvation through grace, Levi Peterson approaches O'Connor in subject method, and effectiveness. He teaches the Atonement better than any Mormon writer and most American writers. And he and [Orson Scott] Card and [Terry Tempest] Williams are wonderful combinations of liberal and conservative qualities, in some ways less orthodox than us and our students, in some ways (such as opposition to racism and violence, concern for earth and family, focus on the Atonement) more orthodox than many of us. We have much to learn from them, despite, even because of, the cultural cringes they produce—and it is one of the tragic prices we are paying for our current lust for cultural correctness at BYU that these fine Mormon authors are neglected and the study of our own heritage has become suspect because our literature and study of it is sometimes critical of conservative elements in our culture.[52]

Teaching what he saw as the lost legacy of past Latter-day Saint authors was not sufficient to fill the void England saw in the current LDS culture. So in 1982, England met with Boyd K. Packer and discussed his frustration at what he felt were limited publishing opportunities given that his interests in "Mormon literature" were not in alignment with secular, professional journals. Packer encouraged England to give some thought to a resolution of his dilemma and England spent months conceiving a grand project that would solve his problem and benefit the church and university. Now England wrote to Packer asking if he could make a presentation, accompanied by a supportive BYU president Jeffrey Holland, to "provide formal leadership of Mormon literary scholarship" under Dean Richard Cracroft's supervision.[53] England's proposal was ambitious bordering on audacious. "I intend to develop a faithful and moral literary criticism. . . . I will use my particular gifts and experience to steer Mormon letters away from the parochialism of superficial Mormonism. . . . I will build a complete Mormon literature archives, . . . develop an endowed Chair in Mormon Letters, . . . and set an example with my own literary and personal essays and poetry. . . . My main focus will be a new publication, edited by me, which will consist entirely of the best Mormon literature past and present."[54]

Sensing support from Packer, England made plans for a new journal. He had gathered a group of like-minded academics, who called themselves "Zion's Campers," a sly reference to the 1834 paramilitary organization that Joseph Smith led—unsuccessfully—to liberate Missouri Saints from the mobs and militia who had expelled them from Jackson County. They appointed England to lead their group, and in February 1983 he made a formal proposal for a monthly periodical called "Wasatch" that would "publish the best 'primary' literature, past and present, that is rooted deeply in Mormon religion and culture." He proposed himself as editor, and articulated the aesthetic by which editorial policy would be guided: "'spiritual realism,' writing that meets the highest traditional standards of fidelity to human experience and the material surface of mortal life but which also maturely engages the important ideas, visions, and symbols of Mormonism."[55] The proposal was sent to the AML, with a request that it consider subsidizing and publishing the journal as its "semi-official" organ.

While England's proposal sounded grandiose, an impressive legacy emerged from his (and others') efforts over succeeding decades. "Wasatch" never saw the light of day, but in 1999 the AML did launch *Irreantum*, a journal of literature and criticism written "by, for, or about Mormons."[56] Over the next several years England would edit the anthology *Harvest: Contemporary Mormon Poems* (with Dennis Clark, 1989), the short story collection *Bright Angels and Familiars: Contemporary Mormon Stories* (1992), and the literary criticism collection *Tending the Garden: Essays on Mormon Literature* (with Lavina Fielding Anderson, 1996). The archives he proposed now exists as the "Mormon Literature and Creative Arts Database," and is "a direct legacy from Gene," in the words of its principal curator.[57] And though he did not found a chair in Mormon studies— a number of such academic positions or programs now exist, scattered from the United Kingdom to Virginia to California.

8

HERESY, ORTHODOXY, AND
THE PERILS OF PROVOCATION

I'd be a different shade of green on church issues,
but I admired him. Time was on his side.
—Richard Lloyd Anderson, interview with author, 3 May 2016

Even as he was bringing Latter-day Saint literary achievement into the spot-
light, England's immersion in the BYU classroom brought him into daily contact with students long accustomed to a more orthodox strain of teaching. He
was a popular lecturer and was frequently invited to give campus talks. As
a professor in the church's flagship institution he did not have the luxury of
couching his unorthodoxy under the heading of free expression in an independent journal. His buoyant optimism about the university as a marketplace of
ideas left him unprepared for what seemed to him a hypervigilance attending
his every word:

> I remember thinking, and I've thought many times since, as others have
> really chastised me for the disturbances [I have] caused the General Au-
> thorities, that for some reason I just can't get concerned about worrying
> people whose faith is strong. That doesn't seem to me one of the Lord's
> major concerns. If you're trying to help people strengthen their faith,
> the fact that that may cause some sleepless nights to people who have
> faith, I've never been able to worry about. But clearly . . . many do in the
> Church, and I think that's part of this thing that Bob Thomas communi-
> cates to me—being able to sense counsel and not do anything that would
> disturb the General Authorities. I can understand it but it really is hard
> for me to get in that frame of mind.[1]

Why could England not conform to the cultural orthodoxy of his own faith tradition? Influence and authority operate within the LDS church in ways fundamentally at odds with their workings in a normal university environment. BYU is not a typical university, functioning as it does as an official church institution that is directly supervised by the church's leadership. Yet England stubbornly insisted that intellectual freedom and faithfulness to the church should—and could—be seamlessly practiced. An exchange between Richard Bushman and England clearly illustrates where England's demeanor challenged the unspoken rules of the Latter-day Saint community pertaining to what Bushman called "speaking out." Bushman's letter is important because it bears eloquent witness to a particular communitarian philosophy, rather than mere timidity, as the foil to England's moralism. This difference is the fault line that time and again cast England in the role of provocateur.

> You want to have the courage to stand against the tanks, to pit your conscience against power and abstractions. . . . What really matters most to you, I came to think, were the moral principles. . . . We go off in all directions on moral truth depending on our situations in society. Although we like to think of them as eternal verities, in their concrete applications . . . they are historically contingent, so much so that I am not inclined to go to the barricades for what I happen to think is the moral truth. You have a fixed, concrete, and certain sense of what is obviously moral. I am less assured, and can see merit and truth in positions quite different from my own—including the assertions of hawks who actually make me furious. What I think lasts is the stories. . . . I feel a deep communion with all who believe the Joseph stories, even if they are members of the NRA or even if they smoke and drink. I think we are a people of the sacred stories . . . .
>
> All of this comes around eventually to the question of speaking out. My first loyalty is to God and secondly to the community of believers. I want to support the believers, to give them courage, and I want to sustain the community where belief is nurtured. . . . I do not wish to see the Church converted into a democratic society where parties struggle to obtain power and where alert citizens watch out for every abuse of power and resist it. . . . I think ultimately my confidence rests in the goodness of the Saints and the beneficent interest of God. In the long run, the right will prevail, even if we wobble along . . . .
>
> I know I have failed you when you wanted me to speak out. It is so contrary to my nature that I have felt hapless when the call has come. . . . But I will never appear on the barricades. I am more committed to tearing

down barricades then to fighting on them. It is a tell-tale fact that I was scarcely touched by the sixties when you were transformed by them.[2]

It was not only his communitarian instincts but also a particular view of ecclesial authority that distinguishes Bushman's position from quietism or passivity. In Catholic and Protestant tradition, mystics, devotional writers, and theologians vie with popes and archbishops for influence. Religious luminaries are not confined to ordained orders, so C. S. Lewis and Mother Teresa and Garry Wills compete for column space with Pope Francis and Rev. N. T. Wright. Not so in Mormonism. The LDS church's faithful, by contrast, look to and cite only ordained authorities; going outside the official canon is frowned upon, generally forbidden to church instructors and impractical in any case, since alternate voices have few outlets in Latter-day Saint media. When figures in their classroom or in their publications attract an enthusiastic following, they are often viewed with suspicion. And so it was with England. "Is he trying to attract a following?" was a question that dogged him. In Latter-day Saint culture the only legitimate authority is ordained, apostolic authority; charisma poses a dangerous challenge.

England's friend, Robert Rees, bristled at allegations that England had "groupies." Some of the more orthodox figures at BYU did have their fervent acolytes, he said. "Wherever they go people kind of gather around to hear the latest thing they have to say. Gene didn't have that because of the very nature of what he was doing. When you are challenging the axioms, when you are raising the hard questions, when you are willing to risk confronting those institutions, you will never have a big following because people are not secure with that. Groupies want assurance. They want entertainment."[3] Others who knew him were less generous, seeing in his popularity the siren call of celebrity. "He couldn't resist the allure of a following," said one former student.[4] Another colleague said he was a "pied piper," who developed "a cult among students and a coterie among colleagues."[5] And as a friend recognized in summarizing England's predicament, "Mormonism doesn't do celebrity."[6]

England's variety of intellectualism was particularly unwelcome given this moment in the church's history. And the reactions he elicited were anticipated early on by colleague Ed Geary, who wrote him with wry hyperbole, "I fear you may find that it is a riskier business at BYU to defend Joseph Smith than dirty movies, since we are apparently to understand that Joseph, while not an apostate or heretic, was mistaken."[7] What he likely meant was that Smith's intellectual adventuresomeness, lack of dogmatism, and open embrace of truth from across sects and culture found little place in that particular historical moment of the church's evolution. To some extent that was doubtless true. We saw above how the church correlation program emphasized conformity and orthodoxy over autonomy and creativity. The aftershocks of the 1960s, the advent of feminism, and the more LDS-specific challenges of the New Mormon History with its revisionary challenges to official narratives about the priesthood ban and a polygamous past—these were genuine threats to traditional constructions of faith, and England felt their challenge was needful and could be constructive. He was unwilling to give any quarter in the face of an idealism that could at times be self-indulgent. He frequently cited New Testament passages in defense of himself and the social gospel; he never cited Paul's counsel to the Corinthians: "take heed lest by any means this liberty of yours become a stumbling block to them that are weak" (1 Cor. 8:9). He could be provocative because he had the luxury of perfect faith to see him through those provocations. As one colleague noted, England's "questioning and uncertainty" could be "too bold for his students. He can seem to leave one clinging to a skeleton of what was once a complete and solid reality."[8]

In 1975, in the very month he had first been denied BYU employment, England had been invited to speak to the university's honor society, Phi Kappa Phi. (Such mixed signals perfectly typified his lifelong relationship to the church establishment.) Driving past the welcome sign en route to his talk, "I felt a deep shock of recognition, and my heart said to me, 'This is home.' I had never been a student at BYU and at that time had no hope of ever being on the faculty, but I felt, 'This is where I belong.' If BYU really took such a motto seriously ["enter to learn, go forth to serve"], I thought, it could well be the greatest university in the world—at least in God's eyes."[9] To understand his years at BYU, it is necessary to see his hopes that the school had the potential to fully realize what St. Olaf College had failed to bring about: the fruitful merging of Christian discipleship with intellectual integrity.

At the venue, his address was an impassioned, Emersonian call to intellectual arms. He saw church culture at a crossroads, an intersection of epochs that he himself bridged: "I propose to you *the Mormon scholar*, the Latter-day Saint intellectual of the last generation before 2000. . . . My call to your generation is that you help establish a new tradition in intellectual service to God and his Kingdom, a new style founded in part on the great tradition of the pioneer intellectuals and with the benefit of the example of the successes and an understanding of the failures of some in this past generation or two." These lines were dense with pathos. He had in mind failures typified by the unwillingness of the institutional church to recognize the heroic honesty of scholars like Juanita Brooks, who suffered "almost total rejection . . . by her own people because of her [1950] book on Mountain Meadows," a painfully objective account of an 1857 massacre of immigrants perpetrated by Latter-day Saints. He also had in mind his own rejection by the church of which he had just learned, based on his association with an independent, edgy journal. The young audience likely missed his cryptic allusion: "I have been part of the growing pains and mistakes of the recent past, of improperly resolved loyalties and defensiveness and uncertain role in the Kingdom."[10]

Two years later, on the cusp of his successful reapplication, England succeeded in placing an article with a kindred tone in the church's own monthly magazine, the *Ensign*. The article was a coup of sorts. It was as subversive a piece as the *Ensign* was ever likely to publish, bringing England's message to the orthodox masses; and that venue gave a kind of official imprimatur to his plea. The essay is a blatant appeal for a cultural shift in the direction of more frank dialogue, and less fear of offending the guardians of orthodoxy. "We need to cultivate moral courage. It seems clear that most forms of insincere and unloving speech arise from fear: fear of serious reflection on what we most care about and want to be, fear of exposing our limited selves, fear of the opinion or power of others."[11]

One can also read the article as a personal apologia for England's own provocative writings and speaking: "If we will only begin to take some risks, speaking the truth lovingly and boldly even though we feel inept or weak or exposed, the Lord will keep his promises and we will be surprised at the response in others and in ourselves. . . . If we can develop the courage to take some personal risks and can learn to rely on the Spirit as we break out of old inhibitions and prejudices, we can be more effective in both vigorously defending the faith in the world and in lovingly challenging people in the church to live the gospel better."

Since members of the church are cautioned against unauthorized exhortation of others to "live the gospel better," it is surprising that England's prod in this direction passed the censors, especially since the example he gives is poorly concealed autobiography: "A new member of our ward spoke in sacrament meeting some years ago on how gospel principles might be translated into politically liberal social and economic action in our nation. The next week, a politically conservative brother used testimony meeting to rebut the newcomer and to question by implication his faith and religious orthodoxy." Tempted to take offense, the advocate of political liberalism instead apologizes to the conservative, and "they became good friends, continuing to differ and sometimes openly disagree, but serving as a powerful example to all of us in the ward of brotherhood and the value of open, sincere, but loving, expression."

The publication of that essay was in some ways a high-water mark in England's career to this point. In an official publication he had urged moral courage in challenging not just the Latter-day Saint cultural status quo but also, one could argue, the leaders themselves (what else can "speaking the truth to power" versus "fearing the power" mean in the LDS church setting?). He had narrated a successful instance of publicly advocating a politically liberal interpretation of the restored gospel with a result of brotherly dialogue rather than censure or ostracism. He had advocated taking risks, had done so by writing the essay, and been endorsed by the institutional church. No wonder that it was with a good bit of optimism that England took his position at BYU, in spite of cautions from Bushman and others. And during his first years, the energies he devoted to Mormon literature bore substantial fruit. However, his continuing attraction to and participation in matters theological, rather than academic, would collide brutally and publicly with his optimistic aspirations for a more unrestricted public square.

Like many other denominations, the Church of Jesus Christ was in the 1970s feeling the currents of sexual liberation, drug culture, postmodernism, and other developments as destabilizing forces. And both Bruce R. McConkie and Boyd K. Packer in particular felt the path of safety was in making crystal clear the lines of demarcation separating worldly voices from prophetic (or apostolic) dictate. And by apostolic, they meant coming from *ordained* apostles. In a sermon that captured these polarities, Packer contrasted opinions of "evil men and seducers" from pronouncements of "one who has authority, and it is known he has authority and has been regularly ordained by the heads of the church."[12] Emphasizing that God's voice only came through authorized channels, he insisted that "revelation is always vertical. There is no horizontal revelation in the church." In this context, Elaine Englehardt's assessment, which she shared with England, makes sense: "What you don't understand is that you are in some ways presuming the role of prophet and telling the truth to our community. The other prophets who are called to that position don't like that. They see you as a rival."[13]

Gene England's quandary—and response to his historical moment—was both like and unlike those of other Christian figures caught up in the modernist crisis that wracked Protestantism (and Catholicism) in the twentieth century. One has to understand the Church of Jesus Christ's unique conception of authority and of history to comprehend why its crisis was delayed by more than half a century. The common root of modernism's challenge to religion was what Grant Wacker calls "the dilemma of historical consciousness." The Higher Criticism that spread from German universities to the American landscape posited convincingly that "what Scripture is, and how Scripture was composed and put together is a matter of history, and to investigate those matters fully is a duty to truth."[14] This challenged the old evangelicalism, the view that "the biblical writers" were "enabled by the Holy Spirit to transcend their social and cultural settings in order to articulate truths of timeless and universal validity." Since all authority was vested in those scriptures, this modernist impulse called into question, in Charles Hodge's words, "whether Christianity is historically conditioned . . . or whether it is, as it claims to be, one final religion."[15]

The Latter-day Saint leaders were never products of theological training, and were thus largely insulated from these developments in biblical criticism. More crucially, Latter-day Saint claims to religious authority resided not in the biblical canon but in something very similar to the Catholic principle of apostolic succession (though routed directly from Peter to Joseph Smith and his successors). Consequently, they were virtually impervious to the modernist crisis that struck Protestantism. However, both Mormonism and Catholicism were vulnerable to a different challenge to authority. For the Latter-day Saint church mirrored "the Vatican's identification of the religious tradition with its institutional embodiment."[16] This was one of the most substantive differentiations between Protestantism and both Catholicism and the Church of Jesus Christ. In the latter cases, the church was both the locus of authority and the indispensable entity through which alone saving sacraments were authoritatively administered. If the burgeoning historical consciousness were to historicize that embodiment in the same way it did the canon, a comparable crisis of authority would result. And indeed, the insights of Higher Criticism—and indirectly those of Darwinian evolution—did raise the troubling question of "how to preserve the idea of divine revelation given the new historical consciousness." Not just scripture but also institutional forms and "all expressions of religious sentiment" were susceptible to the new consciousness. Modernists warned that the alternative was "to embrace and elevate to normative status the particularities of the culture" of the founding context.[17] If revelation could not claim a transcendent, historically unconditioned status, then the church was no more reliable as a source of authority than the scripture. No wonder that a concerned Pope Pius X declared modernism "the synthesis of all heresies" in a 1907 encyclical.[18]

A historical consciousness struck just as deeply at the roots of Latter-day Saint claims to authority and a tradition of ongoing divine revelation. The determinative difference was that in the case of LDS history, the details of the church's founding and early development had been carefully stewarded and safeguarded by a church historian's office whose productions were carefully curated to instill faith. A consciousness of the sometimes-messy details of Latter-day Saint history were only emerging in the 1970s.

The professionalization of the Historical Department inaugurated that process; the internet in another few decades would accelerate and amplify it a thousandfold. When church archives were closed to the public and the church historian's office occupied by Joseph Smith's great-nephew and future president Joseph Fielding Smith (in which historian's office he served for most of the twentieth century) such a narrative was relatively easy to maintain. With the appointment of Leonard Arrington as church historian in 1972, these seminal, founding narratives began to find clearer, unsanitized exposition. As Arrington gathered professional historians around him, these adjustments to the official narrative of church history and theology were both urgent, inevitable—and profoundly disrupting.

When England joined the Historical Department in 1975, "Camelot," as nostalgic historians would remember the Arrington years, was about to be prematurely erased from the Mormon map. Arrington's brand of history never had the full support of the leadership. We saw earlier how his 1959 revisionist essay on the church's health code, the Word of Wisdom, argued that its enforcement by Brigham Young was economically, rather than divinely, motivated. It appeared in the inaugural issue of the new journal, *BYU Studies*—and prompted the journal's immediate suspension by BYU president Ernest Wilkinson.[19] The "New Mormon History" coming out of the Historical Department in the 1970s aroused renewed concern and opposition. Neither Arrington nor England knew it, but Arrington was just two years away from abrupt dismissal. But England would suffer very public repercussions of retrenchment first.

No wonder the religious historian Martin Marty could observe in 1983 that "Mormon thought is experiencing a crisis comparable to but more profound than that which Roman Catholicism recognized around the time of the Second Vatican Council (1962–65). Whatever other changes were occurring in the Catholic Church, there was a dramatic, sometimes traumatic shift in ways of regarding the tradition. One of the conventional ways of speaking of this shift comes from the observation of philosopher Bernard Lonergan. He and others . . . argued that Catholicism was moving from a 'classic' view of dogma to a thoroughly 'historical' view of faith. In the classic view, Catholic teaching has come intact, as it were, protected from contingency, from a revealing God."[20] In the case of Mormon studies, "ways of regarding the tradition" are certainly contested, but the church's leadership was hardly likely to respond with anything parallel to Vatican II.

THE ENGLAND HOME: REFUGE AND SALON

England was certainly popular as well as controversial. The home he and Charlotte built in Provo became a combination salon, hostel, and social nexus for
intellectuals, students, and any number of visitors in financial or emotional
distress. Their open and welcoming home environment was traceable to their
Palo Alto years. David Barber was a law student at Stanford in the early 1960s.
He remembered attending "some kind of evening get together in Eugene and
Charlotte's home." His initial impressions capture the magnetism that would
draw hundreds into the England circle over the years, friendships forged in the
intimacy of a living room salon. "As I walked in, there was a different kind of
feel, a different kind of energy to anything I had experienced in the Mormon
Church before. Experiences that I had until then were kind of formal, kind of
impersonal, and this was very personal. This was an energy of wanting to know
what you thought, what your feelings were, what your struggles were. . . . It
was not authoritarian; it wasn't like he kn[e]w more than you did. It was very
emotional actually."[21]

Moving to Provo, the Englands designed a house in which they could create
this same environment. Erin Silva was the architect of their Provo home. "I
remember how Charlotte trusted me to design a home that would be for many,
mission control, the center of their universe for a time, and a home away from
home for countless students and friends. . . . And I remember thinking to myself, 'My God, this house is so big it is more of a hotel than house. Now I know
why.'"[22] Gene's mother thought the result was "sorta Mormon pioneer style.
It is two-story, pinkish brick, with bay and dormer windows. They found old
brick and cleaned it and used old doors, etc. Charlotte helped and is patient,
living in a mess of unfinished building. Eugene worked all summer and was
his own contractor."[23] It was large enough to house the ever-present additional
family members. "He has helped hundreds of students and others mend their
live[s] and keep their faith. He and Charlotte always have two or three foreign students living in their house and have other student[s] they're hel[p]ing
through school," noted a colleague.[24]

Every Thursday night, Charlotte recalled, "we had something, music or recitals (a lot of student recitals because we designed it with a room that would
be good for music) and Leslie [Norris] came in and read us poetry. New people
that came into the department were invited to come and talk about their dissertation, to get acquainted, that kind of stuff. So we just had a whole variety
of things; that went on for a few years. Sometimes people would call up, who
didn't know us or anything, but they'd say, 'I heard you're going to have this

The home England and his family built in Provo, Utah. Forum for their
famous soirees and a virtual hostel for students and others in need, 1978.
(Courtesy Charlotte England)

event.' So they'd come. Every Thursday, we just had a great gathering, served
up good refreshments, and people enjoyed it and it was great."[25] Scott Bradford
wrote of those halcyon days that "the door was always open. I never knocked,
just walked right in. There is usually someone here. Even when there wasn't
you know just pick up a magazine. Chill out for a while. Look in the fridge see
what is in there. [Laughs.] I felt like family. I am sure I am one of hundreds who
feel things like this."[26] Thanksgivings, they made room for students who stayed
in Utah for the holiday. One student recalled that it was like having "surrogate
parents. Gene and Charlotte. Just surrogate siblings with you all. It was a family environment while being 2,000 miles from home."[27]

Charlotte's hospitality was legendary. So was her bread and ice cream (she
opened her own shop in 1984). Everyone agreed that she was as memorable
a presence in that setting as was Gene, whose esteem and love for her was
evident to all. One friend recalled, "When he first introduced Charlotte to me,
it was like he was introducing the light of the world. I came to see her as the
still point of the turning world for him. He thought she was the most beautiful
woman."[28] Another intimate said, "Charlotte made things possible for him.
She was the foundational support of his entire enterprise. And he adored her.

I don't know if she will ever understand how necessary she was to everything he did."[29]

He wrote in his journal of one occasion when he waited for her on the eve of a Shakespeare play: "Across the pond and fountains from St. Giles Church, I felt something turn my head out toward the water and caught sight of Charlotte's face turning toward me. Glory."[30] A student and family friend wrote to him, "I'd always thought that whoever you were married to must certainly be a lucky woman because you were so inspired and smart, but (this is the truth) the moment I saw Charlotte I *knew*: you were the lucky one."[31] He knew it as well. And he wasn't shy about proclaiming it. A counselor in his bishopric remembered England showing up late for a Sunday morning meeting. Walking in, he calmly stated: "Brethren, when I woke up, I had to make a decision about whether or not to go out into the cold, snowy weather to meet with you or stay in bed and snuggle with my beautiful wife. The choice was easy!"[32] "The way Gene and Charlotte love is the way love ought to be," noted his friend and tennis partner Steve Walker.[33] "My heart is reconfirmed in its integrity and accuracy by my continuing life with Charlotte," he confided to his journal in the midst of one of his frequent bouts of self-doubt.[34]

She did not begrudge Gene his more expansive freedom; his career was a joint decision. He was a branch president while the children were young, yet he was deeply involved at home—just seldom exclusively. "If he was feeding one of the babies he had a book in his hand. Which I would too if I could, but I was usually taking care of the other kids too."[35] At the same time, he was notorious for being immersed in his work, at the center of a hurricane of youthful energies, while remaining oblivious to the commotion surrounding him. Frustrated on one such occasion at his neglect of the kitchen garbage, Charlotte placed it in the doorway to block his path. Sure enough, he stepped smoothly over it distractedly without missing a beat.[36]

He was a devoted father, but his five girls admitted to feeling a bit "neglected." England conceded the point. "I'll always have to live with that. That's the truth. I mean I spent a lot of time with you kids. . . . But definitely not as much as I should have or wish I had."[37] His laissez-faire approach was partly due to his own experience of oppressive parental expectations. While admitting he had been "too laid back," he hoped his children "should find what they enjoy and experience the good results of that. I think that was partly a reaction of my own parents. They were very ambitious for me."[38] Still, he managed to provide a consistent environment of spiritual direction. "In many ways," remembered Katherine, "we were about as orthodox as they come. We had Family Night every Monday, and morning scripture study. We had long, long family prayers. On our knees. We never shopped or traveled on Sunday." In many, but not all, ways. Few LDS fathers took their children out of school "to participate in peace marches." Or, as he did with Katherine, "once to drive up to San Francisco to take food to the American Indians who were occupying Alcatraz in protest of broken treaties."[39] His children also loved the energy and passion of the salon-like atmosphere at home, the constant stream of scholars, students, transients, and the curious passing through their doors—and often taking up lodging. Others, however, were less enthusiastic about the goings-on there.

Spurred by either jealousy or phobia of unauthorized gatherings, rumors spread "that we had a cult going over here and [Charlotte] thought, 'Well why didn't they come and find out?'" His soirees were "seen by enemies as attempts to curry followers," said his friend Doug Thayer.[40] The joie de vivre surrounding the practice diminished, and friends warned England to keep future events under the radar. Still, he stubbornly persisted in "stuffing the boxes of the department with flyers."[41] By 1992, the English Department was balkanized. England arranged a recital at his home. "As usual I passed out about 40 invitations, mainly to English Department people, and no one came." Except one, a visiting scholar from Germany.[42] In one revealing instance of adverse effects of his popularity, Saints in an eastern state were overheard referring affectionately to him as "the thirteenth apostle."[43] That was precisely the problem. The LDS church only has room for twelve.[44] As England was about to learn.

MCCONKIE WARS

> God, forgive my pen its trespass,
> And I forgive thee the sweet burning
> That drives it on through thy dominion.
>
> God, if what it might encompass,
> If shapes of love, thy face, or being
> Itself are challenged in its question,
>
> Indulge the hand that ventures into flame,
> Suffer my searching, for you share the blame.
> —England, "The Firegiver," 1966

Latter-day Saint culture is replete with expressions like "continuing revelation" and "living prophets" and "open canon." Such terms paint a picture of a dynamic tradition that unfolds and expands through time. However, Latter-day Saint understanding of the faith often assumes the Restoration as event rather than ongoing process. Smith is often said to have "restored the fullness of the gospel" in the brief span of his career, one that he traced from 1827 and that ended with his death in 1844. In this narrative, the Restoration *happened*, as a fait accompli. In such a view, all the crucial doctrines, ecclesial structure, priesthood authority and organization, temple theology, and sacramental forms were laid down in linear fashion before his passing. Except for minor adjustments, early canonization of key scriptures and the effusive dispensing of divine revelations to Joseph Smith established once and for the last time the pure and authorized kingdom of God on earth.

The historical record, of course, is quite different. Priesthood orders (Melchizedek and Aaronic) were superimposed on offices that had been in place for years (elders, teachers, etc.) before conferral of priesthood itself became normalized as a prior, separate ordinance. Rebaptism signifying recommitment was common, then ceased. Women administered healing ordinances, before the practice was curtailed. Smith taught of eternal spirits that God adopted, before Orson Pratt and then subsequent prophets taught of heavenly parents conceiving and birthing human souls on the human model. The Light of Christ was a synonym for the Holy Spirit until, in the twentieth century, it became identified with a separate and distinct force experienced as the universal faculty of conscience. And so forth. Nineteenth-century Saints were fully comfortable with a religious understanding that took seriously the modifiers "continuing," "living," and "open," as they referred to revelation, church, and canon respectively.

When Wilford Woodruff announced to the entire church in April 1894 that temple "sealings," sacraments that bonded individuals into eternal relationships, were predicated on a mistaken model creating dynastic rather than family units (children generally being sealed to prophets rather than parents), members and leaders alike took the change in stride. The practice of disrupting the natural connections of children to their parents simply felt "wrong," he said.[45] As prophet, he sought "more revelation concerning sealing under the law of adoption," and was answered by the Spirit of God, who told him, "Let every man be adopted to his father."[46] One listener to the major course correction wrote his uncle, "Why does the Lord permit things to go on in a wrong or loose way, where the dearest rights and tenderest feelings of the human heart are involved?" Then answered his own question: We have to "gain knowledge and wisdom by repeated trials and mistakes, He has left us in a measure free to act and see what we would do."[47]

In implementing plural marriage through various phases and forms, leaders acknowledged some missteps; as apostle Amasa Lyman said from the

Tabernacle, "We obeyed the best we knew how, and, no doubt, made many crooked paths in our ignorance. We were only children."[48] When baptism for the dead was revealed, Saints initiated the practice without order or record-keeping and had to retreat and restart. Wilford asked the congregation rhetorically, "Why did we [act precipitously]? Because of the feeling of joy that we had," he explained.[49]

A few years later, another prophet reminded the church of a Restoration still in progress, with leaders as well as members liable to err and stumble and grow: "Seventy years ago this Church was organized with six members. We commenced, so to speak, as an infant. We had our prejudices to combat. Our ignorance troubled us in regard to what the Lord intended to do and what He wanted us to do. . . . We advanced to boyhood, and still we undoubtedly made some mistakes, which . . . generally arise from a . . . lack of experience. . . . When we examine ourselves, however, we discover that we are still not doing exactly as we ought to do, notwithstanding all our experience."[50]

By the late twentieth century, however, the dominant narrative was one that closely approached infallibility on the part of prophets, flawless linearity in the church's history, and near-perfect harmony in the manifold doctrinal pronouncements of the leadership through time. England's experience in the Historical Department had given him unusual access to—and comfort with—a less airbrushed understanding of the church's history and leadership. In 1979, only two years into his BYU appointment, England had become interested in a particular point of disputed theology in the Latter-day Saint tradition: the meaning of a "progressing" God. In his most radical challenge to Christian orthodoxy, Smith had proposed in a late sermon that "all Gods have [progressed] from a small capacity to a great capacity, from a small degree to another, from grace to grace . . . from exaltation to exaltation." Yet he had also endorsed the absolutist definitions of God as having all knowledge and power. Subsequently, each strain of thought had its expositors and critics among the church leadership.

That fall, England was invited to give a talk in an honors lecture series on education. He approached the topic by positing that in some way God was a progressing Being. Almost immediately, he received a phone call from Joseph McConkie, a very conservative member of the ultraconservative religion faculty and son of the highly conservative—and powerful—apostle Bruce R. McConkie. He informed England that because he was preaching false doctrine, he was no longer comfortable attending the temple with him. Unruffled, England responded that his talk had in fact been so well received that he had been asked to repeat it in a larger forum—the University's Varsity Theater.

In a gesture that was both generous and inevitable, given his passion for civil dialogue, he invited McConkie to offer a rebuttal to his coming presentation. England "thought it would be useful for students to see the process of two teachers talking through their differences."[51]

England's talk traced the well-documented Latter-day Saint history of the teaching that, in Lorenzo Snow's formulation, "as man now is, God once was," and that he continues to progress, from its origins in Smith's King Follett Discourse, through Brigham Young, B. H. Roberts, John Widtsoe, Hugh B. Brown, and Spencer W. Kimball. In his characterization of the idea, God "is perfect in respect to us and the sphere we inhabit" but is in some sense progressing in other spheres. In other words, he harmonized the two perspectives.

McConkie's verbal response to England's presentation was neither generous nor collegial. He likened England to a frog, "hopping from lily pad to lily pad of evidence," and denounced England's ideas as "trespassing on sacred ground."[52] In a gesture that drew mocking "oohs" from the audience, he then played his trump card on the subject. Invoking his connection to the Smith family ("prophets whose blood flows through my veins") and citing the pronouncements of his father, Bruce McConkie, and his grandfather, Joseph Fielding Smith, he was claiming his bona fides as Latter-day Saint royalty and a relative to the two most dogmatic voices in the church. In tone-deaf disregard for John the Baptist's mockery of those who stand upon lineage in their claim to righteousness, McConkie was engaging in a familiar practice that continues to sow resentment in a church more convert than blue-blood in its twenty-first-century composition: citing one's pioneer ancestry like Boston Brahmins conjuring the names of their Plymouth ancestors.

"If another man wants to worship a progressing God, an imperfect God, a God without all knowledge and wisdom, I feel to allow him that privilege," McConkie thundered, "but I would want it announced from the housetops that that is not my god." He, by contrast, would worship "the God that my father testified of, . . . in which he bore witness that Joseph Smith's God was a God of absolutes, a God who did not and could not progress in the attributes of godliness. That talk was given with the full approbation of my grandfather Joseph Fielding Smith, who forthrightly and constantly taught and testified of the same absolute God." Then McConkie brought two more relatives into the fray, citing the testimony of Joseph F. Smith and Joseph Smith's brother Hyrum, who said, "I would not serve a God that had not all wisdom and power."[53]

One listener interpreted the gist of his position to be, "My prophets trump Brother England's prophets." To see the encounter in such terms, and it may have appeared such with McConkie's words in mind, would be to tragically misread England's entire purpose that evening. And that, in turn, would be to misunderstand the church's underlying dilemma, whose eruption into full-blown crisis England was trying to avert. For differing points of view on the question there had certainly been—espoused not by amateur theologians and English professors but by prophets presiding over the church. And England's driving motivation was to bring divergent positions, if not into harmony, at least into dialogue. This was the noble but tragic intention that spurred so much of England's work. Nowhere in his life was his prescience more sorely needed, and so summarily rejected, as in his efforts to address the human elements in the Latter-day Saint present and past. He understood, as nineteenth-century Saints had before him, the imperfect trajectory traced by prophets seeking to articulate divine truths and to enunciate God-ordained practices. Believing in a church presided over by God, he was confident that contradictions could be minimized and apparent conflicts reconciled. This is everywhere apparent in England's writings and public presentations; it is typified in the title he gave to the published form of his Varsity Theatre presentation: "Perfection and Progress: Two *Complementary* Ways to Talk about God" (my emphasis). England noted, "My simple thesis . . . is that, in fact, these statements are not contradictory. These Church leaders were using two different, but complementary, ways of talking about God based on two different aspects of the Mormon understanding of God, both of which . . . are essential to our theology and must be maintained."[54]

The McConkie family, however, was not interested in England's project, in the general or the particular case. The first hammer blow would fall nine months later. Apprised (probably by his son Joseph) of England's remarks, the apostle McConkie had waited for an appropriate public forum in which to make his condemnation of England's views known. His June 1980 talk titled "Seven Deadly Heresies" called out England clearly and unambiguously, with McConkie's anathema pronounced against heresy number one: "There are those who say that God is progressing in knowledge and is learning new truths. This is false—utterly, totally, and completely."[55] Other teachings McConkie labeled heresies actually enjoyed—and still enjoy—wide or even majority support among the leadership, such as that evolution is real and that people may progress through the heavenly kingdoms after death. For this reason, at least according to England's report of a conversation with Marion D. Hanks, "the brethren were just livid" because McConkie made doctrinal claims "which were not in any way official. So they chastised him and told him he had to change it."[56] Edward Kimball reported that President [Spencer] Kimball "responded to the uproar by calling Elder McConkie in to discuss the talk. As a consequence, Elder McConkie revised the talk for publication so as to clarify that he was stating personal views and not official Church doctrine."[57] Unfortunately, reported Hanks, the rebuke backfired. "So he changed part of it. Mainly just the part about evolution. And then circulated it with the statement saying it had been approved by the first presidency."[58]

If England felt the sting of public repudiation, he was more concerned with the way McConkie had only aggravated the underlying problem, the sleeping dragon of which this particular confrontation was but one relatively insignificant but entirely typical foreshadowing: how to faithfully assimilate competing narratives; how to reconcile discordant statements of the leadership; how to acknowledge disagreement, error, and fallibility without forsaking the principle of an inspired and authoritative church leadership. As he would later explain in frustration, "I have students aware of the fact that prophets have said God is progressing, other prophets have said he is not. They come to me with their questions about this apparent disagreement."[59]

In other words, a systematic, univocal theology was not England's goal, here or elsewhere. Dialogue, respectful listening, and a more commodious acceptance of an imperfect tradition in perpetual process of harmonization was. As he agonized in an unpublished letter written in the talk's aftermath, "Students who know that there is indeed difference of opinion, or at least official withholding of judgment on these items, are confused; and we need to know how to help them. We . . . sustain . . . Elder McConkie as a special witness of the Lord Jesus Christ, . . . and we teach our students to feel the same, to take his witness as from the Lord. Now they see him speaking, in what seems direct opposition to clear statements of other prophets and apostles and official Church pronouncements. How can we help our students make proper distinctions and retain and build their essential faith in the apostolic witness?"[60]

He did not mail that draft, but he did send a different, meekly beseeching letter to Elder McConkie three months after the latter's BYU address. This was September 1980, a full year after his original Flea Market talk. It was probably a naive gesture, given the vehemence of the denunciation. But England persisted in his conviction that rapprochement between the two schools of thought was possible. He told the apostle he had revised his paper to make clearer and more emphatic his acceptance of the Joseph F. Smith/McConkie position and that he believed this new synthesis would pass the apostle's scrutiny: "It would be gracious of you to read my paper and give me some response if you feel there is need." And then he added a line that was beyond all question a reflection of his naivete and inability to gauge his standing with his own critics. "If you have any question about my ability or good faith before you take the time to read my work, you could check with Elder Boyd K. Packer," who "know[s] well my mind and spirit."[61]

McConkie's reply was to disregard England's good faith efforts and publicly damn his ideas again, this time in the world broadcast of the October 1980 session of General Conference. Before an audience of millions he derided "the almost unbelievable theory that God is an eternal student enrolled in the University of the Universe, where he is busily engaged in learning new truths and amassing new and strange knowledge that he never knew before. How belittling it is—it borders on blasphemy."[62]

In January 1981 England flew to London as assistant director of BYU's study abroad program. (He would direct it seven times in the future.) And it was while he was there that England's revised paper, thoroughly digested by McConkie, now turned a private follow-up letter of rebuke into a public scandal that forever after dogged both apostle and professor. McConkie had taken his time to respond, but in February he wrote a darkly worded indictment that threatened spiritual doom and destruction upon the head of the earnest peacemaker. "This may well be the most important letter you have or will receive," it began portentously. McConkie indicated that it was contrary to his custom to respond to individual queries. That he did so was purely "out of respect for your parents, G. Eugene and Dora, and for your own personal well-being and for your guidance." From McConkie's perspective, England's views were not just wrong but spiritually dangerous. That was why "I am extending to you the hand of fellowship though I hold over you at the same time, the scepter of judgment." England's theory on the controversial subject was "false— utterly, totally, and completely. There is not one sliver of truth in it. It grows out of a wholly twisted and incorrect view of the King Follet Sermon and of what is meant by eternal progression. . . . How belittling it is—it borders on blasphemy—to demean the Lord God Omnipotent."

At last acknowledging that England's efforts were in the direction of reconciliation and harmonization of diverse strands of LDS thought, McConkie declared, "There is no need to attempt to harmonize conflicting views when some of the views are out of harmony with the Standard Works." Finally, after nine single-spaced pages, with harsher language than England had yet heard, or was ever likely to again, he was unceremoniously silenced: "You should cease to [speak on this topic]. . . . It is not in your province to set in order the Church or to determine what its doctrines shall be. It is axiomatic among us to know that God has given apostles and prophets 'for the edifying of the body of Christ,' and that their ministry is to see that 'we henceforth be no more children, tossed to and fro, and carried about with every wind of doctrine, by

the slight of men, and cunning craftiness, whereby they lie in wait to deceive.'
(Eph. 4:11–16.) This means, among other things, that it is my province to teach
to the Church what the doctrine is. It is your province to echo what I say or to
remain silent."[63]

It was less common for leaked documents to "go viral" in the preinternet
age—but this letter certainly did. The leak was evidently from McConkie's
office.[64] If England felt humiliated, he didn't say so. After all, he had already
been implicitly condemned in two public rebukes—at BYU and in worldwide
General Conference—by the most authoritarian of Latter-day Saint apostles.
But the stinging judgment and medieval language of damnation now widely
disseminated were harrowing for his family. England said the only people who
were cc'd on his letter to McConkie were Elder Packer and Joseph McConkie;
he presumed the latter recipient had leaked the denunciation to further embarrass England.[65] He wrote to Elder McConkie, clarified that he had not promulgated his views on the subject subsequent to McConkie's first public rebuke,
and that he would not speak or write on the subject further. Nevertheless, he
hoped for a meeting to discuss the topic. He managed to secure a meeting, but
McConkie was unwilling to address the controversial material. "So we talked
about my parents and just kind of made light conversation, but he wasn't willing to talk about the progression of God."[66]

Elder Packer felt called to be a "watchman on the tower," in the midst of
gathering forces of darkness (that phrase was in fact the subtitle of his biography published by the church-owned Deseret Books). McConkie felt himself
endowed with the responsibility "to determine . . . the doctrine," of the church.
"If I lead the Church astray, that is my responsibility, but the fact still remains
that I am the one appointed. . . . The Lord's house is a house of order and those
who hold the keys are appointed to proclaim the doctrines."[67] In an earlier age,
Parley P. Pratt had the same apostolic calling, the same doctrinal influence,
and the same sense of an enormous burden he must discharge faithfully, if un-
popularly. As Pratt confided to a congregation in a moment of self-revelation,
there was a reason his companions found him dour and humorless. "A spirit of
solemnity rests upon m[e]. I cannot bring my mind down to the trifling joys or
amusements of life. It is not that I consider them particularly sinful. . . . It is
not that I am opposed to the enjoyments of the young. But the feeling [is] like
this: I cannot bring my mind to stoop, [I cannot] center my mind to waste my
time in much amusement that way. . . . I tremble considerably under the weight
of responsibility that is rolling upon us."[68]

There was much personality intruding in McConkie's exchange with England, but there was much history as well. In an age before the internet, it

was still reasonable to believe the church could control the narrative about its own past. And only the particulars of Latter-day Saint history can explain the compelling desire to do so—a history that extended its reach directly into the McConkie family. Joseph F. Smith, Hyrum Smith's son, was not yet six when he stood by his father's bullet-riddled body as it lay next to Joseph's following their murder by an armed mob in 1844. As an adult, Joseph F. would preside over the church until 1918, while his son Joseph Fielding (McConkie's father-in-law) served as assistant church historian from 1908 to 1921, and then as church historian until 1970. In other words, the man who supervised (or assisted in supervising) church history for more than half a century, and led the church until 1972, would have heard the story of the martyrdom from the lips of a father who witnessed its immediate, bloody aftermath. Doubtless the family history of the Smiths and McConkies, coupled with a lingering sense of injustice and alienation, contributed to a protective disposition in church history writing and archival access by those charged with its oversight. Educationally, the CES mandate delivered by Clark ("The Charted Course of the Church in Education") was still in full force, buttressing the institutional narrative throughout the church.

In September 1981, as England worked through the trauma of his public rebuke, his father described his own interaction with the church president: "On September 12th, I met President Kimball as he was entering the temple through the tunnel. He held my hand with a strong grip and kissed me like my son does. I commented to him about our missionary work. He embraced me and kissed me again."[69] Meanwhile, McConkie's public and private denunciations of England's efforts were implicitly seconded that same summer of 1981 by the only apostle of comparable influence: Boyd K. Packer. Packer's address to church educators, titled "The Mantle Is Far, Far Greater than the Intellect," incorporated four "cautions." The second of them referred to "a temptation for the writer or the teacher of church history to want to tell everything, whether it is worthy or faith promoting or not. Some things that are true are not very useful."[70]

The address was fuel for the fire already raging over the "New Mormon History" and brought about increasingly sharp lines of demarcation. Elder Ezra Taft Benson had given a 1985 talk decrying the tendency "to underplay revelation and God's intervention in significant events, and to inordinately humanize the prophets of God so that their human frailties become more evident than their spiritual qualities."[71] Packer's talk made it clear that apostolic concern was not abating. A student group of history majors at BYU asked D. Michael Quinn, a popular history professor, to respond to these developments in a small group setting. In a move virtually unheard of at the church school, Quinn directly and harshly condemned the statements of the two leaders. Rejecting their many criticisms of professionalizing Latter-day Saint history, he concluded that "the Mormon History of benignly angelic Church leaders apparently advocated by Elders [Ezra Taft] Benson and Packer would border on idolatry." Of Packer in particular, he wrote, "He demands that Mormon historians provide only a church history diet of milk to Latter-day Saints of whatever experience. . . . But a diet of milk alone will stunt the growth of, if not kill, any child." He protested what he saw as a demand "that historians write Church history from a siege mentality." Quinn asked indignantly, "Why does the well-established and generally respected Mormon Church today need a protective, defensive, paranoid approach to its history?"[72]

Quinn was at pains to insist that his objectives were the same as Packer's and Benson's, though his prescription differed: "A so-called 'faith-promoting' Church history which conceals controversies and difficulties of the Mormon past actually undermines the faith." Quinn ended his talk by urging that "if we seek to build the Kingdom of God by ignoring or denying the problem areas of our past, we are leaving the Saints unprotected." That was precisely the position England had staked out the year before, though in much subtler fashion. Quinn and England were both faithful scholars, though the latter managed his provocations (slightly) more successfully than the other. Quinn's words were a journalist's dream, and the *Newsweek* religion writers (and famous anti-Mormons) Jerald and Sandra Tanner were quick to capitalize. Three months later, "Apostles vs. Historians," as the *Newsweek* article was titled, accurately reflected the growing fractures.

England felt the sting of Packer's wide brush strokes and convened a group of colleagues, including Quinn, to discuss the remarks. England sought a conciliatory response, but Quinn was livid. ("I admired his bridge-building," Quinn later reminisced, while "I was more of a bridge burner.")[73] From this point on, the concerns and choices of England and Quinn diverged even more sharply.

Meanwhile, in the immediate aftermath of the Packer talk, BYU students were joining the fray as well. The same year of his address, the newly founded *Seventh East Press*, which England was wholeheartedly supporting, conducted an interview with outspoken Latter-day Saint dissenter Sterling McMurrin, in which he lobbed bombshells at Packer, the Book of Mormon, and Joseph Smith's credibility. The Packer talk was "reprehensible and odious," McMurrin declared, announcing that "you don't get books from angels and translate them by miracles; it is just that simple."[74] When the interview appeared in 1983, BYU officials withdrew campus distribution privileges, and the paper folded. With Arrington's Historical Department disbanded, the *Seventh East Press* defunct, and the Mormon History Association flourishing, the energies and passions swirling around Mormon intellectual life were channeled into polarized camps. Publishing outlets for Latter-day Saint books were likewise increasingly categorized as orthodox (the Foundation for Ancient Research and Mormon Studies [FARMS], *BYU Studies*) or liberal (Signature Books, Smith Research Associates). England's dreams of dialogue were not faring well.

CONSCIENCE AND AUTHORITY

In the extremely rare cases where prophetic authority seems to ask us
to do or believe something that goes against conscience, that is, in
what could be called an "Abrahamic test," we are responsible to
know absolutely . . . that the demand comes from God.
—England to Neal A. Maxwell, fall 1990

McConkie had delivered his first stinging public rebuke of England in June 1980. He had again condemned England's ideas four months later in the General Conference, broadcast worldwide. In neither instance did he mention England by name, but his target was unmistakable to any familiar with England's speculations on the nature of a progressing God. And that would include hundreds of his colleagues at BYU and thousands more in the wider Latter-day Saint intellectual culture. If England felt personally humiliated by the censure, he never gave any indication in his public or personal record. No doubt exists, however, that it provoked some of his most intense introspection, and reflection on the question of conscience, dissent, and discipleship.

In September 1980, sandwiched between McConkie's two addresses, England delivered his oblique response.[75] The occasion was his presidential address for the Association for Mormon Letters. The previous year's president, Richard Cummings, had spoken on "the Mormon Identity Crisis." England picked up the theme, turning it into a thinly veiled account of his own agonizing spiritual crisis. "The most anguishing problem in Mormon experience [is] the struggle to maintain individual integrity, to be true to ourselves in the face of pressures to obey, to conform, to overlook what seem to Cummings and others to be 'clear fallacies or even tyrannies in the strictly authoritarian pattern,' especially to keep faith with ourselves in the face of misunderstanding, hostility, even ostracism from our brothers and sisters and disapproval, even disciplinary action, from those in authority over us in the Church."[76]

England's resolution of the conflict was to celebrate the paradox. True to the church's founding narrative of an Edenic dilemma steeped in cognitive dissonance (forbidden fruit, needful-to-be-eaten fruit), he embraced "the tension between the conflicting values of individual integrity on the one hand and on the other obedience to a God we believe is acting through his servants." He contrasted his view with Cummings's depiction of the matter as a simple contest between "individual integrity" and "blind obedience." England's assessment was more theologically incisive. For a Latter-day Saint, the dilemma of sovereign self versus inspired institution is complicated, and not simply because conflicted loyalties are always soul-wrenching.

Latter-day Saints occupy a uniquely fraught territory that is easy to mischaracterize. That is because Latter-day Saints are a people of a hyper-Protestant sensibility operating within a hyper-Catholic structure. That conflict may go far toward explaining some of the most traumatic episodes in Latter-day Saint history, where deference to authority trumped personal conscience at appalling cost—from polygamy to the Mountain Meadows Massacre to a racial priesthood ban. Polygamy, the most culturally catastrophic such instance, entailed widespread anguish among Latter-day Saint women (and men) that continues to the present and almost led to the dissolution of the church through punitive federal legislation. Such habituation to an Abrahamic surrender of conscience to divine mandate arguably facilitated the atrocity at Mountain Meadows, where Saints under the direction of local priesthood leaders murdered over 120 immigrants.[77] The same deference was what made it possible for progressives like England to sustain a race-based policy of exclusion from the priesthood in spite of their personal revulsion. Without using that vocabulary, England perceived the dangerous allure of simplistic solutions that, like Scylla and Charybdis, beckoned to the idol of conscience, on one hand, and the golden calf of blind submission, on the other.

The Church of Jesus Christ emerged in an America that was thoroughly Protestant in background and sensibility. To the Protestant emphasis on individual conscience, Smith added a cosmology and a human anthropology that radically accentuated and more powerfully grounded that human autonomy. Smith reconstituted a primal war in heaven, in which the contested values were not between simple Good and Evil but between the defenders of moral agency and the promoters of a human destiny stripped of freedom and accountability. In addition, Smith affirmed an eternal existence to the human soul, making it coextensive with God's eternal past and future alike. Thus, human autonomy was in the Latter-day Saint case exempt from the problem first intimated by Aristotle and revisited by subsequent nineteenth- and twentieth-century philosophers, that only what is self-existent and uncreated can be truly free.[78] As eternal beings, humans are inherently, inalienably, free. Those environmental backgrounds and theological foundations go a long way in explaining what one philosopher calls an "almost obsessive Mormon concern for free moral agency."[79] A most prominent consequence of this philosophical ground is the Latter-day Saint emphasis on personal, individual, dialogic revelation. "Man, being created but little below the angels, only wants to know for himself," proclaimed the first issue of the church newspaper, which Smith oversaw.[80]

At the same time, Smith made sacramentalism the very core of the Restored Gospel—a sacramentalism that was the indispensable conduit of salvation and was rooted in an apostolic authority every bit as literal and continuing as that of the Roman Catholic Church. Theologian Stephen Webb's assessment is absolutely correct: Joseph Smith "was, in a way, reinventing Catholicism for a time and a place that did not have access to a truly Catholic presence."[81] Church authority in this scheme is absolute, vested in living oracles whose words Saints are to receive "as if from [Christ's] own mouth" (D&C 21:5). As the church's website declares, "Jesus Christ guides and directs His Church through revelation," received by prophets and apostles who have priesthood keys to act in his name.[82] How, then, to negotiate the competing demands of sacred conscience and divinely directed church?

In the aftermath of the twin developments of Reformation and the Enlightenment, as Bernd Wannenwetsch observes, "to think of ourselves as governed or directed by oughts pronounced by an authoritative Church came to be regarded as demeaning of human freedom. . . . Insofar as Christian thinkers have accepted that Enlightenment critique, the only role left for the Church to play in our moral life is that of motivator."[83] Or in another formulation, "It is part of the conventional wisdom that the Reformation was based upon the assertion of freedom of conscience, the autonomous human conscience against the heteronomy of church and state."[84]

Emerging out of a Protestant (and Jacksonian) milieu, and flourishing in a radically individualistic American culture, the Latter-day Saint church—and its members—bear the unmistakable imprint of that sensibility, which is only buttressed by the church's theological moorings in the spirit's uncreated eternity and autonomy.

However, as sacramentalist believers in prophets, priesthood keys, and a priestly, salvific authority, the Saints cannot really conform to a paradigm in which the church is simply morally fortifying rather than salvationally indispensable. They are, on the contrary, logically bound to a position closer to the Catholic view of conscience—which is its own variety of a paradox alien to fierce individualism. As one Catholic ethicist notes, "Under no circumstances should one violate one's conscience—one must always follow even an erring conscience."[85] The paradox is that a devout Catholic will in this view suspect the error lies in himself, not the church. This paradox—that even an erring conscience is binding on us—was clearly taught by Thomas Aquinas. However, Aquinas complicates his maxim. To act against personal conscience is always wrong. But that doesn't mean, he adds, that acting consistent with conscience is always good. For to be good, the will must be good in both intention and in effect or substance, that is, the will must be both well motivated and itself in harmony with divine law.[86]

From these two propositions traceable to Aquinas, the Catholic teaching on a conflict of conscience is clear. When one finds oneself in discord with church teaching one must follow one's conscience. But one must do so cognizant of both the fallibility of human reason or conscience (we are, after all, fallen creatures) and the contrasting infallibility of the church (as embodied in teachings of the magisterium). In other words, a fully committed Catholic, who believes a church teaching is in error, is bound to follow his conscience, while recognizing that he is acting erroneously.

In the modern era, Cardinal John Henry Newman reiterates the principle with only slightly more moderation: "It is never lawful to go against our conscience." At the same time, in the case of an individual's conflict with papal pronouncements in particular, "Prima facie it is his bounden duty, even from a sentiment of loyalty, to believe the Pope right and to act accordingly." In other words, a presumption of the Pope's correctness is the given, even as the demands of conscience trump the presumptive reality. Newman quotes Cardinal Dominicus Jacobatius to this same effect, that conscience is supreme and binding, but the principle does not imply that one is on that basis immune from either error or deserved sanction: "If it were doubtful," he says, "whether a precept [of the pope] be a sin or not, we must determine thus:—that, if he to whom the precept is addressed has a conscientious sense that it is a sin and injustice, first it is duty to put off that sense; but, if he cannot, nor conform himself to the judgment of the Pope, in that case it is his duty to follow his own private conscience, and patiently to bear it, if the Pope punishes him."[87] In sum, as the *Catholic Encyclopedia* states, "Even where due diligence is employed conscience will err sometimes." Therefore, "he who follows authority contrary to his own private judgment should do so on his own private conviction that the former has the better claim."[88]

If there had been such theological precedent in his own tradition, England's spiritual journey might have been a bit more illuminated. Sadly, a pervasive bias against Catholic theology has long afflicted Latter-day Saint culture, reflected in an absurdly inaccurate perception of the Reformation as a kind of proto-Mormonism.[89] Logically, Latter-day Saints should find themselves fully in accord with the Catholic critique of the Protestant view: "On Protestant grounds, the task of explicating the relationship between conscience and authority is not merely Herculean. It is impossible," writes one Catholic. The reason is simple: "Protestantism has no adequate notion of 'Church.' Not only do they have no way to guarantee the rightness of private conscience, but neither can they establish the rightness of the 'Church.'"[90]

On the fallibility of personal conscience, Brigham Young had no doubt. "Never do a thing that your conscience, and the light within you, tell you is wrong."[91] Nevertheless, like the Catholic theologians, he emphasized the social formation of conscience, and its consequent unreliability. In fact, he repeatedly echoed the Catholic position to a startling degree, making the identical arguments about the unreliability of conscience and the need to bow to the judgment of a divine institution that carries what a Catholic writer calls a "claim to authority . . . based on a divine guarantee."[92]

Young preached that "should you thus go, from one people to another, throughout all nations, you would find that they differ in their religions and national customs, according to the teachings of their mother, and the priest. In this manner the consciences of mankind are formed—by the education they receive. You know this to be true, by your own experience." More starkly, he insisted that "conscience is nothing else but the result of the education and traditions of the inhabitants of the earth. These are interwoven with their feelings, and are like a cloak that perfectly envelops them."[93] On another occasion, he reminded his audience that "their consciences, have been formed by parents, teachers, ministers, and others, who have exercised an influence over the young and tender mind."[94]

Latter-day Saint leaders have consistently referred to the Light of Christ, generally understood to be conscience, as a universal endowment. Nevertheless, ever the realist, Young was simply acknowledging the social realities of environment and influence, and teaching that even a divinely implanted seed needed to be nurtured by a sure source of truth and authority. "We may so live our religion every moment, and so watch our own conduct as to not suffer ourselves in the least to do anything that would infringe upon a good conscience *that is formed and regulated by the Priesthood of God*."[95] Or again, we would do well to "bend our stubborn wills, dismiss every prejudice, and doubt the correctness of our consciences until they are formed by the revelations of Jesus Christ."[96]

England's faith in the institutional church was correspondingly absolute. So was his devotion to the communal essence of the Latter-day Saint faith. He understood that, as the theologian Gilbert Meilaender writes, "the church's shared life requires that obedience be asked even of those who still feel themselves unable to make sense of the church's teaching."[97] And his confidence in his own powers of spiritual discernment was never absolute. Self-doubt coexisted uneasily with a disposition toward precipitous judgment and action. And yet, he did have a blind spot in his deference to institutional authority. For a Catholic, this would be the difference between the magisterium as the embodiment and voice of church authority, and the pronouncements of individual clerics presuming to speak with its authority. In its Latter-day Saint equivalent, England came painfully late to the recognition, in his words, that no one church apostle spoke for the institution. He didn't realize, he said, that his responsibility was to "'Follow the *Brethren*' not 'Follow the *Brother*.'"[98] No one mortal voice could be equated with the voice of God; but he had lived most of his career intimidated by the specter of such a chimera. He had come to see God's mind and will as so mediated by individual church leaders that it was their individual pronouncements, rather than official church teachings, that created virtually all the conflict within his conscience. He knew he loved and revered the church, and could not understand his tormented relationship to the institution. The truth is, he was never at war with the church—though he let himself be misled into thinking that was the case.

A position of public nonconformity comes comfortably to many. For England, however, there was always something self-tormenting about his perpetual provocations. Many tensions wracked England's spiritual equanimity, but none were more constant than what Martin Buber refers to as the contest between "I" and "Ego," by which the Jewish philosopher meant the drive to place oneself in relation as a feeling, caring, subject with other centers of consciousness, with the "Ego" resisting this aspiration of the "I." The "I" wills to enter into genuine community as a full participant in loving and listening mutuality; while the "Ego" demands to assert one's voice, to differentiate it from the chorus of humanity, and affirm one's integrity, one's authentic selfhood. Religious community amplifies that tension, since it requires commitments that will inevitably collide at some point. To embrace institutional religion is to affirm a community that will never adequately express the particularity of one's most private path to the divine. The Christ of Mark's gospel summoned those he healed to the desert places, but England could never fully accustom himself to the loneliness of discipleship in the context of a tribal and corporate people. "I felt again the hunger," he once lamented in his journal, "that 'so-called liberals' in the Church have to find each other and share their trials for a while."[99]

FOOD FOR POLAND

Only a moral bigot could lecture passionate Christians like Mihajlo Mihajlov, Armando Calladares, or Aleksandr Solzhenitsyn . . . on why they must show their love for communist enemies by not only forgiving them but by trusting them in the future.—Bryce Christensen to England, 23 September 1986

Meanwhile, as the controversies over Latter-day Saint historiography and England's personal theological differences with individual apostles heated up, he had found a calling far removed from doctrinal disputation. In May 1981, from the Study Abroad Center in London, he went to Rome, hoping to see a public appearance of Pope John Paul II. On May 13, he found himself in St. Peter's Square during just such an occasion. "I was in the throng, next to his car, just reaching out to touch his hand," when a shot was fired, passing by close enough to cause his ear to ring.[100] In Charlotte's recollection, in typical fashion, England had insisted on worming his way closer to the pope. "The shooter was right behind Gene and when we heard that shot, I just thought, 'Oh my gosh, Gene's down there.' Of course, there was chaos. The ambulance came around; they were chasing the guy through the colonnade, and finally, we caught up with each other. The crowd kind of dispersed a little bit, and his ear was just ringing cause that bullet had gone right past him and I just thought, 'I can't let this man out of my sight ever again.'"[101] A published photograph of the assassination attempt clearly captures the worried face of England, mere yards from the pained expression of the wounded pope.

He didn't learn until later that night, on a train departing Rome, that the pope had survived. England thought John Paul's escape from death a miracle —one that was followed by another, related miracle that summer, when the Polish Communist Party declined to crush Solidarity, the workers' social movement agitating for liberalization. Still, the movement and its supporters suffered horrible deprivations, and England felt that the world was doing too little to support a heroic people. He also felt a personal connection. Some time before, he and Charlotte had taken in some Polish and Lithuanian immigrants. As Charlotte recalled, "They lived here with us until we could find a home for them and a job and things like this, so we started being very connected to Poland in many ways."[102]

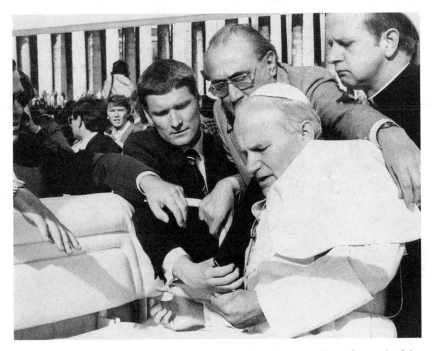

An anxious England (*background left, facing camera*) in the immediate aftermath of the assassination attempt on Pope John Paul II, 13 May 1981. (Courtesy Charlotte England)

Returned to Provo from London, Charlotte remembered, "We were sitting around the table—the family, plus whoever else was there, there was always somebody—and we were talking about this and we said, 'What can we do? How can we help the Polish people?' We bounced around with it and he said, 'There's got to be a way to get food to them, medications, clothes, anything.' The wheels were always going with Gene."[103] Through the Catholic theologian Michael Novak, England was able to make contact with Bronislaw Geremek, chief adviser to Solidarity. "He said the children were starting to die of dysentery. He asked that we send dried milk, detergents, and technicians to help them build privately controlled small businesses and that we do it soon, by plane. We organized Food for Poland."[104] England's proud father noted in his journal, "On November 6, 1981, Gene Jr. visited with Elder James E. Faust about helping with Food for Poland—milk powder for the infants, etc." By December, they had collected a planeload of goods. Days before they could ship, the Polish government declared martial law, and Geremek was arrested. Undeterred, England learned the military was not impeding aid. He secured

England (*seated, front left*) at a Food for Poland rally, 1982.
(Courtesy Charlotte England)

approval from the U.S. State Department, and a few weeks later, he was on TV loading goods for their first relief shipment to Gdansk by truck, then train, then ship. Half a dozen more shipments of food, medicine, and clothing followed, including 90,000 pounds of milk England secured from the church.[105] England obtained guarantees the Catholic Church would get the goods to the right people.[106]

On 8 March 1992, England described the rationale behind the effort in a press release: "It requires an act of faith to think that sending food into ambiguous and changing conditions is worthwhile. But our hearts tell us that feeding the hungry is right, whatever their politics." The valiant cause of the Polish workers added urgency: "Children who starve now will not win the long struggles of the future."[107] Mitch Davis, who served as the group's executive director, described the response to England's crusade: "There were rallies in Salt Lake City and Logan, Utah. There was a statewide proclamation by then-governor Scott Matheson. There was a sneak preview of Polish filmmaker Andrez Vajda's pro-Solidarity film."

England tried to muster congressional support, but given the political complexities of the era they failed to secure nationally prominent sponsors. Still, another leader of the initiative recalled, "Gene's efforts gained many converts. Hundreds, possibly thousands, of volunteers worked during those years in almost every state across the nation." "In the end," said Davis, "we hit upon the idea of a nation-wide 'Fast for Poland!' which encouraged individuals across the country to skip two meals over their Christmas holiday and send the money saved on those meals to us. The idea caught hold . . . and we raised more than a million dollars."[108]

In the fall of 1984, England announced that Food for Poland was succeeding: "The government is to give 1,000,000 pounds of powdered milk at the cost of 5 cents per pound; there is representation from Poland to be at BYU; and the government of Poland will allow missionaries into the country. (Four have already been called.) The Lord takes care of those who trust Him and ask for good things to happen." England continued to court the support of public figures but failed to score any influential names. He decided, in disappointment, that he wasn't cut out for fundraising. His efforts had added "perhaps $1 million worth of supplies to the Polish relief effort. That is pitifully little," he lamented.[109] True enough, he was excellent as a nurturer and teacher, but it's doubtful that he ever engineered a successful public relations coup in his life. Still, the memories and after-effects were indelible. Charlotte remembered that "over the years, we would be in touch with a Polish person and they'd say, 'I'll never forget when that happened, it was like Christmas, I opened up this package and there inside . . . .'"[110]

Even his selfless humanitarian work earned him detractors. It stung that the organization he led was "accused of glory-seeking, of being liberals indulging in do-goodism instead of the true religion of doctrinal purity."[111] After a long-distance phone conversation about his troubles in the department, his friend Bert wrote to console him.

I'm sorry for the problems you are having in the English Department. I've thought a lot about possible reasons for your difficulties. . . . Some feel you are trying to set up a cult, or independent kingdom, through the sessions you hold at the house. Some argue that you debilitate yourself by working on projects like "Food for Poland"—now you are talking about changing our government's immigration policy. Some say that you misguidedly focus on Mormon studies when you should be spending more time with the mainstream. . . . The problem, I believe, is that in this cynical and corrupt world, most people, including members of the BYU English Department do not know how to deal with a genuinely good person. . . . I don't see much hope that things will change and can't recommend anything except continued courage.[112]

VALIDATION AT LAST

The year 1982 ended with patience fraying at both ends of England's relation-ship with the BYU administration. In November, President Jeffrey Holland had written to England about the professor's desire to move forward the cause of a Mormon literature, which desire he had earlier expressed to Boyd Packer. Hol-land's report mentioned a general "uneasiness" on Packer's part with England's publication venues. England responded to Holland with a lengthy description of all of his forthcoming writing projects (more than a dozen). At the same time, he protested "the simple irrationality of being judged not by *what* I write but solely *where* it is published." He criticized the fact that the *New York Review of Books* "published more faith-destroying and anti-Mormon material than *Dia-logue*," yet he was being "tarred" for publishing in the latter. "A strange way to build the kingdom," he complained.[113]

Holland responded in some frustration. "You asked me to give you a leg up on to your horse and then bellowed because you didn't like the way I cupped the hand," he chided. Then he admonished England to simply "do whatever you think best within the traditional departmental and college channels. That works for everyone else and may resolve the irritation both of us are feeling."[114]

England's frequent appeals for approval and clarification may have been fatiguing to some and his standing controversial to others; as 1983 approached, however, validation came at last on a number of fronts. As the year 1982 closed, he visited with Marion Hanks. He wrote of the encounter, "It was very good for me to see you briefly today. I have felt for some time that I had lost (forfeited in some way?) the special bond of love that nourished me through the '50s and '60s. But I felt that bond again briefly today."[115]

He also wrote a letter to Packer full of new commitments. He affirmed, perhaps too emphatically, his desire "to follow the counsel of my file leaders in the Kingdom, in fact to be absolutely obedient to all instructions given in righteousness." He excused his long relationship with *Dialogue* as having been in the absence of any strict prohibition from the leadership. He reported, like an offender on probation, that "right now I am being obedient, as you know, to a constraint by Elder McConkie which is much more painful and difficult to understand than not editing *Dialogue* could ever have been" (a reference to McConkie's admonition "to echo what I say or to remain silent"). In clos-ing he insisted that "if I have seemed disobedient, it has been simply my own misunderstanding of the intent of the counsel. I ask you to continue to be pa-tient with me."[116] A few years before, he had quoted to BYU students Thomas More's advice to Richard Rich, that he concern himself with "your students, your friends, God. Not a bad public that."[117] For England, God's approbation could only be felt through the affirmation of those men he took to be his appointed representatives. He included with his letter a copy of his latest "effort to follow your counsel to 'build faith'"—a chapter defending the Book of Mormon's historicity.[118] At the close of 1983, Holland was expressing appreciation for his suggestions about improving the intellectual climate at the university, and was sharing his "Excellence for the Eighties: Four Specific Proposals" with administrators.[119]

Though he still gave some of the Brethren heartburn, England was called to be a bishop again—this time of a congregation of young married members at BYU consisting of 120 young couples. Since that calling has to be personally approved at the level of the First Presidency, he found the news reassuring. As he had done leading the branch in Minnesota, England set about creating a close-knit community steeped in mutual love and service. One member recalled, "We had Pioneer-Day sacrament meetings outdoors in Provo Canyon. We had post-temple-night socials at the Englands' home with Charlotte's homemade ice cream. And best of all, we had weekly short sermons from Bishop England."[120]

England saw particularly difficult challenges as opportunities for the soul-stretching that life in community requires, and two such catalysts stood out. The first was a young couple with a

> spastic quadriplegic child. . . . I had known the crippled child's mother for nearly a year. After I had spoken on the Atonement at her sacrament meeting, she had come to me for counsel and help with her anger, guilt, and loss of faith as she tried to understand the failure of hospital care that had made one of her twins into a desperate physical, emotional, and financial burden, one that had ended her husband's education and intended profession, severely tested their marriage and their faith as priesthood blessings seemed to fail, and left her close to breakdown and apostasy. Now, as I prayed for guidance in organizing a new ward, I felt clearly as I ever had those 'strokes of intelligence' Joseph Smith described, telling me that I should, against all common sense, call her as my Relief Society president. I did, and despite being on the verge of moving away, she accepted. She became the main source of the unique spirit of honest communication and sense of genuine community our ward developed.

The second was a handicapped couple he met "wandering through the halls of our ward house on our first Sunday." The ward made "a major expenditure of our ward resources—time, welfare aid, patience, tolerance—as we worked to get them employed, into decent housing, out of debt, capable of caring for their bright, energetic child, and tried to help them become less obtrusive in meetings and less offensive socially." England, along with his ward, "learned to expand greatly our ideas about 'acceptable' behavior and especially our own capacities to love and serve and learn from people we would otherwise never know."[121]

Meanwhile, the Food for Poland effort was continuing to contribute aid to those in need. That same year, England was promoted to full professor. Though he had been denied a tenure-track spot at St. Olaf eight years before, BYU had hired him at the associate rank. The subsequent promotion evinced recognition of his accomplishments as a teacher and scholar. He received the prestigious Honors Professor of the Year award for the 1981–82 term. Just before, in 1980, he had published a biography of Brigham Young, *Brother Brigham*. (The church publisher had rejected the manuscript in 1976, during the time Arrington said England was blacklisted; the independent LDS publisher Bookcraft published it.) In 1983, he received the AML award for Mormon literary scholarship. The citation noted that "his name has become synonymous with Mormon Letters."[122] In early 1984, he received a note of thanks from the immensely popular LDS leader Paul H. Dunn, who said he had "long been one of your fans and appreciated you so much" for his "sensitive balance on delicate subjects."[123] Another, unprompted letter arrived from the First Presidency's personal secretary, Arthur Haycock. Haycock congratulated England on his call as bishop, thanked him for three of his recent articles (grudgingly in one case, for "as you are aware, I am not a particular fan of *Dialogue*"), and commended him for "your ability, your loyalty, and your faithfulness, and for the great contribution which you make to the kingdom."[124] The tide seemed to be shifting in his favor. Even better, in 1984 England published a collection of essays that placed him firmly at the forefront of Mormon letters, but this time as producer rather than chronicler.

9

ENGLAND AS ESSAYIST

Gene wrote about war, he wrote about politics, he wrote about the environment,
he wrote about families, he wrote about what's going on with minorities—his mind
was a far-ranging intellectual mind and because of his broad background in the
humanities, he was able to bring all kinds of interesting perspectives to bear on
whatever it was that he was writing about. He had a lot to say but he said [it] well.
He was a wordsmith.—Robert Rees, undated interview with Mark England

Gene never had a thought he didn't write about.
—Philip Barlow, conversation with author, 2018

Most, but not all, of England's many publications up until 1984 were with
Latter-day Saint-related presses and journals (the overwhelming majority in
Dialogue with *BYU Studies* a close second. In fact, he was the most published
author in the latter).[1] He published poetry and reviews, but his forte was the
personal essay. In 1984, he produced his first collection in this genre, *Dialogues
with Myself: Personal Essays on Mormon Experience* (Signature Books). Many
of the pieces for which he was most famous—and most controversial—were
gathered in this collection. These included his essay on atonement, as we saw
above, and "The Mormon Cross," which was first published in 1973, five years
before the priesthood ban was lifted. Republishing the work in 1984 gave notice that, for England, the racial issue was not resolved.

Not all of England's essays were theologically controversial. This collection
also revealed England's literary gifts that found few Latter-day Saint parallels,
before or since, in the personal essay form. Mary Bradford captured the logic
of England's preference for this genre—both as critic and as practitioner. She
said that England was "devoted to the essay as a logical extension of that vital
form—the testimony."[2] In 1829, Oliver Cowdery had prepared the "Articles of

the Church of Christ" at Joseph Smith's behest (later supplanted by Smith's own version). In those Articles, it was stipulated that "the church shall meet together oft for prayer & supplication casting out none from your places of worship but rather invite them to come. And each member shall speak & tell the church of their progress in the way to Eternal life."[3] The practice was a stepchild of the Puritan custom requiring candidates for membership to narrate a conversion experience attesting to God's saving grace. In Latter-day Saint culture, the monthly "testimony meeting" offers to one and all a public confessional, in a safe and accepting environment. While many expressions are banal and formulaic, some narrate members' unvarnished, remarkably beautiful, and vulnerable encounters with the divine in all its manifestations. Testimony meetings, journal keeping, personal histories—all these Latter-day Saint practices combine to cultivate gifts of introspection and an awareness of sacred immanence. Such a sensibility often could manifest in church culture as a startling collapse of sacred distance, demonstrated in one of England's most popular essays.

"BLESSING THE CHEVROLET" (1974)[4]

John Gary Maxwell remembered a debate among the group of four teenage
friends of which he and Gene were part. One asked, "What should one do if there
is an emergency need for one's automobile and it will not start?" Max took the
position that one should lift up the hood of the car and look for the cause of the
problem and attempt to repair it. Gene took the position that the best plan was to
place one's hands on the hood of the car and give it a blessing. . . . I have spent
much of my professional life looking under the hood to see what
could be fixed. Gene remained a man of the spirit and of faith.[5]
—John Gary Maxwell to Charlotte England, undated

"At various times I have heard and read, with mild curiosity, of the anointing of animals by the power of the priesthood in pioneer times, but it wasn't until I found myself with my own hands placed in blessing on the hood of my Chevrolet that I really felt what that experience meant to those early Saints, who depended on their animals, as we do our cars, for quite crucial things." Performing a healing ritual on an animal seems a bit odd but not an unreasonable thing to do. God loves all creatures, and Catholics and Anglicans alike bring animals to be blessed on the feast day of St. Francis of Assisi (4 October). That love, combined with the urgent needs of animal-dependent pioneers, seems sufficient warrant for such a variation on the Latter-day Saint practice of anointing and blessing a sick individual.

England was at the time serving as the branch president of his Minnesota flock. His car was in the garage, stubbornly resisting every effort to start its engine. The mechanic was stymied, England had pressing branch business to attend to, so "when my anxiety reached a certain point, I found that it was quite natural, while the mechanic was helping at the gas pumps out front, to literally place my hands on the car and give it a blessing, explaining to the Lord that I was about His work, that my branch needed me, and I needed some extraordinary help to get there. The mechanic came back, made another adjustment, and half-heartedly tried the starter again for the hundredth time. So help me, I was not even surprised when, after a few mild growls, the engine started."

To perform a priesthood ritual on a car engine seems either blasphemous or comical, although the analogy England points to is logical enough. Our estrangement in the face of such a ministration, in actual fact, is the illogical, unreasonable reaction. Brigham Young thought one of Joseph Smith's principal achievements was that he "took heaven, figuratively speaking, and brought it down to earth; and he took the earth, brought it up, and opened up, in plainness and simplicity, the things of God; and that is the beauty of his mission."[6] The seamless continuity between the sacred and the banal was, to early observers, laughably absurd. The famous newspaper editor James Gordon Bennett jibed that those Mormons "are busy all the time establishing factories to make saints and crockery ware, also prophets and white paint."[7]

Latter-day Saints belong to a practical religion; its strength resides in an ethos of hard work, sacrifice, community-building, and community-bonding. It has no tradition of mysticism, deep piety, spiritual exercises, or spiritual retreats. Its spirituality lies largely in the doing. Still, most all of the religiously inclined generally hunger, whether by cultural training or by psychological disposition, to stand with trepidation in the face of the "mysterium tremendum," or, in the phrase of William James, to have objects to which we can attach "adjectives of mystery and splendor."[8] The religion of Brigham Young, however, is one in which a pause to reflect on the sacred imponderables can appear a self-indulgent distraction from practical religion. One of the tradition's greatest novelists accurately captures the strain in Smith's successor, having Young counsel Brother Mac to always "pay your debts, keep your bowels open, walk uprightly before God and you will never have a care."[9]

But there are other palpable, culturally pervasive indications of the Latter-day Saint tendency to thoroughly infuse sacred space with seemingly pedestrian elements, or to conflate heaven and earth. It is everywhere true of the Saints, as it was of their founder, according to Josiah Quincy, that "no association with the sacred phrases of Scripture could keep the inspirations of this man from getting down upon the hard pan of practical affairs."[10] The same prophetic voice of Joseph could one minute dictate revelations of sublime poetry: "The earth rolls upon her wings, and the sun giveth his light by day, and the moon giveth her light by night, and the stars also give their light, as they roll upon their wings in their glory, in the midst of the power of God" (D&C 88:45), and the next, invoke the same revelatory power and authority to declare in the voice of God, "Let my servant Oliver Cowdery have the lot which is set off joining the house, which is to be for the printing office, which is lot number one, and also the lot upon which his father resides" (D&C 104:28). England's essay provokes amusement or wonder only to the extent that his readers let their yearning for transcendence and God's radical otherness overwhelm the Restoration's—and its God's—emphasis on "the hard pan of practical affairs." That is why, for himself, England insists that, subsequent to his ministrations, "so help me, I was not even surprised when, after a few mild growls, the engine started."

In the nineteenth century, Latter-day Saint church newspapers often compiled regular lists of reported miracles, generally involving healing of the sick. In the early twentieth century the practice desisted—whether for lack of material or to dissuade the sensationalizing of sacred experiences is unclear. As in many religious traditions, the Saints experienced their faith's founding, Pentecostal phase not only with healings but also with frequent reports of angelic ministrations, speaking and singing in tongues, prophesying, and even raising the dead. England's essay is a not so subtle attempt to suggest that while the dramatic forms of God's intervention are still available to us, as his "healing" of a Chevrolet indicates, most of his still plentiful ministrations are less conspicuous but equally miraculous.

Some time after the miracle indicated in the title, England relates, "I found myself gripping the steering wheel with a special intensity and giving the car a blessing again. I told the Lord that my family was in danger and that our branch needed us the next day and it was time once more for some special help." This time, a more conventionally Latter-day Saint result followed. "I felt impressed to take the next exit, which led us to a town some distance from the freeway, and without any surprise felt directed to a certain station." There, a savvy mechanic recognized an unusual problem (a collapsed double-walled muffler) and effected the solution that saw them safely home. Stories of spiritual promptings that direct individuals to safety, rescue, or remedies of any sort, are legion in Restoration culture. They were particularly conspicuous in England's life.

England is reflective enough to recognize the objections such stories of divine guidance as his elicit: "How to fit all this with the Lord's assurances that he makes his sun and rain to come down equally on all his children—the just and the unjust? How about all that suffering, apparently uninterrupted by God, in the Sub-Sahara famine, Southeast Asia's constant bloodshed, the animal-like packs of deserted children in South American cities, the emotional destruction during slow death in American nursing homes?" Perhaps it has to do with God's greater concern for souls than lives, he conjectures. Or perhaps the decisive factor is not need but the susceptibility of humans to gentle promptings that must never contravene agency. Ultimately, he concedes, "I don't know. . . . The opportunities, the needs, come often, and the Lord's response forms a bright thread in the texture of gospel living. But I don't fully understand why or how. I only know that I continue to ask—and to acknowledge the Lord's hand in all things."

"ENDURING" (1983)[11]

"I grew up in a safe valley," he begins this meditation. The Edenic image is well chosen. Like Wordsworth's great "Ode" ("There was a time . . . "), the passage inscribes a childhood of innocent bliss, even as it portends the intrusions of a fallen world: "Even the Second World War seemed far away, unconnected, intruding only for moments when I rushed outside at a sudden roar one overcast morning to see a strange, double-bodied, P-38 fighter plane just passing over our house, hedgehopping down the valley toward Pocatello under the low clouds. Or when the oldest Bickmore boy was shot through the chest by a sniper on Okinawa and came home to tell about it in Sacrament Meeting."

The safe valley, though he doesn't expressly say so, ultimately proves a more potent metaphor for Mormonism than for childhood. Latter-day Saints, as we saw above, grow up in a culture immersed in the rhetoric of certainty, in boundless optimism about humankind's divine origins and potential, and in cohesive, tight-knit communities. In other forums, England had tried to make room for unresolved tensions in church doctrine, uncertainties, and hard questions. This essay, in contrast, is a window into his own intermittent existential angst, a condition he finds that Restoration theology can aggravate as well as mitigate.

How is it then that sometime in those years I first felt my own deepest, most hopeless, fear, the fear of being itself? It is a fear I have never been able to write about until now nor imagined anyone else knew about or could understand, a fear so fundamental and overwhelming that I feel I must literally shake myself from it when it comes or go mad. And yet I felt it as a child in that safe valley. I've forgotten, perhaps blocked away, the time it first came. Probably it was during one of those long summer evenings when Bert Wilson and I would sleep out on our large open front lawn and watch the stars come. The stars in that unpolluted sky were warm and close and dense. . . . I began to learn from my father . . . about the worlds without number God had created and that we had always existed and always would, destined to explore and create forever in that infinite universe. . . . My own deep fear seems unique, precisely because of those unique Mormon beliefs that have given me my greatest joy and security.

And here the Latter-day Saint contrast with other Christian paradigms becomes double-edged:

It is one thing to wonder, as traditional Christians do, why an absolute, perfectly self-sufficient God would bother to create me and this strange, painful universe out of nothing, to feel the proximate mysteries of this "vale of tears" but also an utter dependence on an ultimate being who can indeed reduce me and the universe to nothingness and thus painlessness again. . . . The restored gospel provides the best answers—the most adventuresome and joyful—to the basic questions about how I came to be here and about my present and future possibilities. But there finally is no answer to the question of why and how I exist in my essential, Being. . . . And the answer of Joseph Smith, that it did not come to be but simply always was, is marvelous—until I let the horror intrude.

Words like "restoration" and "fullness" and "continuous revelation" imbue the faith community with profound confidence in the meaning of life and the ultimate value of suffering. England finds in his own life, however, that glib optimism in the face of life's experiential horrors is its own kind of blasphemy.

I know a young couple whose two-year old boy, because of cerebral palsy, is a spastic quadriplegic, apparently blind and deaf. His twin brother is perfectly healthy. As a new high councilman, I gave a sacrament meeting sermon at my assigned ward on the grace of Christ, his unconditional love for sinners. Susan, the mother, came up, grateful for what I'd said and wanting to talk more about how she could cope with her struggles and feelings, her guilt about her son. What neglect had caused the fever in the hospital that produced the palsy? Or, if a genetic "accident" was to blame, why had God allowed—or caused—it? Why had priesthood blessings that promised recovery not yet been fulfilled? How could she go on holding Allyn almost twenty-four hours a day to keep him from bracing back and choking? How could she be forgiven for her anger at him, striking him, sometimes wanting him dead? . . .

I wasn't much comfort. I could testify about Christ's understanding and unconditional acceptance of her and about the real benefits to her son of gaining a body, however imperfect now, and of feeling her love while he lived, however dimly. But I could not tell Susan I found Allyn's trouble a blessing in disguise or evidence he was an especially righteous spirit who had volunteered for such trouble or that he would be compensated in some extra way in the next life. . . . She listened, [and] wept.

And he tells other stories that must be told. Not to destroy faith, but to encourage its refinement.

I know of a couple whose first baby was born with a gaping cleft lip, the eyes squeezed almost into a cyclops, no muscle tone, and profound retardation. It lived ten days, requiring very expensive care at enormous cost to the parents. A chromosomal check available in recent years revealed the mother to be a carrier of trisomy 13, Patau's syndrome, and the doctors presented the options: no more children except by adoption, amniocentesis in future pregnancies to check the chromosomes of the fetus and abortion in case of abnormality, or having children with a high percentage of carriers and abnormalities. On the basis of their opposition to birth control and abortion (and thus to amniocentesis that would assume abortion as an option), and with faith in an optimistic priesthood blessing and strengthened by the fasting of their ward and stake, the couple went ahead with another child. It was born with trisomy 13, lived thirty-three days, and put the parents in debt over $100,000.

He concludes his essay, as his theme by now requires, without resolution. "If I let it (sometimes I invite it), the horror deepens, because neither that atomized, inertial, spinning chaos nor my strange ability to sense and order and anguish over it have any real reason to exist."

Then, he adds a postscript. Developments subsequent to writing have taught him—or reminded him—that in the overall calculus of the world, reasons for hope and reasons for despair maintain a fragile equilibrium. Such is the ground of genuine faith.

We are sending, in cooperation with the LDS Welfare Program, another large shipment of food and clothing to help the Poles through this winter. . . . Our third daughter, who was born with a diaphragmatic hernia and who almost died from a resulting intestine block last June, while she was on a mission—came home, was operated on, slowly recovered, and is going back into the field in January. Our oldest daughter is in love. I lie awake sometimes now, as the nights begin to shorten, my mind besieged by woe and wonder.

Edgar to his blind father in *King Lear*:
Men must endure
Their going hence even as their coming hither.
Ripeness is all. Come on.

"EASTER WEEKEND" (1988)[12]

If only one of England's writings were to survive, "Easter Weekend" would most accurately preserve the essence of the inner man: his foibles, his insecurities, and his distinctive discipleship. The title unfolds as a multilayered meditation on the atonement: It specifies a particular Easter spent on the road, chronicles a descent into a private hell, and narrates an episodic ascent toward insight and understanding—all against the backdrop of a divine mystery that escapes rational articulation even as it permeates every moment of the journey.

Walking the streets of New York en route to a conference, England pauses to watch some street hustlers bilking a naive mark with card tricks. England discerns the pattern, and marvels at the dupe's simplicity. After observing helplessly, he is given an opportunity to show how the game works and lays down his money for what seems to be a gratuitous opportunity to double his own meager resources. The naïf, of course, was no dummy. Before England can fully absorb the shock, he has lost all the money he had to see him through the entire conference trip, save a few dollars. As he reels, "the crowd left, and the dealer, Black Beret, Stretch Pants, and Red Tie walked quickly together toward Broadway, leaving me frozen, spent, swirling in a tempest, damned, gaping, clear only about one thing—I was the mark, the only mark. As I stood there and then walked east I was absolutely serene and absolutely violated."

His fall and his predicament are the more powerful for being so sudden, so pedestrian, so recognizably human. England experiences his micro-catastrophe through the lens of the atonement theology he has spent years developing.

The existential pain that follows is not that of the victim, or the offender. He is himself thoroughly implicated in the fractures of this set piece that typifies the fallen world. Greed, precipitousness, racism, irresponsibility; and most of all, a diffused sense of guilt that cries out for repair. "My mind had come unfrozen enough to begin to calculate how I could make it home on my remaining twenty-nine dollars cash without getting any more money or admitting my plight—and in a way that would make me suffer (that seemed very important)."

Still stinging from the con, he attends a Sam Shepard play, "A Lie of the Mind," a harrowing tale of brutality and sacrifice and redemption—as unlikely but as beautiful as "fire in the snow." No coincidence, then, that recollecting the play incites thoughts of his own redemption. For England, the key lies not in Christ's payment for a debt incurred by our sin but in Christ's perfect empathy bought at the cost of his immersion in our pain:

> It hurts very much to think of you. How could you suffer not only our pains but our sicknesses and infirmities? Did you actually become sick and infirm or merely feel, with your greater imagination, something like what we feel when we are sick and infirm? . . . I don't want you to hurt like this, like I do now, to be ashamed, to hate the detailed, quotidian past. Yet I want you to know the worst of me, the worst of me possible, and still love me, still accept me—like a lovely, terrible drill, tearing me all the way down inside the root, until all the decay and then all the pulp and nerve and all the pain are gone. . . .
>
> Could it be that your very willingness to know the actual pain and confusion and despair of sin, to join with us fully, is what saves us? It's true, I feel your condescension in that; I feel you coming down from your formidable, separate height as my Judge and Conscience. . . . So how can I refuse to accept myself, refuse to be whole again, if you, though my Judge whom I hide from, know exactly what I feel and still accept me? . . . Who is it can withstand your love?

The next day, Good Friday, in Montreal, he finds a Protestant service and sings with the congregation, Bach's Chorale from the St. Matthew Passion. That afternoon, he is in a cathedral. "At 2:50 the priest quickly finished his talk and a complete silence fell over the congregation until 2:55, when a group of priests, white-robed and hooded, evidently representing all of us, filed up to the altar and gazed up at the crucified Savior until 3:00. The signal of the moment of death was a sudden lighting of the brightest altar lights; all the congregation stood and remained in silence for a few minutes. Then slowly we left."

Another set piece intrudes, a report he imagines his guardian angel ancestor is preparing on England's life to date. (Again, note the deliberate juxtaposition of himself with the spiritually accomplished father figure.) It is the most confessional of England's writings:

> The main problem is that Gene understands what is right to do but does not do it. He knows more about the Atonement than I did when I was branch president in Lyme Regis—or even when I became a patriarch in Plain City after the crossing to Utah. He writes constantly about it, even when he is writing for the gentiles about literature. Many people praise him for what he says; they write letters to him telling how he helped them live the gospel better and helped them understand repentance. But he still does terrible things. It is still hard for him to be honest. He covers up his mistakes with lies. He pretends he knows things or remembers people or has read books when he has not. I think he loves to do right, but he has a hard time being honest or kind when the chance to do so is sudden or embarrassing or when he is in pain or lonely. If he has time to think, he is very often good, but not when he is surprised.

Back in New York for Easter Sunday, England's religious pilgrimage comes full circle. Street hustles, plays of redemption, pilgrimages to Protestant churches and Catholic cathedrals culminate in the familiar family circle of a Latter-day Saint meetinghouse. The closing line, in its poignant inarticulateness, is the perfect image of England's own yearning beyond language.

> The bishop bore his testimony, not about the resurrection but about the power of repentance, which he had experienced personally. An elegantly dressed businessman picked up the theme by confessing, in a careful, broken voice, how Christ had changed him twenty years before, suddenly, completely. A short man with a beer belly, thinning, long black hair, and a black leather jacket, almost a caricature of the aged hippie, spoke softly of his long, slow, still-backsliding conversion. And a young Puerto Rican on the bench in front of me, whom I had noticed struggling for courage to get up, spoke last. He told how a few weeks before he had made a Saturday trip to see this strange part of New York, had wandered into the LDS visitors' center on the main floor just below us, and had met some missionaries and joined the Church. He tried to describe his former sins and how he had changed. "I'm sorry in all the world," he kept saying. "I'm sorry in all the world."

"MONTE CRISTO" (1993)[13]

One key to understanding England's enduring influence and compelling appeal is the lyrical simplicity he brought to gospel living and Latter-day Saint writing. Stanford-trained and a published scholar, an accomplished historian, and a speculative theologian, his strength was nonetheless in his exemplification of the counsel he once gave a recently married student couple: "Experience church service and communion with common people in common struggles." Our purpose, he believed, is to expose ourselves to the refining cycles of "loving and being hurt, making mistakes and being forgiven."[14] His best essays, the finest in the Latter-day Saint tradition, are unadorned, unpretentious windows into the richness of the quotidian, infused by intimations of an eternal significance to the evanescent.

England's personal favorite was "Monte Cristo," a simple account of his first experience fly-fishing with a friend and teacher in the South Fork of Ogden Canyon. Intentionally or not, the story serves as a fully realized microcosm of the human odyssey—and the fragility, the contingency, the giftedness of a life that always exceeds our thirst for control. An arduous and uncertain trek culminates in arrival at a remote, beautiful riverbank. The day is well spent in developing mastery of the artful form of casting the fly, setting the hook, and landing the fish. Interspersed with the telling is recollection of recollections and stories within the story. England relates how beloved church prophet David O. McKay had lived in the area. "I pointed at the sagebrush-covered hills to the north. 'He said he rode his horse many times out onto those foothills and knelt and begged the Lord for some manifestation, but that when he got up he always had to admit nothing had happened.'" His companion, Frank Odd, relates the tragic tale of friends whose beautiful young daughter is murdered by a jilted boyfriend. When Frank asks the mother, a year later, how she fares, she responds with potent economy. "I am a happy woman who cries a lot."

England soon follows with his own story, one of subtle self-revelation. Invited to speak in a student's home ward, he happily obliges. His talk is a sermon on the evils of materialism, an exhortation to live the temple covenant of consecration and an echo of the Lord's reproof to a world steeped in inequality: "We should be equal in temporal things or we cannot be equal in spiritual things." Soon thereafter, England is chagrined to learn that, yet again, his words have elicited complaints to church headquarters and a chastisement from his supervisor. Obtaining the name of the complainant, he sallies forth "defensive and full of desire to condemn him." To his surprise, he finds the man a kindly, amiable person, who describes a ward England had never paused to appraise. "Full of widows and elderly couples on fixed incomes." England ends the story there, as if the implied reproof needs no further explication. More intent on preaching than ministering and more attuned to his own spirituality than his audience's impoverishment, his relation of the story was about a painful moment of recognition. Is such pain always the price of progress?

The narrator then returns to a fishing day full of splendor, love of creation, and reveling in friendship, a day that strikes the reader as beautiful but unexceptional. But the story ends with a subtle extrapolation from the tragedy of the young girl's death to the common thread of every mortal joy: eruptions of the sublime into the commonplace are moments of grace we cannot will into repetition or persistent visitation.

> The year after that, I tried to take Charlotte and my children but found the gate locked where we had turned off the upper logging road—I learned later that the Deseret Cattle Company, which leased the land, had decided to keep people out. It was much too far to walk to the river from there, so we turned back. I think often of Monte Cristo and the river that flows on with no human visitation, without the arc of Frank's perfect cast and without his softening voice. I think of deer that come down to the beaver ponds to drink and how they spook the fish, how the hummingbird appears and is gone. I think of those red-throated fish measuring the pools in their shadowed flight, swift as the jet shadows measure, in silent noons, that continuing valley.

"WHY THE CHURCH IS AS TRUE AS THE GOSPEL" (1999)[15]

One unanticipated consequence of the Protestant Reformation was that it made the church as an institution suddenly no longer indispensable to all. For a Catholic, as Adolph Harnack noted decades ago, "assurance of salvation can only come when an imperfect faith is supplemented by the doctrinal authority of the Church on the one side and by the Sacramental Church institution on the other."[16] With priestly authority and sacraments no longer considered essential to salvation, the institution lost its central place in the whole scheme. And so in the country of England, for instance, Benjamin Hoadly argued that individual "conscience" and "sincerity" trumped apostolic authority and "external communion"; in so doing he ignited a debate involving fifty churchmen and seventy-four pamphlets in 1714 alone. Anxious fellow Protestants correctly perceived his argument would effectively "dissolve the Church as a Society."[17] In America a century later, the young Abraham Lincoln drew the same logical inference from Reformation thought as did numbers of Protestants: Lincoln embraced the Bible but felt no need for any formal religious affiliation whatsoever. "I am not a member of any Christian church, but I have never denied the truth of the Scriptures."[18]

The full ramifications of that revolution in the standing of the church are still playing out—now more conspicuously than at any time in recent memory on the American landscape. The unprecedented growth of the "nones," those affiliating with "none of the above," is currently a riptide. As a Pew study noted in 2012, "A third of adults under 30 . . . are religiously unaffiliated today, the highest percentages ever in Pew Research Center polling."[19] Seven years later, that share had grown to 40 percent.[20] Once again, England showed himself prescient. His thesis offered a new take on the post-Reformation question of why a church is necessary—and in so doing he dismantled the most persistent myths in Latter-day Saint culture:

> One cliché Mormons often repeat is that while the gospel is true, even perfect, the Church is, after all, a human instrument, history-bound, and therefore understandably imperfect—something to be endured for the sake of the gospel. Nevertheless, I am persuaded . . . that, in fact, the Church is as "true," as effective, as sure an instrument of salvation as the system of doctrines we call the gospel—and that is so in good part because of the very flaws, human exasperations, and historical problems that occasionally give us all some anguish.

The myths he was hereby dismissing were those of prophetic infallibility and of church history as an error-free linear narrative without bumps and false starts along the way. So much was England an advocate of the social gospel and a lived discipleship that he wanted to call the essay (and the collection it headlined) "Why the Church Is More True than the Gospel." He was overruled by editors.

One consequence of too much religious certitude, as England recurrently worried, was lack of maneuvering room when realities failed to meet expectations. A related danger of epistemological certainty was too little room for reverence before a never fully fathomable Divine. Latter-day Saints have a particular hostility toward language of ineffability, transcendence, and mystery. Their God is anthropomorphic, their angels are resurrected humans, and even their spirits are conceived of as "more refined matter." Believing in literal heavenly parents, and in Jesus Christ as their "elder brother," their hostility to creedal irrationality can veer off in the other direction, landing dangerously close to glib familiarity. England wanted to call Saints back to a posture of reverence and meekness in the face of our own littleness. Restoration scriptures actually emphasize prophets as "weak things" and describe revelation as "given unto my servants in their weakness, after the manner of their language" (D&C 124:1; 1:24). Smith, the revelator and translator, complained emphatically about communicating his sublime visions from the "little narrow prison almost as it were total darkness of paper pen and ink and a crooked broken scattered and imperfect language."[21] Brigham Young reminded his flock that "when God speaks to the people, he does it in a manner to suit their circumstances and capacities."[22]

England found in such caveats "a remarkably complete and sobering inventory of the problems involved in putting God's knowledge of the universe into human language and then having it understood. It should make us careful about claiming too much for 'the gospel,' which is not the perfect principles or natural laws themselves—or God's perfect knowledge of those things—but is merely the closest approximation that inspired but limited mortals can receive." Once disciples recalibrate their expectations of how nearly a church—the Latter-day Saint church in particular—can mirror divine intentions and designs, they are prepared to reinterpret the salvific efficacy of those flaws they can no longer ignore or flee from. Luther famously referred to marriage as "the school of love." The Latter-day Saints have particular reason to adapt that metaphor to the church with remarkable force. The crucial parallel with marriage that is virtually unique in the case of Saints is the thoroughgoing immersion—spatial and temporal—of the individual in the institution. Without parallel in modern Christendom is the church's organization according to strict geographical boundaries, and the church's constant presence in the daily existence of its members. Protestants and Catholics can flee a congregation or parish for more congenial fellow parishioners or clerics and can relegate their interactions with the institution to set occasions. Latter-day Saints can do neither. They are tied to their church family (by ward boundaries) as inescapably as any spouse honoring a marriage bond. And intragroup bonds that challenge sociologists for appropriate nomenclature (tribe? subculture? quasi-ethnicity?) further push the family analogy well beyond mere metaphor. What this creates, as England points out, is a human laboratory from which one cannot opt out at the first signs of discomfort, dislike, or irritation.

Marriage, as England quotes Michael Novak, "is an assault upon the lonely, atomic ego. Marriage is a threat to the solitary individual. Marriage does impose grueling, humbling, baffling, and frustrating responsibilities. Yet if one supposes that precisely such things are the preconditions for all true liberation, marriage is not the enemy of moral development in adults. Quite the opposite."[23]

So too, in the Church of Jesus Christ, ward organization—respected by "almost all Mormons—brings them directly and constantly into potentially powerful relationships with a range of people and problems in their assigned congregation that are not primarily of their own choosing but are profoundly redemptive in potential, in part because they are not consciously chosen." As he himself admitted of his time in a rural Minnesota branch, "Of the seventy or so members I got to know, at most four or five were ones I would ever have chosen for friends." And they would doubtless have expressed similar misgivings about befriending him, being "properly suspicious of a liberal intellectual from California." And yet, after months of frequent interaction in common service, they "had come to feel in their bones, from direct experience, that indeed my faith and faithfulness to them was 'stronger than the cords of death.'"[24]

Paradox, contraries, and opposition were central components of England's theological understanding. He would often cite Smith's aphorism that "by proving [testing] contraries, truth is made manifest," and the Book of Mormon's proposition that "there must needs be . . . opposition in all things" (2 Nephi 2:11). The tensions inherent in a community of struggling saints compressed into uncomfortable and frequent proximity was his classic example of the generative power of contraries and opposition. "The Church's paradoxical strength derives from the truthful paradoxes of the gospel it embodies, contraries we need to struggle with more profoundly in the Church." Therefore, he warned in conclusion, "If we cannot accept the Church and the challenges it offers with the openness and courage and humility they require, then I believe our historical studies and our theological enterprises are mainly a waste of time and possibly destructive. We cannot understand the meaning of the history of Mormonism or judge the truth of Christ's restored gospel unless we appreciate—and act on—the truth of the Church."

England first delivered the essay as a talk at a Sunstone conference, published it in that journal, and then republished it as the title essay of his 1986 collection. England considered "Why the Church Is As True As the Gospel" to be "the most influential thing I've written."[25] Today, it is the most read of anything he wrote, a testament to its enduring—more likely increasing—relevance to a Latter-day Saint public increasingly skeptical of institutional trustworthiness. The value of organized religion *as* a human-staffed and run institution is irreplaceable:

If we cannot stand the misery and the struggle, if we would prefer that the Church be smooth and perfect and unchallenging rather than as it is—full of nagging human diversity and constant insistence that we perform ordinances and obey instructions and take seriously teachings that embody logically irresolvable paradoxes—if we refuse to lose ourselves wholeheartedly in such a school, then we will never know the redeeming truth of the Church. It is precisely in the struggle to be obedient while maintaining integrity, to have faith while being true to reason and evidence, to serve and love in the face of imperfections and even offenses, that we can gain the humility we need to allow divine power to enter our lives in transforming ways.

10

FRAYING OF THE FABRIC

He seemed to be in anguish all the time.
He was fighting a many-front war.
—Mitch Davis, interview with author, 3 May 2016

By the end of 1984, England was in a relatively good position, having received tenure, promotion, and a teaching award, and published a new collection of essays. Perhaps new confidence in his status, perhaps lingering resentment at his 1980 public censure, or maybe a confluence of the two precipitated a very public avowal of his controversial heterodoxy. England had been a supporter of the Sunstone Education Foundation for almost a decade, contributing articles to the journal and participating in its popular symposia that were launched in 1979. In the summer of 1984, he prepared a presentation that he would deliver at the new year's Salt Lake symposium—the basis of the essay referenced above: "Why the Church Is More True than the Gospel." However, his 1985 presentation began with a section omitted from subsequent published versions. He states as this thesis that "relationships and experiences of salvation" are "more true, more dependable, than the vagaries of abstract theology we call 'the Gospel.'"

By way of "extreme illustration" of the principle, England invokes McConkie's 1980 condemnation of "the Seven Heresies [of Mormonism]"—which of course included England's own thesis on a progressing God. In his awkward reference to McConkie's sermon, however, England implies a different moral than the one he, England, ostensibly intended. For if this instance of confronting "the flaws, exasperations, historical problems, etc. that give us . . . liberals so much anguish" is supposed to eventuate in the greater sanctity of the individual and the greater love and harmony of the community, England fails utterly. Rather, he has just publicly called out an apostle for teaching doctrines he is unwilling to accept ("I missed out on four of the seven"). The focus quickly moves to England's own justification for discord: having already situated McConkie at the nexus of "flaws, historical problems and [liberal] exasperation," he now adds that "because the Church has not taken official positions on any of those four, I feel no obligation to agree with Elder McConkie."

England goes on to insist that he loves McConkie, recognizes his authority, and sustains him as a leader. But the moral about relationships and spiritual experiences having greater efficacy than doctrine has faded out of sight. The principle that emerges instead is one of personal integrity, not community: "I have and will be influenced by him in my beliefs—but only as I am persuaded by reason and by my own confirming inspiration. . . . [I] will do what he tells me to do in my Church duties, at any sacrifice short of my integrity."[1]

The delivery of the remarks to a receptive audience may have been cathartic. (They especially laughed at his aside, "I'm not going to tell you which . . . of the seven [heresies I embrace].")[2] For England, it was a rare instance of publicly aligning himself against a church authority, of publicly rejecting an apostle's interpretation of doctrine, and doing so with unapologetic defiance. Those words never appeared in print, however, and it is difficult to know if the performance was reported up the line—but given the hundreds in attendance it is more than likely. All the references to his dispute with McConkie were omitted from the print versions; the tone was further softened by the change of title: "*More* True" became "*As* True."

LITERATURE AND SCANDAL

This afternoon I went alone to *Cinema Paradiso*. It's a painfully tender poem about a boy growing up in Sicily loving films and learning from the local projectionist. . . . At the man's funeral, he finds for himself, in the old theatre being torn down, the film clips the local priest had censored out of movies over many years—all the kisses. The film ends with him playing them all in sequence—a wonderful evocation of human love and the strange idiocy of censoring that love.
—England, journal entry, 5 January 1994

Latter-day Saints have long been characterized as sexually repressed, producers and consumers of a hyperpuritanical culture. (One consequence was the salacious novel *Fifty Shades of Grey*, which began as fan fiction and escalated into a reaction against the restrained sexuality of Latter-day Saint author Stephenie Meyer's *Twilight* saga.)[3] Chastity, sexual purity, and continence are indeed inculcated in young Latter-day Saints with demonstrable success,[4] and the Saints consider such a culture of sexual virtue a supreme achievement in a fallen world roiling in carnality. The downside, however, is an overavoidance of sexual themes that at times can become absurd. In 1997, BYU administrators, caving to pressure from ultraconservative Saints, would ban an exhibit of four Rodin statues portraying nudity. Some students would counterprotest the decision, carrying signs that said, "We Can Protect Ourselves" and "Would We Have to Put Shorts on (Michelangelo's) David?"[5]

Such overscrupulosity is ironic, given the legacy of the church's "art missionaries" several decades earlier. Church leaders did not find it incongruous, or at least not intolerably so, to send some of their most promising artists to Paris to improve their talents, having in mind their subsequent assistance with the interior decoration of Latter-day Saint temples. The use of church funds for artists to practice drawing nude models in fin-de-siècle Paris in preparation for adorning the sacred inner precincts of a temple is surely one of the most delightful ironies of religious history. Sometimes, however, ascertaining an appropriate balance between religious imperatives and artistic freedom is genuinely worthy of debate. And many such cases would be found in literary works that graphicly depict sexual subjects. England's decision to emphasize literary art over moral concerns, pedagogical freedom rather than restraint, led to some of his most damaging censures by church authorities.

England spent a good deal of his life in the church writing responses to aggrieved students and parents. One incident in the summer of 1988 grew out of a class he delivered to a public audience at "Education Week," a kind of huge lyceum held annually on the BYU campus. In this class on "Mormon literature," he praised the research—though not the conclusions—of Fawn Brodie, author of the controversial Joseph Smith biography *No Man Knows My History*. He also spoke highly of the work of Levi Peterson, whose work struck many Saints as irreverent and sexually edgy. An alarmed student sent a complaint to the church commissioner of education, Elliot Cameron, who in turn directed England's dean, Todd Britsch, to have England respond. He did so, with more grace than the hysterical accusations merited, in two letters.

To Britsch (and copying a half-dozen administrators) he wrote: "I have [responded] because I am an obedient citizen of this community, but I wish here to object in the strongest terms to such a procedure. . . . It seems dishonorable to me to 'suggest a response to the issues raised' . . . especially since the writer of the letter was not 'raising issues' but was simply complaining about me, behind my back, to higher authority. Both professional and gospel standards seem to me to suggest a different procedure." The letter of complaint, he noted, should have been "returned to her for her to take up with me directly."[6]

In the Gospel of Matthew, he pointed out, the aggrieved are admonished that "if thy brother shall trespass against thee, go and tell him his fault between thee and him alone" (Matthew 18:15). Latter-day Saint revelation confirms the principle in virtually identical language: "And if thy brother or sister offend thee," one is to handle the matter "between him or her and thee alone" (D&C 42:88). As a general rule, church practice reflects this principle, insofar as complaints received at headquarters—when a matter of personal conflict—are *supposed* to be remanded back down the chain with instructions to resolve the matter at the individual or local level.

In his response to the woman, England defended his choice of Levi Peterson—whose frank engagement with taboo subjects she criticized as "shock tactics." It was clear from her other complaints that England's willingness to criticize the church's cultural and historiographical sanitizing was at the heart of her protest. She would not be the last. Even staff in the English department protested when he asked a secretary to process a piece for publication that she deemed "garbage." "Please don't ask us to type material such as this again," she huffed.[7]

A few years later, a classroom incident in an advanced literature class precipitated another protest, this time directed to the board of trustees. In 1991, England invited to his class a rising star on the national scene, and one of the most prominent writers with any Latter-day Saint connection, Walter Kirn. Kirn claimed he was a Mormon by background, but his familiarity with Latter-day Saint culture was actually scant, and he was a Saint by neither practice nor conviction. He had just published to wide acclaim his first short-story collection, *My Hard Bargain*. One of his stories, "Planetarium," details the shame and travails of a Latter-day Saint youth struggling to overcome masturbation. The very topic was one unlikely to be heard in a Brigham Young University class, and the public reading of a relatively graphic scene on the topic was undoubtedly without precedent. But that was the story—and the scene— that Kirn chose to read aloud to a class of some hundred students. England claimed he had specifically requested Kirn to read from another work so as to "avoid discomfort to some students," but he did nothing to interrupt the proceedings when they unexpectedly unfolded. (The selection England had approved, "Whole Other Bodies," was read by Kirn subsequently at a meeting at the England home.)

Whether Kirn's choice was based on misunderstanding or his provocative nature is not too hard to fathom. Neither was the reaction, and the inevitable complaints that went directly to the board. England explained to the class that he had not approved the reading of "Planetarium." Some students, while surprised, felt that it reflected "a kind of risk-taking consistent with the ethic of candid inquiry that governed our course of study." Like the brutally honest novels focused on the harrowing lives of polygamous wives, here was an "unimpeachable commitment to a kind of faith history that, because it was candid, was more faithful."[8] For others, the episode was simply the most extreme instance of a morally problematic syllabus. "I found myself reading pornography in the form of literature," one student complained. The student's distortions were patent ("my professor commented that this [story] was a God-inspired, spiritual experience" and that he plans to "take out some of the cleaner, more uplifting literature" in the next iteration of the class).[9] Distressingly, as with its antecedents, the complaint was not dismissed or returned. Rather, once again, England was called upon by the administration to defend himself.

He wrote several pages in reply, most of them again directed at process rather than the complaint itself. Regarding the latter, he insisted that "all the allegations are false, absolutely false with regard to tone and essentially false with regard to the content of our class experience and discussions." As for the central controversy, however, he was unrepentant. And rather than blame Kirn for his lack of discretion, he took occasion to insist that "by any dictionary, legal, or common sense definition of pornography, there was absolutely none" in the controversial passages or elsewhere in the syllabus.[10] England's chair, Bert Wilson, defended him to the administration. "I do not find the student's complaint worthy [of] the attention it has been given," he wrote to Stan Albrecht. And he mirrored England's protest that the procedure itself was inappropriate.[11] Nevertheless, he did admit to Albrecht that he "would have felt uncomfortable reading or having read to my class" the controversial selection.[12]

So exasperated was England with these back-channel complaints that had dogged him since Palo Alto that he prepared a class handout titled "Some Notes on Ethical Matters for My Students." Like virtually every teacher in the profession, England included a definition of plagiarism and the associated sanctions. Unlike every other teacher in the profession, England included as part of this personalized honor code item number 3: "If someone offends us, we are first to go privately to them and seek understanding and reconciliation—and *only* if that fails seek a resolution from some higher authority. . . . You should not talk or write to others about my mistakes or failings before seeking such a reconciliation."[13] This remarkable document, a kind of desperate prophylactic against further conflicts with the administration, was probably more alarming to students than conducive to the ends he sought. Why would students need to be warned about proper protocol for resolving grievances against the instructor? they must have wondered. At the same time, one might interpret the action as placing a safety net for the high-wire acts he refused to avoid in the interests of safety and conformity.

England continued defending himself against such recurrent criticisms up through his last years at BYU. A 1996 complaint chastised him for assigning such "disturbing" readings as the great Mormon novel *The Giant Joshua* and Harold Bloom's celebration of "The Religion-Making Imagination of Joseph Smith."[14] Not all complaints were knee-jerk provincial screeds. One student cited the apostle M. Russell Ballard in support of her decision to withdraw from a class she found offensive. And England himself had counseled BYU students in a 1996 devotional, "If you choose to read anything that contains material that is contrary to the moral standards of the Church, then you are placing yourself and your own wisdom above the counsel of God's prophets."[15]

Even at the secular Utah Valley State College (UVSC), now Utah Valley University (UVU), in his later years, England continued to offend, though he was freed from the onus of administrative reproof. One student in his Mormon literature class withdrew because of the readings she found offensive (early readings in the syllabus dealt with lesbianism, fractious divorce, and other topics England admitted were "a bit strong").[16] The student told England he was "a good man, trying to do good," but was "misguided and leading the class into evil." He let her withdraw but privately expounded his own thoughtful but unrealistic justification for exposing students even to objectionable images and themes: "I feel very strongly that agency is always involved in the translation process—certainly of symbols and even of raw visual images—into the mind and spirit. Otherwise, we live in a very strange and quixotically dangerous universe that I just don't believe is the one God designed."[17] Apparently, he believed there were no exceptions to the principal that "to the pure all things are pure."

To say these conflicts were cultural is not to reduce them to a simple problem of differing sexual ethics or sensitivities. Mormonism is also a culture that is relentlessly positive, optimistic, and harmony-driven. And that comes with a cost. In chapter 4, we saw him complain to a colleague, "Must we measure the value of all discussions and teachings by whether 'the Spirit' is present, defined narrowly as a feeling of complete agreement and peace?" He continued, "In order to achieve that apparently good goal are we willing to let students who *do* in fact disagree or misunderstand hide their feelings and confusion in order to keep the insisted on appearance of peace and agreement?"[18] As his friend Gary Browning astutely observed, "Provocative to Gene was not a negative word."[19] As early as 1973, England had complained to Dallin Oaks that "our official church literature has perhaps tended to err in the direction of the dishonesty of sentimentality, of inappropriate or unearned feeling." Then he added, "I think the same problems face us in teaching in the church."[20]

As if to counteract his growing reputation as iconoclastic and dangerous, but out of heartfelt conviction, England launched in 1988 a faith-building project that collected "Book of Mormon conversion stories." His aim was to fulfill the recent challenge of President Ezra Taft Benson to "strengthen our faith and prepare great missionaries" and to "let us know how the Book of Mormon leads us to Christ."[21] Later, true to not just his love of paradox but also his embodiment of it, England would write an essay notorious among the orthodox, alleging that the Book of Mormon prophet Nephi, in a famous episode of spirit-directed killing, was actually committing nothing more than rationalized murder. ("Gene loved the Book of Mormon but he loved it differently," observed one colleague.)[22]

BEGINNING OF THE END

Recently a chill has come over my heart.
—England, letter to the *Daily Universe*, 5 April 1989

England had enjoyed fifteen years at BYU, marked by highs (teaching awards and promotion) and lows (the imbroglio with McConkie, controversies over his syllabus). In 1988, Oaks had written to England, expressing his personal "confidence in Eugene England, both as to what he has done and to what he will do. That is trust and a trust."[23] Oaks had recently cited England in an essay on "purity of heart in intellectual endeavors," to England's great delight.[24] He could hardly ask for more significant affirmation. After that high point, the early 1990s marked the beginning of a downward spiral in his relationship with both the BYU administration and the church leadership. This had far less to do with his political or theological positions than with his naive confidence that his outspoken criticisms would be taken in a spirit of dialogue. He simply couldn't remain quiet when he felt he had constructive suggestions to make—or heartfelt protests to lodge.

An example of the first was a letter he had written to BYU president Oaks as a recent hire back in 1979. In what he clearly considered a remarkable feat of self-restraint, he introduced eleven pages of impressions and criticisms by pointing out that he had waited a full two years before offering the president "a general evaluation." He admitted up front a "personal weakness" that made him "outspokenly evaluative about any environment" he found himself in, but he believed his two-year self-restraint made his contribution now "appropriate."[25]

An example of the second had come in 1988, when developers were preparing to tear down the historic Brigham Young Academy on University Avenue. The architect for this predecessor to BYU was Young's son Don Carlos, and according to tradition, the plans for the building were sketched by Karl Maeser following a dream-vision in which Brigham Young appeared to him. It was a magnificent monument to Latter-day Saint educational aspirations, and the home to great teachers from Maeser himself to Philo Farnsworth, who invented television in its basement. England was convinced that BYU erred in selling off the building in 1975, and that the leadership was unprepared to acknowledge the mistake. "Is institutional repentance simply impossible?" he asked of his two more frequent apostolic contacts. What was called for, he rather audaciously suggested, was for Oaks or Maxwell himself—"with both clout and humility"—to proclaim a change of heart.[26] Maxwell responded a little impatiently: "I hardly know how to respond. I don't get a feeling that there is any need for 'institutional repentance.'" Even so, he said to soften the blow, "I am genuinely reluctant to disappoint."[27]

In the familiar pattern, England apologized for his "hasty and overly-passionate letter" and for his use of the term "institutional repentance," even as he maintained stubbornly that "I have no evidence I am wrong." And then he attached some of his "recent writing" as an addendum.[28] The postscript to the episode? A citizens' group formed a foundation, sued the city of Provo to block demolition, and funded a restoration a few years later.

The day before Maxwell penned his reply, England was alleging the same need for "institutional repentance" to then BYU president Jeffrey Holland. England was nothing if not persistent in trying to enlist anyone and everyone in a position of authority to his causes. The appeal followed three other complaints he was making to Holland in the same letter. First, he objected to the policy he had heard reported that BYU administrators were not allowed to attend Sunstone symposia or publish in *Dialogue*. The policy was "insulting," "irrational," and censorship by "prior restraint." (That policy, formal or not, would soon extend to potential hires as well.) Second, he protested the continuing necessity of having to defend himself or others from complaints lodged with General Authorities—in the most recent case for endorsing a controversial work of fiction by a colleague. And third, he was upset to learn he had been barred from teaching religion classes, based on his work in "speculative theology," undoubtedly referring to the piece he had written the year before, "On Fidelity, Polygamy, and Celestial Marriage."[29]

That decision was not a total surprise. The publication grew out of his 1986 Sunstone talk, "Sweet Are the Uses of Fidelity: Why Celestial Marriage Is

Monogamous."[30] If the ban against Black priests was the "Mormon Cross," England was here addressing the second-most pervasive (and more seldom-acknowledged) pain in the Latter-day Saint church: polygamy. Carol Lynn Pearson has documented a sampling of the many thousands of women who think of the Latter-day Saint heaven as "a celestial glory that I dread with all my heart," given the specter of having "sister wives" in the hereafter.[31] Since 1912, church teaching has been that plural marriage is not requisite for eternal life.[32] However, though depicted as a now defunct nineteenth-century practice, polygamy is a continuing reality for deceased polygamous ancestors, as well as for living women who are sealed in the temple to previously temple-sealed widowers. (A widower may remarry and be sealed to subsequent wives even if he was sealed to a first wife; a widow may remarry but not be sealed to a second husband.) Thus, a man in the modern church may still effectively have multiple "eternal wives," whether or not the first wife in such cases consented.

Few propositions could be as welcome to multitudes of Latter-day Saint women as the assurance that monogamy is the exclusive order of marital associations in heaven. That was the thesis of England's Sunstone presentation. His talk made no theological innovations; it was essentially an exposition of the obvious, if threatening, view of companionate marriage as the highest form of human union. He introduced his talk as an experiment in "speculative theology." The speculative dimension of his remarks alluded to his interpretation of past polygamy as an Abrahamic test of temporary duration, as inconsistent with sexual equality, and a clear violation of the "one flesh" mandate of Genesis 2:24. If his arguments were deficient, it was because they were devoid of any supportive statements from the leadership, and relied upon abstract if compelling principles rather than an exposition of the actual costs and damages that decades of polygamy inflicted on the psyches and sensibilities of the men and women thus engaged. "Even the best relationships were bittersweet," was as far as his criticism extended; and he was careful to affirm his belief in the inspired origins of the practice. The closest he came to explicit condemnation was his assessment, "from talking with Mormon women, that the devaluation of women inherent in the expectation of polygyny is destructive of their sense of identity and *worth now*." Hence, even though "it was once an inspired practice, [it] is not an eternal principle," he opined.

Doubtless his talk, a bold gesture by a church employee in the heart of Latter-day Saint culture, was gratefully and hopefully received by most listeners. It was, however, immediately attacked by church conservatives. Robert J. Matthews, one of the most highly regarded professors in the religion department, who served as both chair of ancient scripture and dean of religious education, wrote to England personally with a twelve-page critique. The normally congenial Matthews was unrestrained in attacking England's logic, his motives, and his spiritual standing. The letter was almost panicky, to the point of logical incoherence. England had committed the offense of "interpreting scripture" rather than "learning from the scriptures." His "rationalization" did not "carry the same Spirit as is found in the scripture." "Even if Eugene were correct in his doctrine, . . . he seems out of order to advocate publicly." England's invocation of Shakespeare on the value of "fidelity . . . does not prove a thing." His worries about the sexual temptations inherent in polygamy "throw some doubt . . . upon the lives of the Prophet Joseph, President Brigham Young, Abraham, etc." Did he presume that "Young, President John Taylor or Wilford Woodruff would accept this reasoning and rationalization?"

Finally, with a rationale highly demeaning to women while being both naive and presumptuous about the celestial order of things, Matthews pointed out that the gestational requirements of women made an eternal plurality logical in the case of women, but not of men. In sum, though England's was an essay in speculative theology, not direct action, he was "plac[ing] his own views above obedience." Then, Matthews turned from condemnation to threatening England's future as a sometime instructor in the religion department. "What will he directly and indirectly teach his students about understanding the scriptures? Will they learn true faith and a desire for obedience . . . or will they learn how to question?"[33]

England responded with understandable alarm. "Since you are in a position of great authority and influence, your misunderstanding of me and any conveying of that to others (as the style of your reply suggested you might intend to do) could have very serious consequences."[34] He was particularly offended at Matthews's portrayal of him as "some kind of dangerous enemy, critical of Church leaders and Church policies, devoted more to 'skepticism and rationalization' than to the Gospel of Christ." England attempted a temperate rapprochement, but his feminist indignation got the better of him. "I think you quite wrong if you teach (as you say on page 8 you believe) that the essential difference between men and women is that 'it is women who have the babies' and that thus the essential purpose of eternal marriage is 'to bear children in the next world' and that given 'the periodic nature of women, the basic essential biological reproductive difference between men and women,' polyandry would be absurd in heaven but polygyny would make things more efficient. . . . It is terribly demeaning to women."[35]

Matthews responded again, politely but firmly. He was unmoved by England's defense (or his analysis of what he saw as Matthews's misogyny). The bottom line for Matthews was that England, a person of "stature, influence, position, reputation, and opportunity," was publicly teaching private speculation to impressionable people.[36] Darkly hinting of sanctions, he closed by saying, "We have to guard against that as teachers and reduce the risk." And in fact, Matthews did act immediately to bar England from teaching any religion classes in the future. Alerted by his department chair Bert Wilson, England reacted sharply. He wrote Matthews, "I have never and would never, while a covenant church member, knowingly teach or write contrary to official Church doctrine or practice. If I must be disciplined in some way for speculating that polygyny may not be the ideal celestial order and may not be required of us . . . then so be it. But I object strongly to being disciplined and my character questioned and my reputation injured for things I have not done and would not do."[37] A ban on teaching in the religion department would turn out to be the least of the repercussions from this talk.

It was no surprise that some of the severest criticism of England came from the religion faculty. After being barred from their classrooms, he attempted an end run by appealing directly to the president of BYU, now Rex Lee. First, he expressed his view of his religion colleagues indirectly but clearly: "The religion department is seen by many others as narrow, provincial, anti-intellectual, not doing respectable work and not really worthy of being part of a genuine university. On the other hand many in that department see the rest of us as apostate, pinko eggheads leading the youth of Zion astray." Then he proposed a two-part solution: appoint Richard Bushman dean of religion and recommend to religion faculty that they award religion credit for England's Modern Mormon Literature class ("one of the best LDS religion courses on campus," he wrote).[38]

If England now found himself in a hole, he only dug deeper. In 1990, in a clear sign that the Brethren believed he had crossed the line from provocation into opposition, England learned that he was being excluded from a proposed encyclopedia of Mormonism (published under that title in 1992). Although not an official church publication, it was to be edited by BYU religion professor Daniel Ludlow, and apostles Dallin Oaks and Neal Maxwell, along with BYU president (and later apostle) Jeffrey Holland, had supervisory roles. In April 1990, England was informed that his participation in the project had been "turned down at the General Authority level." As the preeminent scholar on the topic, he had hoped to author articles on Mormon literature, but he learned he would have no role whatsoever. Devastated, he wrote to Maxwell a few months later, "It has continued to trouble me, to hurt increasingly, not only because I have become the chief scholar of Mormon literature. . . . Editing or even turning down my article would have been fine. But to turn *me* down as some-how unworthy or inappropriate, even before seeing what I might say—and then to give the job to Leslie Norris, a non-member who . . . knows very little about Mormon poetry—was humiliating."[39] He was hoping for an explanation. "What have I done—what am I doing—to merit such extreme judgment? I have made mistakes but am not aware of ever having written or said anything against the Church. . . . What should I be repenting of?"[40] (Adding salt to the wound, two other editors wrote England and asked whom they should include in the category of "top-ranking essayists.")[41]

Maxwell agreed to meet, but England's request for a reply turned into an apostolic summons, and England was told Elder Dallin Oaks would be attend-ing the 12 October encounter as well.[42] Then, three days before the meeting, England wrote yet a third time, copying a laudatory letter about himself from Robert Rees to Truman Madsen and Robert Thomas and including an essay he had recently published in *Sunstone*, which "a number of people from around the Church . . . found . . . accurate and helpful." At the same time, he acknowl-edged, "I have also recently been told that some members of the Quorum of the Twelve were concerned about me because of this essay, with no other details. If you know what those concerns are and you can tell me Friday, I certainly want to know."[43]

"Are All Alike unto God? Prejudice against Blacks and Women in Popular Mormon Theology," had appeared in *Sunstone* that past April—just before he was excluded from the encyclopedia project—yet the oblivious England did not suspect a connection. He could hardly have been in any doubt as to the alarm his essay had caused the apostles. His own stake president, BYU Law School dean Reese Hansen, had told him days earlier that he was calling England in for a conversation in response to their wishes. And Hansen told England explic-itly that the essay was rife with alarming material. Reese pointed out that En-gland had expressed "embarrassment" for Brigham Young, referred to Joseph Fielding Smith as "fooled . . . into false belief," and said Bruce McConkie had not "taken the . . . obvious step . . . to rid the church of false doctrine on races." He intimated that Young was "racist" and Smith "gullible and foolish."[44] This was the essay he had sent to First Counselor in the First Presidency Gordon B. Hinckley, hoping he "might be interested" in reading it.[45]

Presenting Oaks and Maxwell with a copy of the most inflammatory ar-ticle he had yet written, *after* his meeting with Hansen and even while await-ing a meeting to better ascertain *why* he was considered a dangerous pro-vocateur almost strains belief. He was gifting his judges with a smoking gun on his way to his own trial. The essay was a full-frontal assault on prophetic infallibility—extending to a devastating excavation of systematic racism and sexism alike in past Latter-day Saint leadership. He had criticized institutional racism before, and he had earlier criticized polygamy as inherently demeaning to women. He ramped up the latter critique in this article, calling polygamy a "clearly sexist practice" and claiming that in its aftermath "the Church . . . developed a semi official sexist theology to support it."[46] Whether they saw his gesture, on the eve of their meeting, as willfully provocative or merely naive is impossible to say. It would not have escaped their notice, either, that the very title was a direct and explicit challenge to Elder McConkie, who had given an address, in 1978, titled, "All Are Alike unto God."[47] England was throwing the church's embrace of that proposition into doubt, slapping a question mark onto the apostle's title.

England's essay first addressed racism in the modern church by tracing its roots to the 1850s. Contesting the thesis of Latter-day Saint historian Ronald Esplin, who has ventured that Brigham Young is unlikely to have introduced changes in racial positions that Smith did not himself initiate, England lays the blame for the origins of Latter-day Saint racism squarely at Young's feet. The evidence England musters for Young's personal racism is bitter medicine to modern ears: Young described Negroid features as "the mark of Cain," declared summary death the fitting punishment for miscegenation, and made other painful statements. More disturbing, England found enduring echoes of such racism well into the twentieth century among church leaders. Equally problematic to England was the continuing prevalence in Latter-day Saint culture of the very mythology that Joseph Fielding Smith had himself relinquished (according to England's 1973 account, which he now repeated), that the priesthood ban had been a punishment for subpar valiance in the preexistence. England noted that even prominent Latter-day Saint leaders had acknowledged error in their previous explanations (like Elder McConkie's famous act of contrition: "Forget everything that I said . . . that is contrary to the present revelation. [I] spoke with a limited understanding"). Yet, remarkably, noted England, even McConkie continued to publish his view that "the race and nation in which men are born in this world is a direct result of their pre-existent life," and other races arise from "racial degeneration" and "apostasy."[48] Other Latter-day Saint figures, like the venerated Orson Pratt and B. H. Roberts, provided further examples of "popular but false theology."[49]

It is hard to imagine that England did not anticipate the inflammatory effects of his litany; first, the array of prophetic, apostolic, and Seventy-level voices constituted, in his demonstration, not a prophetic misstatement later contradicted but rather a prolonged, systematic, authoritative consensus that was later determined to be false. (Though the church has stopped short of declaring the priesthood ban itself an error, it has pronounced the various rationales that had sustained it to be mere speculation.)[50] Second, England indicted Bruce R. McConkie for *post*-1978 words that continued to justify racial disadvantage. Prefacing his indictment of McConkie, he praised the apostle for his public humility and courage in the aftermath of the ban's revocation. At the same time, unfortunately, McConkie "left complete [in *Mormon Doctrine*] his old entry under 'Races of Men,' in which he continues to suggest that other races than the white arise from 'racial degeneration' and 'apostasy' from 'our common parents.'"[51] Whether England was intimating simple carelessness or intransigent racism, the effect was to call into question the integrity and good faith of a revered apostle who had died only five years before.

One could see England's efforts as an attempt to exorcise the demon of racism by confronting it fully and honestly. One Black member from South Africa wrote to thank England for confronting the racism that still pained him personally, and which "none of the [local] priesthood leaders is bold enough to deal with . . . head-on."[52] In the twenty-first century, the legacy of the ban and lingering racism continues to be a searing burden for a growing Black membership (which, at present, is virtually the same proportion of total membership as that found in mainline Protestant denominations).[53] In 1971, Darius Gray, a convert from the 1960s, was assigned by the church leadership to the presidency of a Latter-day Saint support group for Blacks called Genesis. When asked in 2018, almost fifty years later, and forty years after the priesthood restriction was lifted, if the day was coming when an organization like Genesis would be unnecessary in the church, he replied unhesitatingly that at this point we are "not even close." If anything, racial tensions have "only increased" in recent years. One explanation he gives is that Black members who have been "wounded" are expected to put the past behind them and concentrate on the healing effects of the atonement. "Wait," he responds. "I didn't cause the problem. When we speak of the Atonement, are we doing it to hinder a conversation about something that is [still] occurring that needs to be spoken to?"[54] Womanist scholar and Black member Janan Graham-Russell agrees: "The lack of consistent dialogue within the Church about the bans has created confusion about the restriction's origins and the official LDS position on racial issues. The seeming reluctance by some Mormon leaders to speak about the violence faced by its black members in the United States has brought many black Mormons to points of frustration."[55]

Rather than excuse or contextualize, England presented as unstinting and unfiltered a catalog of Young's (and others') racist views as he could muster, almost as an act of public confession and penance on behalf of the church. Alternately, one could interpret the essay (as others apparently did) as an unfair and ahistorical crucifixion of Young, too smugly presentist and gratuitously defamatory to be a good-faith effort at understanding the cultural universe of a nineteenth-century prophet. Something of the twenty-year-old Samoan missionary, full of zeal, naivete, and moralizing "outburst," is still evident in England the author-crusader, now approaching the age of sixty with the publication of "Are All Alike?" Certainly the persistence of prejudice merits condemnation; yet it was possible to see the dogged showcasing of a litany of the painfully racist rhetoric of the salty Brigham Young speaking a century and a half ago in slaveholding and Reconstruction America, quoted against pious assurances that he was "a man I love and respect," as more a parading of moral outrage than a particularly useful commentary addressed to modern manifestations of racism. A few years later, England listened to a Black member tearfully narrate his own battle with lingering Latter-day Saint prejudices. England confided his suspicion that this member's "kind of patient, humble, forgiving testimony does more good than all my talk about continuing racism in the Church and my attacks on the false theologies of racism."[56]

Racism and apostolic error were not the only inflammatory charges England leveled in his essay. Equally disturbing, and equally presumptuous to official eyes, was his forceful return to daring speculations regarding the sacred cow of polygamy. In his first writing on the subject, "On Fidelity, Polygamy, and Celestial Marriage" (1987), which he called "an essay in speculative theology," England had offered a persuasive and eloquent defense of the principle of marriage equality—here and eternally. Hence, his essay could not have been more divisive: welcomed by a substantial constituency of readers who bridled at the notion that a painful relic of the past would reappear in celestial garb, and resisted by those who felt it called into question both the meaning of pioneer principles endured at such tremendous cost and the durability of serial marriages made in the present era.

Three years later, he returned to the subject with even greater intensity. First, he not only argued for the purely provisional status of plural marriage as a nineteenth-century practice but also emphasized its deleterious impact:

By 1852 the Church openly adopted a clearly sexist practice—polygamy —and then developed a semi-official sexist theology to support it. The Church, by revelation, ended that practice in 1890, but it has not repudiated the sexist popular theology that went with it, the notion that the ideal form of celestial marriage is not an equal yoking of one woman and one man in an eternal union of polar opposites that makes possible a continuation of the seeds forever, but rather one patriarchal man and plural wives. I have presented in an essay elsewhere five reasons why I believe that though nineteenth-century Mormon polygamy was revealed to Joseph Smith from God, it was for mortal purposes and not to be practiced in heaven.

Though speculative and to some minds deeply subversive, England's position was not entirely without historical support. Even during its practice, the perception—and comparison—of polygamy as a temporary purgatory was apparently prevalent enough among Utah women that Heber C. Kimball tried to squelch it. "The principle of plurality of wives never will be done away although some sisters have had revelations that, when this time passes away and they go through the veil, every woman will have a husband to herself."[57] But the protests were legion: "In obeying this law it has cost [us] a sacrifice nearly equal to that of Abraham. . . . There is nothing that would induce me to . . . lose my hold upon that crown which awaits all those who have laid their willing but bleeding hearts upon the altar," said one plural wife.[58] Young's second wife, Mary Ann, concurred: "God will be very cruel if he does not give us poor women adequate compensation for the trials we have endured in polygamy."[59] Lorena Bent found nothing to praise in a "principle which had caused so much sacrifice, heartache, and trial."[60]

Heavenly continuation of those trials would hardly constitute compensation. But England was swimming against a long historical current. Following polygamy's demise at the turn of the century, the status of the principle entered a theological limbo. Probably reflecting the uncertainty of thousands, a member queried the First Presidency in 1912, "Is plural or celestial marriage essential to a fulness of glory in the world to come?" He was answered that "celestial marriage is essential to a fulness of glory in the world to come, as explained in the revelation concerning it; but it is not stated that plural marriage is thus essential."[61] The statement was far from a repudiation of the eternal validity of multiple temple sealings to a man.

Latter-day Saint discourse at times invoked the logic of a "higher law" behind polygamy, and the human need to overcome "selfishness." But the decades-long acknowledgment of the principle's difficulty, the pervasive, wrenching heartache it engendered, its consistent practice by only a minority, the practice's incompatibility with contemporary expressions of companionate marriage, and a dominant view of polygamy as a trial not a blessing all make polygamy's eternal perpetuation undesirable if not unlikely to most Latter-day Saints (with the possible exception of those involved in remarriage after the death of a spouse).

Only in very recent times has the church come to a position that approaches England's view that the practice was a temporary diversion from an otherwise immutable law. An official press statement proclaims that "the standard doctrine of the Church is monogamy, as it always has been, as indicated in the Book of Mormon (Jacob, chapter 2)." In the spring of 2013, the church elevated that position to the status of virtual scripture, introducing the canonized manifesto ending plural marriage with a new introduction that uses similar language: "Monogamy is God's standard for marriage unless He declares otherwise."[62] Even so, the statement does not declare polygamy a nonfactor in the eternities.

But this was 1990, and England was declaring doctrine when no statement on the status of polygamy as God's higher law had been issued since the abandonment of the practice a century ago. No one of note was prepared to defend racism, but plenty of traditionally oriented Latter-day Saints were prepared to defend polygamy's celestial status, especially given the church's unwillingness to pronounce specifically on that question. England, of course, was unaware of the exact motive behind the meeting on 12 October 1990 and did not even know if these apostles had read his "Are All Alike" article. He would soon learn that they had indeed. He had experienced years of tense interactions over his public pronouncements and activities, but this was different. This was the only time he had been directed to appear to defend his writings before the apostles. And the strength of their reaction to his article took him off guard. "I felt like they were my antagonists in some way. . . . Like I was part of the enemy. . . . I had never felt that way before."[63]

The apostles expressed apprehension that England's portrayal of Young and McConkie would tend to undermine faith in the church leadership. In some alarm, England sensed that he no longer had the support of either apostle, with both of them mentioning concern over the appearance of a church-sponsored "platform"—that is, his position at BYU—for England's controversial teachings.[64] He was chastised and cautioned "not to write on 'speculative' subjects like polygamy or material that could seem to undermine the authority of church leaders."[65]

He took the chastisement meekly and remarked afterward to his son, "I am always willing to give them the benefit of the doubt. I really believe they are called of God and that they are apostles. I still say maybe they know something I don't know."[66] In his journal, he continued to refer to both men as his "heroes."[67] (His daughter remembered that "never, never in my entire life, even in intimate discussions, did I ever hear him say a single unkind, critical, or derogatory remark about any Church leader—or any person.")[68] At the same time, England could not desist from defending his motives, if not his methods. A letter he wrote the apostles in response to their meeting is one of the most concrete and frank illustrations of the seismic strains England was trying to bridge: institutional reluctance to acknowledge the limitations of an authoritarian church culture colliding with intellectual ferment, historical revisionism, and the new information age.

He begins with contrition: "I have thought much about your concerns and counsel, and I believe they will help me better fulfill the vocation I feel from the Lord to write and teach in ways that will convey love and integrity and help build faith and strength in the kingdom. I have already been able to make a few 'course corrections.'"[69] But when he turns to the core of the issue, it was the same as in the Bruce McConkie episode exactly one decade earlier: Members of the church were increasingly aware of prophetic inconsistencies in the historical record but were called to operate in an environment of effectual infallibility. In 1980, Bruce R. McConkie had refused to engage England about this collision of competing narratives, opting instead to invoke his apostolic authority to pronounce doctrine, ignoring the larger historical reality and competing apostolic voices with which rank-and-file members had to contend. In his role as a teacher, a scholar, and an apologist, England insisted, he could not avoid his responsibility to wrestle with such conflicts.

In England's motives and analysis, with the benefit of hindsight, we find a striking prescience vindicated in subsequent years. Only in 2016, with the church finding its growth in the Northern Hemisphere stymied and disaffection increasing, did the church issue a statement that emphatically signaled a new directive for a new age. The Clark talk of the 1930s, which emphasized the discontinuity of secular and religious training, and insisted church educators not concern themselves with their interrelation, was inadequate and inappropriate to a church in the midst of the information revolution. Senior apostle Russell Ballard, recognizing that a new church pedagogy was necessary to a spiritually healthy and resilient membership, enunciated a radically new ethos. Signaling a self-conscious shift in response to historical developments, he said, "As Church education moves forward in the 21st century, each of you needs to consider any changes you should make in the way you prepare to teach, how you teach, and what you teach."[70] More specifically, "It was only a generation ago that our young people's access to information about our history, doctrine, and practices was basically limited to materials printed by the

Church. Few students came in contact with alternative interpretations. Mostly, our young people lived a sheltered life. Our curriculum at that time, though well-meaning, did not prepare students for today—a day when students have instant access to virtually everything about the Church from every possible point of view."

Ballard continued, "Gone are the days when a student asked an honest question and a teacher responded, 'Don't worry about it!' Gone are the days when a student raised a sincere concern and a teacher bore his or her testimony as a response intended to avoid the issue." Then, directly countering the anti-intellectual attacks and controversy-avoidance of the 1980s, he recast brutally honest scholars—of the type England was—as assets rather than challengers of the faith. "If necessary, we should ask those with appropriate academic training, experience, and expertise for help. . . . Inoculate your students by providing faithful, thoughtful, and accurate interpretation of gospel doctrine, the scriptures, our history, and those topics that are sometimes misunderstood. To name a few such topics that are less known or controversial, I'm talking about polygamy, seer stones, different accounts of the First Vision, the process of translation of the Book of Mormon or the Book of Abraham, gender issues, race and the priesthood, or a Heavenly Mother." "Gospel transparency" and "spiritual inoculation" are the "best antidote," he summarized, encouraging teachers to "study . . . the best LDS scholarship available," describing almost precisely the strategy that had cost England the goodwill of the leadership.

Ballard's talk was, though muted, a partial validation of England's harsh indictment years earlier when he wrote to a friend that since Lowell Bennion's firing the CES had experienced "a general decline into a focus on 'pure doctrine,' obedience, proof-texting, piety, a conservatism purged of its traditional moral rigor and example and an anti-intellectualism cloaked in mechanical scholasticism and a 'CD-Rom theology'. . . . There are no longer course[s] open to the questioning needs of individual students struggling to unite faith and reason."[71] England's protest was practical and personal, not theoretical. As he defended himself to Maxwell and Oaks almost three decades before Ballard's revision of the Clark mandate, "I often deal with sincere, troubled young people who believe they see contradictions among statements or teachings of Church authorities. . . . Many seem to have been taught that unless they change their minds and believe each new thing as they hear it from authority, they are not worthy members. So they think they have to either violate their integrity or throw the Church over entirely. I suggest that they make a distinction between, on the one hand, Church policies and official statements of doctrine that . . . they must obey or at least accept as binding, . . . and, on the other, regular teachings of Church authorities that they are to take very seriously. . . . But I suggest that the latter category is not *binding* upon them." He was trying to create a larger space for spiritual independence, by narrowing the domain of orthodoxy. He had been making this same argument for years. As he had earlier pleaded with a colleague, "Why must we assume that *all* teaching must be declaration of the absolute, inspired truth? Is there no room at a university for sincere, thoughtful exploration of possibilities?"[72]

England records no reply to this plea. Meanwhile, his exclusion from the encyclopedia project was to have devastating consequences for a personal friend. Bob Rees wrote a letter declining to have his name associated with the encyclopedia in protest at the blackballing of England. When the name of Rees himself was later forwarded to the board of trustees with a recommendation to hire, Neal Maxwell mentioned his letter by way of background on the candidate. In response, the committee decided, "We'll turn him down, then."[73]

That England received no direct reply is not to say that authoritative voices weren't continuing to tell him—or scholars in general—that they were undermining rather than edifying Zion. In February 1991, Boyd K. Packer gave the devotional address at Brigham Young University, "I Say unto You, Be One." The theme was a restatement of his earlier chastisement of academics titled "The Mantle Is Far, Far Greater than the Intellect." On this occasion, he addressed those in the academic community who felt the Latter-day Saint leadership "may not understand the mysteries of the world of academia and therefore are not fully qualified to set policy, standards, and direction for a university."[74] However, he said echoing words of a decade earlier, "Theirs, and theirs alone, is the right to establish policies and set standards under which administrators, faculties, and students are to function—standards of both conduct and of excellence." And their underlying philosophy of education, he concluded, was comprised in two sentences: Don't even teach "the alphabet or the multiplication tables without the Spirit of God," and "seek learning, even by study and also by faith."[75]

In response, England wrote Packer what he thought was a note of appreciation for the talk but received in reply a thinly veiled rebuke—which in all likelihood he did not take as directed at himself. "One thing that has puzzled me over the years," Packer responded, "has been the willingness of some few individuals to accept salaries that are drawn from the tithes and yet . . . remain as persistent echoes and supporters of the voices of those who carry the spirit of criticism rather than sustaining and of common unity. . . . If one's values are different from those for which the University has been founded surely there is a place where the values of an employer will match their own." Ostensibly,

Packer was responding to England's expressed surprise that "there were some who questioned the right of the Board to give direction." But given events preceding this exchange and England's dismissal a few years later, it would appear that Packer was firing a none-too-subtle shot across the bow.[76]

One catalyst behind Packer's pointed remarks to England was a communication Packer had received just months earlier from Richard Cracroft, then president of the group England had helped found—the Association for Mormon Letters. England had contributed his latest installment to the adumbration of a Mormon literature by publishing an anthology of Latter-day Saint poetry in 1989, *Harvest: Contemporary Mormon Poems*. Cracroft, we saw, had actually produced the first anthology of Mormon literature in 1974 with *A Believing People; Literature of the Latter-Day Saints*. And Cracroft clearly did not see England as sharing in his vision of just what a Mormon literature should look like, as he made clear in a 1990 review of England's new anthology. Cracroft found much to praise but lamented the paucity of "that distinctively Latter-day Saint voice, the sensibility of the believing poet."[77] He assumes that absence is attributable to England's coeditor Dennis Clark rather than England himself, but the condemnation is stark: "The poems . . . seem to spring less from the spiritual and mythic roots of Mormonism than from the self-fascination of much contemporary poetry."[78] And so the battle was joined.

England had been driven by his recognition of the raw authenticity of the early Saints' distinctive voice, and his efforts to win legitimacy for a Mormon literature were rooted in his respect for a human saga couched in unadorned simplicity and freighted with sacralizing sacrifice. No one would impute technical proficiency to the pioneer materials out of which England hoped to construct the foundations of a Mormon canon. But Cracroft and others believed that in his poetry anthology he was being suborned by the standards of modernity, and about to make a devil's bargain—winning plaudits from the secular academy but losing Mormonism's soul. For Cracroft, the soul-struggle was between secularism and discipleship, the sexy allure of Babylon with its vapid values confronting the solid if technically safe expression of the good, the true, and the beautiful. For England, the choice was rather between authentic if edgy art and a stultifying cultural conformity. Cracroft's attack deeply hurt England, who saw himself as embodying the precise model of Christian self-sacrifice that Cracroft failed to see. As England would later write, "[Our relationship with] . . . God the Father and Mother, [and] the community of Saints . . . require that we curb our radical egotism in obedience and self-sacrifice, even at the cost of what seems our precious integrity."[79]

England's colleague and friend Bruce Jorgenson fired back at Cracroft, defending England's enterprise while questioning the very existence of an essential Mormon identity to be reflected in the tradition's literature. Cracroft had recently replaced Jorgenson as the new president of the AML, and he used his presidential address to make a more prolonged argument than he had in his review. Borrowing terms from Latter-day Saint scholar Hugh Nibley, Cracroft replaced Boyd Packer's dichotomy of the mantle and the intellect with the similar "mantic" and "sophic" distinction (evoking a contrast between the prophetic "mantle" and the worldly "sophist"). The sophic poems in England's collection were marked by an "earth-bound humanism," he lamented, were "mislabeled Mormon," and lacked the Mormon "essence." Mantic Mormon literature, by contrast, was infused with "ethereal but real, ineffable but inevitable spiritual analogues and correspondences that convey Mormon realities, and without . . . which no literature could be essentially Mormon."[80] These sentiments were a clear echo of Orson Whitney's nineteenth-century call for a uniquely Mormon literature: "It is from the warp and woof of all learning, so far as we are able to master it and make it ours, that the fabric of our literature must be woven. . . . [But] above all things, we must be original. The Holy Ghost is the genius of 'Mormon' literature. . . . No pouring of old wine into new bottles. No patterning after the dead forms of antiquity. Our literature must live and breathe for itself. Our mission is diverse from all others; our literature must also be."[81]

More specifically, Cracroft faulted England for espousing a hollowed-out version of Latter-day Saint "orthodoxy." England, he complained, equated the LDS sensibility with a commitment to "the optimistic view of life, to faith in Christ and his Atonement, . . . to a liberal concept of the nature of humans and of God and to a conservative moral life." As Cracroft rightly remarked, "Such a definition . . . makes no differentiation between Christian and Mormon."

More effectively, perhaps, Cracroft drew attention to England's lavish praise of a celebrated and reviled passage in a Levi Peterson novel, a character's "culminating, deus ex-machina vision that comes as he zips up his pants before a flushing urinal in which he suddenly sees an aw-shucks Cowboy Jesus who straightens Frank out by dispensing, while rolling and smoking a Bull Durham cigarette, homely counsel about Frank's sexual hangups, his guilty sensual indulgences with his wife, and his longstanding quarrel with a vindictive, . . . God."[82] As secular art it succeeds, opines Cracroft, but it is at the same time a "profanation of Christ," portrays a "grotesque God," and reflects a "quasi-Calvinistic—but decidedly not LDS—theology."

England resented what he saw as a "vehement—not to say vicious" attack.

He clearly believed that the real controversy was about prudery, not morality or Mormonness. For few scholars had shown more concern with the morally edifying power of literature than England; his whole Shakespearean scholarship was witness to that fact, and he had himself lamented to a friend "what has happened to our profession—apparent loss of moral concern in preoccupation with theoretical frameworks and jargon."[83] But more hurtful and consequential than the personal affront was what Cracroft later related to England. Cracroft had sent a letter to Boyd Packer and included a copy of his AML address, both to distance himself from the likes of Levi Peterson (and, of course, by implication his admirers like England) and "to show how passionately he was advocating a faithful and moral Mormon literature and criticism." Packer wrote back to Cracroft, praising his actions and clarifications, "because [Packer] *was* very concerned about what was happening in the English department." In his note to England, Cracroft then added, with pathetic understatement, "I probably didn't do you any good with Elder Packer."[84]

On other fronts, England was also finding himself mired in bitter conflicts. He spoke and wrote repeatedly in opposition to the Gulf War (August 1990– February 1991). In response to one such article,[85] a member of the religion faculty, Kelly Ogden, wrote a vehement counterattack, explaining why some might view antiwar voices as "traitorous" (the word was England's).[86] England fired off a letter of complaint to the faculty council, alleging that Ogden's assault on dissent in a time of conflict was an assault on academic freedom itself. The council rejected England's complaint as unjustified: "You got mugged in an editorial," their representative from the religion faculty Stephen Robinson responded. "You are too quick to identify your views with the side of the angels and academic right."[87] Robinson's criticisms were largely on target. England's editorial had criticized rationales for the Gulf War, and then to the faculty council he condemned his silent colleagues as guilty of "moral cowardice and dereliction of their academic duty." Ogden had only accused England of "pessimism" and scriptural cherry-picking. Apparently, Robinson chastised, "You want the freedom to tweak the nose of the majority with vigor and with passion whenever you feel the urge (and you feel the urge quite often), but at the same time you demand protection from any vigorous or impassioned response from the majority."[88]

To the first issue, England replied that his point was not technical or legalistic; rather, his concern was that "the use of religious sources by a religious authority to brand dissent improper is unusually effective in discouraging expression of dissenting viewpoints among students and young faculty—and thus doubly dangerous."[89] To the second, England could only react with hurt. "I was disappointed that you could not sense more accurately my pain." As he had vowed so often before, "Staying out of the arena for a while may be the answer."[90] That, of course, was hardly possible.

THE SYMPOSIA STATEMENT

> You can convey . . . your slightly slant, wryly intelligent and realistic view of
> the Church and the culture without putting anyone's teeth on edge (Do you
> detect envy here?).—England to Jeffrey Holland, 18 January 2000

The principle of academic freedom and the prerogatives of religious oversight were on a collision course that culminated at BYU in 1991, as simultaneous declarations emerged on both sides of these twin imperatives. England was, of course, at the center of this storm. By disposition, he placed intellectual freedom at the center of his whole system of ethics—a freedom he thought was well exemplified in his hero Joseph Smith. ("I want the liberty of thinking and believing as I please. It feels so good not to be trammeled.")[91] And, of course, the journal he cofounded as well as the later *Sunstone* were the venues in which the free expression of Latter-day Saint scholars—especially those employed by BYU—was increasingly stymied by the leadership. England had learned in 1986 that "administrators are advised not to publish in *Dialogue* . . . or to participate in *Sunstone*'s symposia."[92] That fact compounded what England saw as an almost simultaneous attack on academic freedom: BYU's refusal to allow the campus distribution of the independent *Student Review*, founded that same year. (An even earlier independent, *Seventh East Press*, had folded in 1983 when administrators banned its campus distribution.) England now took his dismay public, publishing an op-ed in the official BYU paper, the *Daily Universe*, in 1989. While acknowledging reasonable limits on expression at a church college, he criticized "prior restraint and guilt by association [as] serious violations of the freedoms championed in the Constitution and [as being] particularly rejected in the tradition of free academic inquiry at universities."[93]

His hope for more "open discussion, by faculty and students, of this crucial issue" found little support. In 1991, a BYU committee began drafting a Statement on Academic Freedom; that was also the year that the First Presidency issued a statement that clarified certain limits on academic expression. In 1989, Dallin H. Oaks, the onetime law professor and BYU president who was now an apostle, had given a talk called "Alternate Voices" at the church's semiannual General Conference. Among the voices Oaks warned about were the ones "heard in magazines, journals, and newspapers and at lectures, symposia, and conferences."[94] At the same General Conference, Elder Russell M. Nelson said that a true "stalwart" of the church "would not lend his or her good name to periodicals, programs, or forums that feature offenders who do sow 'discord among brethren.'"[95] The allusions were clear to Latter-day Saints: Sunstone was the only organization of note holding regular public symposia that became forums for critics and dissenters as well as faithful scholars and researchers.

Presentations at their symposia continued to concern some in the leadership. Concern turned to alarm by 1991. That year, presentations included "Goals and the Temple Endowment," "Parting the Corporate Veil . . . of Church Finances," and perhaps most threateningly, "Child Sexual Abuse in the LDS Community." In the latter case, the abstract described the church as promoting "comprehensive youth programs and a reverence for authority which gives perpetrators of sexual crimes unique access to fresh victims."[96] Weeks after the August Sunstone Symposium, the First Presidency, together with the Quorum of the Twelve Apostles, took the unusual step of issuing a joint statement in response to these symposia, which was published in the *Deseret News* (August 23) and the next month in the church's official magazine. While acknowledging that not all presentations were objectionable and that some speakers were actually there to defend the church or its programs and teachings, the leadership nonetheless sent a clear message of disapprobation of members who chose to participate. Two types of presentations were held out as particularly objectionable. The first was "public discussions of things we hold sacred," such as topics "relating to the House of the Lord, the holy temples." The second, more cryptic, category included "matters that were seized upon and publicized in such a way as to injure the Church or its members or to jeopardize the effectiveness or safety of our missionaries. . . . There are times when it is better to have the Church without representation," the statement concluded, "than to have implications of Church participation used to promote a program that contains some (though admittedly not all) presentations that result in ridiculing sacred things or injuring The Church of Jesus Christ, detracting from its mission, or jeopardizing the well-being of its members."[97]

The reaction from the liberal wing of the church was immediate and furious. Even the universally admired, saintly Lowell Bennion declared, "It is a poor religion that can't stand the test of thinking." At least two individuals who wrote letters of protest to the First Presidency were called in for worthiness interviews by local leadership.[98] Earlier symposia had featured some of the church's most highly respected—and unquestionably orthodox—figures, including Church Historian Leonard Arrington, leading apologist and polyglot

Hugh Nibley, future BYU president Rex Lee, and the chair of BYU's Department of Ancient Scripture.[99] Nevertheless, the symposia statement seemed unequivocal in directing even the faithful to refrain from attending forums where presentations could be subversive of the faith.

England had convinced himself that the statement did not implicitly forbid BYU faculty from attending the symposia, and he had written a letter to the BYU newspaper to that effect. Weeks later, he was called into the office of Provost Bruce Hafen. There, he learned that the statement had, indeed, been intended to dissuade BYU faculty from attending Sunstone symposia, but without explicitly saying so. As England perceived the situation, "They want to restrict freedom without having to pay a political price for it."[100] The deliberate ambiguity of the statement incensed England, who had made academic freedom a leading plank in the platform of his irrepressible activism. His protests against the war and racism had been transmuted, at BYU, into a dogged battle for academic freedom that was part of his holistic concern for dialogue and dignity alike. Looking back on the era of his Vietnam radicalism, he explained, "It's really important to break through the absolutism of power and realize that anytime you make anything into an absolute government or church, that is a form of idolatry. The natural tendency of human organizations is to move in that direction. It takes really active opposition from within to stop it. Openness and freedom for all points of view [are imperative]. If anything in our society represents that, I think the university does. That's one of the reasons I guess I get so upset at the infringements of academic freedom at BYU."[101]

Meanwhile the pattern initiated in Palo Alto of resistance to his public provocations continued. Even as he attracted admiring readers and students, he garnered back-channel complaints. "I can't quite figure out why they released me from the Gospel Doctrine Class," he mused, even as he answered his own question: "apparently because someone complained about my unorthodox ideas, especially against the Gulf War and in favor of stopping [school] prayer."[102] England was hugely popular with students; he had a good number of detractors among them as well who did not appreciate what they saw as an opinionated liberal undermining church orthodoxy. "Not afraid to tell us his opinions"; "had a good secular viewpoint"; "seems to make up his own doctrine"; "set in his opinions and lets us know it"; "he thinks that the official church viewpoint is wrong."[103] Such criticisms are sprinkled throughout his student evaluations. Although a minority among his students, such unhappy voices would have registered with administrators, especially given England's fraught history. Another index of conflict between his worldviews and those of the dominant Latter-day Saint culture came that same year. As Packer and his colleagues were trying to unite Zion, England chided his colleagues for their "monoculturalism," distributing to faculty a Barbara Ehrenreich editorial on the subject. "I would have thought that Mormons, who have been among those victimized by monocultural prejudice," would be "especially empathetic" to the multiculturalism Ehrenreich defended, he added in his own note.[104]

Months later, and shortly before returning home from another study abroad in London, England had a conversation with Jeffrey Holland—previously England's university president and now a General Authority Seventy. He confided to Holland his fear "that perhaps my usefulness at the Y had ended, given what seemed increasing anxiety, even hostility, from church and university leaders over the past two years." Holland offered to look into England's concerns, adding, "It troubles me that someone as ingenuous as you, without, it seems, any hidden agenda or animosity and as honest and faithful in your writings, arouses any anxiety in the Brethren.'"[105] Weeks later, reason for such anxiety would be all too clear to everyone.

11

J'ACCUSE!

BEGINNING OF THE END

Mark: Do you think he opposes the church?
Dora: I don't think he does but he gives that attitude.
Mark: Yes, but even so there are certain leaders who may think that . . .
Dora: He should keep still and keep on the side.
—England's son and mother, undated interview with Mark England

A year after the Symposia Statement, its impact was greater pushback than compliance. Fifteen hundred participants showed up to the next session, from BYU professors willing to dare the symposia denunciation to independent scholars and dissidents. Most impactful by far at this August 1992 meeting was the presentation by former *Ensign* editor Lavina Fielding Anderson. Anderson was one of the trustees of the Mormon Alliance, founded the month before "to identify and document ecclesiastical/spiritual abuse in the Church of Jesus Christ of Latter-day Saints."[1]

At the symposium her paper, "A Dialogue toward Forgiveness: A Chronological History of the Intellectual Community and Church Leadership," combined the language of rapprochement and meekness with expressions of outrage and indignation. (She had delivered a version months earlier in Washington, D.C., but it passed largely under the radar.) In her "dialogue toward forgiveness," Anderson declared she was performing the role of "witness, not a judge," and set out to view the landscape with "more charity" than she had in previous decades. But those sentiments did not dampen her denunciations of "an abusive church," its "scapegoating" of independent voices and "blacklisting" of troublesome figures. Her talk was largely a systematic catalog of the intimidation, silencing, and church disciplining of feminists and intellectuals from 1945 to the moment of her 1992 speech. The bombshell accusation, however, was her revelation in her talk's closing moments of "an internal espionage system that creates and maintains secret files on members of the church."[2]

England had not planned to attend Sunstone. After his most recent meeting with BYU provost Bruce Hafen, he was told his "doing so would be an act of defiance to him, which I wasn't quite ready to do." His son Mark found Gene's name missing from the advance program, which provoked a heated exchange with his father, the son feeling his father was being intimidated.[3] But what likely changed England's mind was his meeting at that time with BYU's out-going academic vice president, Stan Albrecht. In that encounter, he related, "I learned from him that one reason he had resigned was his difficulty carrying out university business because of complaints from BYU religion faculty about other faculty members' writings, made to the Strengthening Church Members Committee, which seemed to him to be an ad hoc middle-management committee that kept files on the writing and activities of certain Church members. I began to think about friends who had been called in to discuss their writing or had actually seen their own file, in one case containing press clippings on their activities as a Young Democrat in college, and my anxiety and pain increased."[4]

England had therefore been primed for Anderson's protest, and needed only this spark to explode. When Anderson added more names to the list of those injured, he lashed out in a fully human urge, in his words, "to punish those who had hurt people I loved."[5] First to rise in dramatic outrage at the talk's conclusion, pointing his finger and borrowing from "J'accuse!," Émile Zola's open letter during the Dreyfus Affair, he rose to his feet, identified the committee responsible for monitoring dissident activity—the Strengthening Church Members Committee—and stabbing the air with his finger declared in a fury, "I accuse that committee of undermining our Church." It is, he said, "an ad hoc Church group without General Authority standing but apparently great influence, headed by one William Nelson."[6]

In Lavina Anderson's account, "Associated Press bureau chief Vern Anderson (no relation), who was sitting at the end of a row at the south end of the hall, quietly stood up and walked into the lobby. The next day, Saturday, 8 August 1992, an AP story under Anderson's byline appeared. It quoted church spokesman Don LeFevre's acknowledgment that such a committee "provides local church leadership with information designed to help them counsel with members who may hinder the progress of the church through public criticism."[7]

Lavina Anderson's publication of her exposé factored into her excommunication months later. For England, the repercussions of his very public and

made-for-media denunciation forged yet more links in the chain of events leading to his ouster from BYU and alienation from the church leadership. Days
after the outburst, the *New York Times* reported on the bombshell exposure
of the committee in an article titled "Secret Files."[8] What turned the explosive episode into personal catastrophe was the surprising revelation of who
comprised the secret committee: two apostles, James E. Faust and Russell M.
Nelson. England was mortified now at what he had done. In contravention
of his personal moral code, as well as the terms of his BYU contract, he had
engaged in a highly public attack on the leadership of the church. This was the
beginning of the end for England.

In a telling admission to his son, England confided that "the Lord tried to
warn me" in advance of my outburst. "I had this kind of feeling maybe I should
keep quiet. . . . But of course I never pay attention to those," he said, with wry
self-reproach.[9] He was gradually coming to realize a sad truth about himself. As
he acknowledged to his colleagues in the aftermath of a departmental conflict
in this same era, "I might have seemed to be taking sides on certain ethical
and political questions and thus deepening divisions rather than helping to
bring peace."[10] Richard Bushman had warned him of just such dangers to his
approach just months earlier. "In [your] healing essay you lament adversarial
escalation and the divisions that rend our communion. In the Nibley essay you
seem to foster those very divisions. You use Nibley to attack wealth, putting
everyone who pursues money in Babylon and the others, presumably people
like you and me, in Zion."[11]

In the present Sunstone fiasco, he immediately wrote a letter to Elder Faust
and Elder Nelson apologizing. At the same time, he felt compelled to attest to
the personal harm that such behind-the-scenes investigations inflicted on their
subjects. "It breaks my heart to think that I and these devout members I know
that have been called in, apparently on private reports from your committee,
are seen as enemies, to be compared to those who raped and murdered the
Missouri Saints."[12]

He also drafted a letter to Maxwell, but it displayed little contrition: "The
anger which led to my outburst is not directed at the Church or its appointed
leaders. I am completely loyal to the Church and would rather die than impede its righteous work." Nevertheless, he said of the apostle-led committee,
"If what I have learned is even mostly true, then the activities in question are
not the Church. In fact, they terribly undermine the Church."[13] At the urging of
Rex Lee, to whom he showed his draft, he struck the passage and instead copied Maxwell and Oaks on his revised apology to the two committee members.
Oaks chose not to reply, but Maxwell, having a longer history with England,

did. A private apology was a good start, he noted to the repentant England, but a public attack warranted public contrition. He said, "What happened was regrettable. Your concern is commendable. It would be admirable if, in some way, you could set the record straight publicly as you have done privately."[14] Faust and Nelson responded to the same effect: "Because of publicity given to quotations attributed to you by the media, there may be a public perception of your contention with General Authorities which may differ, in fact, from your private expression to the Brethren. You may wish to consider how you could correct this perception."[15] England perceived in these responses a clear message: "They had gotten to a point that they were not going to put up with that stuff anymore."[16] Exacerbating his position with BYU was the fact that he had promised Hafen that he would not present at Sunstone anymore. The televised shots of his comments gave the impression that he was a featured panelist. And in any event, the leadership had made clear that *any* participation in Sunstone was anathema.

In predictable fashion, with what had now become a pattern, England attempted to compensate with the same energy that had gotten him into trouble to start with. He apologized to members of his ward in the monthly testimony meeting. He apologized to his colleagues in the English department at BYU (tactlessly using the occasion to complain that "I have been stereotyped by some colleagues as a 'liberal.' This hurts me.").[17] He wrote a letter to *Sunstone* and apologized to the organization. He wrote to Hafen, whom he had promised personally he would not speak at further Sunstone conferences. After explaining his misidentification in news reports as a speaker, he made his situation worse by intensifying rather than repenting of his criticism.

On the one hand, he wanted to insist to himself and others that he would not have publicly criticized the committee had he known it was composed of two apostles. On the other hand, he indicated to Hafen that such knowledge would have changed little: "Let me tell you, on reflection, what I wish I had said: 'I have recently learned of the existence of a committee at Church head-quarters called the Strengthening Members Committee. . . . One of its functions seems to be to scan newspapers, periodicals, etc. for materials by and about Church members that make those members dangerous . . . and to report those members' names . . . to other Church groups . . . for action against those members.'" With escalating vehemence, he concluded "I am outraged, . . . I am devastated . . . and well aware of how similar such actions are to what we have condemned in the Catholic Inquisition and modern dictatorships." Then, with guileless honesty, he added, "Well, that wasn't exactly temperate either, I guess.

Sorry."[18] England sent a copy to BYU president Rex Lee and intended to send a copy to president of the Quorum of the Twelve Apostles, Howard Hunter, but Lee dissuaded him from that impolitic move.[19]

Following this secondary explosion, England did in fact continue a series of public apologies: in sacrament meetings, in departmental memos, in his public speaking and writing. By the next year, his persistent apologies were noted—and becoming awkward. In April, the two apostles sent him a note: "Could we suggest that, so far as we are concerned, there is no need for you to make further expressions of public apology."[20]

Repentant but undeterred, England continued to advocate on a wide range of issues. Even as he was publicly denouncing the Strengthening Church Members Committee, he was privately encouraging the leadership to reverse course on the politics of public prayer. In August 1992, he had written to Dallin Oaks, who had testified before Congress on the subject of religious freedom. England criticized the practice of public prayer and even suggested that Latter-day Saints in Utah, "as the dominant religion," might voluntarily exercise a moratorium on the practice "as an act of mercy" toward those of minority faiths. "I've wondered if we need to be more sensitive to that in Utah," he urged.[21] Oaks responded politely but firmly. "The considerations pertaining to public prayer outlined in your letter have been discussed in our circles many times in the last several years. . . . The course we are following is the course we felt impressed to follow, and we are united in it."[22]

As England became more frustrated by his conflicts with BYU administration, which was itself indissolubly linked to and at times indistinguishable from church headquarters, he began to lose his equanimity. Learning of the blackballing of Robert Rees for presuming to protest England's treatment, he despaired, "This is all so devastating because it comes at the climax of two years of increasing difficulty of this strange, sickening, Kafkaesque kind. I thought that as author of 'Why the Church Is As True As the Gospel,' that I was relatively immune to the challenge of all this. But it seems now so concentrated, irrational, continuing, and ultimately devastating to the Church I love and believe is true that I'm beset with self-doubt. . . . Where is God in all of this?"[23] Four days later, England was pricked by guilt at his own felt disloyalty: "That last comment was somewhat extreme," he noted in his diary.

At BYU the conflicts over the limits of academic freedom intensified. In late 1992, the university's board of trustees had vetoed without comment the invitation of Pulitzer Prize winner and Harvard historian Laurel Thatcher Ulrich. She had been slotted to speak at a campus women's conference. In

September 1992, a faculty committee released its final draft of an academic freedom statement, which was accepted by the faculty and the board of trustees. The document conceded that limitations on faculty speech were reasonable "when the faculty behavior or expression *seriously and adversely* affects the University mission or the Church." Trying to thread the needle, the writers offered as an example of such speech any that "contradicts or opposes, rather than analyzes or discusses, fundamental Church doctrine or policy."[24]

Many faculty members were happy with the final product; reservations came from precisely those quarters where conflicts had arisen in the past: the social sciences and the humanities, two domains where Mormon studies was finding a growing number of practitioners. Packer replied to such critics the next month in a General Conference address: "For those very few whose focus is secular and who feel restrained as students or as teachers . . . there are over 3,500 colleges and universities where they may find the kind of freedom they value."[25] The next week, counselor in the First Presidency and chair of the board of trustees Gordon B. Hinckley struck a more conciliatory tone: "You have the trust and confidence of the governing board. I am confident that never in the history of this institution has there been a faculty . . . more loyal and dedicated to the standards of its sponsoring institution." At the same time, he added, "Every one of us who is here has accepted a sacred and compelling trust. With that trust, there must be accountability."[26]

LOW STAKES AND HOT TEMPERS: ENGLISH DEPARTMENT TURMOIL

Don't jump, Neal. It isn't high enough.—Faculty member seeing the newly
appointed English department chair looking out his window

And exactly what *was* happening in England's BYU English department that heightened Packer's concern? "Academic politics is so vicious because the stakes are so low," reputedly opined Henry Kissinger, and never were those words more applicable than to American English departments of the 1980s and early 1990s. Since midcentury, English departments were largely bastions of an unchallenged formalism, also known as New Criticism (whose most influential exponent was perhaps the Latter-day Saint scholar-critic Wayne Booth). New Criticism emphasized poetry as a self-contained, formal structure, whose aesthetic value was disconnected from reference to any external consideration. By the 1970s, this approach was under assault for its indifference to literature's

freighted but unacknowledged ideological agendas. Enter the "hermeneu-
tics of suspicion," a whole gamut of critical approaches (like those of Freud,
Nietzsche, and Marx) that sought more potent meanings concealed beneath
aesthetic trappings.

By the 1980s, English departments were riven by competing ideological
partisans of feminist, Marxist, and Freudian varieties, along with a number of
esoteric approaches that were to literary criticism what quantum mechanics
was to physics: beyond the comprehension of many scholars and certainly most
students. Deconstruction was foremost in the list, but it was taught alongside
phenomenological, structuralist, New Historical, queer, and soon postcolonial
and other schools of theory. As literature became of less interest than new and
esoteric ways of politicizing its study, the discipline entered into steep decline
in American higher education. The Sokol scandal, a famous hoax that resulted
in the publication of a caricature submitted as real scholarship, hurt the credibility of "cultural studies," as did the public defection of leading critical practitioner Frank Lentricchia.[27]

Whether Jane Austen should be read through the prism of a feminist consciousness that challenges patriarchal power structures and the oppressiveness
of the male gaze, or through a Marxist lens that reveals the implicit condoning
of a corrupt capitalist morality in which the aristocracy instrumentalize the
petty bourgeoisie, or via a poststructuralist deconstruction of any stable meaning at the story's core, does indeed seem to be a debate for intellectual elites
with little bearing on the real world of life, labor, and love. At a university run
by the Latter-day Saint church, however, where feminism was seen as an assault on normative family structures and roles, and Marxism was considered
a threat to democratic values and moral absolutes, the Kissinger quotation is
particularly inapt. The problem was not just differing approaches to literature
but attacks on the very value of literature as traditionally understood and of the
role of the teacher as an agent of the transmission of culture rather than radical
critic of such culture. As one professor noted, "In the post-modern world, some
of those working within literature are using literature as an instrument to try
to affect social change. . . . In the new era, once literature becomes politics,
then politics is a matter of contention rather than consensus."[28]

The stakes of such academic debates at BYU were very high indeed. The
growing cleavage in the 1980s between the Latter-day Saint faith and post-
modern secularity was fully enacted in microcosm in BYU's own Department
of English—to the intense concern of its apostle-laden board of trustees. The
most contentious conflicts were those between the old school traditionalists

and the young scholars emerging from graduate programs where poststruc-
turalism was the new governing paradigm for all cultural study, and feminist
theory was front and center.

Pressure to participate in the emerging schools of theory was coming from
departmental recognition that, in England's words, "our students were not
being prepared well to study in the good graduate schools, where the new literary theories had taken firm hold." As a consequence, he explained to apostle
Jeffrey Holland, the department chair Bert Wilson "felt we needed to hire
people trained in the new post-modernisms, including feminism and multiculturalism, and got permission from the administration to do so."[29]

MORMONISM'S CONFLICTED FEMINISM

One of the greatest new insights of the Restoration was to counter the false
Christian tradition . . . that the fall was a mistake and Eve was responsible. . . .
The tendency to believe the false tradition . . . contributes to the
suppression, even abuse, of Mormon women.—England to
President Gordon B. Hinckley, 25 September 1989

For England and like-minded faculty, the most pressing need in the English
department was for qualified feminist scholars. That was a scenario rife with
paradox and strewn with landmines. The paradox resides in the fact that the
Church of Jesus Christ exhibits at once the most feminist and the most anti-
feminist theology imaginable. On the feminist side of the ledger, the faith is
virtually alone among Christian denominations in subscribing to Elizabeth
Cady Stanton's dictum that "the first step in the elevation of woman to her
true position, as an equal factor in human progress, is the cultivation of the
religious sentiment in regard to her dignity and equality, the recognition by
the rising generation of an ideal Heavenly Mother."[30] Latter-day Saints emphatically rupture the patriarchal monopoly of heaven by teaching of a literal,
personal, embodied Divine Feminine who copresides with the Father.

In addition, Latter-day Saints assign to Eve a role unique in Christendom.
For generations Latter-day Saint leaders have taught that "Mother Eve bestowed upon her daughters and sons a heritage of honor, for she acted with
wisdom, love, and unselfish sacrifice."[31] At one blow, then, the Latter-day
Saints repudiate a historical tradition that sees God as a solitary male and Eve
as the prototype of vulnerable, fallen woman, Milton's weaker vessel and the
universal temptress. Those ideas seem prescriptions for the most progressively
feminist theology to be found. On the other side of the ledger, however, is the

nineteenth-century practice of polygamy—never repudiated as a principle and effectively still intact as a condition of postmortal life for some. In addition, Latter-day Saints restrict the priesthood to men. Women have no authority anywhere in the church to preside over men, or to administer baptisms, the Lord's Supper, or blessings of the sick. The church structure, in other words, is unapologetically patriarchal.

One Latter-day Saint woman (herself a world-renowned radiologist and wife of a General Authority) writes defensively that "no religion holding as one of its fundamental tenets that the seed of godhood is in every man and every woman and that neither can achieve it without the other could by any reasonable, fair definition be called sexist."[32] To some women and observers, that seems scant theological counterweight to the male monopoly on priesthood, the consequent exclusion of women from the highest ranks of congregational and church-wide leadership, and a history (and persisting intimations) of a heaven organized polygamously.

To be a Latter-day Saint woman, then, is arguably to be ipso facto a feminist—but of a very particular sort. Many of the positions advocated by the majority of contemporary feminists, however, are incompatible with moral positions affirmed publicly at the highest levels of the church. Hence, the minefields. The church, for example, opposed passage of the Equal Rights Amendment and maintains an emphatic opposition (with rare exceptions) to abortion.

A third challenge for feminists in the church is not political or moral but cultural: The Saints have long subscribed to highly traditional norms regarding gender roles. As recently as 1995, an official proclamation affirmed that "by divine design, fathers are to preside over their families . . . and are responsible to provide the necessities of life and protection for their families. Mothers are primarily responsible for the nurture of their children."[33] Hence, professional women—including female professors at BYU—often had to contend with frequent bias and hostility. In 1992, for instance, an unsuccessful applicant for a BYU position in biology was asked, "Wouldn't it be better for her family for her to be at home?"[34]

The church first confronted feminism directly and dramatically in 1976 when the First Presidency issued a statement opposing passage of the Equal Rights Amendment. The document cited the amendment's encouragement of a "unisex society" and its potential to threaten the family as an institution by failing to recognize traditional gender roles and differences.[35] Negative reaction to the church's position increased with the publicized excommunication of famous ERA proponent Sonia Johnson in 1979, who insisted that her beliefs, rather than her public attacks on church leaders and church missionary work, were the basis for church sanctions.[36] Ultimately, the church's ability to mobilize member opposition to the amendment was seen as decisive in its 1982 defeat, though widespread support for passage was by then waning nationally.[37]

With the Sonia Johnson imbroglio only a few years in the past, BYU's administration nonetheless approved the English department's decision to brave the rough waters, and so BYU hired, among the new crop of young scholars, a number of outspoken feminists. Predictably, some of them would turn the department upside down. England seldom criticized his colleagues to administrators, but he made an exception when two untenured members vocally objected to feminism as "against the gospel" and referred to progressive colleagues as "evil."[38] One of them was so determined to publicly demonize England and other "liberals" that England took the unusual (for him) action of voting against the colleague's promotion.[39] Meanwhile, other interdepartmental memos circulated with charges and countercharges of "palpable arrogance," "benighted antifeminism," and "self-aggrandizing claptrap" along with demands to "get off your platform" and promises to "set you straight."[40] England himself prepared to fire off a memo calling a department member's actions "irresponsible and personally offensive" but softened the final version, instead "pleading with you my brother." His revised version elicited a courteous reply.[41] Too few faculty members, however, manifested his restraint. At the same time, England circulated a *Time* article titled "Teach Diversity—with a Smile."[42] Not content to let the essay speak for itself, he appended a few words, indicting "most of us at BYU [as] still so enmeshed in the evils of monoculturism."[43]

England then came under attack when it was learned that he had offered his home as a forum for a group of English students who wished to express criticisms of the English department and its faculty. His complicity, a "shocked and angered" colleague alleged, "breaches acceptable professional conduct and violates the principle of collegiality."[44] Others joined in the criticism, which dissipated only when England explained that the group had approached the departmental chair for an opportunity to provide input, and the students met with the department's Professional Development Committee, not England alone.[45] On occasion England wrote personal notes expressing hurt and asking forgiveness—to which one aggrieved colleague responded thanking him for his "gracious spirit."[46] In general, such reconciliations were in short supply. When the exchange of hostile memos escalated to anonymous notes left in mailboxes, tempers flared even more. One exasperated professor damned the "vicious" practice as "psychologically childish, socially irresponsible, and morally reprehensible."[47] A few years earlier, a colleague had sent England a note:

"Everybody in the department likes you very much, including me. A lot of us question some of your ideas, which I find half the time harebrained, half the time downright inspired; and I sometimes question the situations in which you choose to express them."[48] With the explosion of the culture wars, such good-natured differences became a thing of the past. England lamented "the defensiveness (on both sides but mainly from the old guard) that makes discussion of any of the new critical challenges difficult, that seems to require that differences of opinion or interpretation . . . be seen as not merely different and interesting, worth considering, but matters of absolute right and wrong, even of good and evil, and as coming from enemies."[49]

Cecilia Konchar Farr, who unapologetically defined herself as a "radical feminist . . . in social, economic, political, and religious philosophy,"[50] was among those recruited into this hotbed of new contention. Given her unabashed self-description and the competition between the department's mandate to engage contemporary critical perspectives and the fierce hostility toward feminism expressed by church leadership and many departmental faculty, her position was virtually untenable from day one. She had written a master's thesis at BYU employing feminist theory (the school's first such thesis) in 1987. Prior to the Fall 1990 semester, BYU hired her with the specific mandate to teach feminist theory. She quickly volunteered as a faculty adviser to a student feminist organization, VOICE (Visionary Organization Intent on Creating Equality). Her second semester, she laid the foundations for her own demise when she published an article in an independent student weekly, the *Student Review*, openly advocating abortion rights. More conspicuously, she gave a very public speech in January 1992 in which she emphatically declared "to our leaders" that "the abortion choice should be available and must be women's."[51] Most provocatively, she insisted that "whether or not the embryo is a life" was a "secondary question." Quoting Catherine MacKinnon she asked, "Why should not women make life or death decisions?" In publicly advocating unrestricted abortion rights while a church employee, she ignited a furious controversy.

ABORTION AND THE LDS CHURCH

Brigham Young and other early Latter-day Saint leaders, like the first Christians, referred to abortion, infanticide, and "child-killing" as related crimes, recognizing little distinction from murder.[52] "Infanticide is . . . not so boldly practiced as is the other equally great crime, which no doubt, to a great extent, prevents the necessity of infanticide," said Young in reference to abortion. George Q. Cannon and John Taylor agreed that the practice was a "black art," "a damning evil," and constituted "murder of the unborn," and was so rampant that America had become "a nation of murderers."[53] This language doubtless explains the oblique reference to abortion in Latter-day Saint scripture: "Thou shalt not . . . kill, nor do anything like unto it" (D&C 59:6). Catholic prohibitions against abortion admit of no exceptions, based on the doctrine of the seamless garment: Life is sacred from conception to death. Latter-day Saint theology of abortion blends the sanctity of life with a rigorous grounding in moral agency. This sounds ironic, and for some liberal Latter-day Saints it is precisely the church's emphasis on agency that makes the pro-choice position appealing. (Indeed, Farr herself invoked the Latter-day Saint principle of "free agency" in her argument.)[54]

In possible response to Farr, Elder Packer commented at the next church-wide General Conference that "the 'pro-choice' argument . . . is badly flawed. With that same logic one could argue that all traffic signs and barriers which keep the careless from danger should be pulled down on the theory that each individual must be free to choose how close to the edge he will go."[55] Years later, apostle Dallin Oaks further critiqued such reasoning: The sanctity of one agent's choice can never trump the sanctity of the other's life. Given the status of the unborn child as a human individual, two human agents, and two vested interests, must be weighed accordingly. Oaks's comments also have the virtue of interpreting the particular moral freedom, as taught in the Book of Mormon, as assuming a sacrosanct link between choice and consequence. As Oaks reasons, "The effect in over 95 percent of abortions is not to vindicate choice but to avoid its consequences. Using arguments of choice to try to justify altering the consequences of choice is a classic case of omitting what the Savior called the 'weightier matters of the law.'"[56] Ironically, in this vision, those who seek to safeguard the human products of conception are the actual defenders of the principle of choice. The moral logic of Latter-day Saint opposition to abortion being based on the principle of choice is evident in the church's granting of an exception in the case of rape, where no choice was made by the mother of the child.[57]

Given the Latter-day Saint leadership's emphatic public stand against abortion, Farr's dissent directed at "our leaders," while working as a church employee, was bound to complicate her tenure prospects. Knowing even before her public opposition to church teachings that her tenure as a feminist at BYU was a perilous prospect, England was her champion from the start. Farr later fondly remembered the image of England, "who I still see vividly in the back of my classroom, where he sat through nearly an entire semester of my Modernism class so he could experience and testify to what I really teach. The same Gene England who constantly invited me to guest-lecture his Mormon literature classes because he could see that I, a convert and feminist, belonged there."[58]

Her public advocacy of abortion rights was not troubling to England because he shared them. With rare moral and logical obtuseness, he privately characterized abortion restrictions as more in the nature of "sumptuary laws"—restrictions on food, drink, or dress—than involving high moral stakes.[59] He railed against Oaks's public teachings on the subject (again, in private), though Oaks's position was entirely consistent with an unbroken tradition of similar statements; his was simply the most analytical defense of the church position. Apostle Russell M. Nelson, later church president, used equally emphatic language in 2008, also stating that the personally opposed but politically supportive position was logically untenable and morally inconsistent with church teachings: "A woman's choice for her own body does not include the right to deprive her baby of life." In any case, he pointed out, rape and incest aside, "When conception does occur, that choice has already been made."[60]

It is not clear what informed England's thinking on the subject of abortion, though it was likely his late but unreserved embrace of contemporary feminism, with perhaps some overcompensation for his tardiness to the party. A few scattered epiphanies find space in his journal, narrating the slow recognition of his general conformity to the pattern of patriarchal obliviousness. In one entry, he finds, "It amazes me now to think of how childish I can be with [Charlotte] when I love her with all of my being. Perhaps it is defensiveness, a kind of guilt because I don't really think I'm carrying my share."[61] And yet, a few months later, he confessed a stubborn myopia. He gave a sacrament talk that infuriated a member and offended "a number of Bishops and others" who were present. Gene recognized the criticisms were legitimate—"it was an over-zealous, self-righteous, insensitive blast at people I didn't know." Among other gaffes, he had proclaimed to the audience that he possessed "the gift of knowledge and words" while "saying that Charlotte did not." He had meant to illustrate the diversity of gifts, but his tone-deafness to how an audience would respond to the seeming self-promotion and the slight of a nonacademic spouse would manifest itself recurrently over the years.[62] One former student recalled, "He was raised in the 'old school' and still he tries to make adjustments in his own life to coincide with his changing attitudes."[63]

With England slow to recognize the general disadvantages of women in the church, the Palo Alto years had been particularly hard on Charlotte. "I always thought anybody else, I don't care who it was, anybody else was smarter than I was." "I kept trying to fit in to his life, his role and until I realized that me trying to fit into the academic crowd that he worked with was an impossible thing."[64] Removed from the hyperintellectual environment of Stanford, she found her bearings in the more congenial atmosphere of St. Olaf, taking classes and developing her talent in music and art (today, her hand-painted postcards are treasured by recipients). Like many women of her generation, she had a happy marriage but one unsettled from time to time by her not-yet-articulated intimations of dissatisfaction with her place in a patriarchal order. These she traced to the first meal she shared with Gene as a newlywed wife. "Gene asked me to say the prayer and I thought, why does he ask me to say the prayer?" Something disturbed her about the abrupt assumption of authority. "It was just kind of strange to me that he was all of a sudden not just a boyfriend, a husband, but now he was in charge." She said nothing at the time, because whatever it "stirred up" in her couldn't yet find expression.[65] Decades later, she still silently bridled at Latter-day Saint norms more cultural than theological. At George Sr.'s ninetieth birthday she challenged, rather tardily, a claim he made at her wedding four decades earlier: "When Dad told me that I no longer belonged to my family and . . . that I was [now] his, I knew something wasn't quite right about it."[66]

A family friend remembered one moment of Gene's awakening in particular: "We were sitting around a table and Charlotte in her hesitant sweet way says, 'you buy as many books as you want. Why can't I do the same?' He was suddenly being exposed to a point he hadn't thought about."[67] Before long, Eugene was strongly encouraging Charlotte to take courses to develop her writing, for which she also had a natural gift. A colleague whose cause he championed (unsuccessfully) recalled in 1998 what she took to be his complete transformation. At a quilting bee to which he was invited, she saw "Gene England, who had never made a quilt in his life, [sit] into the wee hours sewing. He didn't participate in the sewing with the all-female quilters in order to display his support of feminists. Rather, he had temporarily moved to the moment all feminists look forward to—a time when there will be no need for feminism anymore. . . . Sewing his awkward stitches in the quilt, Gene had transcended his culture's limited views of gender, and in doing so, he found what has always been most important to him—a place in which to share the profound and pure love of Christ."[68]

By the time of Farr's hiring, England's stance toward feminism evinced not just sympathy but a touch of atonement. One evening found him sitting on the periphery of a campus meeting of VOICE, led by the new professor. An angry male student, intent on disrupting the meeting, rose and challenged Farr directly: "Do you believe that the Mormon patriarchy is abusive?" he demanded.

Farr refused to let him hijack the discussion, but he persisted. Suddenly, re-counted an attendee, England rose from the back and looked the student di-rectly in the eye. "I have been a bishop," he said, "and I'll answer your question. Regardless of how sensitive I may have tried to be, I know that I must have abused the authority somewhere." The student sat down, silenced.[69]

On a particularly contentious faculty retreat, England again displayed a pro-pensity to reverse his gendered perspective—and Farr was the agent of change. In February 1992, following heated exchanges among department members, England proposed that all members "work to love and forgive each other based on the idea that the department is much like a family." Farr immediately rose to object. She argued that the term "family" had pernicious connotations for some women, and she herself wasn't about to be cast as "anyone's dutiful daughter." Far from being offended, England was won over to her point. For the majority in attendance, however, critiquing the use of family metaphors in a Latter-day Saint setting was rather like attacking Moses at a bar mitzvah. They would remember her words.[70]

On her present-day webpage, Farr says that "good teaching is, in bell hooks' words, 'teaching to transgress.'"[71] In the classroom and faculty meetings alike, she made England look like an orthodox shrinking violet. By her own account, she led an entire class to a consensus on support for the pro-choice position. Her energetic hostility to metaphors of family was the final provocative gesture in a family-obsessed community and became a red flag rallying her opponents. Denial of tenure was all but inevitable.

Her third-year review came in 1993, and the surrounding controversy would reach both the *Chronicle of Higher Education* and the *New York Times*. In June she was informed that her contract would not be renewed. She would not even make it to the final year of tenure probation. The divisiveness of the contro-versy was nowhere more pronounced than in the English department itself. Fourteen tenured members had voted for continuing status, thirteen for pro-visional status, and seventeen for termination.[72] Heightening the controversy were the revelations that the Faculty Council's claims in their letter of dis-missal were inaccurate; the stated reason for noncontinuing status was the assertion that her teaching and publication record were unsatisfactory. She appealed the verdict.

Shortly before the final decision was announced, England had written a revealing memo to BYU administrator Neal Lambert: "I am drawn to explicate the religious insights and power of literature and to help students benefit in their own religious journeys. . . . I obviously still have much to learn about how to do this in ways that do not cause so much concern among parents, alumni, and Church leaders." And then adds, "As a citizen [of the university], I hope mainly to be a peacemaker, perhaps by withdrawing a bit from my political activities."[73] And yet, at this moment, along with department chair Bert Wilson, England stepped forward as Farr's only colleague to defend her against the decision of her colleagues and administrators.

He emphatically disputed the grounds for her dismissal: In less than three years she had produced two book chapters, an article, essays, one book manuscript, and part of a second. Her scholarly productivity could not seriously be called into question. Neither could her teaching record. Even as those categories were the ostensible complaints, it was clear to everyone involved that the real point of dispute concerned the nature of her "citizenship." What blew the controversy wide open was the question, fair enough in a church-sponsored and church-funded institution, of how justifiable and proper it was to interpret citizenship as encompassing church loyalty—and what that loyalty meant. According to one administrator, the problem was deliberate rebellion, manifest by "daring publicly to contradict the Church's teachings and its leadership," and publishing an essay in support of abortion after being warned that "no BYU professor should take a public pro-choice position."[74] By defending not just her scholarship but her right to publicly contradict those teachings, England was again making himself a conspicuous symbol of disruption in the eyes of the apostles, who constituted the BYU Board of Trustees. In a letter to the (church-owned) *Deseret News* he flatly denied that Farr's public advocacy of abortion rights "contradicted LDS Church positions."[75] This in spite of the fact that BYU president Rex Lee had relayed the verdict of the board that "there was no place at BYU for faculty members who were 'pro-choice'" about abortion.[76]

A few years before, as we saw above, Packer had personally and powerfully communicated to England the principle on which Farr's dismissal would be based. He had said the words with thinly veiled reference to England, but the relevance now was undeniable. "One thing that has puzzled me over the years," he had said on that occasion, "has been the willingness of some few individuals to accept salaries that are drawn from the tithes" and yet fail to support the church leadership and its teachings. "If one's values are different from those for which the University has been founded surely there is a place where the values of an employer will match their own."[77] England had not seen himself as the target of those words in 1991, and he did not believe they were a reasonable rationale for denying Farr tenure now. For England, academic freedom trumped institutional loyalty. Farr was offered a settlement before the appeal was litigated, and left for another university. Henceforth, England would become as passionately committed to fighting for a very broadly defined academic freedom at the church school, as he had been in promoting his other social agendas.

Wilson, England's closest friend and former department chair (until 1991) was equally disheartened but stopped short of carrying the campaign to the public. In his journal, he wrote that the experience "makes me wonder if there is any place left for me in the institution for which I once would have sacrificed almost anything."[78] He resigned a few years later from what he called "one of the most fractious English departments in the world."[79] England's fervent advocacy of Farr further alienated him from those who had prevailed in her ouster, and definitively branded him before leaders like Packer as a partisan of those who openly defied church teaching. Not only had England failed to muster sufficient support for Farr or for an absolute academic freedom, but he was also out of sync with prevailing sentiments at the institution regarding the conditions under which professors worked and taught. Surveys of that period revealed that college professors rated their jobs as satisfactory or very satisfactory at numbers between 64 percent (at public institutions) and 72 percent (at private ones). At BYU, the number was 85 percent. Clearly, the English department, or its most outspoken members, were outliers.[80]

Even while BYU contended with the controversial firings of Farr and some of her colleagues (notably the anthropologist David Knowlton), other prominent figures were finding not their tenure but their church membership itself in jeopardy. Stirrings that began decades ago were coming to a convulsive conclusion in the 1990s. The independent journals, a flourishing Mormon History Association, a professional scholar running the church Historical Department, and new access to the rich archives were producing a flood of historical research—much of which was increasingly threatening to the uncomplicated faith-promoting narratives members had inherited.

The temperature continued to rise toward the boiling point. In 1985, the historian Michael Quinn was Eugene England's BYU colleague. In that year he had published a groundbreaking article, "LDS Church Authority and New Plural Marriages, 1890–1904."[81] Latter-day Saints, as well as the general public, are usually aware that the church banned plural marriage with an official manifesto in 1890; it's even a part of the scriptural canon (D&C Official Declaration 1). Quinn's article demonstrated convincingly—and uncomfortably— that the church's standard narrative of polygamy's demise was seriously deficient. Few inside the church—including the apostles—were even aware that the manifesto ostensibly banning the practice in 1890 was not the definitive end to plural marriage it had seemed. The leadership had continued to sanction plural marriages until a second, lesser-known manifesto with real teeth was issued in 1904.

Quinn's revelation—disconcerting to laity and leadership alike—was precisely the kind of nontraditional narrative that England was at pains to address and assimilate into a more capacious and honest embrace of the Latter-day Saint tradition. However, the church was clearly unprepared to make the transition from the history that the leadership had carefully curated for a century and more to the unencumbered free-for-all boded by professionals given unrestricted access to church archives. Quinn's stake president was directed to discipline Quinn but chose to protect him instead.[82] Quinn followed up a few years later with a monograph that, in the eyes of many, was a sustained attempt to thoroughly dismantle the sacred foundations of the church itself. Relying in part on documents later found to be forgeries, he argued in *Early Mormonism and the Magic World View* (1987) that Smith reconfigured a wealth of nineteenth-century folk magic traditions along with a number of highly esoteric traditions and artifacts in producing the Book of Mormon. In words that sound remarkably like England's self-appraisal, Quinn saw himself as "hunting for ways to justify contradictions between simplified official accounts and messy human history," believing that "these two halves of his personality were complementary, that he would use them to build up the faith he loved."[83] Under continuing pressure, Quinn resigned from BYU in 1988, referring thereafter to his former place of employment with bitter overstatement as "an Auschwitz of the mind."[84]

Other scholars were similarly threatening the borders of orthodoxy. Maxine Hanks edited a daring essay collection called *Women and Authority: Re-emerging Mormon Feminism* (1992). She prefaced it with the clarification that her purpose was "to illustrate women's religious equality, not to lobby or persuade."[85] And indeed, the book was not an argument for ecclesiastical power or priesthood; it was, however, a reinterpretation of the status and prerogatives of women, relying in part upon little-known historical precedents. Like Quinn's work, Hanks's efforts to animate Latter-day Saint women by an appeal to precedent revealed the disruptive potential of the New Mormon History.

In May 1993, in an address to the All Church Coordinating Council, Boyd K. Packer delivered one of his most stinging rebukes of the church's liberal wing. "There are three areas where members of the Church, influenced by social and political unrest, are being caught up and led away," he declared. These "dangers" were the "relatively new" feminist and "gay-lesbian" movements, and "the ever-present challenge from the so-called scholars or intellectuals."[86]

Packer may well have had England's forays into speculative theology in mind when he added, "The doctrines of the gospel are revealed through the Spirit to prophets, not through the intellect to scholars." Just months later, in the span of one month, Quinn and Hanks along with four other writers and scholars were excommunicated (or disfellowshipped, a lesser sanction, in one case). The group was thereafter known as the "September Six." The six were forthcoming about the exact charges behind their discipline to varying degrees, and the church does not discuss details surrounding any church discipline. However, the most common factor was scholarship that challenged orthodox narratives—whether about the meaning of Isaiah, details of Heavenly Mother doctrine, or Latter-day Saint history. The disciplinary actions were widely perceived as orchestrated by the leadership as a powerful warning about the limits of intellectual inquiry that would be tolerated.

England's response to the unfolding fissures in Latter-day Saint culture, published just months before the September Six disciplinary actions, was an essay, "On Spectral Evidence," published in the Spring 1993 issue of *Dialogue*.[87] The essay was in equal measure a lament, a confession, and an exculpation. As the title indicated, England was likening the mechanisms and mentality of surveillance to the hysteria surrounding the Salem witch trials of 300 years earlier. He decried "the increasing passions and anxieties, jealousies and name-calling, low morale and scapegoating, an increasing tide of judgments and even punishments based on spectral evidence [he had] seen in the church lately—mainly at Brigham Young University." Much of the problem was bottom-up. As he had been experiencing from his Palo Alto days to the present, church members wrote to the First Presidency (or BYU administrators) when they found a church talk or a professor's lecture offensive. In some cases, the letters were returned. Too often, however, they were given credence and—likely referring to the recent cases of himself, Farr, and some of the September Six—the targets were "rejected from a teaching position, or denied publication, . . . or denied due process, . . . or treated in [ways] that disregard their rights and feelings as longstanding, proven, virtuous members of the church."

He stopped short of identifying the top-down power dynamic; it had been alleged by many that church discipline and administrative actions had been ordered from the highest levels, in spite of policies that directed church discipline to be locally inaugurated and administered. On the contrary, he argued in his essay that leaders at the center of recent controversies—he mentioned Dallin Oaks by name—were as victimized by liberals on the left as church intellectuals had been by conservatives on the right. And the respective terms were now invoked as self-authenticating evidence of disvalue and demerit.

At the same time, his essay includes a small but significant conversion narrative about his own coming of age in his efforts to reconcile faithfulness and intellectual independence vis-à-vis these church authorities. "I have come, through careful study and trial, to the following approach: I am bound by my beliefs about their calling *to be attentive* and receptive to everything any of the Brothers say—*to listen charitably* and invite the Spirit to confirm, to be fundamentally believing and submissive. I am bound by covenant *to obey* the official directions of the president, the First Presidency, and the Quorum of the Twelve—and to obey according to the best understanding that plain sense and the confirmation of the Spirit can give me, and not according to the claimed understanding of any other person." Recognizing that essential distinction between dogma as taught by consensus and views pronounced by individuals is why, he explained, he felt justified, back in 1989, in publishing the talk (on God's continuing progression) that had earned him official and public censure by Bruce McConkie.

And yet, in concluding his essay, he can be fairly understood to be still at war in himself over unresolved tensions. He recaps the "J'accuse" episode in the final pages, again evincing regret and contrition for his ill-considered "outburst," and again effectively apologizing to Elders Faust and Nelson. And yet, of course, his repentance is undercut by the entire thrust—and pointed title—of the essay itself. For the committee he attacked with his now repented eruption is the elephant in the room. That Strengthening Church Members Committee, whose exposure was the flash point for all that followed, would seem to be the fullest incarnation of an official sponsorship of that very "spectral evidence" he protests.

No wonder that his parting note is one of pessimism. A "'graceless perversion' of honorable motives and of true Mormonism," he fears, "is increasing now and may yet lead to much destruction of faith and love—as well as the pain many are already feeling." Even scripture, he concludes, foretells that "iniquity shall abound and the love of many shall wax cold." Even if those rare exceptions who "endure to the end . . . shall be saved" (Matthew 24:12–13).

Meanwhile, England had been continuing in the antiwar efforts he had aligned himself with in the 1960s. He wrote a letter to Gordon B. Hinckley opposing basing of the MX missile in Utah in the 1980s.[88] In March 1988, he had written in the *Deseret News* that supporting the Contras in Nicaragua would not "bring either peace or democracy."[89] Months later, his full-blown pacifism was evidently beyond compromise when he wrote an op-ed piece with the provocative title, in reference to World War II, "Was Chamberlain Right?" Against the odds, he maintained that "we have more to learn from Chamberlain than from those who dismiss or attack him on this anniversary."[90] In 1990, he published a critique of the recently launched Gulf War. In it, he not only invoked New Testament and Book of Mormon principles about loving and praying for enemies but pushed the envelope by justifying Saddam Hussein's invasion of Kuwait on historical grounds (comparing it to the Federal army's forcible reincorporation of seceded Southern states in the American Civil War).[91] Following the Gulf War, in a 1992 meeting with BYU's provost, England vented his anger with the public statements of President Thomas Monson, counselor in the First Presidency, "praising Mormon anxiousness to support President Bush and go to war in the Gulf, even early on when other churches were counseling patience and reliance on sanctions—a position that in my view contradicts Gospel principles and even previous statements by the First Presidency."[92] Hours later, England delivered a paper on pacifism to a session of the Christian Philosophers symposium held at BYU. "No religion professors around that I could see," he noted sourly.[93]

In March 1993, England spoke at a "Mormon Peace Gathering" at St. James Catholic Church in Las Vegas ("risking incarceration for trespassing on federal land in Nevada as part of a witness against nuclear weapons testing," according to one report).[94] Elder Henry Eyring, commissioner of education, sent a letter of concern to Rex D. Lee, president of BYU, who contacted England. Two concerns were paramount: (1) the event included plans for civil disobedience, a "crossing the line" onto federal property in order to protest nuclear weapons testing and (2) the event brochure identified England as a BYU professor. He wrote to Eyring, clarifying that he was neither engaging in nor advocating civil disobedience. He had merely fulfilled a request to give a scripture-based talk on the subject of peace, and he did not intend for his BYU affiliation to be indicated on the printed material. He requested its removal and promised more vigilance in the future.[95]

Meanwhile, the leadership's efforts to sanction what they saw as dissident scholarship showed no signs of success. By Fall 1993, BYU professors were still, in large numbers, disregarding the Symposia Statement. Leonard Arrington noted dozens of BYU names on that year's program. "Of all those, I personally do not know of a single one who was 'critical of the Brethren' or who has other than a deep attachment to the Church and its leaders," he wrote.[96] It was believed that old-guard members passed the name of attendees on to Elders Ezra Taft Benson, Mark E. Peterson, and Boyd K. Packer. "These then dressed down [BYU President] Jeff Holland in a very forceful way. [BYU historian] Ron [Walker] understands that he was lashed so heavily that he was ill the next day."[97]

STUDY ABROAD EXPERIENCES

We left early for Ann Hathaway's cottage and after the tour I invited all the
students to the Shakespeare Tree Garden for a group picture. I surprised Charlotte
by gathering our children on the bench that I had purchased for our fortieth
anniversary, which has a brass plaque: For Charlotte and Eugene England, "The
Marriage of True Minds—Sonnet 116."—England, journal entry, 17 June 1994

England found frequent respite from departmental wars and controversial
symposia, and presumably his colleagues and church leaders found relief as
well, during his time directing a study abroad program in London. Along with
Tim Slover, England had created the London Theatre Study Abroad program
in 1992, and ran it regularly until the year before his death. Shakespeare, theater, London, students, and time with Charlotte: Five great passions of his life
converged and he was in another dimension of happiness. He gave running
commentaries on bus rides, held energetic discussions after the group attended
plays, taught and tutored, ministered to troubled students, led field trips and
city explorations, managed the money and quietly provided needed loans, and
presented regular firesides to the students.

Even there, however, his provocations continued as he pushed the envelope of safe orthodoxy with his students. He presented a fireside on the topic
of "Your Religious Questions" which concerned even his generally supportive
wife. It "upset Charlotte and possibly some others because it seemed to get
negative and unresolved."[98] With his own unfiltered honesty, he added his own
doubts to the mix, realizing too late that his questions about "the inefficiency
of God" (too few Saints to evangelize and transform the earth) were elicit-
ing alarm and even tears from some of the more fragile of faith ("They'll be
writing letters home about faithless directors," groused Charlotte). By way of
repair, Charlotte organized a subsequent fireside on the more edifying topic,
"People and Events That Have Influenced My Testimony or Conversion." Gene
followed up with a newsletter proffering his own solution to the problem he
had raised. Invoking the Latter-day Saint doctrine of postmortal evangelization, he opined that "in his infinite love [God] has provided a way to extend
our mortal probation beyond this life until we all . . . hear the gospel fully." But
the problem continued to haunt him, and arose repeatedly in his conversation
and writings alike.

Meanwhile, Charlotte continued to show concern "about the effect of
[Gene's] bald openness," and even as he tried to temper his provocations, he
seemed oblivious to boundaries. For example, after challenging students to

England with a study abroad group in London, 1989. (Courtesy Charlotte England)

write letters home reflecting the fruits of their Shakespeare study with him, one newly liberated student followed up his lecture on *King Lear* with a letter to her father "about her determination to be independent of him . . . and *not* to be like her sister who was too dependent." "Very honest and possibly the beginning of a healthy relationship," England noted to himself with satisfaction.[99] In his element and removed from the tensions at BYU, his joy was infectious, and so was his kindness. His codirector claimed that "Gene . . . never had a business relationship with anyone in his life, certainly not in London. . . . All were his friends, and all came to love him dearly: the father and sons whose buses we hired, the people who cleaned and serviced our flats, ticket sellers at theatres. He knew all their names and their lives."[100]

While in London he blazed across the city like a meteor, attending plays and museums frenetically, racing from tube stop to tube stop, running for buses, and squeezing in every performance he could. One typical day catches a man consumed with a passion to wring every drop from the London theater scene: "I left in plenty of time to see Mad, Bad, and Dangerous, . . . starring Derek Jacobi." However, it was not plenty of time. "I ran back west along Baywater to see if I could get a bus. . . . It was moving so slow I took off and caught another one on Oxford Street. Then it got slowed down so much I took off but ran into a police barrier just before the Oxford Circus station, skirted it around to Regent Street and crossed over and ran along Great Monmouth St. to Charing Cross and down to the theatre, arriving breathless and sweating at 7:55—just in time to get a student standby ticket."[101]

His ploys for getting better seats, or finding room in sold-out venues, or gaming the system, became legendary. One student recalled wonderingly "the plays that we got into that were sold out but got in anyway because Gene would just lead us down to the front row."[102] In another typical instance, as he recorded, "I noticed that students were using the Radcliffe Camera reading room [in Oxford] and the guard was occupied, so I slipped in, asked some questions about sixteenth-century medical books and their location as a cover so I could look around at this marvelous circular space."[103] Later the same day he slipped into a guided tour of the Bodleian Library when no one was looking. On another occasion, England made plans to see a match at Wimbledon. He announced he was going there with the one ticket but invited a student to accompany him. He bought a cheap seat for the young man. Early on in the match, they saw a dropped ticket. Gene motioned to the ball girl to retrieve it for him, which she did. Nonchalantly, he took the ticket and, a surprised student at his side, just walked into the high-priced stands, where they sat on the front row, center court.

Another day at Wimbledon, he learned from a local how to bypass the long lines. And then wanting to see top-billed action, he "flashed my ticket at a gate on center court and was let in to watch [Boris] Becker play three games." He then rushed off from the match to another Shakespeare play, arriving at the Barbicon Centre with fifteen minutes to spare.[104] When he arrived too late at Wimbledon on another occasion, he climbed a tree to see John McEnroe

England and Charlotte on the bench with a plaque commemorating their
anniversary in the Shakespeare Garden at Ann Hathaway's Cottage in
Stratford-upon-Avon, England, 1997. (Courtesy Charlotte England)

playing Andrei Olhovskiy.[105] Friend Mary Bradford visited him in London.
"When we found ourselves sitting in the balcony, actually in back of the stage
in the Folger Theatre, Gene spotted empty seats only four rows from the front
and herded us into them."[106]

One ruse at Royal Festival Hall gave him a remarkable view of an Itzhak
Perlman performance: "I went down at the interval to an empty seat on the
front row, right in front of him, so I could see him labor up the specially con-
structed ramp with his two crutches. . . . When he was listening to the orches-
tra, he sometimes pursed out his lips and seemed to be popping his breath
in time and enjoying the music; while playing himself he would occasionally
purse his lips and raise his eyebrows in a beatific kind of concentration and
pleasure at a difficult or purely moving passage. His last cadenza was unbeliev-
ably complex and sure, and the audience gave him a standing ovation. I looked
back to see Charlotte weeping."[107]

Back in New York, "a Kennedy Center production of Swan Lake was sold
out, but we saw it anyway and from good seats."[108] Daughter Katherine remembered him leading the family in backward through the exit to a sold-out art

exhibit in Venice. "Daddy always finagled the best seats. It's like he had to be a part of what was going on on stage."[109]

Bob Rees described this infectious zest for life in all its variety:

I would find myself in London . . . and I can remember so well him say-ing come on we just have time to get to this great play . . . if we run and jump on the right Tube we can get there, and running across the bridge with him and just making it and going in and seeing this wonderful play with your father and somehow he had been able to get the tickets to it and he wanted to share it with me. I can remember going to see The Passion Play and going to Fortnum & Mason after the play and having a meal or going to a great Indian restaurant out at south Kensington or going to the British Museum or going to the Victoria and Albert Museum, run-ning someplace to catch something that was not to be missed. He had an enthusiasm for life, love of life, love of literature, love of music, love of drama and wanted to share that. That was the thing about Gene, he just wanted everybody to go with him. He wanted everybody to see what he saw and experience what he saw: the great taste of Indian food, this not to be missed play or this great dessert, and I just think there is something wonderful about that. His life was marked by the devotion and the love but also the infectious enthusiasm and passion for the world.[110]

"He loved his life," reminisced daughter Katherine. "I am convinced he woke up every morning and thought, 'I am the luckiest man alive,' and then he went out and did amazing and extraordinary things that most of us only dream about."[111]

12

THE WRITING ON THE WALL

> It's a bit shameful that my yearning for some kind of validation in my life
> sometimes takes the form of being obsessed with sports—or at least with success
> of a particular team—as if it mattered at all to my soul, or that of the universe.
> —England, journal entry, 4 January 1997

Throughout these troubled years, several members of the department wrote letters to Elder Boyd K. Packer complaining about England. Jay Fox became chair of the English department in 1995 (it took the administration two hours to convince him to take the job).[1] He described the environment as "worse than arbitration with Israelis and Palestinians." He was called to a meeting with Elders Packer and Neal Maxwell, who came with a "very thick file," and he listened to their concerns about England. Fox told them, "That's not the Gene I know."[2]

England had opened his journal for the new year of 1994 with a play on Wordsworth's famous ode: "Intimations of mortality," he headed the entry. He had had a fright over what turned out to be harmless blood in his stool; then after a choking episode, he was diagnosed with a Schatzki ring—"that sometimes formed around the esophagus in older folks," he was told. In addition, he experienced bouts of tachycardia, with a racing pulse that reached 240 beats per minute. England was only sixty, and still had a full head of hair and boyish good looks. But the incidents turned his mind to questions of his own mortality and legacy. "Things seem so unsettled in the Church right now," he mused, "that it seems a bad time to leave."[3]

He started the year off reading a collection of essays on science and Mormonism (*The Search for Harmony*),[4] and was moved by Richard Smith's account of growing up a Latter-day Saint in the 1930s, "being encouraged in his early love of science by apostles like Talmage and Merrill and mentored by Henry

Eyring in a conviction that began with Joseph Smith and Brigham Young and Orson Pratt—that science was a welcome part of Mormonism."[5] Such nostalgia deepened the pain of the tides wearing down faithful Latter-day Saint intellectual culture. In his journal, England directed his anger not at those leaders, but at "the intellectuals themselves" in positions of influence—"those who have failed or refused to find ways to oppose anti-intellectualism and denigration of both science and humanistic learning," whether BYU professors or quorum members.[6] Even while damning their inaction, he lamented that he, outspoken as ever, had been "increasingly rejected and marginalized by the Church and BYU over the past four years." "Clearly with the approval or at least permission of men I believe are apostles of the Lord Jesus Christ," he added. The first lament was merely painful. The second was his enduring cross.

As 1994 rolled on, England sensed a growing wave of opposition, and all the signs led him to despair of his survival in the Church Educational System. "I have to start rethinking everything," he confided to his journal after cataloging the setbacks. Blackballing from participation in the encyclopedia of Mormonism; the October chastisement at the hands of Oaks and Maxwell; the publicized fiasco that erupted over the Strengthening Church Members Committee; denial of tenure for Professors Cecilia Farr and David Knowlton, both of whom he had championed; the excommunications of the September Six.[7] That fall, BYU president Rex Lee called him in to rebuke him for publishing two articles on celestial polygamy, in spite of a promise to avoid the topic in future. England explained that both were products of years past; one was a talk published without his permission. The second had been committed to print before his pledge.[8]

Just before Christmas 1995, England made an appointment with Lee, who was leaving the position that month. In the course of their visit, England mentioned that he was considering a position likely to open up for him at the University of Utah's new campus. England was clearly hoping that Lee would try to dissuade him, and insist upon his vital role at BYU. Lee, to his great hurt, did not. England had enjoyed a robust correspondence with Lee since he assumed the presidency in the summer of 1989. England had called him visionary, thoughtful, and deserving of faculty trust. Lee had called England "one of the most talented people I know."[9] But Lee had run interference for some years now. Fatiguing of the role, "Rex responded very enthusiastically about me going to the U and implied . . . that it would be best for me to leave the Y. This surprised me, and I asked if I should talk about this with President [Merrill] Bateman, who was about to take office, and Rex said yes." England had provided the opening Lee had clearly been hoping for, and Lee was willing enough to speed along England's departure that he offered to set up a meeting with Bateman, who could add his weight to Lee's judgment.[10]

After the meeting with Lee, England considered his predicament. For the first time, he considered that maybe it was indeed time for him to move on. He wrote to Lee on 29 December: "I spent the worst Christmas of my life, partly because of our conversation. ... I've just about decided that I simply cannot go on having experiences where I learn that men I believe with all my heart are apostles of the Lord Jesus Christ are displeased with me, that some even distrust me. . . . The options are to stop writing about Gospel and Church matters or leave BYU—possibly both."[11] What he really hoped for were affirmations that the church—and BYU—valued him and encouraged him to stay. Bateman was not about to provide either.

Years earlier, Bateman had been the ecclesiastical leader who fielded member concerns about England's teachings on atonement. The complaints clearly lodged in his mind. Taking advantage of Lee's offer to arrange a meeting was "probably a mistake" he later admitted to his son, but that was his standard operating procedure: meet the persons in power to establish rapport and engage any preconceptions.[12] At this meeting, over the course of several awkward minutes together, Bateman was chilly to England to the point of rudeness. This coldness surprised England, because (clearly forgetting the circumstances of their earlier encounters) he "thought he knew my testimony and devotion."[13]

When England offered to "possibly give him one useful perspective on what was happening in the English department" (still famously riven with strife and controversy), Bateman declined, saying "he didn't want to hear it."[14] Seeing at a glance that his future prospects were indeed grim, he queried Bateman about a possible move to the position at the University of Utah Sandy Center. Bateman was blunter than Lee: "He said, 'I think you should. I think you'd be happier elsewhere,'"[15] and added that "'the Brethren' were unhappy about some of my writing but gave no details."[16]

In what transpired next, England once again revealed his imperviousness to the obvious: Bateman "gave no details" about those leadership concerns, he wrote, but then "he asked what I believed about the Atonement." This was clearly no offhand non sequitur but as precise a signal as one could ask for. It is a bit astonishing that England seemed to have forgotten that Bateman, in his role eight years earlier as England's stake president, had been the authority fielding Milton Wille's allegations of heresy against England—and that they centered on his publicly expressed views on the atonement. Yet the explicitly named "details" failed to register even then. Mistaking the query for one about

256

THE WRITING ON THE WALL

personal commitment rather than theological orientation, England bore his testimony of Christ's sacrifice, and of its centrality to all his teaching. He then offered to send Bateman his article on atonement, believing it would alleviate his concerns, when of course it would only confirm them. Here, once again, is painfully evident England's almost willful resistance to the gaping chasm between the content of his heart and the impact on his audience. He continued to believe that his writings were a monument in print to the centrality of Christ in his discipleship, a legacy of which he was proud; this he believed, even though two senior and hugely influential apostles, Packer and Maxwell, had clearly conveyed their interpretation of his atonement theology as heresy plain and simple.

After leaving Bateman's office, England considered that the Sandy slot would be a good recourse if he decided to go that route, but he still felt no immediate threat to his position. Days later, the friend he was counting on to secure the Sandy post for him lost her own position. The timing could not have been worse. Bateman called England back to his office in March 1996, and informed him that he didn't have to resign immediately; he could teach half-time during his transition to total severance, if finances were a concern. England left the office in a daze.

He spoke to his chair, Jay Fox, who thought the storm might pass, and advised England to keep quiet and do his work. He left to direct the theater program in London shortly thereafter, and for the next months he lay low and hoped for the best, but the decision had already been made, and the wheels were grinding away. That December, his usual application to teach honors courses was turned down at the behest of the vice president, Alan Wilkins. Religion classes were also vetoed. For England and others, it was looking like a purge, not just one squeaky wheel. As England wrote a correspondent: "The administration has . . . turned down most of the people we have recommended for hiring this year, including all of the women. . . . Good teachers and scholars, like Bert Wilson and Darrel Spencer, are leaving, and the best young prospects are not even considering coming here. Worst of all, many of the students are picking up the vigilante spirit. . . . We are starting to lose and will lose many of our most bright and faithful young students—lose them to BYU and possibly to the Church."[17]

England was at a low point and confided in close friend Robert Rees. "I'm even losing confidence in my teaching, losing that sense of assurance that I've always had that what I was doing was truthful and kind and therefore approved of by the Lord." After his meeting with Lee, "I felt completely humiliated and helpless, . . . just suspicion and condemnation and implied threats. Then, on

Christmas day, I got word my mother had suffered a heart attack. The two events produced the deepest depression I've ever felt. I couldn't get out of bed most of Christmas day."[18]

The following summer, in July 1997, Fox was pressured to reduce England's load to one course per semester—at the behest of President Bateman, it turned out.[19] And in addition to the early prohibition against teaching in the religion department, he was now banned permanently from teaching in the Honors Program he had once codirected.[20] Hearing the news, Bert Wilson wrote in sympathy, "I can imagine, but probably can't really know, the pain you must feel. . . . This on top of all the other setbacks you have suffered at the hands of those who neither know nor care about you. You have never wanted anything other than to serve the Lord and help his children find their way home. . . . You should be aware, though, that you serve in ways you may not recognize. Not many people could endure the course you have been forced to run and endure. But you have."[21]

The proximate cause given for the course reduction, only the latest in a long list of offenses, was his publication in 1994 of another *Dialogue* article, "'No Respecter of Persons': A Mormon Ethics of Diversity." That rationale was dubious, given its relatively innocuous content, and its appearance a few years before. But three decades of provocations had predisposed the powers that be to the least generous reading of his text. None of his themes were new: generosity of spirit, unconditional love, respect for all; but probing so many tender pressure points in one cumulative package was too much. He hinted at a future gender-less priesthood, pining for "a theology of gender and church practices that [would] release . . . enormous spiritual energy and moral impetus," creating a "true gender equality and family relationships unfettered by the sinful traditions of the fathers." He questioned the church's canonical scriptural exceptionalism: "Every people has the word of God, much of it in written form, from the Hindu Bhagavad Gita to the Oglala Sioux Black Elk Speaks." He wanted to contextualize and historicize prophetic revelation: "Even prophets can be at times affected by their cultural conditioning." And finally, he challenged the Mormon monopoly on salvation as the "only true and living Church," by invoking Karl Rahner's universalism: "Christ's grace must have been operating in non-Christian peoples all along." Even those who are non-Christian we should recognize as in reality "an anonymous Christian," in Rahner's phrase.[22]

Ecclesiastical patience was exhausted. "'The Brethren' had indeed brought pressure . . . to let me go."[23] Jay Fox delivered the news. One of England's favorite films was *A Man for All Seasons*, a celebration of that martyr to conscience, Thomas More. To his daughter Margaret, More had written, "I am . . . the

King's true faithful subject and daily beadsman and pray for his Highness and all his and all the realm. I do nobody harm, I say none harm, I think none harm, but wish everybody good. And if this be not enough to keep a man alive, in good faith, I long not to live."[24] A kindred sentiment became England's own. England fantasized about unleashing his personal hurt, his disappointment in his church, and his indignation at ecclesiastical wrong-doing in a manifesto to be sent to the full array of administrators and apostolic overseers. Like More, he realized such an outburst would serve his friends and family poorly, and like More, his postjudgment anger subsided, in the pages of his journal, into pained resignation instead: "I came to BYU with a sense of religious mission, convinced I could relate the Gospel to literature in ways that would . . . help build intelligent, lasting faith in young Latter-day Saints and thus contribute to the building of God's kingdom. I have worked hard . . . to fulfill that mission. . . . I have never opposed official doctrine or practice or . . . spoken evil of my leaders, but instead have defended and expounded upon my testimony concerning all of these. If this is not enough to keep me at BYU, then I dearly wish to be gone."[25]

Even so, England attempted one more time to receive a personal, face-to-face clarification behind his ouster. He met with Alan Wilkins, BYU's academic vice president and former associate academic vice president for faculty. Charlotte accompanied him. In England's retelling, she alluded to hundreds of communications from students profoundly affected by England's teaching over the years. Had the administration one letter in support of his dismissal? "And he said, 'No, we just have a feeling that there might be a danger there.' That's when she finally blew up and he had a statue of Christ on his desk and she said, 'You are not a Christlike person. You are not doing what he would want you to do' and walked out. We were both stunned."[26]

With nothing to lose, England continued to protest policies and practices that struck him as wrong—even craven. Controversy erupted in late 1997 over the aforementioned exhibit of Rodin sculptures—nude sculptures. Caving to community pressure by the puritanical minority, BYU removed some of the statues. England fired off a letter to the *Deseret News*, deploring the fact. "'BYU officials, bowing to the lowest common denominator of 'community standards,' rather than trying to inform and raise those standards, have undermined the patient, loving work of hundreds of their faculty by directly contradicting what they have taught students'—the difference between pornography and true art."[27]

Days later, he sent a stark memo to Fox: "This then is the formal notification that I will retire at the end of the 1997–98 school year."[28] With his resignation

England's last day in his BYU faculty office, 1998. (Courtesy John Snyder)

submitted and accepted, he then composed a long letter (seven single-spaced pages) to Jeffrey Holland, ordained an apostle three years earlier. He had heard that Holland had been appointed to a two-man committee to look into the England problem.[29] His purpose was not to ask for intervention—he made clear that his departure was no longer the issue. But what he saw as unethical and un-Christian engineering of his ouster was, and he wanted all those in the leading councils of the church to be aware of what had transpired. He hoped not just to instill a shared outrage but to inspire change in the governance and conduct of BYU and its administrators. Holland forwarded the letter to church president Gordon B. Hinckley, noting to England that he was "not on the BYU Board of Trustees and [had] no assignment with the larger Church Board of Education."[30] Disappointed and confused, England decided to move on with his life.

A friend reminded him of the unjust exile of his mentor Lowell Bennion from the CES in 1962, and Bennion's gracious response. England doubted he could match Bennion's spiritual triumph over the forces that had conspired to eject Bennion from the system. He did show a loyal restraint—but barely. Writing to his friend Marion D. Hanks, he admitted to a barely repressed "angry impulse to write every G[eneral] A[uthority] I knew, including all the Twelve and First Presidency!," protesting his firing. His exit was not on the epic scale of a Christian martyr. Still, his last years had been "a constant humiliation," and his dismissal "feels like disgrace," he wrote. The hardest blow was confirmation that it was not "overzealous administrators" who engineered his ouster but "General Authorities, men I believe called of God."[31] He did vent his dismay to Holland: "I left BYU in the summer of 1998, under duress, with a feeling that my heartfelt and reasonably effective life's work had been disdained and I had personally been humiliated and even lied to. I was not only told 'the Brethren' wanted me out of there, at least by age 65, but that I was to have my teaching load cut in half to minimize the danger of my exposure to students. . . . Finally, all opportunity after retirement to teach an occasional class in Mormon literature or Shakespeare in England . . . or even to address a fireside of BYU students in London—was taken away, with the clear implication that I was some kind of leprous pariah whose mere contact would contaminate students."[32]

In September 1998, Utah Valley State College in Orem (now Utah Valley University) extended to Gene a position as writer in residence, asking him also to teach Mormon literature. He noted to Hanks that he would be consulting there "on writing and teach Mormon literature—just call me apostle to the Gentiles!"[33] His jest masked a great pain. His last gesture as a BYU and church employee was a forgiving one. Just prior to his resignation from his beloved school, he gave a deeply personal address that was at once a kind of apologia for his own commitments, and a warning to the institution and his fellow faculty: "Now, twenty years later, I find myself labeled a liberal, publicly attacked and privately punished, not for violating the academic freedom document prescriptions against criticizing Church leaders or opposing Church doctrine, but for violating cultural taboos that are mistakenly made into religious issues: for publicly opposing war, for exposing my own and other Mormons' racism and sexism, even for teaching nationally honored but liberal Mormon writers."[34]

England ended his address by speaking, in Samoan, a repentance and reconciliation blessing, one that invoked both mutual forgiveness and joint healing.

Ou te faamagalo atu ia te outou i o outou 'aleu uma ia te a'u, ma ole atu ia outou faamagalo mai fo'i ia te a'u. Ou te ole atu i le Atua ia faamanuia mai ia i tatou, a tatou faia ia mea, 'o le a Ia faamalolo mai i ese'esega ma manu'anu'a o la tatou matagaluega, ma faafouina i tatou i lo tatou malosi e faia lalei ai la tatou galuega ma tusa ai ma le finagalo o le Atua.

[I forgive you for all your offenses against me and ask you to forgive me as well. I ask God to bless us, that if we do these things, he will heal our department of its divisions and wounds and renew us in our ability to do our work well and according to God's will.][35]

THE GENESIS OF MORMON STUDIES

Eugene Senior once told me that he said if the Lord gave him a son, he would dedicate that son to the Lord's service. Gene never had a choice. He became the person that he had to be. Then he turned to me and said, "Look what they've done to my boy. I've given millions of dollars to the church and look at what they do to my boy."
—Clifton Jolley, interview with author, 12 June 2017

England left BYU quietly, but inwardly he was conflicted. Unsure if he was himself to blame for the long debacle, he continued to agonize, searching for a single concrete fact or episode or sin that would make sense of it all. In that respect, nothing had changed from his first rebuff by BYU almost a quarter-century earlier, when he lamented an undefined "past action or present un-worthiness" affording "no apparent way to repent."[36] A few years before England died, his son Mark posed the question: Might his father have found a less contentious path, a voice more amenable to church leadership? Was a more conflict-free way open to him? "Probably not," Gene replied. "I have thought about that a lot and Charlotte has too. She is always talking about, 'well, if you do this and that differently, you would be better received.' Maybe she is right but I don't think so. . . . We've become even more divided on that. . . . Maybe it's just a matter of time. Maybe it's hopeless."[37]

Student editors at the *Student Review*, which England had supported, were so grieved at his ouster that they dedicated an entire issue to him. Tributes poured in from students, colleagues, and nationally renowned scholars like Wayne Booth. One expressed the sentiments of hundreds: "Despite the ungracious way in which both the University and the Church had rewarded his years of service, there were a great many of us whom he had touched, mentored, fathered, and loved on our respective paths to understanding. I told him that I felt lucky to be part of the chorus of those who would forever sing his praise."[38] The tributes that filled the pages were effusive in attesting to his life-changing impact on myriad students, friends, and colleagues. A common refrain was the recognition that England's essays, or England's personal interactions, were responsible for the writer's abiding faith in the face of contrary winds.

After his departure from BYU, England continued to be a fly in the Brethren's ointment—and now he was unhampered by fears of administrative reproach. A week after accepting UVSC's offer, he sent Hanks a copy of an address given to a Latter-day Saint LGBT group. ("It probably doesn't look like I'm keeping my head down," he remarked wryly).[39] Predictably, he continued attempting to thread the needle of edgy loyalty to church teachings. His address

to the group Affirmation recommended "a hope for change and faithful obedience now." He counseled "celibacy to gay Mormons as long as that is the
church's position," while advocating prayer and patience that the leadership
would soon countenance gay marriage. He thought the analogy with the 1978
removal of the 1852 priesthood ban was apt.[40]

A few months later, he was interceding in the church court of a friend,
Elbert Peck. Peck's position as editor of *Sunstone* was being construed by his
stake president as an instance of "apostate activities which foster and lead to
disparagement, ridicule, and making light of sacred matters." In his letter to
Holland, England pointed out that Peck was actually a mere employee of the
board, of which England himself was a member. That fact was hardly likely to
help Peck's standing—or his own.[41]

At UVSC, his energies were undiminished. His duties were simple: to serve
as the writer in residence, and to direct the London study abroad program.
The first position he filled by just being Gene. He wrote, gave lectures, invited
prominent writers like Leslie Norris and Orson Scott Card, and did public readings. In the second, he immediately infused new life into a middling program.
"Only a dozen or so students" peopled the diverse programs before his coming.
His popularity drew enthusiastic students and the London version became "a
resounding success," which spilled over into other versions that "flourished
throughout the world," in the words of one administrator.[42] Over eighty students
studied with England in London each of the two years he directed. Now, in the
twilight of his career, he made one of the most substantial contributions of his
life. Through his anthologies, classes, and mentoring of Latter-day Saint authors, he had done more than any figure to establish the contours of an authentic Mormon literature. Now, he undertook to expand that mission. Soon after
settling in as writer in residence, he made an ambitious application to the National Endowment for the Humanities (NEH) to establish an entirely new sub-
field in religion. His project was titled, "Enriching Humanities Curricula: Mormon Studies."[43] England was an unabashed promoter of Mormonism's unique
cultural contributions, and felt his coreligionists, too timid to trumpet their
faith's cultural achievements, were guilty of "provincial anti-provincialism."
"'Nothing good can come out of Panguitch,' they say. Or 'We can't be so provincial as to write or read *Mormon* literature when there are all the great and
universal *human* themes in our *world* literature.'"[44] To the faculty and administrators of his new home, he proffered his rationale for the initiative:

> If we were talking about a university that was 70 percent Black or Jew-
> ish, the point would be immediately clear. If such a university . . . did not

have courses in Black or Jewish culture (literature and history and sociol-
ogy, etc.), most likely taught by Black or Jewish scholars, that university
would be a laughingstock; in fact, its academic reputation might well be
compromised and its accreditation in serious trouble. But, even more seriously, it would be failing to seize a great educational opportunity—that
is, to engage the majority of its students where they can most directly
and easily be reached, that is in reference to their own culture and belief
systems. Such a university would thus neglect material and approaches
that could be a great help in achieving perhaps the main purpose of a college education, which is to understand, both critically and appreciatively,
the diversity of human cultures, including one's own, and thus become a
genuine citizen of the national and world community.[45]

The proposal went forward with the endorsement of the UVSC administration,
who wanted to see a Mormon studies program established at the school. The
assistant vice president for academic affairs, Elaine Englehardt, was tasked
with overseeing the initiative.

Sunstone hosted a session on the project: "The Academic Study of Religion:
Prospects and Perils."[46] The organizers noted that "such a program . . . has
also raised concerns on two fronts. Some have begun to worry that such a
program could easily become a forum for Mormon apologetics, even proselytizing, while others voice concerns about it as 'yet another forum for Mormon
bashing.'" England's remarks in the session apparently aggravated rather than
alleviated concerns—probably because he was neither basher nor conventional
apologist but rather the scathingly loyal but honest critic of Mormonism's cultural forms. "It was nip and tuck to keep Eugene on after the Salt Lake Tribune
report" on the conference, said Englehardt.[47]

The substantial grant was successful on the first round (an unusual coup)
and provided funds for a year-long faculty seminar and lecture series. Astonish-
ingly, the UVSC Board of Trustees, largely filled with Latter-day Saints, urged
the administration to decline the award. They were "threatened by the past
work and reputation of Eugene England," according to Englehardt.[48] That his
outspoken engagement with the church's troubled past on race and other issues unsettled many Latter-day Saints was well established and understandable. That an institution would reject an NEH grant to establish the academic
study of Mormonism on that basis was alarming. At the same time, as a public
institution with a majority Latter-day Saint student population, and located in
a state with an LDS-dominated legislature, UVSC was financially dependent
on maintaining good relations with the church. That fact doubtless weighed

on those fearing a Mormon studies program under England's leadership. In response, England made a case for Mormon studies as an appropriate academic fit for a student population whose interest in the subject was self-evident; of greater moment, he argued, suppressing the initiative would be a blatant violation of the principle of academic freedom. To drive home that point, England urged the sponsoring of a UVSC conference on academic freedom. The administration consented, and at the venue he spoke forcefully on the topic, as did UVSC president Kerry Romesburg and Baylor University provost Donald Schmeltekopf. The grant was accepted.

The administration directed England to partner with the college's Center for the Study of Ethics, and the collaboration created tremendous synergy, as did teaming up with Brian Birch, who was directing the college's Religious Diversity Program. Englehardt described the successful execution of England's agenda:

> The grant was used to strengthen the library in Mormon studies, providing texts and periodicals essential for the academic study of Mormon culture by individuals. A study group of scholars from throughout the state was formed to study recent texts by Mormon scholars, and discuss the implications of these texts on the overall religion. The scholars writing the most current texts were invited to the UVU campus to conduct these study groups and also public seminars which were free and open to the student body and community. All of the authors who were part of the grant were from the Mormon community, and had impeccable reputations nationally as scholars and writers. While on campus the scholars participated in the seminars and gave public lectures. [After England's death, the series took the name of the "Eugene England Religious Studies Lecture Series."]

Steve Carter, who worked with the Ethics Center, remembered being at the center of historic developments, birthed in humble soil but fertilized by Gene's frenetic energy.

> Fifty feet down the hall, in a converted broom closet, stood the outer satellite of the Center: Eugene England's office. . . . The closet burst with the lawn signs he had made by the dozens to advertise the conferences he sponsored on campus, and my ever-ringing phone provided a constant background noise to the office activity. Nine times out of ten, it was Gene on the other end. When people familiar with his projects, articles, and books discovered I worked for Gene, then Writer-in-Residence at UVSC,

most of them assumed I must spend my days talking theology with him or researching his next essay. It is true that I talked with him a lot—maybe once every three minutes. Gene's mind, I found, works on the fly. He called to talk about anything that came into his mind—the moment it came into his mind. I could hear Melanie giggling sometimes when my phone rang for the thirtieth time that day. "Steve? Gene here. I want you to get fifty more copies of the conference flyer and put them in my box. Oh, and I want to change the lawn signs this time to include the time and place for the keynote speaker. Do you think you can get Gustav to do that?" Five seconds later the phone rang again. Gene had remembered that he also wanted engraved invitations for the local dignitaries, a copy of the article on the Bear River Massacre that may have been published in October by the *Salt Lake Tribune*, and addresses for three people who had just moved. By the time I had opened the word processor to print out the flyer, Gene was on the phone trying to remember if the conference participants had been paid and if, by any chance, I had found that *Tribune* article yet.

As ever, England was anxious for the ministerial as well as academic side of discipleship. The year 2000 found England in his most beloved church calling, teaching Sunday school once again. The great literary critic and mildly disaffected Latter-day Saint Wayne Booth found himself attending Gene's ward in the open air and wrote up the experience in his journal.

The first hour was an abominable sermon, the old guy giving the class no chance to interact. . . . The entire message was obedience! . . . I walked away so disgusted I was thinking seriously about getting myself excommunicated. Then I suddenly remembered that Gene England would be teaching the next class, and I returned to the chairs under the sacred trees. His hour was so thoughtful that I changed my mind: I'm not going to bother about getting excommunicated. In fact, I found myself thinking: any religion or culture that can produce a man like Gene, a man who can get away with unpopular, deeply thoughtful interpretations with a congregation like that, is worth belonging to. So why not become active again? The answer: because I could never endure attending more services like that first hour.[49]

As the semester wore on, the Mormon studies program flourished but England's energy flagged. He would not live to finish the full year of the NEH-funded initiative. The repercussions of his experiment, however, continue to reshape religious studies to this day. He had founded what is now generally considered the first Mormon studies program in the country.[50] Today, university presses from Illinois to Oxford have substantial lists in Mormon studies, and chairs and programs in Mormon studies have been established, following in England's footsteps, at Claremont Graduate University, the University of Utah, the University of Virginia, and Utah State. Other initiatives are in development or under discussion at the University of Southern California, the University of Wyoming, the University of California at Santa Barbara, and Graduate Theological Union, Berkeley. If Leonard Arrington is the father of Mormon history, Eugene England has the parallel distinction as the founder of Mormon studies. That he established its foundations as a disciple-in-exile was but the final irony of his tempestuous career.

DEPARTING THE STAGE

He was looking for God when he didn't have
anything to offer God anymore.—Steve Carter

The first week of the new millennium, England drove Sholly to the Country Club Inn, a Salt Lake City hotel where they had spent their honeymoon forty-six years before. "It was a small, tacky, 1950's" establishment, and they managed to find the very room where they had spent their wedding night. Sholly woke several times during the night with troubling dreams. It was a poignant, but not fully satisfactory, anniversary. Their marriage had been under strain lately. Sholly was working through long-repressed after-effects of childhood traumas; Gene had been uncharacteristically depressed and listless. He had weathered years of conflict and opposition and the grief of being perpetually misunderstood. But this was different. Steve Carter, a student who worked as his assistant, said everyone noticed he was losing energy, "like a marionette, nodding and trying to stay awake." At long last, Carter noted, "his high idealism was tempered, and he was full of melancholy."[51]

Except for a few sporadic entries, England's diary comes to an end in these months. His personal papers, however, reveal a spiritual torment that occludes all other concerns in his life. Although his new position was satisfying and he was finding the support, recognition, and respect he had yearned for at BYU, he could not make peace with his dismissal of two years past. On 18 January, he wrote a letter to the apostle in whom he still placed his greatest trust— Neal Maxwell. In it, he rehearsed and explained once again the final series of conflicts with the administration beginning in 1994. He narrated the events up to 1998, when President Bateman had directed his chair to terminate him. Compounding the pain, he added, he had learned from Wayne Booth, who had visited BYU shortly before, that "President Bateman had said, without specifics, that I was a 'person who could not be trusted.'" He had considered legal action and resistance to what he saw as an unjust firing. But the report of Booth changed everything. His concern now was for his own soul and standing, not justice.

> It hurts me terribly to think I am—or am seen as—a person who can't be trusted or doesn't tell the truth. . . . So I ask your forgiveness. If the reason for all of this is that I did not properly follow the counsel you gave . . . and the follow-up counsel Rex [Lee] gave, . . . I am truly sorry. . . . I only wish someone had talked to me straight about this. I certainly recognize that I am passionate, probably self-deceiving, even arrogant at times. . . . But I hope you know I am not defiant, unrepentant, dishonest, or inclined in any way to hurt the Church or its leaders. If I have done so in any way, please forgive me.[52]

England did not send the letter—apparently realizing that his long series of attempts to be understood and validated had come to naught and were unlikely to be fruitful at this stage. Throughout the year, his despondency persisted. He taught, built upon the foundations of the Mormon studies program, and fulfilled his duties—but family and friends grew concerned at his unprecedented change in demeanor. The day after Thanksgiving, he had written in his journal, "I'm suffering more than any time I can remember. I have a constant hurt in my stomach that is not sharp like an ulcer just dull, but seems the result of some inner stress. I find myself reviewing my past and thinking of decisions and actions I would like to go back and change and thinking of my future as rather bleak because of those decisions and actions." The upside he strove to find was in a determination "to repent and live differently. . . . Less scattered, less pushy and self-confident about doing things my own . . . way."[53]

Like a drowning man caught between two banks, he fled first to one side and then the other. No sooner had he committed to acknowledging personal "failure of some kind" and maintaining his "focused, repentant mode" than he switched direction and found the culprit in the institution he loved. He became "increasingly convinced my pain is due to a lack of voice, of expression of my heart's core." His sense of "humiliation and loss" was attributable to the "unfairness of being asked to leave BYU by President Bateman on behalf of the 'Brethren.'" Never imputing any wrong to England, the church had never given him a "chance to repent if need be."[54]

Two days later, his resolve to let the matter lie broke down, and he wrote another letter to Maxwell. He incorporated much of the year-old draft, omitted some details, but returned even more poignantly—and pathetically—to his spiritual pain. "I feel now that I should have been more vigilant, and I apologize to you that I wasn't. I repent sincerely and . . . am 'trying again' constantly in what I see as my task to be the kind of writer whose work only builds faith. Please tell me if this failure is the reason I have been thought untrustworthy or if there is something else I need to know and do and be to regain that trust. It is a constant, piercing pain in my soul to think that I have done something that might prevent me from serving the Church with the gifts I know God has given me." And then, in desperation, he reverts to his familiar pattern of invoking character witnesses one last time: "Bishop Borland and my stake president, Jim Toronto, have expressed complete confidence in me, and though I sought it, I have felt no chastisement from the Lord, but my soul is still not at peace. Can you help me?"[55]

Revisiting the past had not been cathartic—it had only intensified his turmoil. After sending his letter to Maxwell, his anxiety spilled over. Days before, UVSC's vice president, Brad Cook, had told England that he was "a great treasure" of the college. But such praise did nothing to assuage his despair. That was not the approbation he craved. He confided in his journal, "I'm getting close to a panic attack. I lay in bed this morning for almost an hour, just barely hanging on. My mind keeps circling, circling, over past failures, mistakes, omissions, wishing I could go back and change things. Nothing attracts me, fills me with desire to do, accomplish, feel. As I think of what I must do, it all seems banal, petty, doomed to failure."[56]

He anxiously awaited Maxwell's reply. On 20 December, he wrote in his journal, "I'm getting afraid of total collapse. . . . Charlotte feels I need to face my ultimate anxieties concerning the Church and authority but that she's not sure I can resolve them—or that she can stand the process."[57] Uncharacteristically, the apostle did not respond. England continued to puzzle through his guilt, desperately seeking to pinpoint a sin he could make the focus of his repentance. Perhaps, he considered, it was in publishing, after McConkie's death, the essay the apostle had condemned. "I felt I was being honest but I may have been guilty of self-deception. . . . God help me be true."[58] He supplemented his repentance with antidepressants, but still wondered whether he was being "fitly punished with much sorrow and a withdrawal of the spirit."[59]

In London a few months before, England had attended the final moments of one of his favorite dramas, a medieval religious play called *The Mysteries* that chronicled the history of the world from Lucifer's fall to final judgment. The play was almost over, but a befriended house manager let in the two couples (Gene, Charlotte, and their friends Tim and Mary Slover). They entered the back as Jesus was imposing judgment. Tim Slover described what followed.

> Jesus turned to a section of audience who had unknowingly sat on a bit of stadium seating that he had marked out for damnation. "Ye cursed caitiffs of Cain's kin," he said to the startled theatregoers, "that never me comforted in my care, from me flee, in hell to dwell without an end." By this time, Gene, who knew the drill, had worked himself over to the section of those who were to be saved. Jesus turned to him and smiled. "My blessed bairns on my right hand," he said. "Your life in liking shall ye lead, in this kingdom that to you is due for your good deed. Heaven shall be your rest, in joy and bliss to be me by." Gene, I noted from where I stood in tears, beamed beatifically back at him.[60]

Now, gravely ill (though still undiagnosed) and finding no solace, and after a lapse of six silent weeks since his letter to Maxwell, England wrote to the apostle again. He enclosed a copy of the original letter, and appended a note with additional details of his harrowing dark night of the soul, sounding like a medieval monk mercilessly debasing himself in a fruitless quest for absolution: "I have continued my process of self-examination and prayer for guidance and forgiveness on a daily basis—with many sleepless nights. I am worried that I may be sinking towards a serious depression and so am asking again if there is any help you can give. . . . The Lord warns that 'the rebellious shall be pierced with much sorrow.' [But] I don't feel I'm rebellious, in fact, I've bowed my head and said yes many times when it was not only hard but unexplained and seemed unjust. . . . But I have realized, in my late night struggles with conscience, that I may have been proud and rebellious at times that I managed to rationalize in terms of being true to my conscience." And then he assured Maxwell, "All of you Apostles are the Lord's chosen servants to whom I should be especially obedient. . . . I have never spoken ill of you or been knowingly untrue or intentionally disobedient. If pride or rebelliousness has ever dimmed my judgment I am profoundly sorrowful and ask your forgiveness."[61]

The same day, he wrote his final journal entry—where he sounded a still-defiant note. Referring to the church that had deprived him of his position at BYU, he quoted Walter Lippman, who wrote of the "'necessary opposition.' His point was that the leaders of any institution must allow their opponents the right freely to challenge official positions, not out of any generosity of heart, but because the leaders desperately need to hear opposing views in order to keep their own excesses in check."[62] As with Goethe's Faust, two spirits were at war in his breast to the very end.

Maxwell broke the silence nine days later, but rather than offer either absolution or comfort he effectively confirmed England's fears. The reason for the delay, he responded in late January, was in "pondering how best to respond to you." Then he said, "It would be unprofitable to meet merely in order to reprocess incidents from your personal history with their attendant concerns." Perhaps, in struggling with his own leukemia that would prove fatal, Maxwell recognized that England had to find his own way to a peaceful exit from a life of fraught discipleship. Especially since, as he suggested, England might not yet have come to terms with his own culpability in this tragic denouement to his career. "You mentioned that 'I have felt no chastisement from the Lord,' but you also wrote that 'I have realized . . . that I may have been proud and rebellious at times.'" And then, with words that must have aggravated England's already considerable misery, Maxwell added, "Frankly, your struggles may reflect having lived so long in the intellectual world that you might be 'past feeling' in terms of the precious process which may be under way." Only at the end of his letter did Maxwell almost, but not quite, soften the blow. He would consider meeting at a "spiritual level," he granted, meaning past history and past controversies were off the table. There would be no reexamination, no resolution, of the fractured past. But even such a concession to allow England a final meeting with his spiritual confessor—death was now mere months away—was contingent on "your receptivity to counsel about discipleship."[63]

The letter must have come as a devastating final blow. The rebuff was a tragedy beyond mere emotional pain. It represented England's ultimate failure to secure the goodwill of the hierarchy he had so earnestly sought to serve throughout his life. Yet perhaps, even in the tragedy, one may discern a kind of *felix culpa*, a lovely grace that emerges from the ashes of a broken communion. What endures in England's fraught discipleship is his determination, to the very end, to make peace. Levi Peterson recalled, months before England's death, the depths of his sorrow. His faith was undiminished, England told the novelist, though his treatment had been unfair.[64] Years before, Michael Quinn had been furious with England, yet grudgingly admiring of him— that "wonderful big hearted person who could love those who had blacklisted him as much as he loved those who were his [devoted fans]."[65] His children remembered that he never once discussed his public humiliation at the hands of Bruce McConkie, and a student recalled how he convened the entire study abroad group to pray on McConkie's behalf when he was struck with cancer.[66] Days after a rebuke by two apostles, delivered in tones that surprised him by their iciness, he referred to them in his journal as his "heroes."

And then, too, there was the consolation in his final agonies of Sholly, to whom his last poem was addressed.

> I woke to hear you breathing next to me
> And knew you'd wakened often in the night
> To help in what is now my being's fight—
> To stay alive and get my body free
> Of cancer and paralysis. I knew
> You'd wake again to help: read me to sleep
> Or rise to fix me healing food and keep
> Me clean and warm and dressed—or teach me not to rue
> My life.
>
> We talked of all we'd forged together—home
> And children, faith and vows that make us one—
> And all we might still make in Kingdoms where
> None can sever us from continued seed forever
> Or me from your comfort close by.[67]

On 21 February, three weeks after he received Maxwell's response, Gene collapsed. A CAT scan and MRI revealed a mass with hemorrhaging and swelling in his brain. The neurosurgeon on call, Dr. Howard Reichman, operated immediately and removed four golf-ball-sized cysts and a large tumor from his right temporal lobe. (England's children, in the throes of both sorrow and bitterness, named each cyst after a different BYU administrator, rumor had it.) Initially, the unexpected trauma was thought to be good news of a sort. His months of unprecedented and unaccountable depression now had an explanation. The surgery appeared successful and England's postoperative recovery appeared at first excellent.[68]

Gene's collapse interrupted his winter semester at UVSC. When he had recovered sufficiently from his surgery, he insisted on visiting the class he had left so abruptly in the hands of substitutes. A student recalled, "We were honored by his presence in a surprise visit that he made in his wheelchair with his sweet wife on a cold and rainy day. He came to encourage us and to bear his testimony of the gospel. . . . He spoke longer than Charlotte was comfortable with, and it was obvious that it had taxed him immensely to come, but his students were of utmost concern to him. We were told that when he came out of the brain surgery and could begin to respond, his first request was that Charlotte call this number and take care of his students."[69]

England was flooded with expressions of love, support, concern—all attesting to a man whose life had registered profound and lasting impact on hundreds directly and thousands more through his writings. Most were somber, even poignant. Some provided welcome humor. Lavina Anderson shared her latest J. Golden Kimball story (he was a famously and excruciatingly irreverent Seventy of the late nineteenth century): "A sweet little old lady in Circleville delivered Kimball's wisdom to a priesthood gathering. 'There are three types of men in the Church, brethren. One type learns from reading good books and the scriptures. One learns about life from observations. And then there's the third type who just has to piss on the electric fence himself.'"[70] No one doubted which type Gene was.

Frank Odd, who had served with him in leading the small Minnesota branch a quarter century earlier, closed his last letter: "I begin my days in prayer and end them in kneeling benediction, and you, my friend, are there in every prayer. How could you not be, when thoughts of you accompany me through all the hours? I grieve for your ordeal, hard beyond my experience or imagination, revere your courage, yearn for your recovery, pray God to sustain and comfort you, and thank Him for the blessing of calling you friend. For what a friend you are, Gene: a true friend, a friend for all seasons—mentor, guide, teacher, companion, confidant, true Israelite without guile—sustaining me at [all] times. And what times they have been for me, all the unforgettable occasions when you challenged me to deepen my discipleship and become more selfless in service."[71]

Bert Wilson wrote constantly from where he was serving in Finland. Gene's respite had been temporary, false solace. As his condition now plummeted, Wilson wrote: "Dear sweet, gentle, kind friend. What a mess you have gotten yourself into now. I wish I could write still one more letter to extract you from your difficulty as I have in the past. But this time I'm powerless." He then recalled their shared boyhood. "I have a claim on you none [other] can match. I have known you since we were both five years old. Who else can claim to have lain with you on the canal bank behind your home and pulled the legs off water skippers? Who else has camped with you on your farm, only to have your dad come roaring in like a bear and scare us half to death. Who else has memorized with me the shortest page in our fourth grade history book so we could mass produce it to meet the punishments Miss Salvesen meted out—one page copied from the history book for each of our misdeeds. . . . Who else has faced you with a loaded rubber band gun from across the narrow space of your dad's grain silo. . . . Who else has lain out with you under Idaho's star-studded skies and dreamed dreams of grandeur?"

Then he closed with a fond wish. "In your last letter to me [before Gene's collapse], you wrote: 'We look forward to seeing you in about a year and to being better friends than we have been in the past, to share more of our lives and confidences and pleasures. . . . I hope we can teach a class together.' I'm going to hold you to that, dear friend."[72] It was not to be. In Gene's last reply to his friend of sixty-three years, he told him, "Though sleepless, lonely nights, thoughts of you come like a sweet melody."[73]

For the next months, England's condition deteriorated further. There was to be no remission. Mary Bradford had earlier written from Ireland, "You have cared for us and about us as long as we can remember. Please stay with us. You can lick this as you have so many other trials and tribulations."[74] Now, days before he died, Mary Bradford crawled onto the bed of the unresponsive England, covering his face with kisses and crying, "Oh, my eternal brother." Doug Thayer came every day. Daughter Jane read to him Wallace Stegner's novel *Crossing to Safety*.[75] On 19 August, in the presence of his beloved children and his incomparable Sholly, he passed across the veil.

13

LEGACY

A DANGEROUS DISCIPLESHIP

Take some risks. Leave something unresolved but deeply felt.
—England's comment on a student's paper

The nineteenth-century apostle Orson Pratt, the most original theologian the Latter-day Saint tradition ever produced, frequently locked horns with Brigham Young. Like England, Pratt was publicly rebuked from the stand and required to repudiate some of his teachings. But Young's famous tribute to Pratt could also be said of England: "If Elder Pratt was chopped up in pieces," Young proclaimed, "every piece would cry out 'Mormonism is true.'"[1] At England's funeral, many constituencies wanted to claim him as theirs: for the intellectuals, he was a role model; for the liberals, he was a rare outlier; for the disaffiliated and marginalized, he was a bridge-builder. Last to speak was England's stake president, James Toronto, and he played a tape of England's last spoken testimony. It may have been Toronto's way of mirroring Young's tribute to Pratt; many constituencies claimed England as their own but from his first breath to his last England was a true believer.

At his own father's funeral just five years before, Gene had spoken of "the most comforting witness—the direct life changing contact with spiritual realms, with the Savior, in those spiritual realms that my father and I and many others have experienced. . . . I witness that I have had intimations from behind the veil, from across the boundary between our world and the eternal world where God and Christ . . . live."[2] Now, at his own funeral, those in attendance heard England's recorded voice bearing his last witness, given in February 2001, just months before his own death and wracked with a still-undiagnosed brain cancer. Standing for the last time in his Provo Pleasant

View ward, he acknowledged that perhaps his daughter was right. Perhaps "my problem was that I was trying to save the world and I neither had the ability nor was it my assignment." His current condition, which he experienced as a bewildering and enervating depression, "has been hard in many ways but it has given me time to reflect on my testimony. The conviction came to me very early in life and has continued strong to the present that Jesus Christ is our Savior, that he is the greatest reality in the Universe. He restored his church to help us learn to love each other and all human beings as he loved us." As his faith in the institutional form that "Restoration" took was undiminished, the "prophet and apostles chosen by the Lord Jesus Christ . . . speak as special witnesses of him."[3]

In considering the wide-ranging legacy of his life, Eugene England was above anything else a disciple of Jesus Christ, and a devout believer in that version of the Christian Good News articulated by Joseph Smith. Friend Gary Browning offered the same summation of England's life: Wherever the questing of a conversation led, however many the digressions or speculations, the "journey ended up at the same place, and that was with his incredible, unmoveable, unshakeable faith."[4]

With the distance of decades, two ironies are paramount in considering the life and impact of Eugene England. First, England was arguably more orthodox than his contemporaries—if orthodoxy is measured as consistency with the words and spirit of the church's founder, Joseph Smith. One such indication emerges in a paper published under the title, "Becoming a World Religion: Blacks, the Poor—All of Us." England was perennially troubled by what he saw as the apparent "inefficiency" of God. The charge to revitalize Christianity, evangelize the world, and redeem the billions of its inhabitants, living and dead, seemed to him clearly beyond the scope of a tiny religion mustering a fraction of a percentage of earth's population (less than 1 percent are committed Latter-day Saints).

He found a path forward in the writings of Catholic theologian Karl Rahner, who recognized a parallel problem in Catholic theology. Though Catholicism has far more members than do the Latter-day Saints, its numbers still pale against the many billions of uncatechized and unbaptized across the world's many cultures and pre-Christian centuries. The Jesuit theologian developed a notion of the "anonymous Christian" and held that "a person lives in the grace of God and attains salvation outside of explicitly constituted Christianity . . . because he follows his conscience."[5]

England wanted to find a way to emulate Rahner's generosity of vision by employing the resources of the Latter-day Saint tradition, without apparently realizing how abundant they were. The Church of Jesus Christ was birthed in a soteriology that was far closer to universalism than even England was aware of because it had been eclipsed in his day by sharp opposition. Charlotte Haven was a Nauvoo, Illinois, resident who heard Joseph Smith say that a spirit in the lowest kingdom "constantly progresses in spiritual knowledge until safely landed in the Celestial."[6] The temple ritual Smith instituted itself recapitulates this form. In its most basic outline, temple ritual charts the progress of the individual from premortal life through mortality and into the beyond, passing through the lower two kingdoms and culminating with entry into a representation of the celestial kingdom itself. Excepting only those few who will refuse Christ's love till the end, Smith later taught, man "cannot be damned through all eternity, there is a possibility for his escape in a little time."[7] Joseph's brother Hyrum also believed that no salvific state in the hereafter was static.[8]

Brigham Young was exactly in line with Joseph's thinking. He was teaching in 1855 that those who fail to secure exaltation by the conclusion of their earthly probation "would eventually have the privilege of proving themselves worthy & advancing to a Celestial kingdom but it would be a slow progress."[9] Fifth president of the church Lorenzo Snow was in accord,[10] as was the tradition's eminent theologian and Seventy B. H. Roberts, who explicitly interpreted Smith's near universalism to imply a steadfast progression through the kingdoms of glory. Though scripture was vague, he argued, the ministry alluded to in each kingdom seemed meaningless "unless it be for the purpose of advancing our Father's children along the lines of eternal progress."[11] James Talmage, virtually the only apostle to produce a theological treatise (two actually) under official imprimatur, wrote in his first edition of the *Articles of Faith* that the answer was implicit in the principle of eternal progression itself: "Advancement from grade to grade within any kingdom, and from kingdom to kingdom, will be provided for. . . . Eternity is progressive."[12]

However, by England's day, two of midcentury Mormonism's dominant voices, those of Joseph Fielding Smith and Bruce R. McConkie, had emphatically declared such eternal progress for all to be damnable heresies. ("The scriptures say there is no progression from one kingdom to another. This really should settle the matter," McConkie told one questioner. Then he added, surprisingly, that "I am not aware of any of the present or past General Authorities ever thought any differently than this.")[13] His colleague Neal Maxwell was more circumspect. To an institute director he wrote on the same subject, "We know only so much about this matter beyond which anything is speculative."[14] Maxwell's views were privately expressed, while McConkie made his emphatic claims public. As a consequence, rigorous and permanent lines of demarcation separating the saved from the vastly more numerous nearly saved were taken for granted by most all Latter-day Saints from that era going forward. England insisted that "surely the Restored Gospel does not merely substitute *four* divisions of judgment for two" [the three kingdoms of glory and outer darkness in place of heaven and hell]. In a similar vein, he argued that "judgment will be simply our complete self-knowledge and our consequent acceptance of the best opportunities and environment for further progress."[15]

Like McConkie, apparently not familiar with the extensive precedents, England operated largely by simply extrapolating from Enoch's depiction of a God of infinite love. As he wrote in that same essay, "God did indeed love us infinitely, and he would indeed never stop loving us and helping us repent—and he would accept our repentance and welcome us into his presence and eternal life whenever we chose to turn to him, even after any imagined 'final' judgment."[16] He was profoundly influenced by both the theology and the iconoclastic role played by not just Rahner but his personal mentor, Robert McAfee Brown of the Reformed tradition. England served as the latter's teaching assistant at Stanford, and may have glimpsed his own future in Brown's outsider status. He recalled a moment when Brown was lecturing on God's infinite, unconditional love. Then, with tears in his eyes, Brown told the class, "I'm considered a heretic in my own church because I can't accept its teaching that, when we die, we are judged and go to heaven or hell. . . . The God of perfect love I know . . . would *never* stop loving us and trying to save us." So, too, did England "rejoice in God's . . . permanently offered forgiveness."[17]

England was of course well aware of the Restoration doctrine of vicarious salvation—that those unexposed to the gospel in mortality would be evangelized in the hereafter and posthumously baptized in Latter-day Saint temples. However, that seemed a thin theology, a salvational plan mired in inefficiency, if only the smallest percentage of inhabitants were able to maximize the purpose of mortality for which the earth was created. A lot of work to go to, a vast scheme of creation, for so few to benefit from in the here and now. And so England drew out another aspect of Restoration teaching—that embodiment with its immersion in the crucible of earthly schooling is itself a prime purpose of mortality, and is accomplished irrespective of one's faith tradition: "In saner moments, I . . . open my imagination to the billions of diverse lives who have learned about and experienced that love in many diverse ways. I realize that the mortal experience of those billions is not wasted because they don't have the version of the gospel that I have. They are learning and experiencing vital things, . . . important spiritual growth, even as they are being prepared—just as I am—to eventually hear the fullness of the gospel."[18] That was the only refuge he could find from what he later would call "the greatest challenge to my faith."[19] Almost buried in those words was another provocative implication. That members of other faiths were being prepared, "just as I am—to eventually hear the fulness of the gospel" suggested that as a Latter-day Saint he had neither a monopoly on nor a totality of the truth. Mormon culture is replete with language of a "gospel fulness" restored by Joseph Smith. The words may have been a gesture of ecumenical humility—or England may have had in mind the seldom-noted Book of Mormon prophecy, referring to Smith's mission of "bringing to pass much [not all] restoration" (2 Nephi 3:24).

England's inclination toward a more universal soteriology also led him toward a more liberal conception of revelation than was welcome in his twentieth-century church. The Book of Mormon had explicitly insisted that "*every* nation has been given, directly, in their own tongues, some manifestation of Christ."[20] This demanded, to England, an openness to the inspiration of diverse cultures and traditions. "Christ's grace has come to all, that *every* people has the word of God, . . . [and that] part of our mission is to learn from them and delight in the diversity of revelation God has given."[21] Joseph Smith, like England, was himself far from proprietary about truth monopolies. Smith said late in his ministry, "If the Presbyterians have any truth, embrace that. If the Baptists and Methodists have truth, embrace that too. Get all the good in the world if you want to come out a pure Mormon."[22]

The statement could well have been England's personal mantra. In the reconciliation of contraries not only peace, but truth and wisdom were to be found. In his last public discourse, England's voice broke on this very point. "We must protect the right of our opponents to speak because we must hear what they have to say. . . . [Pauses]. . . . Because freedom of discussion improves our own opinions, the liberties of other[s] are our own vital necessity. . . . Freedom of speech . . . may not produce the truth. . . . But if the truth can be found, there is no other system which will normally and habitually find so much truth."[23]

Other aspects of England's nonconformity have become mainstreamed. He wrote about the impediments to female equality that were institutionalized in the church's culture and practices; today, the church is in the midst of numerous adjustments that bring women into many (not all) of its governing councils, eliminate sexist language from temple ceremonies, and more equally apportion resources to the young women of the church. He exuded compassion for the gay community and spoke at some of its early gatherings—at a time when church rhetoric condemned not only the practice but the very condition of same-sex attraction. His position that elicited criticism for pushing boundaries at the time would now be considered regressive in the church.[24]

While the racism he decried may never be thoroughly expunged from all those who call themselves Saints, he would be pleased to see such developments as the church-wide commemoration of the priesthood ban's cessation in 2018, and the invitation extended to President Russell Nelson by the National Association for the Advancement of Colored People to address its annual convention in 2019. Although McConkie's *Mormon Doctrine* continued to be a best seller for a few more years, the church publishing house ceased publishing it in 2010. As long as a scholar's "speculative theology" makes no authoritative claims, it is highly unlikely to be condemned today; in fact, a Society for Mormon Philosophy and Theology was organized in 2003 and publishes its own journal, *Element*. *Dialogue* continues to thrive as a journal, as does *Sunstone*, although their reputation as "alternative voices" to orthodoxy is undiminished.

Most ironic and tragic, perhaps, is the unfolding of the clash with secularism that has taken such a toll on the church's youth—and that England foresaw and tried to assuage. In 1998, as England was being exiled from the institution he had so loved and tried to improve, he made a tragic prediction: "I think we are going to have a situation where these people ['bright and experienced and more liberal in their views'] are just going to leave."[25] Two decades later, a leading Latter-day Saint scholar could retrospectively confirm the prognosis: Speaking of the "twenty-year chill between the church's administrative and intellectual leaders" that began circa 1980, Philip Barlow writes, "The earlier permafrost . . . exacted an ongoing toll on a new generation whose native tongue was the internet. . . . This cacophonic choir introduced a widening public to versions of the historical and social problems that [Leonard] Arrington and his colleagues"—foremost among them being Eugene England—"had earlier attempted to address, with erudition, in the context of faith. The result among an unprepared populace was frequent dismay, even panic, and a sense of betrayal. 'Why weren't we told these things while growing up in the church?' The dismay proved contagious among a widening minority, contributing to the Mormon inflection of a growing societal disenchantment with organized religion."[26]

Perhaps no institutional response could fully satisfy generations steeped in secular values, progressive politics, and a skepticism toward institutional authority reminiscent of the 1960s. However, the Latter-day Saint church has in many cases responded in precisely those ways England advocated, and for which he was often censured, decades ago. He aroused consternation when he gave firesides in which he confronted unflinchingly the Mountain Meadows Massacre, orchestrated by local church leaders, and the Willie and Martin handcart company, an apostle-blessed enterprise that ended with catastrophic loss of life.[27] Such honesty is now part of Latter-day Saint institutional culture: the church sponsored an unflinchingly honest account of the atrocity in 2011;[28] the Joseph Smith Papers project encompasses a comprehensive, unexpurgated record of all Joseph Smith's writings, sermons, and correspondence, and a new multivolume church history is in process, acknowledging with unprecedented frankness Smith's polygeny and polyandry, and the church's follies and foibles as well as its faith-building accomplishments.[29] As we saw, the Church Educational System has a new mantra, admitting the insufficiencies of its past pedagogies and insisting on a more open, historically informed, and liberal approach. Apostles have explicitly acknowledged doubt as a frequent stage on the road to spiritual growth, and reminded the Saints that prophets, while inspired, are fallible.

In England's case, letters and notes by the score attest to the efficacy of his approach. "Gene England almost singlehandedly saved my activity in the LDS Church," wrote one. In another entirely typical homage, a student wrote that "when I couldn't think of reasons to go on, Gene provided them. He still does."[30] "My most involved and significant mentor," "the single most influential force," "the most profoundly influential person," "a moral compass," "the greatest influence for good in my life"—such tributes were common not just at his funeral but throughout his life.[31]

England never railed against his censure or his expulsion from BYU. What his friend Lavina Anderson said of the period of most intense friction between intellectuals and leadership was to him an unquestioned verity: "Someday all of us who have lived through this month, leaders and members alike, will look back and see it as a time when truth and courage meant very different things to very different but equally honorable people."[32] Like his reading of the Garden of Eden narrative, England fully understood that his personal tragedy reflected the inherent and inescapable tension between omnipresent competing Goods. There were no villains or heroes in his conflicted odyssey, only Saints struggling to find ever more productive dialogue, and ecclesiastical authorities trying to safeguard the doctrinal purity of the church they were charged with leading. An antiwar activist who won the prize as outstanding cadet in his Air Force squadron, England knew the greatest show of love and loyalty alike was faithful provocation from within the fold.

While England would likely find a comfortable home in the church of the twenty-first century, his eloquent voice and his compassionate nature would mark him as a distinctive Saint. Those views of his that were never—or are not yet—assimilated continue both to inspire and provoke. One of his profounder contributions was to introduce into Latter-day Saint discourse the intractability of the tragic, its fierce resistance to glib moralizing, facile comforts, or even final explanations—without calling his faith in Joseph Smith's gospel into question. His religious culture was not always prepared to allow such complications into the picture without construing them as the doubt of faithlessness. We saw in this regard his account of the mother carrying trisomy 13 who was warned against further pregnancy. "On the basis of their opposition to birth control and abortion . . . and with faith in an optimistic priesthood blessing and strengthened by the fasting of their ward and stake, the couple went ahead with another child. It was born with trisomy 13, lived thirty-three days, and put the parents in debt over $100,000."[33] In his Latter-day Saint brand of faith, he does not find a certain species of Christian consolation available to him. "I want to take refuge in the mystery that an absolute God made it all out of nothing and will make sense of it or send it back to nothing, but Joseph Smith will not let me."

What he means is that thanks to Smith's divine anthropology, a Latter-day Saint cannot take refuge in God's omnipotence as conventionally understood. "Reality is too demanding for me to feel very safe anymore in the appalling luxury of my moments of utter skepticism. God's tears in the book of Moses, at which the prophet Enoch wondered, tell me that God has not resolved the mystery of being. But he endures in love. He does not ask me to forego my integrity by ignoring the mystery or he would not have let Enoch see him weep. But he does not excuse me to forego my integrity by ignoring the reality which daily catches me up in joy and sorrow and shows me, slowly, subtly, its moral patterns of iron delicacy."[34]

Eugene England was an anomaly in the Latter-day Saint tradition. Just as the church's theology cannot be inscribed in traditional theological categories, neither does England fit the mold of the typical liberal dissenter from a conservative tradition. The liberalism of his progressive social conscience did not infiltrate his simple faith in the personal, embodied, accessible, and interventionist God of Mormonism, the literal apprehension of the church's scriptural canon, or the permeability of a veil that barely partitioned the world of the living and the world of the numinous. He was a charismatic Saint, a believer in healing and prophecy, practicing old-time religion's reliance upon Christ as a personal and attentive Savior. He noted the paradox more than once. "I read the testimony [of pioneer colonizer Joseph Murdoch]," he recorded, and of his "work for the dead in the St. George Temple, where three of his aunts appeared to him. I read his testimony, claiming to have seen them with his natural eyes and talked with them, and I believe him." At the same time, England was troubled and vexed by the particularism of Latter-day Saint theology, its cultural as well as doctrinal claims to privileged status among the great faiths of the world. "So what am I to do with my overwhelming conviction that God does such particular things for Latter-day Saints . . . and my equally strong conviction that he must be an awfully partial, even inefficient God if he indeed reserves such small favors, or even much of his attention, for a very, very small minority of his children. . . . It violates the basic spirit of Christianity itself—and certainly of the Restored Gospel with its incredible new emphases on universal salvation."[35]

His faith was always twofold, a tenuous balancing act that held simple faith and intellectual rigor, belief and skepticism, in fragile tension. He adored the Christ of Restoration teaching and the dream of a universal salvation, but, along with Enlightenment philosophers like G. E. Lessing, he was troubled by the particularism, the failed economy of a minuscule Latter-day Saint discipleship among the earth's teeming billions. He wrote devotedly about the Book of Mormon, engraved on gold plates and translated by seer stones, with its awesome power to convert, yet he also saw its anachronisms and nineteenth-century intrusions. "There is a lot of Joseph Smith in that book," he told a friend. But it was also marked by authentic ancient voices "like Nephi and Alma and Moroni" whom he took to be real people.[36] Few Latter-day Saints, then or now, were marked by such internal contraries. Skeptics who claim Mormon affiliation through their DNA or tribal loyalty are common; England was a true believer, though he asked the hard questions, and was troubled by the disjointed links in the theological and historical chain of the church.

His friend Robert Rees eloquently expressed the "dangerous discipleship" that he and England shared. "[Gene] and I talked a lot about faith. At some point, I observed that living with a dynamic faith is like rebuilding a ship one plank at a time—while in a storm—at sea and that's both hard to do and dangerous to do but you see I think Christ calls us to a life of danger. I think Christ in many ways is a dangerous person because what he asks us to do is dangerous because it is to somehow use the best love that we can in the most dangerous way that love can be used."[37] Gary Browning sensed the same compelling tension: England always enacted a kind of "holy danger."[38] The holiness was in England's commitment to the centrality of Christ in all he said and taught. The danger was in his courageous confrontation with "any issue that faith might raise, no matter how troubling, no matter how vexing the questions it provoked."[39]

Gene was a fly fisherman, and the stories his fishing partners told were legion. One close companion, the novelist Doug Thayer, shared some at his funeral, concluding with a metaphor apt for Gene's life. "Gene had an incredible ability to get hung up, snagged in trees and brush, which was inevitable because he fished that long rod (the tip was perpetually falling off and the handle was loose) and made long casts. But he also had an incredible ability to get those snags undone without losing his fly. He was a hopeful fisherman. . . . I'm going to keep fishing the streams we fished, sometimes alone, sometimes with a friend. The fishing will be rich with memories. And as we move up the creek, I will tell the friend about George Eugene England, who lived his life well and liked to make long casts."[40]

NOTES

ABBREVIATIONS

CDBY   Brigham Young, *Complete Discourses*, edited by Richard S. Van Wagoner (Salt Lake City: Smith-Pettit Foundation, 2009)

CE-C   Private papers in the collection of Charlotte England

D&C   Doctrine and Covenants

DW-C   Dan Wotherspoon collection of Eugene England papers

EE   Eugene England

EEJ   Journals of Eugene England

EE-P   Eugene England Papers, Special Collections, Marriott Library, University of Utah

JD   *Journal of Discourses*, 26 vols., reported by G. D. Watt et al. (Liverpool: F. D. and S. W. Richards et al., 1851–86. Reprint Salt Lake City: n.p., 1974)

ME-I   Interviews conducted by Mark England (seldom dated though approximate dates are often implied contextually and are so indicated)

INTRODUCTION

1. In deference to the wishes of the leadership of the Church of Jesus Christ of Latter-day Saints, that full name rather than "Mormon" will be generally employed in this book, with the understanding that the latter term may occasionally be necessary when referring to entities of which "Mormon" is an integral part: Mormon studies programs, Mormon literature classes, and so on. At times, the word is also used when referring to a more amorphous cultural entity that transcends the institution, or to be consistent with historical context.

2. Mitch Davis, interview with author, 3 May 2016.

3. Cal Rudd to EE, 13 September 1975, CE-C.

4. The question was put by Lavina Fielding Anderson, EEJ, 7 September 1975.

5. John Milton, *Paradise Lost* 1.1–2, edited by David Scott Kastan (Indianapolis: Hackett, 2007), 6–7.

6. Gen. 3:22. Unless otherwise indicated, the King James Bible will be cited since that is the version employed by Latter-day Saints.

7. Andrew Louth, ed., *Ancient Christian Commentary on Scripture: Genesis 1–11* (Downers Grove, Illinois: InterVarsity, 2001), 1:100.

8. John L. Thompson, ed., *Reformation Commentary on Scripture: Genesis 1–11* (Downers Grove, Illinois: InterVarsity, 2012), 1:177.

9. John Chrysostom, *Homilies on Genesis* 7, in *Ancient Christian Commentary*, 1:101.

10. Moses 5:11.

11. John A. Widtsoe, *Evidences and Reconciliations* (Salt Lake City: Bookcraft, 1947), 2:78.

12. EE, "Hawthorne and the Virtue of Sin," *Literature and Belief* 3 (1983): 109.

13. Salvatore Russo, "Hegel's Theory of Tragedy," *Open Court* 3 (1936): 138.

CHAPTER 1

1. *England Family Histories: George Eugene England Sr. and Dora Rose Hartvigsen England*, compiled and edited by Ann Christine England Barker (n.p.: n.p., 2012), 3, CE-C.

2. Barker, *England Family Histories*, 10.

3. Douglas Thayer, "A Fisherman's Heart," *Student Review*, 10 April 1998.

4. Barker, *England Family Histories*, 31.

5. Barker, *England Family Histories*, 40.

6. Barker, *England Family Histories*, 52.

7. Barker, *England Family Histories*, 61.

8. "A Partial Record of the 90th Birthday Party for Eugene England Sr.," 12 March 1994, CE-C.

9. EE, "Growing Up Mormon," typescript, EE-P 91.11. England envisioned this as the first chapter of his autobiography but never moved beyond chapter 1.

10. EE, "Enduring," *Dialogue: A Journal of Mormon Thought* 16, no. 4 (Winter 1983): 103.

11. EE, introduction to Charles Peterson, Family History Symposium, January 1987, EE-P 194.6; Bert Wilson journal, 25 December 1981, EE-P 151.3.

12. Clifton Jolley to author, 12 June 2017.

13. Ed Geary recalled Bert Wilson saying, "Gene was always surprised when as children he and Bert and others got into trouble." Ed Geary to author, 3 May 2016.

14. Ed Geary to author, 3 May 2016.

15. Bert Wilson to EE, 21 April 1992, EE-P 167.12.

16. Bert Wilson to EE, 26 February 1968, EE-P 167.12.

17. Barker, *England Family Histories*, 70.

18. Dora England, ME-I 119, pt. 1.

19. EE, "Born Square: On Being Mormon, Western, and Human," Eugene England Foundation, 2, http://eugeneengland.org/wp-content/uploads/sbi/articles/2001_e_002.pdf. Originally in *Literature and Belief* 21, no. 1 (2001): 275–94.

20. William Wordsworth, "The Prelude," in *The Collected Poems of William Wordsworth*, 637–38 (Ware, U.K.: Wordsworth, 1994).

21. Max Scheler and Bernard Stambler, "On the Tragic," *Cross Currents* 4, no. 2 (Winter 1954): 178–91.

22. ME-I 117, pt. 1.

23. ME-I 117, pt. 1.

24. EE, "Kinsman," *Dialogue: A Journal of Mormon Thought* 21, no. 4 (Fall 1981): 488–89.
25. ME-I 117, pt. 1.
26. EE, "Growing Up Mormon."
27. EE, "Growing Up Mormon."
28. ME-I 119, pt. 2. Also confirmed in ME-I 116. Dora gave slightly different numbers: Over $4 million in donations were funding 2,000 missionaries a year by 1989.
29. Barker, *England Family Histories*, 254.
30. Eugene Sr. mentions a gift of 43 acres (ME-I 101) and a later gift of 430 acres (ME-I 112).
31. Barker, *England Family Histories*, 115.
32. "We helped them with payments on a home, a car—possibly as much as the Danforth." *England Family Histories*, 220.
33. ME-I 119, pt. 2.
34. ME-I 125.
35. EEJ, 14 April 1992.
36. ME-I 117, pt. 2.
37. Floyd Astin, "A Few Memories of My Friend, Eugene England," Eugene England Foundation (n.d.), https://www.eugeneengland.org/eugene-england/remembering -gene-project/remembering-gene/a-few-memories-of-my-friend-eugene-england.
38. EE, "Charlotte Spreads Her Wings," typescript, CE-C.
39. ME-I 124, pt. 1.
40. ME-I 124, pt. 1.
41. EE, "Charlotte Spreads Her Wings."
42. ME-I 124, pt. 1.
43. ME-I 125.
44. See Mary Lythgoe Bradford, *Lowell L. Bennion: Teacher, Counselor, Humanitarian* (Salt Lake City: Dialogue Foundation, 1995), 113.
45. Bradford, *Bennion*, 119.
46. ME-I 118, pt. 2.
47. ME-I 124, pt. 2.

CHAPTER 2

1. A search of mission journals and diaries in the Harold B. Lee Library at Brigham Young University revealed these examples but no such joint calls to nonisland nations.
2. Unless otherwise indicated, all citations in this section are from the mission journal of Eugene and Charlotte England, CE-C.
3. ME-I 124, pt. 2.
4. In addition to maintaining a mission journal, England later recounted his mission experiences in "Mission to Paradise," *BYU Studies* 38, no. 1 (1999): 170–85.
5. EE, "Mission," 173.

6. ME-I 120, pt. 2.

7. ME-I 120, pt. 2.

8. EE, "Mission," 182.

9. ME-I 125.

10. EE, "Letter to a College Student," Eugene England Foundation (n.d.), https://www
.eugeneengland.org/letter-to-a-college-student.

CHAPTER 3

1. ME-I 125.

2. ME-I 117, pt. 2.

3. "Toby" to Charlotte [England], 19 August 2001, EE-P 146.11.

4. A newspaper clipping announced his appointment as editor, 8 May 1957, CE-C.

5. "Induction Statistics," https://www.sss.gov/history-and-records/induction
-statistics/.

6. EE, "Finding Myself in the Sixties," unpublished ms., circa 1990, 11, EE-P 50.4.

7. Toby Pingree, ME-I 109.

8. Email, Thom Parkes to Charlotte [England], 19 August 2001, CE-C.

9. Thom Parkes, "Memories of Gene England," CE-C.

10. "Danforth Graduate Fellowship," https://www.reed.edu/ir/danforthawards.html.

11. EE, "Born Square: On Being Mormon, Western, and Human," Eugene England
Foundation, 3–4, http://eugeneengland.org/wp-content/uploads/sbi/articles
/2001_e_002.pdf. Originally published in *Literature and Belief* 21, no. 1 (2001):
275–94.

12. Anthony W. Ivins, *Conference Report*, April 1911, 118–19.

13. Ezra Taft Benson, "Three Threatening Dangers," *Improvement Era*, December
1964, 1067–68.

14. Boyd K. Packer, *Conference Report*, April 1968, 33.

15. EE, "'No Cause, No Cause': An Essay toward Reconciliation," *Sunstone*, January
2002, 32.

16. Kathleen Petty to author, 8 July 2017.

17. Charlotte England to author, 24 March 2020.

18. George Pace to "Gene," 23 September 1966, CE-C.

19. "History of Joseph Smith," *Millennial Star*, 4 December 1858, 774.

20. *Elders' Journal*, August 1838, 53, Joseph Smith Papers, https://www.josephsmith
papers.org/paper-summary/elders-journal-august-1838/5.

21. Thomas Dick, *Philosophy of a Future State* (Philadelphia: E. C. & J. Biddle, 1845),
1:170.

22. Brigham Young, "The Fullness of the Gospel—Its Power to Unite—Its
Comprehensiveness—Definition of Its Priesthood—Condition of Apostates,"
JD 15:127.

23. Orson Pratt, "Concentration of the Mind," JD 7:157.

24. "A Vision Given to Mosiah Hancock," in *Levi and Mosiah Hancock Journals*, 188
(Genola, Utah: Pioneer, 2006).

25. David J. Whittaker, "Joseph B. Keeler, Print Culture, and the Modernization of Mormonism, 1885–1918," in *Religion and the Culture of Print in Modern America*, edited by James P. Danky (Madison: University of Wisconsin Press, 2006).

26. Leonard J. Arrington and Davis Bitton, *The Mormon Experience* (New York: Random House, 1979), 337.

27. "Projecting Bachelor Degree Recipients by Gender," *Postsecondary Opportunity*, December 2000, 102; Mabel Newcomer, *A Century of Higher Education for American Women* (New York: Harper & Brothers, 1959), 46.

28. B. H. Roberts, *The Autobiography of B. H. Roberts*, edited by Gary James Bergera (Salt Lake City: Signature, 1990): 54.

29. Statistics quoted by Charles Ellis, a non-Mormon, in *Scrapbook of Mormon Literature* (n.p.: Ben Rich, n.d.), 2:151–52. Ranking from *Contributor* 4, no. 5 (February 1883): 183.

30. *Times and Seasons* 5, no. 24 (1 January 1845): 758.

31. Pratt, "Concentration," 157.

32. Cited in Thomas W. Simpson, *American Universities and the Birth of Modern Mormonism, 1867–1940* (Chapel Hill: University of North Carolina Press, 2016), 72.

33. First Presidency of the Church, "The Origin of Man," *Improvement Era*, November 1909, 80.

34. The charges were outlined in a report by Church Superintendent of Education Horace Cummings, recorded in the manuscript "History of Brigham Young University," compiled by J. Marinus Jensen, N. I. Butt, Elsie Carroll, and Bertha Roberts, on file at the Harold B. Lee Library, Brigham Young University, Provo, Utah; cited in Richard Sherlock, "Campus in Crisis," *Sunstone*, May 1985, 32.

35. Simpson, *American Universities*, 92.

36. Russel B. Swensen, "Mormons at the University of Chicago Divinity School: A Personal Reminiscence," *Dialogue: A Journal of Mormon Thought* 7, no. 2 (Summer 1972): 39–40.

37. From a meeting of the Twelve, 7 January 1930. Cited in James B. Allen, "The Story of *The Truth, the Way, the Life*," in B. H. Roberts, *The Truth, the Way, the Life*, edited by John W. Welch, clxxviii (Provo, Utah: BYU Studies, 1994).

38. *Deseret News*, 5 April 1930, 8; qtd. in Allen, "The Story," clxxix.

39. "I can state positively that it was not published by the Church, nor by the approval of the Authorities of the Church," wrote Joseph Fielding Smith; cited in Steven H. Heath, "The Reconciliation of Faith and Science: Henry Eyring's Achievement," *Dialogue: A Journal of Mormon Thought* 15, no. 3 (Autumn 1982): 93.

40. Armand L. Mauss, *The Angel and the Beehive: The Mormon Struggle with Assimilation* (Urbana: University of Illinois Press, 1994), 43.

41. M. Russell Ballard, "The Opportunities and Responsibilities of CES Teachers in the 21st Century," 26 February 2016, https://www.churchofjesuschrist.org/broadcasts/article/evening-with-a-general-authority/2016/02/the-opportunities-and-responsibilities-of-ces-teachers-in-the-21st-century?lang=eng.

42. J. Reuben Clark Jr., "The Charted Course of the Church in Education," *Improvement Era*, September 1938, 573.

43. First Presidency to Franklin L. West, 29 February 1940, Harris Papers; cited in Gary James Bergera and Ronald Priddis, *Brigham Young University: A House of Faith* (Salt Lake City: Signature, 1985), 62.

44. Harold T. Christensen and Kenneth L. Cannon, "The Fundamentalist Emphasis at Brigham Young University: 1935–1973," *Journal for the Scientific Study of Religion* 17, no. 1 (March 1978): 55.

45. Christensen and Cannon, "Fundamentalist Emphasis," 54.

46. "Study Finds Mormon Teens Fare Best," Associated Press, 14 March 2005, www.news14.com. The results are published in Christian Smith and Melinda Lundquist Denton, *Soul Searching: The Religious and Spiritual Lives of American Teenagers* (New York: Oxford University Press, 2005).

47. Mary Lythgoe Bradford, *Lowell L. Bennion: Teacher, Counselor, and Humanitarian* (Salt Lake City: Dialogue Foundation, 1995), quoted on dust jacket.

48. Bradford, *Bennion*, 127.

49. Bradford, *Bennion*, 131–32.

50. England reports these words from a recorded interview he conducted with Hugh B. Brown. The original interview is not known to be extant. ME-I 118, pt. 1.

51. Dian Saderup Monson, "Eugene England—Master Teacher: The BYU Years," *Sunstone*, January 2002, 30.

52. Richard Bushman, "Joseph Smith and His Visions," in Terryl L. Givens and Philip L. Barlow, *The Oxford Handbook of Mormonism*, 117 (New York: Oxford University Press, 2015).

53. Bushman, "Joseph Smith," 117.

54. Gregory A. Prince and William Robert Wright, *David O. McKay and the Rise of Modern Mormonism* (Salt Lake City: University of Utah Press, 2005), 50–52. McConkie's "Seven Deadly Heresies" sermon had a similar history; Marion D. Hanks reported to England that it was privately condemned though publicly circulated. See ME-I 119, pt. 1.

55. Bradford, *Bennion*, 155.

56. Bradford, *Bennion*, 160.

57. Bradford, *Bennion*, 167.

58. Bradford, *Bennion*, 173.

59. Bradford, *Bennion*, 173.

60. Donald Bruce Johnson and Kirk H. Porter, *National Party Platforms, 1840–1972* (Urbana: University of Illinois Press, 1978), 27.

61. The view of sexual sin as second only to murder, as well as being intimated in the scripture cited, Alma 39:5, has been affirmed by several statements by presiding leaders of the church. See "Is Sexual Sin Next to Murder?," https://ldsanswers.org/is-sexual-sin-next-to-murder-book-of-mormon-central-fact-check/.

62. "U.S. Religious Groups and Their Political Leanings," https://www.pewresearch.org/fact-tank/2016/02/23/u-s-religious-groups-and-their-political-leanings/.

63. "An Interview with Eugene England," *Student Review*, 10 April 1998.

64. Ezra Taft Benson, "Beware of Pride," *Ensign*, May 1989, 4–7; Spencer W. Kimball, "The False Gods We Worship," *Ensign*, June 1976, 6.

65. ME-I 125.

66. England implies he taught at the institute as early as 1964. Perhaps he did, however, a letter dated 8 November 1966 acknowledges his formally expressed "desire to enter into the Institute program of the Church." That may be a reference to an inquiry about a career in the CES. William E. Berrett to Eugene England, 8 November 1966, EE-P 172.5.

67. Kathy Shirts to Charlotte [England], 20 August 2001, CE-C.

68. Robert A. Goldberg, "From New Deal to New Right," in *Thunder from the Right: Ezra Taft Benson in Mormonism and Politics*, edited by Matthew L. Harris, 71, 68 (Urbana: University of Illinois Press, 2019).

69. ME-I 116.

70. "Maybe two or three," he recollected. ME-I 116.

71. ME-I 116.

72. ME-I 118, pt. 1.

73. Marion D. Hanks (First Council of Seventy) to EE, 13 September 1965, EE-P 171.9.

74. EE to Marion D. Hanks, 4 November 1965, EE-P 171.9.

75. EE to Marion D. Hanks, 16 November 1965, EE-P 171.9.

CHAPTER 4

1. EE, "The Quest for Authentic Faculty Power," *Soundings: An Interdisciplinary Journal* 52, no. 2 (Summer 1969): 200.

2. Mary Lythgoe Bradford, "In Memory of Dr. Bill," *Dialogue: A Journal of Mormon Thought* 41, no. 3 (Fall 2008): 190–91.

3. "An Interview with Eugene England," *The Carpenter: Reflections on Mormon Life*, Spring 1970, 10.

4. "Interview," *Carpenter*, 11.

5. "Interview," *Carpenter*, 11–12.

6. Gene Kovalenko, ME-I 104.

7. Mary Lythgoe Bradford, "Reminiscence," EE-P 165.15.

8. G. Wesley Johnson, "Editorial Preface," *Dialogue: A Journal of Mormon Thought* 1, no. 1 (Spring 1966): 6.

9. "Interview," *Carpenter*, 13.

10. EE, "'No Cause, No Cause': An Essay toward Reconciliation," *Sunstone*, January 2002, 36.

11. Leonard Arrington, *Reflections of a Mormon Historian: Leonard J. Arrington on the New Mormon History*, edited by Reid Neilson and Ronald Walker (Norman, Okla.: Arthur H. Clark, 2006), 81.

12. "Mormon Scholars Plan a Journal: Independent Quarterly Will Be Issued in February," *New York Times*, 12 December 1965, 80.

13. EE, "Finding Myself in the Sixties," unpublished ms., circa 1990, 11, EE-P 50.4.

14. EE to Richard Marshall, 14 December 1965, Dialogue Collection, DW-C.

15. EE to First Presidency, 15 December 1965, Dialogue Collection, DW-C.

16. EE to Gordon B. Hinckley, 7 March 1966, Dialogue Collection, DW-C.

17. EE and Wes Johnson to the First Presidency, 29 March 1966, Dialogue Collection, DW-C.

18. Harold B. Lee, "New Plan of Co-ordination Explained," *Improvement Era*, January 1962, 36.

19. Harold B. Lee in *Conference Report of the Church of Jesus Christ of Latter-day Saints*, April 1963, 394.

20. Leonard Arrington, "Blessed Damozels: Women in Mormon History," *Dialogue: A Journal of Mormon Thought* 6, no. 2 (Summer 1971): 26.

21. Lee, "New Plan," 37.

22. Kenneth W. Godfrey, "Eugene England: A Man for Whom Faith Won," Eugene England Foundation (n.d.), https://www.eugeneengland.org/eugene-england /remembering-gene-project/remembering-gene-mission-marriage-mit-air-force -stanford-dialogue/983–2.

23. Godfrey, "Eugene England."

24. William E. Berrett to EE, 8 November 1966, EE-P 172.5.

25. Godfrey, "Eugene England."

26. EE, interview by David Bitton, Oral History Program, Church History Library.

27. EE, "The Possibility of Dialogue: A Personal View," *Dialogue: A Journal of Mormon Thought* 1, no. 1 (Spring 1966): 9–10.

28. Dilworth Young to "Bro England," 29 March 1966, EE-P 172.3.

29. EE interview by Davis Bitton, Oral History Project.

30. Elder Boyd K. Packer, "Talk to the All-Church Coordinating Council," 18 May 1993, https://www.zionsbest.com/face.html. England had a copy of the transcript in his files.

31. *Improvement Era*, June 1945, 354.

32. Cited in *Dialogue: A Journal of Mormon Thought* 19, no. 1 (Spring 1986): 38.

33. Memo to Don [Marshall?], 29 May 1987, EE-P 168.5.

34. Susan Lundquist, interview with author, 12 June 2017.

35. *England Family Histories: George Eugene England Sr. and Dora Rose Hartvigsen England*, compiled and edited by Ann Christine England Barker (n.p.: n.p., 2012), 227, CE-C.

36. Theology Lecture Second, II.56, 1835 D&C 25.

37. Stan Larson, "The King Follett Discourse: A Newly Amalgamated Text," *BYU Studies* 18, no. 2 (Winter 1978): 201.

38. As both David Knowlton and Armand Mauss have pointed out, these testimonies, formerly steeped in firsthand experiences, miraculous healings, and spiritual encounters with the divine, have attained a highly formulaic and ritualized dimension, prime evidence of which is the frequent participation of little children reciting the formulas they have imbibed. (In an effort to curb this last trend, at least, the First Presidency issued a statement discouraging that practice in 2002.) See David Knowlton, "Belief, Metaphor, and Rhetoric: The Mormon Practice of Bearing Testimonies," *Sunstone*, April 1991, 20–27; Armand L. Mauss, *The Angel and the Beehive: The Mormon Struggle with Assimilation* (Urbana: University of

Illinois Press, 1994), 28–30; and Letter of the First Presidency, 2 May 2002, https://
www.churchofjesuschrist.org/church/news/first-presidency-letter-testimonies-in
-fast-and-testimony-meeting?lang=eng.

39. EE, "The Possibility of Dialogue," 9–10.
40. EE, "The Possibility of Dialogue," 10–11.
41. See M. Russell Ballard, "The Opportunities and Responsibilities of CES Teachers
in the 21st Century," 26 February 2016, https://www.churchofjesuschrist.org
/broadcasts/article/evening-with-a-general-authority/2016/02/the-opportunities
-and-responsibilities-of-ces-teachers-in-the-21st-century?lang=eng. See also
Jeffrey R. Holland, "'Lord, I Believe,'" General Conference talk, April 2013, https://
www.thechurchnews.com/archives/2013-04-07/elder-jeffrey-r-holland
-lord-i-believe-46398; and Dieter F. Uchtdorf, "Come, Join with Us," General Conference talk, October 2013, https://www.churchofjesuschrist.org/study/general
-conference/2013/10/come-join-with-us?lang=eng.
42. EE, "On Finding Truth and God," *Why the Church Is As True As the Gospel* (Salt
Lake City: Bookcraft, 1986), 111–12. First delivered at the 1985 Sunstone Theological Symposium.
43. Jana Riess, "How Many Millennials Are Really Leaving the LDS Church?," Religious News Service, March 7, 2019, https://religionnews.com/2019/03/27/how
-many-millennials-are-really-leaving-the-lds-church/.
44. R. A. Christmas, "*The Autobiography of Parley P. Pratt*: Some Literary, Historical,
and Critical Reflections," *Dialogue: A Journal of Mormon Thought* 1, no. 1 (1966):
33–43.
45. Frances Menlove, "The Challenge of Honesty," *Dialogue: A Journal of Mormon
Thought* 1, no. 1 (Spring 1966): 44–53.
46. Henry Eyring, "My Father's Formula," General Conference talk (October 1978),
https://www.churchofjesuschrist.org/study/ensign/1978/10/my-fathers-formula
?lang=eng.
47. Wesley P. Walters, "New Light on Mormon Origins from Palmyra (N.Y.) Revival,"
Bulletin of the Evangelical Theological Society 10, no. 4 (Fall 1967): 227–44.
48. Godfrey, "Eugene England."
49. Godfrey, "Eugene England."
50. "Interview," *Carpenter*, 14.
51. "Interview," *Carpenter*, 23.
52. "In This Issue," *Dialogue: A Journal of Mormon Thought* 1, no. 2 (Summer 1966): 2.
53. Sterling M. McMurrin and L. Jackson Newell, *Matters of Conscience: Conversations
with Sterling M. McMurrin on Philosophy, Education, and Religion* (Salt Lake City:
Signature, 1996), 198.
54. Sterling M. McMurrin, "On Mormon Theology," *Dialogue: A Journal of Mormon
Thought* 1, no. 2 (Summer 1966): 136.
55. McMurrin, "On Mormon Theology," 137.
56. McMurrin, "On Mormon Theology," 138.
57. Karl Keller, "Every Soul Has Its South," *Dialogue: A Journal of Mormon Thought* 1,
no. 2 (Summer 1966): 73.

58. Keller, "Every Soul Has Its South," 79.

59. P. A. M. Taylor, "The Life of Brigham Young: A Biography Which Will Not Be Written," *Dialogue: A Journal of Mormon Thought* 1, no. 3 (1966): 106, 110.

60. Taylor, "The Life of Brigham Young," 109.

61. Ray C. Hillam, Eugene England, and John L. Sorenson, "Roundtable: Vietnam," *Dialogue: A Journal of Mormon Thought* 2, no. 4 (Winter 1967): 65–100.

62. Knud S. Larsen, "A Voice against the War," *Dialogue: A Journal of Mormon Thought* 2, no. 3 (Fall 1967): 163–66.

63. Armand L. Mauss gave a provocative overview and critique, "Mormonism and the Negro: Faith, Folklore, and Civil Rights," *Dialogue: A Journal of Mormon Thought* 2, no. 4 (Winter 1967): 19–40; The topic was raised frequently in subsequent articles like Royal Shipp, "Black Images and White Images: The Combustibility of Common Misconceptions," *Dialogue: A Journal of Mormon Thought* 3, no. 4 (Winter 1968): 77–91, as well as in numerous letters and other articles.

64. Steward Udall, "Letter to the Editor," *Dialogue: A Journal of Mormon Thought* 2, no. 2 (Summer 1967): 5–7.

65. Udall, "Letter," 6.

66. D. Arthur Haycock to G. Eugene England, 26 May 1967, EE-P 172.7.

67. EE to D. Arthur Haycock, 24 June 1967, EE-P 172.7.

68. EE to N. L. [*sic*] Tanner, 28 June 1967, EE-P 172.6.

69. N. Eldon Tanner to EE, 22 June 1967. The date of one of the two letters is apparently in error, since Tanner's is a reply to England's, EE-P 172.6.

70. William E. Berrett to EE, 6 June 1968, DW-C.

71. ME-I 118, pt. 1

72. Godfrey, "Eugene England."

73. ME-I 118, pt. 1

74. Marion D. Hanks to EE, 24 September 1968, EE-P 171.9.

75. EE to Marion D. Hanks, 5 September 1968, EE-P 171.9.

76. Marion D. Hanks to EE, 19 September 1968, EE-P 171.9.

77. Marion D. Hanks to EE, 24 September 1968.

78. EE to Marion D. Hanks, 1 October 1968, EE-P 171.9.

79. Marion D. Hanks to EE, 4 October 1968, EE-P 171.9.

80. EE to Marion D. Hanks, 5 September 1968.

81. EE to Marion D. Hanks, 13 May 1969, EE-P 171.9.

82. EE to Marion D. Hanks, 21 March 1974, EE-P 171.9.

83. ME-I 118, pt. 1.

84. Lester Bush, "A Commentary on Stephen G. Taggart's *Mormonism's Negro Policy: Social and Historical Origins*," *Dialogue: A Journal of Mormon Thought* 4, no. 4 (Winter 1969): 86.

85. Bush, "Commentary," 103.

86. Bush is quoting from a letter of Sterling McMurrin to Llewelyn McKay, cited in Stephen G. Taggart, *Mormonism's Negro Policy: Social and Historical Origins* (Salt Lake City: University of Utah Press, 1970), 79.

87. EE, "No Cause," 34.

88. Details of Brown's response to Bush's article are recounted in a memo written by Paul Salisbury, the day of their meeting, dated 29 September 1969, EE-P 172.9. Brown's article, "An Eternal Quest: Freedom of the Mind," was perfectly chosen to show thematic as well as symbolic support for the journal. Delivered to the BYU student body in 1969, it was not published in the journal until several years later. *Dialogue: A Journal of Mormon Thought* 17, no. 1 (Spring 1984) 77–83.

89. Lester Bush, "Writing 'Mormonism's Negro Doctrine: An Historical Overview' (1973): Context and Reflections, 1998," *Journal of Mormon History* 25, no. 1 (Spring 1999): 250. Bush had shown the manuscript to Janath Cannon, who passed it on to Packer on her own initiative but with Bush's approval (247).

90. Bush, "Writing 'Mormonism's Negro Doctrine,'" 252. His research was published as "Mormonism's Negro Doctrine: An Historical Overview," *Dialogue: A Journal of Mormon Thought* 8, no. 1 (Spring 1973): 11–68.

91. Lester Bush to EE, 23 August 1973, EE-P 171.27.

92. EEJ, 6 March 1992.

93. Bush, "Writing 'Mormonism's Negro Doctrine,'" 265–66.

94. Lester E. Bush Jr., "Looking Back, Looking Forward: 'Mormonism's Negro Doctrine' Forty-Five Years Later," *Dialogue: A Journal of Mormon Thought* 51, no. 3 (Fall 2018): 7.

95. Mary Lythgoe Bradford, *Lowell L. Bennion: Teacher, Counselor, and Humanitarian* (Salt Lake City: Dialogue Foundation, 1995), 166.

96. Bradford, *Bennion*, 166.

97. EE, "The Mormon Cross," *Dialogue: A Journal of Mormon Thought* 8, no. 1 (Spring 1973): 78–86.

98. EE, "The Mormon Cross," 78.

99. EE, "The Mormon Cross," 78–79.

100. Joseph Fielding Smith, "The Negro and the Priesthood," *Improvement Era*, April 1924, 565.

101. He repeats the story in another essay on race, "Are All Alike unto God? Prejudice against Blacks and Women in Popular Mormon Theology," *Sunstone*, April 1990, 21–31.

102. EE, "The Mormon Cross," 85.

103. "Race and the Priesthood," Church of Jesus Christ of Latter-day Saints, 2016, https://www.lds.org/topics/race-and-the-priesthood?lang=eng.

104. Laurel Thatcher Ulrich, "The Pink *Dialogue* and Beyond," *Dialogue: A Journal of Mormon Thought* 14, no. 4 (Winter 1981): 29.

105. "Interview," *Carpenter*, 14.

106. "Interview," *Carpenter*, 10.

107. "Interview," *Carpenter*, 22.

108. ME-I 117, pt. 2.

109. Charlotte England, "Finding Bearmont," personal essay, CE-C.

110. Jack Zenger, personal communication with author, 2 March 2020.

CHAPTER 5

1. Karl Keller to EE, 3 May 1968, EE-P 166.6.
2. He was offered a contract as assistant professor of English on 22 December 1966. Fred F. Harcleroad to Mr. George Eugene England Jr., CE-C.
3. EE, "'No Cause, No Cause': An Essay toward Reconciliation," *Sunstone*, January 2002, 33.
4. ME-I 116. See "EE, "Finding Myself in the Sixties," unpublished ms., circa 1990, 11, EE-P 50.4.
5. EE, "The Quest for Authentic Faculty Power," *Soundings: An Interdisciplinary Journal* 52, no. 2 (Summer 1969): 196–217.
6. Kenneth W. Godfrey, "Eugene England: A Man for Whom Faith Won," Eugene England Foundation (n.d.), https://www.eugeneengland.org/eugene-england /remembering-gene-project/remembering-gene-mission-marriage-mit-air-force -stanford-dialogue/983–2.
7. EE to Boyd K. Packer, 20 May 1974, EE-P 171.21; EE to President Sidney A. Rand, 26 May 1970, EE-P 193.1.
8. Albert Finholt to EE, 23 July 1970, CE-C.
9. "United Methodists Claim LDS Not Really Christian," *Idaho Statesman*, 11 May 2000; "Striving for Acceptance," *Washington Post*, 9 February 2002. In this same period, I was present at a hearing of the Faith and Order board of a state affiliate of the National Council of Churches, listening to a Latter-day Saint petition for a shift from observer status to membership (more by way of testing the issue than in earnest presumably). During the proceedings, a Methodist representative concluded that, "based on our own criteria" (according to the World Council of Churches constitution, members constitute "a fellowship of churches which confess the Lord Jesus Christ as God and Saviour according to the scriptures"), "Mormons are as Christian as any here." However, he was overruled by another member who insisted repeatedly and vehemently, "But they don't accept the Trinity." The meeting took place in Charlottesville, Virginia.
10. The talk was reprinted as "Are Mormons Christians?," *Dialogue: A Journal of Mormon Thought* 5, no. 4 (Winter 1970): 71–76. The talk is said to have been given in 1970, but this is inaccurate: England was not at St. Olaf until that fall and delivered the talk the next March. The "winter" issue was apparently printed behind schedule.
11. EE, "Are Mormons Christians?," 71–76.
12. Owen Jordahl to EE, 1 March 1971, EE-P 193.1.
13. Steve Miles to EE, 14 June 1972, EE-P 193.1.
14. Charlotte England to author, 2 April 2016.
15. Charlotte England to author, 2 April 2016.
16. Charlotte England to author, 2 April 2016.
17. Charlotte England to author, 2 April 2016.
18. EEJ, 14 August 1975.
19. "Faribault Branch History," CE-C.

20. EE, "No Cause," 34.

21. "Faribault Branch History," CE-C.

22. Christine Carlicci to Charlotte [England], 20 August 2001, CE-C.

23. These details are given in his letter to Harold B. Lee, 17 October 1972, EE-P 171.15.

24. Joan Odd, "Memorial Service for Eugene England," CE-C.

25. EE to Neal A. Maxwell, 30 June 1970, EE-P 171.18.

26. EEJ, 21 June 1992.

27. Neal A. Maxwell to EE, 6 July 1970, EE-P 171.18.

28. EE to Neal A. Maxwell, 18 March 1971, EE-P 171.18.

29. Neal A. Maxwell to EE, 20 September 1971, EE-P 171.18.

30. Joseph J. Christensen to EE, 13 April 1971, EE-P 172.20.

31. Neal A. Maxwell to Dean EE, 15 February 1973, EE-P 171.18.

32. Neal A. Maxwell to EE, 18 May 1984, EE-P 171.18.

33. Albert Gelpi to EE, 27 October 1971, EE-P 193–91.

34. EE to Marshall Craig, 25 October 1972, CE-C.

35. Dallin Oaks to EE, 9 January 1973, EE-P 171.20.

36. Lloyd Svendsbye to EE, 31 August 1972, EE-P 148.13.

37. Memo, EE to Lloyd Svendsbye, 14 March 1973, EE-P 148.13.

38. EE to Dallin Oaks, 3 January 1973, EE-P 171.20.

39. Sidney Rand to EE, 16 March 1973, CE-C.

40. Lloyd Svendsbye to EE, 31 August 1972, EE-P 148.13.

41. Ivo Struttal [?], 30 January 1973, EE-P 193.1.

42. Sidney Rand to EE, 12 February 1974, EE-P 193.1.

43. England discusses the conflict over Svendsbye's authority in EE to Gerald Thorson (English department chair), 11 December 1975, EE-P 8.5.

44. Charlotte Hansen, "Eugene England's Calculated Risk: The Struggle for Academic Freedom and Religious Dialogue," MA thesis, University of Utah (May 2010), 3; EE, "Speaking the Truth in Love," *Ensign*, April 1976, 51–55.

45. Memo, Ronn Farland to Gerald Thorson, 17 January 1974, EE-P 8.1.

46. EE to Bruce Clark, 31 January 1974, CE-C.

47. EE to George [Holling], 28 January 1975, EE-P 193.1.

48. Sidney Rand to EE, 14 February 1975, EE-P 193.1.

49. EE to Marvin Rytting, 19 February 1975, EE-P 193.1.

50. EE to President [Sidney] Rand, 20 February 1975, EE-P 193.1

51. Sidney Rand to EE, 25 February 1975, EE-P 193.1.

52. EE to President [Sidney] Rand, 28 February 1975; Sidney Rand to EE, 12 March 1975; EE-P 193.1.

53. *The Messenger*, 2 May 1975.

54. EE to Clifton Jolley, 25 February 1975, EE-P 193.1.

55. Michael Massing, *Fatal Discord: Erasmus, Luther, and the Fight for the Western Mind* (New York: HarperCollins, 2018), 676.

56. Karl Keller to "Gene," 12 January 1973, EE-P 166.5.

57. Neal A. Maxwell to EE, 21 February 1974, EE-P 171.18.

58. EE to Marion D. Hanks, 21 March 1974, EE-P 171.9.

59. EE to Marion D. Hanks, 21 March 1974, EE-P 171.9.

60. Dallin H. Oaks to EE, 16 August 1974, EE-P 171.9.

61. Gerald Thorson to EE, 15 January 1975, EE-P 193.1.

62. EE to Dallin H. Oaks, 20 February 1975, EE-P 171.12.

63. Bruce Clark to EE, 3 March 1975, EE-P 193.1.

64. EEJ, 12 August 1975.

65. EE to Dallin H. Oaks, 20 February 1975, EE-P 171.12.

66. England acknowledged this in a journal entry the next year, 16 March 1976.

67. EE to Boyd K. Packer, 9 April 1975, EE-P 171.21.

68. Harold Hunker replied to his application noncommittally. Harold Hunker to EE, 14 April 1975, CE-C.

69. Charlotte England, interview with author, 29 July 2017. He had mentioned the idea in passing to Dallin Oaks in 1971. EE to Dallin Oaks, 6 May 1971, EE-P 171.20.

70. EE to Sir Walter Lindal, 3 February 1975, EE-P 193.1.

71. EE to Dallin H. Oaks, 20 February 1975.

72. EEJ, 4 March 1992. England also said that Hanks confirmed the account, and he speculated that Hanks's open dissent on this and other board of trustees decisions was why he was never made an apostle. ME-I 118, pt. 1.

CHAPTER 6

1. EE to Leonard Arrington, 5 February 1975, EE-P 165.5.

2. Leonard Arrington to EE, n.d., EE-P 165.5.

3. EE to Robert D. Hales, 7 May 1975, EE-P 171.8.

4. *England Family Histories: George Eugene England Sr. and Dora Rose Hartvigsen England*, compiled and edited by Ann Christine England Barker (n.p.: n.p., 2012), 238, CE-C.

5. Leonard Arrington, *Confessions of a Mormon Historian: The Diaries of Leonard Arrington, 1971–1997*, edited by Gary James Bergera (Salt Lake City: Signature, 2018), 2:84.

6. ME-I 118, pt. 1.

7. EEJ, 12 August 1975.

8. EEJ, 15 August 1975.

9. EEJ, 4 September 1975.

10. EEJ 4, 16 September 1975.

11. EE, "Easter Weekend," *Dialogue: A Journal of Mormon Thought* 21, no. 1 (Spring 1988): 26.

12. Barker, *England Family Histories*, 119.

13. EEJ, 13 August 1975.

14. Sterling McMurrin, "On Mormon Theology," *Dialogue: A Journal of Mormon Thought* 1, no. 2 (Summer 1966): 140.

15. Charles Buck, *Theological Dictionary* (Philadelphia: Joseph Woodward, 1830), 582; Theology Lecture First, I.Q1, 1835 D&C 9; John Taylor, "Communism—Sectarianism—The Gospel and Its Effects," *JD* 5:240.

16. McMurrin, "On Mormon Theology," 136.

17. Parley P. Pratt, *The Millennium, and Other Poems: To Which Is Annexed, a Treatise on the Regeneration and Eternal Duration of Matter* (New York: Molineux, 1840), 137.

18. Wilford Woodruff, "Discourse by President Wilford Woodruff," *Millennial Star,* 6 June 1895, 355–56.

19. Bruce R. McConkie, *Mormon Doctrine* (Salt Lake City: Bookcraft, 1958), 5.

20. This is the subtitle of his authorized biography. Lucile C. Tate, *Boyd K. Packer: A Watchman on the Tower* (Salt Lake City: Bookcraft, 1995).

21. EEJ, 24 January 1994.

22. B. H. Roberts, "Book of Mormon Translation," *Improvement Era,* July 1906, 713. Cited in "Unto All Nations: Becoming a World Religion," version in EEJ, 11 January 1997. Unpublished ms. prepared for a writer's group to which EE belonged.

23. EE, "Unto All Nations."

24. John Harris, "Risk and Terror," *Dialogue: A Journal of Mormon Thought* 26, no. 4 (Winter 1993): 153–58. England's apologist comment was made to me in 2001.

25. EEJ, 24 January 1994.

26. Augustine, *De Civitate Dei,* 13, 21. Clement of Alexandria, *Stromata,* 4, 8. Both cited in Elaine Pagels, *Adam, Eve, and the Serpent: Sex and Politics in Early Christianity* (New York: Vintage, 1989), 120, 52. Her book is an explanation of how this "radical departure" unfolded and became orthodoxy (132).

27. Stan Larson, "The King Follet Discourse: A Newly Amalgamated Text," *BYU Studies* 18, no. 2 (April 1978): 201.

28. Eliza R. Snow Smith, *Biography and Family Record of Lorenzo Snow* (Salt Lake City: Deseret, 1884), 46.

29. *CDBY* 2:1088, 5:3139.

30. Theology Lecture Seventh, 1835 D&C, 66–67.

31. Charles W. Penrose, *"Mormon" Doctrine, Plain and Simple: Or, Leaves from the Tree of Life* (Salt Lake City: Juvenile Instructor Office, 1888), 49.

32. EE to Dallin H. Oaks, 30 November 2000, EE-P 171.20.

33. EEJ, 24 January 1994.

34. ME-I 117, pt. 1.

35. EEJ, 24 January 1994.

36. "Lecture on Theology" II.2, 1835 D&C, 12.

37. EE, "The Weeping God of Mormonism," *Dialogue: A Journal of Mormon Thought* 35, no. 1 (Spring 2002): 73.

38. My emphases. The groundwork for the shift in interpretation was the rendering of the Greek *dikaioun* (to make righteous) into Latin as *iustificare* (to justify). This point is made by a combined Anglican/Roman Catholic International Commission statement, "Salvation and the Church." See Stephen Sykes, *The Story of Atonement* (London: Darton, Longman and Todd, 1997), 58.

39. "Simul justus et peccator," in the original. "The Saints are at the same time sinners while they are righteous." In one gloss, Luther explains that "outside himself (i.e., before God) [the saved man] is wholly and without exception unrighteous." Martin Luther, *Lectures on Romans,* edited and translated by Wilhelm Pauck (Louisville: Westminster, 1961), xlv, 79.

40. James E. Talmage, *Articles of Faith* (Salt Lake City: Deseret, 1899), 97.

41. Thomas Weinandy, "Does God Suffer?," *First Things*, November 2001, https://www.firstthings.com/article/2001/11/does-god-suffer.

42. John Calvin, *Isaiah*, edited by Alister McGrath and J. I. Packer (Wheaton, Ill.: Crossway, 2000), 75.

43. Sterling M. McMurrin, *The Theological Foundations of the Mormon Religion* (Salt Lake City: University of Utah Press, 1965), 35.

44. Joseph Smith, *Elders' Journal*, July 1838, 44.

45. Andrew F. Ehat and Lyndon W. Cook, eds., *The Words of Joseph Smith* (Orem, Utah: Grandin, 1991), 63.

46. Anselm, *Cur deus homo?*, 1:xi–xiii; cited in Henry Bettenson, ed., *Documents of the Christian Church* (New York: Oxford University Press, 1947), 196–97.

47. Friedrich Nietzsche, *The Genealogy of Morals*, trans. Horace B. Samuel (Stilwell, Kan.: Digireads, 2007), 47.

48. Stephen Finlan, *Problems with Atonement* (Collegeville, Minn.: Liturgical, 2005), 84.

49. Quoted in Rita Nakashima Brock and Rebecca Ann Parker, *Saving Paradise: How Christianity Traded Love of This World for Crucifixion and Empire* (Boston: Beacon, 2008), 292.

50. Diana Butler Bass, *A People's History of Christianity: The Other Side of the Story* (New York: HarperCollins, 2010), 116. Bass also cites the Abélard passage referenced above.

51. Hastings Rashdall, *The Idea of Atonement in Christian Theology* (London, n.p.: 1919), 357–62; cited in Peter Abelard, *Commentary on the Epistle to the Romans*, trans. Steven R. Cartwright (Washington, D.C.: Catholic University of America Press, 2011), 44.

52. B. H. Roberts, *The Truth, the Way, the Life*, edited by John W. Welch (Provo, Utah: BYU Studies, 1994), 405–08; 453–54.

53. Russell M. Nelson, "Addiction or Freedom," *Ensign*, November 1988, 7.

54. Boyd K. Packer, "The Mediator," https://www.churchofjesuschrist.org/study/general-conference/1977/04/the-mediator?lang=eng.

55. Boyd K. Packer, "Atonement, Agency, Accountability," *Ensign*, April 1988, 69.

56. Roberts, *The Truth, the Way, the Life*, 453–54.

57. A growing consensus has it that Pelagius was generally misrepresented by his opponents, and did not assert the possibility of salvation outside of Christ's grace, however aided by human effort.

58. Neal A. Maxwell to EE, 20 February 1968, EE-P 171.18.

59. This phrase was Milton G. Wille's characterization of England's own account, which England did not dispute. See "Report of Milton G. Wille to President Bateman and Bishop Andrus," 18 October 1988, EE-P 171.30.

60. "Report of Milton G. Wille to President Bateman and Bishop Andrus."

61. EE, "'No Cause, No Cause': An Essay toward Reconciliation," *Sunstone*, January 2002, 38.

62. EEJ, 21 June 1992.

63. EE, "Cordelia and Paulina, Shakespeare's Healing Dramatists," *Literature and Belief* 2 (1982): 79–81.

CHAPTER 7

1. EE, "Letter to a College Student," *Dialogue: A Journal of Mormon Thought* 8, no. 3/4 (Autumn/Winter 1973): 178–80.
2. EE, "Great Books or True Religion? Defining the Mormon Scholar," *Dialogue: A Journal of Mormon Thought* 9, no. 4 (Winter 1974): 47.
3. EEJ, 16 March 1976.
4. Richard Bushman, personal correspondence with author, 1 August 2017.
5. EEJ, 16 March 1976.
6. EE to Boyd K. Packer, 9 April 1975. England mentions their "pre-conference" meeting, indicating it was shortly before the first weekend in April, EE-P 172.17.
7. Clifton Jolley (author of the poem), said England related the episode to him. Interview with author, 12 June 2017. The poem is found in *Dialogue: A Journal of Mormon Thought* 7, no. 3 (Autumn 1972) 64. Jolley refers to his piece as that "awful poem."
8. EE to Boyd K. Packer, 9 April 1975, EE-P 172.17.
9. EE to Boyd K. Packer, 10 February 1976, EE-P 172.17.
10. Boyd K. Packer, "The Arts and the Spirit of the Lord," *Ensign*, August 1976, 61.
11. EEJ, 16 March 1976.
12. EE, "Letter to the Editor," *Sunstone*, Winter 1975, 5.
13. EEJ, 17 March 1976.
14. EEJ, 17 March 1976.
15. EEJ, 7 September 1975.
16. *England Family Histories: George Eugene England Sr. and Dora Rose Hartvigsen England*, compiled and edited by Ann Christine England Barker (n.p.: n.p., 2012), 52, CE-C.
17. Donlu Thayer, conversation with the author, 15 September 2018.
18. EEJ, 23 September 1999.
19. Eyring was the most distinguished and lauded scientist in LDS history. He won the Wolf Prize, the National Medal of Science, the Berzelius Medal, and would have won the Nobel if not for his religious affiliation, according to John F. Kennedy's commissioner of education, Sterling McMurrin.
20. Barker, *England Family Histories*, 61.
21. ME-I 117, pt. 1.
22. Mary Lythgoe Bradford to EE, 31 October 1974, EE-P 165.15.
23. ME-I 119, pt. 2.
24. EE, "Finding Myself in the Sixties," unpublished ms., circa 1990, 11, EE-P 50.4.
25. The remarks were made to Mary Lythgoe Bradford, EEJ, 13 August 1975.
26. "George Eugene England. Jr.," typescript, EE-P 2.5.
27. EEJ, 24 March 1976.

28. EEJ, 24 March 1976.

29. "Apostle David B. Haight wrote to us in appreciation for our fund for the missionaries and said he had heard Eugene Jr. give a good talk on Brigham Young. He said they had a good visit. He was Eugene's stake president in Palo Alto. I hope he pulls for him to get a job at BYU." Barker, *England Family Histories*, 243.

30. ME-I 118, pt. 1. Holland later confirmed his role in England's hiring: "I'm assuming your employment at the university is a vote of confidence. Certainly I'm willing to see it that way inasmuch as I tried to help in obtaining it for you"; Jeffrey Holland to EE, 1980, EE-P 171.12.

31. "I don't know what [was now different]. Really nothing had changed from their original objections" of two years ago, he told his son. ME-I 118, pt. 1.

32. Leonard Arrington, *Confessions of a Mormon Historian: The Diaries of Leonard Arrington, 1971–1997*, edited by Gary James Bergera (Salt Lake City: Signature, 2018), 2:390–91.

33. Ezra Taft Benson, "God's Hand in Our Nation's History," in *1976 Devotional Speeches of the Year*, 310, 313 (Provo, Utah: Brigham Young University Press, 1977).

34. Arrington, *Confessions*, 2:478.

35. Richard L. Bushman to EE, 23 May 1975, EE-P 165.18.

36. Ralph Waldo Emerson, "The American Scholar," *Complete Writings of Ralph Waldo Emerson* (New York: Wise, 1929), 25, 36.

37. Orson Whitney, "Home Literature," *Contributor* 9, no. 8 (June 1888): 300.

38. *Golden Multitudes: The Story of Best Sellers in the United States* (New York: Macmillan, 1947), 310–11.

39. "Salutation," *Contributor* 1, no. 1 (October 1879): 12.

40. EE, "Without Purse or Script: A 19-Year-Old Missionary in 1853," *New Era*, July 1975.

41. Richard H. Cracroft and Neal E. Lambert, *A Believing People: Literature of the Latter-day Saints* (Provo, Utah: Brigham Young University Press, 1974), 5. William Mulder began his essay on Mormon literature with the same observation, exactly two decades earlier. See "Mormonism and Literature," *Western Humanities Review* 9 (January 1955): 85.

42. Vardis Fisher, *Children of God* (New York: Harper and Brothers, 1939); Maureen Whipple, *The Giant Joshua* (Boston: Houghton Mifflin, 1941); Virginia Sorensen, *A Little Lower than the Angels* (New York: Knopf, 1942 [repr. Salt Lake City: Signature, 1997]).

43. EE, "Born Square: On Being Mormon, Western, and Human," Eugene England Foundation, 6, http://eugeneengland.org/wp-content/uploads/sbi/articles/2001_e_002.pdf. Originally published in *Literature and Belief* 21, no. 1 (2001): 275–94.

44. Cracroft and Lambert, *A Believing People*, 5.

45. EE, "Mormon Literature: Progress and Prospects," in *Mormon Americana: A Guide to Sources and Collections in the United States*, edited by David J. Whittaker, 477 (Provo, Utah: BYU Studies, 1995).

46. EE, author's foreword to *Dialogues with Myself: Personal Essays on Mormon*

Experience (Midvale, Utah: Orion Books, 1984), x. This text originally appeared in a slightly different form in *BYU Studies*, Spring 1975.

47. EE, "Born Square," 4.

48. Spencer W. Kimball, "Second Century Address," *BYU Studies* 16, no. 4 (1976): 445–57.

49. Thomas Alexander to EE, 1 March 1979, EE-P 168.1.

50. Cited by Dean L. May, "Mormons," in *Harvard Encyclopedia of American Ethnic Groups*, edited by Stephan Thernstrom, 720 (Cambridge, Mass.: Harvard University Press, 1980).

51. Sydney E. Ahlstrom, *A Religious History of the American People*, 2nd ed. (New Haven, Conn.: Yale University Press, 2004), 508.

52. EE, "'No Cause, No Cause': An Essay toward Reconciliation," *Sunstone*, January 2002, 38–39.

53. EE to Boyd K. Packer, n.d. Two drafts exist; it is not known if either was ever sent. EE-P 171.21.

54. EE to Boyd K. Packer, n.d., with annotation of "1982?," EE-P 171.21.

55. Memo, EE to the Association of Mormon Letters, 5 February 1983, EE-P 103.

56. "About Us," *Irreantum*, https://irreantum.associationmormonletters.org/about -irreantum/.

57. Personal communication with Gideon Burton, 6 February 2020.

CHAPTER 8

1. EE interview by Davis Bitton, Oral History Project.

2. Richard L. Bushman to EE, 21 August 1994, EE-P 165.18.

3. ME-I 103.

4. The former student made the comment in a confidential memo to the author.

5. Wes Johnson, interview with author, 3 May 2016.

6. Doug Thayer, interview with author, 3 May 2016.

7. Memorandum, Ed Geary to EE, 13 September 1979, EE-P 168.1.

8. Joseph W. Hales to Elouise Bell, 21 February 1989, EE-P 165.10.

9. EE, "Learning to Serve as Brigham Young's University," in *The Quality of Mercy: Personal Essays on Mormon Experience*, 78–83 (Salt Lake City: Bookcraft, 1992); quotation 78.

10. EE, "Great Books or True Religion? Defining the Mormon Scholar," *Dialogue: A Journal of Mormon Thought* 9, no. 4 (Winter 1974): 38.

11. EE, "Speaking the Truth in Love," *Ensign*, April 1976, 53.

12. Boyd K. Packer, citing 2 Tim. 2:13 and D&C 42:11 in untitled address to student body, BYU Hawaii, 14 January 1977, EE-P 145.10.

13. England reported her remark in ME-I 110.

14. Grant Wacker, *Augustus H. Strong and the Dilemma of Historical Consciousness* (Macon, Ga.: Mercer University Press, 1985).

15. Wacker, *Augustus H. Strong*, 11, 140.

16. R. Scott Appleby, *"Church and Age Unite!" The Modernist Impulses in American Catholicism* (Notre Dame, Ind.: University of Notre Dame Press, 1992), 5.

17. Appleby, *"Church and Age Unite!,"* 115.

18. "Pascendi Dominici Gregis: On the Doctrine of the Modernists," Papal Encyclicals Online, https://www.papalencyclicals.net/pius10/p10pasce.htm.

19. Gregory A. Prince, *Leonard Arrington and the Writing of Mormon History* (Salt Lake City: University of Utah Press, 2016), 137.

20. Martin E. Marty, "Two Integrities: An Address to the Crisis in Mormon Historiography," *Journal of Mormon History* 10 (1983): 3.

21. David Barber, ME-I 104.

22. Email, Erin Silva to Gene and Charlotte, 8 March 2001, CE-C.

23. *England Family Histories: George Eugene England Sr. and Dora Rose Hartvigsen England*, compiled and edited by Ann Christine England Barker (n.p.: n.p., 2012), 248, CE-C.

24. Douglas Thayer, "A Fisherman's Heart," *Student Review*, 10 April 1998.

25. Charlotte England, interview with author, 2 April 2016.

26. Scott Bradford, ME-I 113.

27. Scott Bradford, ME-I 113.

28. Sue Lundquist, interview with author, 12 June 2017.

29. Diane Saderup, interview with author, 12 June 2017.

30. EEJ, 21 June 1992.

31. "Dian" to EE, 12 March 2001, CE-C.

32. Mark Richards, "'Out-of-the-Box' Bishop," *Sunstone*, January 2002, 19.

33. Steve Walker, "Heavenly Tennis," *Sunstone*, January 2002, 20.

34. EEJ, 1 January 1994.

35. ME-I 120, pt. 1.

36. ME-I 120, pt. 1.

37. ME-I 117, pt. 1.

38. ME-I 117, pt. 1.

39. Katherine England, "Life with Daddy," *Sunstone*, January 2002, 21.

40. Doug Thayer, interview with author, 3 May 2016.

41. Charlotte England, interview with author, 2 April 2016.

42. EEJ, 6 March 1992.

43. Susan Lundquist traced this anecdote to Claudia Harris. Lundquist, interview with author, 12 June 2017.

44. Technically, there are generally fifteen apostles at any given moment: the Quorum of the Twelve plus the members of the First Presidency.

45. Wilford Woodruff and George Q. Cannon, "The Law of Adoption," *Deseret Weekly* 48, no. 18 (April 21, 1894), 543.

46. Woodruff and Cannon, "The Law of Adoption," 542–43.

47. Darius Clement, 20 April 1894, to Warren Foote. In Warren Foote, *Autobiography*, 3:14, http://wchsutah.org/people/warren-foote-journal1.php.

48. Amasa Lyman, "Marriage: Its Benefits," *JD* 11:207.

49. *Collected Discourses Delivered by President Wilford Woodruff, His Two Counselors, the Twelve Apostles, and Others*, edited by Brian H. Stuy (n.p.: BHS, 1999), 4:71.

50. Lorenzo Snow, "Opening Address," *Seventieth Annual Conference* (Salt Lake City: Deseret, 1900), 1–2.

51. Kathy Petty, "Report on the England/Bruce R. McConkie Episode," typed ms., CE-C. Petty, a close family friend of the Englands, wrote up a fully researched report on the exchange and its aftermath for inclusion in the Eugene England Papers.

52. ME-I 118, pt. 2.

53. "The Only Living and True God," transcript of remarks by Joseph McConkie at Flea Market, September 1979, in EE-P and posted on Eugene England Foundation website, http://www.eugeneengland.org/a-professor-and-apostle-correspond -eugene-england-and-bruce-r-mcconkie-on-the-nature-of-god.

54. EE, "Perfection and Progress: Two Complementary Ways to Talk about God," *BYU Studies* 29, no. 3 (Summer 1989): 31.

55. Bruce R. McConkie, "The Seven Deadly Heresies," BYU devotional, June 1, 1980, https://speeches.byu.edu/talks/bruce-r-mcconkie/seven-deadly-heresies/.

56. ME-I 118, pt. 1.

57. Edward L. Kimball, *Lengthen Your Stride: The Presidency of Spencer W. Kimball* (Salt Lake City: Deseret, 2005), 101.

58. ME-I 118, pt. 1.

59. EE-P 171.28.

60. Petty, "Report."

61. EE to Bruce R. McConkie, quoted in Petty, "Report."

62. Bruce R. McConkie, "The Lord God of the Restoration," *Ensign*, November 1980, 50.

63. Bruce R. McConkie to EE, 19 February 1981. McConkie's letter was circulated widely, in thousands of copies. Many online sources for the document exist. This version comes from "Bruce McConkie's Letter of Rebuke to Professor Eugene England," http://www.eugeneengland.org/bibliography/unpublished-items.

64. As England explained in a letter to McConkie, friends saw circulating copies of the letter before the original even reached England in the United Kingdom. EE to Elder Bruce R. McConkie, 29 October 1982, CE-C.

65. ME-I 118, pt. 2.

66. ME-I 118, pt. 2.

67. Bruce R. McConkie to EE, 19 February 1981.

68. Parley P. Pratt, sermon, 9 January 1853; cited in Terryl L. Givens and Matthew J. Grow, *Parley P. Pratt: The Apostle Paul of Mormonism* (New York: Oxford University Press, 2011), 397.

69. Barker, *England Family Histories*, 125.

70. Boyd K. Packer, "The Mantle Is Far, Far Greater than the Intellect," address given to BYU religious educators, August 22, 1981, https://www.churchofjesuschrist.org /study/manual/teaching-seminary-preservice-readings-religion-370–471-and-475 /the-mantle-is-far-far-greater-than-the-intellect?lang=eng.

71. Ezra Taft Benson, "God's Hand in Our Nation's History," in *1976 Devotional Speeches of the Year*, 310, 313 (Provo, Utah: Brigham Young University Press, 1977).

72. D. Michael Quinn, "On Being a Mormon Historian," speech given to the BYU Student History Association, Fall 1981.

73. D. Michael Quinn, ME-I 103.

74. Blake Ostler, "Interview with Sterling McMurrin," 19; originally published in *7th East Press*, 11 January 1983, Harold B. Lee Library Special Collections, box 4, folder 5.

75. Published versions date England's talk to October. However, his presidential address was given at the Fifth Annual AML Symposium, Weber State College, Ogden, Utah, 27 September 1980. See http://mldb.byu.edu/amlproceedings/amlproce .htm#1979.

76. Quotations are from the text published subsequently in England's essay collection *Dialogues with Myself: Personal Essays on Mormon Experience* (Midvale, Utah: Orion Books, 1984), 19–38.

77. See Ronald W. Walker, Richard E. Turley Jr., and Glen M. Leonard, *Massacre at Mountain Meadows* (New York: Oxford University Press, 2011).

78. Aristotle, *Metaphysics* I.2. For several related positions, see Terryl L. Givens, *When Souls Had Wings: Pre-mortal Existence in Western Thought* (New York: Oxford University Press, 2009), 200–237.

79. Sterling M. McMurrin, *The Theological Foundations of the Mormon Religion* (Salt Lake City: University of Utah Press, 1965), 52.

80. *Evening and Morning Star*, June 1832, 7.

81. Sean Salai, S.J., "Catholic and Mormon: Author Q&A with Professor Stephen H. Webb," *National Catholic Review*, https://www.americamagazine.org/content/all -things/catholic-and-mormon-author-qa-professor-stephen-h-webb.

82. "Lesson 23: The Savior Restored His Priesthood, Church, and Gospel," *Jesus Christ and the Everlasting Gospel Teacher Manual*, 2016, https://www.lds.org/manual/jesus -christ-and-the-everlasting-gospel-teacher-manual/lesson-23-the-savior-restored -his-priesthood-church-and-gospel?lang=eng.

83. Paraphrased by Gilbert Meilaender, "Conscience and Authority," First Things (November 2017), https://www.firstthings.com/article/2007/11/conscience-and -authority.

84. George Forell, "Luther and Conscience," *Journal of Lutheran Ethics* 2, no. 1 (1 January 2002), https://www.elca.org/JLE/Articles/991.

85. Brian Patrick Green, "Catholicism and Conscience" (2013), Markkula Center for Applied Ethics, Santa Clara University, https://www.scu.edu/ethics/focus-areas /religious-and-catholic-ethics/resources/catholicism-and-conscience/.

86. An accessible summary of the position of Thomas Aquinas is "Conscience," Thomistic Philosophy, https://aquinasonline.com/conscience/.

87. John Henry Cardinal Newman, "Letter to the Duke of Norfolk," in *Certain Difficulties Felt by Anglicans in Catholic Teaching*, 261 (London: Longmans, Green, 1914).

88. John Rickaby, "Conscience," in *The Catholic Encyclopedia*, vol. 4 (New York: Robert Appleton, 1908), http://www.newadvent.org/cathen/04268a.htm.

89. Antisacramentalism, deemphasis of ecclesial forms, sola scriptura, sola gratia, sola fide, salvation by imputed righteousness, inability of the living to aid in salvation of their deceased, God's absolute sovereignty, total depravity, predestination, a limited or absent free will, and myriad other Reformation innovations and emphases are much further removed from Restoration theology than are Catholic teachings. This is why Smith felt moved to pronounce, "The old Catholic Church is worth more than all." Andrew F. Ehat and Lyndon W. Cook, eds., *The Words of Joseph Smith* (Orem, Utah: Grandin, 1991), 381–82.

90. Jeff Mirus, "Conscience and Authority: The Protestant Dilemma," *Catholic Culture*, 24 October 2007, https://www.catholicculture.org/commentary/conscience -and-authority-protestant-dilemma/.

91. *CDBY* 4:2507.

92. Mirus, "Conscience and Authority."

93. *CDBY* 1:556.

94. *CDBY* 2:714.

95. *CDBY* 3:1581; my emphasis.

96. *CDBY* 4:2217.

97. Gilbert Meilaender, "Conscience and Authority," *First Things*, November 2007, https://www.firstthings.com/article/2007/11/conscience-and-authority.

98. Ironically, this principle England heard from Boyd K. Packer in a 1991 BYU devotional address. EE, "On Spectral Evidence," *Dialogue: A Journal of Mormon Thought* 26, no. 1 (Spring 1993): 140.

99. EEJ, 26 August 1975.

100. EE, *Dialogues with Myself: Personal Essays on Mormon Experience* (Midvale, Utah: Orion Books, 1984), 200.

101. Charlotte England, interview with author, 2 April 2016.

102. Charlotte England, interview with author, 2 April 2016.

103. Charlotte England, interview with author, 2 April 2016.

104. EE, "Enduring," *Dialogue: A Journal of Mormon Thought* 16, no. 4 (Winter 1983): 201.

105. EE, "Enduring," 201.

106. Barker, *England Family Histories*, 126, 127.

107. Mitch Davis, Michael G. Sullivan, and Ronald J. Ockey, "A Bullet and a Vision: Food for Poland, 1982–1985," *Sunstone*, January 2002, 46.

108. Davis et al., "A Bullet and a Vision," 47.

109. EE, "Enduring," 202.

110. Charlotte England, interview with author, 2 April 2016.

111. EE, "Enduring," 204.

112. Bert Wilson to EE, 26 May 1982, EE-P 167.12.

113. EE to President Jeffrey Holland, 3 November 1982, EE-P 171.12.

114. Jeffrey Holland to EE, 11 November 1982, EE-P 171.12.

115. EE to Elder Marion D. Hanks, 10 December 1982, DW-C.

116. EE to Boyd K. Packer, 24 November 1982, EE-P 172.17.

117. The quotation, from Robert Bolt's "Man for All Seasons" is cited in EE, "Great Books or True Religion?," 49.

118. EE, "Through the Arabian Desert to a Bountiful Land: Could Joseph Smith Have Known the Way?," in *Book of Mormon Authorship: New Light on Ancient Origins*, edited by Noel B. Reynolds, 143–56 (Provo, Utah: FARMS, 1982).

119. Jeffrey R. Holland to EE, 2 November 1983, EE-P 171.12.

120. Boyd Petersen, "Eugene England and the Future of Mormonism," *Dead Wood and Rushing Water*, January 28, 2016, https://boydpetersen.com/2016/01/28/eugene -england-and-the-future-of-mormonism/.

121. EE, "Why the Church Is As True As the Gospel," *Sunstone*, June 1999, 67.

122. Transcript of award speech, n.d., EE-P 168.3.

123. Paul H. Dunn to EE, 24 January 1984, CE-C.

124. D. Arthur Haycock to EE, 30 March 1984, CE-C.

CHAPTER 9

1. In 1999, *BYU Studies* honored England as the most published contributor in their history. See Richard H. Cracroft, "Eugene England and the Rise and Progress of Mormon Letters," *Sunstone*, January 2002, 42.

2. Mary Lythgoe Bradford, "I, Eye, Aye: A Personal Essay on Personal Essays," in *Tending the Garden: Essays on Mormon Literature*, edited by Eugene England and Lavina Fielding Anderson (Salt Lake City: Signature, 1996), 148.

3. *Joseph Smith Papers: Documents*, vol. 1, edited by Michael Hubbard MacKay, Gerrit J. Dirkmaat, Grant Underwood, Robert J. Woodford, and William G. Hartley (Salt Lake City: Church Historian's Press, 2013), 372–73.

4. EE, "Blessing the Chevrolet," *Dialogue: A Journal of Mormon Thought* 9, no. 3 (Autumn 1974): 57–60.

5. John Gary Maxwell to Charlotte [England], n.d., CE-C.

6. *CDBY*, 3:1351.

7. *New York Herald*, 4 August 1842.

8. Rudolf Otto, *The Idea of the Holy*, 2nd ed., trans. J. W. Harvey (London: Oxford University Press, 1950), 12, 13, 28, 146; William James, *The Varieties of Religious Experience* (Cambridge, Mass.: Harvard University Press, 1985), 362.

9. Maurine Whipple, *The Giant Joshua* (Boston: Houghton Mifflin, 1941), 261.

10. Josiah Quincy, *Figures of the Past* (Boston: Little, Brown, 1926): 326.

11. EE, "Enduring," *Dialogue: A Journal of Mormon Thought* 16, no. 4 (Winter 1983): 103–14.

12. EE, "Easter Weekend," *Dialogue: A Journal of Mormon Thought* 21, no. 1 (Spring 1988): 19–30.

13. EE, "Monte Cristo," *Wasatch Review International* 2, no. 1 (January 1993): 84–102.

14. EE, "Monte Cristo," 86.

15. EE, "Why the Church Is As True As the Gospel," *Sunstone*, June 1999, 61–69.

16. Adolf von Harnack, *History of Dogma*, trans. William M'Gilchrist (London: Williams & Norgate, 1899), 6:133.

17. A. K. Walker, *William Law: His Life and Work* (London: SPCK, 1973), 21.

18. Lincoln cited in Nathan O. Hatch, "Sola Scriptura and Novus Ordo Seclorum," in *The Bible in America: Essays in Cultural History*, edited by Hatch and Mark A. Noll, 59 (New York: Oxford University Press, 1982).

19. "'Nones' on the Rise," Pew Research Center, Religion and Public Life, 9 October 2012, https://www.pewforum.org/2012/10/09/nones-on-the-rise/.

20. "In U.S., Decline of Christianity Continues at Rapid Pace," https://www.pewforum.org/2019/10/17/in-u-s-decline-of-christianity-continues-at-rapid-pace/.

21. Joseph Smith to William W. Phelps, 27 November 1832, in *Joseph Smith Papers: Documents*, vol. 2, edited by Matthew C. Godfrey et al. (Salt Lake City: Church Historian's Press, 2013), 2:319.

22. *CDBY* 4:2033.

23. The Novak passage is from his "The Family Out of Favor," *Harper's*, April 1976.

24. EE, "'No Cause, No Cause': An Essay toward Reconciliation," *Sunstone*, January 2002, 34.

25. ME-I 117, pt. 2.

CHAPTER 10

1. EE, "Why the Church Is More True than the Gospel," draft, 17 August 1984, EE-P 94.

2. The original audio is available on the Eugene England Foundation website, https://www.eugeneengland.org/bibliography/video.

3. See Hayley C. Cuccinello, "Fifty Shades of Green: How Fanfiction Went from Dirty Little Secret to Money Machine," *Forbes*, 10 February 2017, https://www.forbes.com/sites/hayleycuccinello/2017/02/10/fifty-shades-of-green-how-fanfiction-went-from-dirty-little-secret-to-money-machine/#fe3d8d0264cf.

4. See both Christian Smith and Melinda Lundquist Denton, *Soul Searching: The Religious and Spiritual Lives of American Teenagers* (New York: Oxford University Press, 2005); and Christian Smith with Patricia Snell, *Souls in Transition: The Religious and Spiritual Lives of Emerging Adults* (New York: Oxford University Press, 2009).

5. Edward L. Carter, "Students' Protest at BYU Is about More than Rodin," *Deseret News*, 31 October 1997, https://www.deseret.com/1997/10/31/19342954/students-protest-at-byu-is-about-more-than-rodin.

6. Anonymous to Elliot Cameron, 1 September 1988; EE to William Evenson, 17 October 1988 (he directed his reply to Evenson, even though the request came from Britsch), EE-P 171.29.

7. The piece in question was "Heel" by C. A. Christmas; "Barbara" to "Gene," 23 June 1988, CE-C.

8. Frank Christiansen, interview with author, 12 June 2017.

9. Anonymous to Board of Trustees [1991], EE-P 169.1.

10. "To the Students from My English 368 Class Who Complained to the Board of Trustees," EE-P 169.1.

11. Bert Wilson to Stan Albrecht, 19 July 1991, EE-P 151.3.

12. Bert Wilson to Stan Albrecht, 19 July 1991, EE-P 151.3.

13. "Some Notes on Ethical Matters for My Students," EE-P 169.1.

14. "K. B. to Dr. Fox," 4 May 1996, EE-P 169.8.

15. Cited in Karen R. Bryce to EE, 4 May 1996, EE-P 169–7.

16. EEJ, 30 January 1999.

17. EEJ, 9 February 1999.

18. EE memo to Don [Marshall?], 29 May 1987, EE-P 168.5.

19. Gary Browning, interview with author, 3 May 2016.

20. EE to President Dallin H. Oaks, 3 January 1973, EE-P 171.20.

21. The book would be published as *Converted to Christ through the Book of Mormon* (Salt Lake City: Deseret, 1989); EE to "Dear Colleagues," 7 November 1988, CE-C.

22. Sue Lindquist, interview with author, 12 June 2007.

23. Dallin H. Oaks to EE, 5 April 1988, EE-P 171.20.

24. EE to Elder Dallin Oaks, 30 March 1988, EE-P 171.20.

25. EE to Dallin Oaks, [1979], draft letter, EE-P 171.20.

26. EE to Neal A. Maxwell, 16 February 1988, EE-P 171.18.

27. Neal A. Maxwell to EE, 17 March 1988, EE-P 171.18.

28. EE to Neal A. Maxwell, 30 March 1988, EE-P 171.18.

29. EE to Jeffrey Holland, 16 March 1988, EE-P 171.12. "On Fidelity, Polygamy, and Celestial Marriage" was published in *Dialogue: A Journal of Mormon Thought* 20, no. 4 (Winter 1987): 138–54.

30. Delivered 30 August 1986, copy in EE-P 60.3.

31. Quoted in Carol Lynn Pearson, *The Ghost of Eternal Polygamy* (Walnut Creek, Calif.: Pivot Point, 2016), 24. Her online survey on attitudes toward polygamy elicited more than 8,000 responses, with fewer than 10 percent expressing "positive emotions" (8–9). She collected dozens of testimonials expressing pain and anguish, from the nineteenth century to the present day.

32. "Celestial marriage is essential to a fulness of glory in the world to come . . . but it is not stated that plural marriage is thus essential." Charles Penrose, "Editor's Table," *Improvement Era*, September 1912, 1042.

33. "Written Reply by Robert J. Matthews," 7 November 1986, EE-P 144.5.

34. EE to "Dear Brother Matthews," 26 November 1986, EE-P 144.5.

35. EE to "Dear Brother Matthews."

36. Robert J. Matthews to EE, 7 December 1986, EE-P 144.5.

37. EE to Robert J. Matthews, 5 February 1987, DW-C.

38. EE to President Rex Lee, 14 November 1990, EE-P 171.16.

39. EE to Neal A. Maxwell, 21 September 1990, EE-P 171.18.

40. EE to Neal A. Maxwell, 21 September 1990, EE-P 171.18.

41. Ronald K. Esplin and John W. Welch to EE, 2 August 1990, CE-C.

42. Neal A. Maxwell to EE, 27 September 1990, EE-P 171.18.

43. EE to Neal A. Maxwell, 9 October 1990, EE-P 171.18.

44. H. Reese Hansen, memo of conversation with EE, 7 October 1990, DW-C.

45. EE to President Gordon B. Hinckley, 25 September 1989, EE-P 171.11.

46. EE, "Are All Alike unto God? Prejudice against Blacks and Women in Popular Mormon Theology," *Sunstone*, April 1990, 23.

47. Bruce R. McConkie, "All Are Alike unto God," address given at BYU, 18 August 1978, https://speeches.byu.edu/talks/bruce-r-mcconkie/alike-unto-god/.

48. Cited in EE, "Are All Alike unto God?," 20.

49. EE, "Are All Alike unto God?," 18.

50. "Church leaders and members advanced many theories to explain the priesthood and temple restrictions. None . . . is accepted today as the official doctrine of the Church." "Race and the Priesthood," https://www.churchofjesuschrist.org/study /manual/gospel-topics-essays/race-and-the-priesthood?lang=eng.

51. Cited in EE, "Are All Alike unto God?," 20.

52. Thomas Dube to EE, 30 March 2001, CE-C. The remark was in reference to England's essay, "Becoming a World Religion: Blacks, the Poor—All of Us," *Sunstone*, June–July 1998.

53. Pew Research Center, "Religious Landscape Study: Racial and Ethnic Composition," 2014, http://www.pewforum.org/religious-landscape-study/racial-and -ethnic-composition/.

54. "Darius Gray: An Interview about the Genesis of Change in the LDS Church," *Faith Matters*, https://faithmatters.org/the-genesis-of-change-in-the-lds-church-an -interview-with-darius-gray/

55. Janan Graham-Russell, "Choosing to Stay in the Mormon Church Despite Its Racist Legacy," *Atlantic*, August 28, 2016, https://www.theatlantic.com/politics /archive/2016/08/black-and-mormon/497660/.

56. EEJ, 28 January 1994.

57. Heber C. Kimball, "Iniquity—Saints Living Their Religion—Early Marriages," *JD* 3:125.

58. Helen Mar Whitney, *Plural Marriage as Taught by the Prophet Joseph* (Salt Lake City: Juvenile Instructor, 1882), 48.

59. Quoted in Richard S. Van Wagoner, *Polygamy: A History* (Salt Lake City: Signature, 1992), 100.

60. Autobiography of Lorena Eugenia Washburn Larsen, quoted in Paula Kelly Harline, *The Polygamous Wives Writing Club* (New York: Oxford University Press, 2014), 138.

61. Charles Penrose, "Editor's Table," *Improvement Era*, September 1912, 1042.

62. Church of Jesus Christ of Latter-day Saints, "Official Declaration 1," October 6, 1890, https://www.churchofjesuschrist.org/study/scriptures/dc-testament/od/1 ?lang=eng.

63. ME-I 118, pt. 1.

64. EEJ, 24 January 1994.

65. Unsent letter of EE to Neal A. Maxwell, 18 January 2000, EE-P 171.18.

66. ME-I 118, pt. 1.

67. EEJ, 24 January 1994.

68. Katherine England, "Life with Daddy," 23.

69. EE to Elder Neal A. Maxwell, EE-P, 22 October 1990, DW-C.

70. M. Russell Ballard, "The Opportunities and Responsibilities of CES Teachers in the 21st Century," 26 February 2016, https://www.churchofjesuschrist.org /broadcasts/article/evening-with-a-general-authority/2016/02/the-opportunities -and-responsibilities-of-ces-teachers-in-the-21st-century?lang=eng.

71. Gene to "Mary," 18 April 1994. No further details are on the memo printed on English department letterhead, CE-C.

72. Memo, EE to "Don," 29 May 1987, EE-P 168.5.

73. The episode was related by Rex Lee, present at the meeting, to the English department chair, Bert Wilson, EEJ, 4 March 1992.

74. Boyd K. Packer, "I Say unto You, Be One," address given at BYU, 12 February 1991, https://speeches.byu.edu/talks/boyd-k-packer/say-unto-one/.

75. The first principle was the counsel Dr. Karl G. Maeser reportedly received from Brigham Young; the second is from D&C 88:118.

76. Boyd K. Packer to EE, 21 March 1991, EE-P 171.21.

77. Richard H. Cracroft, "Harvest: Contemporary Mormon Poems; A Review," BYU Studies 30, no. 2 (Spring 1990): 122.

78. Cracroft, "Harvest; A Review," 122.

79. EE, author's foreword to EE, Dialogues with Myself: Personal Essays on Mormon Experience (Midvale, Utah: Orion Books, 1984), x–xi.

80. Richard H. Cracroft, "Attuning the Authentic Mormon Voice: Stemming the Sophic Tide in LDS Literature," Sunstone, July 1993, 51.

81. Orson Whitney, "Home Literature," Contributor 9, no. 8 (June 1888): 296–300.

82. Cracroft, "Attuning the Authentic Mormon Voice," 55.

83. EEJ, 21 April 1992.

84. EEJ, 21 April 1992.

85. EE, "Scriptures Are Helpful in Renouncing War," Daily Universe, 14 February 1991.

86. Kelly Ogden, "Scriptures Can Justify a Just War," Daily Universe, 27 February 1991.

87. Stephen Robinson to EE, 13 March 1991, EE-P 147.9.

88. Stephen Robinson to EE, 13 March 1991, EE-P 147.9.

89. EE to Stephen Robinson, 15 May 1991, EE-P 147.9.

90. EE to Robinson, 15 May 1991, EE-P 147.9.

91. "History of Joseph Smith," Millennial Star, 4 December 1858, 774.

92. England is here quoting from BYU's Accreditation Report of 1986. In EE, "Academic Freedom Restricted at BYU," Daily Universe, 5 April 1989.

93. EE, "Academic Freedom Restricted."

94. Dallin H. Oaks, "Alternate Voices," General Conference talk (October 1989), https://www.churchofjesuschrist.org/study/general-conference/1989/04 /alternate-voices?lang=eng.

95. Russell M. Nelson, "The Canker of Contention," General Conference talk (April 1989), https://www.churchofjesuschrist.org/study/general-conference/1989/04 /the-canker-of-contention?lang=eng.

96. "Child Sexual Abuse in the LDS Community," 1991 *Sunstone* Summer Symposium, 16 November 2016, https://www.sunstonemagazine.com/sunstone-1991-80-child-sexual-abuse-in-the-lds-community/.

97. "Statement on Symposia," *Ensign*, November 1991, 105–6.

98. Lavina Fielding Anderson, "Landmarks for LDS Women: A Contemporary Chronology," *Mormon Women's Forum* 3, no. 3–4 (December 1992): 14.

99. Those names were publicized as participants in the 1986 Sunstone Conference. "*Sunstone* Schedules Annual Symposium," *Daily Herald*, 17 August 1986, CE-C.

100. EEJ, 16 March 1992.

101. ME-I 116.

102. EEJ, 22 March 1992.

103. Student evaluations, EE-P 194.11.

104. Barbara Ehrenreich, "Teach Diversity—with a Smith," *Time*, 8 April 1991, 84. In EE-P 168.1.

105. EEJ, 21 June 1992.

CHAPTER 11

1. Mormon Alliance Home Page, http://mormon-alliance.org/.

2. This phrase was not included in her first printed remarks in the *Mormon Women's Forum*, but it was restored in her *Dialogue* version. Lavina Fielding Anderson, "The LDS Intellectual Community and Church Leadership: A Contemporary Chronology," *Dialogue: A Journal of Mormon Thought* 26, no. 1 (Spring 1993): 62.

3. EEJ, 16 July 1992.

4. EE, "'No Cause, No Cause': An Essay toward Reconciliation," *Sunstone*, January 2002, 39.

5. EE, "No Cause," 39.

6. Lavina Fielding Anderson, "For the Record," *Sunstone*, April 2001, 4.

7. Anderson, "For the Record," 4.

8. Peter Steinfels, "Secret Files," *New York Times*, 22 August 1992.

9. ME-I 118, pt. 1.

10. EE to "Dear Colleagues," 17 February 1992, EE-P 169.3.

11. Richard Bushman to EE, 18 March 1992, EE-P 165.18. The two essays to which Bushman refers are England's "Healing and Making Peace: In the World and in the Church" (*Sunstone*, December 1991, 36–46) and "Hugh Nibley as Cassandra" (*BYU Studies* 30, no. 4 [1990]: 104–16.

12. EE to Elder James E. Faust and Elder Russell M. Nelson, 17 August 1992, CE-C.

13. EE to Elder Neal Maxwell, 10 August 1992. "Not sent by advice of Rex Lee" penciled in margin, EE-P 171.18.

14. Neal A. Maxwell to EE, 13 October 1992, EE-P 171.18. Maxwell is responding to a 25 August 1992 letter from England not extant.

15. James E. Faust and Russell M. Nelson to EE, 16 September 1992, DW-C.

16. ME-I 118, pt. 2.

17. EE to "Dear Colleagues," 31 March 1993, EE-P 169.1.

18. EE to Bruce Hafen, copying President Rex Lee, 10 August 1992, DW-C.

19. A draft of his letter to Hunter has a notation from England, noting that "on advice of Rex Lee" he is excising a passage promising to send a copy of his Hafen letter, EE to President Howard W. Hunter, 10 April [sic] 1992, EE-P 171.13. (The letter is misdated, since the event discussed transpired in August.)

20. James E. Faust and Russell M. Nelson to EE, 6 April 1993, EE-P 171.6.

21. EE to Dallin H. Oaks, 10 August 1992, EE-P 171.20.

22. Dallin H. Oaks to EE, 10 August 1992, EE-P 171.20.

23. EEJ, 4 March 1992.

24. Cited in "BYU Continues to Debate Academic Freedom Issue," *Sunstone*, March 1993, 63.

25. Boyd K. Packer, "To Be Learned Is Good If . . . ," General Conference talk (October 1992), https://www.churchofjesuschrist.org/study/general-conference/1992/10/to-be-learned-is-good-if?lang=eng.

26. Gordon B. Hinckley, "Trust and Accountability," devotional address delivered to BYU (13 October 1992). This and above reference cited in "BYU Continues to Debate," 65.

27. Yascha Mounk, "What an Audacious Hoax Reveals about Academia," *Atlantic*, https://www.theatlantic.com/ideas/archive/2018/10/new-sokal-hoax/572212/; Daniel T. O'Hara, "Reviewed Work: *The Edge of Night: A Confession* by Frank Lentricchia," *boundary 2* 21, no. 2 (Summer 1994): 40–62.

28. James Applewhite, quoted in Janny Scott, "Discord Turns Academe's Hot Team Cold," *New York Times*, 21 November 1998.

29. EE to Jeffrey R. Holland, 20 August 1997, EE-P 171.12.

30. Elizabeth Cady Stanton, *The Woman's Bible* (New York: Prometheus, 1999), 14.

31. Beverly Campbell, "Eve," in *Encyclopedia of Mormonism*, edited by Daniel Ludlow, 4 vols., 2:476 (New York: Macmillan, 1992).

32. Anne Osborn Poelman, *The Simeon Solution: One Woman's Spiritual Odyssey* (Salt Lake City: Deseret, 1995), 4.

33. The Church of Jesus Christ of Latter-day Saints, "The Family: A Proclamation to the World," 23 September 1995, https://www.churchofjesuschrist.org/study/manual/the-family-a-proclamation-to-the-world/the-family-a-proclamation-to-the-world?lang=eng.

34. Lorelei Harris reported her experience to England, EEJ, 21 June 1992.

35. Cited in Bryan Waterman and Brian Kagel, *The Lord's University* (Salt Lake City: Signature, 1998), 40.

36. Officially, the grounds for excommunication in cases of dissent do not encompass personal belief, only "repeatedly act[ing] in clear, open, and deliberate public opposition to the Church or its leaders." Statement by the First Presidency and the Quorum of the Twelve, 17 October 1993, https://www.lds.org/ensign/1994/01/news-of-the-church/statement-released-by-first-presidency-and-quorum-of-thetwelve? lang=eng. Older church handbooks used the same definition.

37. Neal J. Young chronicles the pivotal role of the church in defeating the ERA in a number of states. See "'The ERA Is a Moral Issue': The Mormon Church, LDS Women, and the Defeat of the Equal Rights Amendment," *American Quarterly* 59, no. 3 (September 2007): 623–44.

38. EE to Rank and Status Committee, memo, n.d., EE-P 24.6.

39. England voted in the negative and included a lengthy explanation, concluding, "The Committee's . . . apparent unwillingness to face [the candidate] with his errors, will simply encourage him and others to act in their unprofessional and destructive ways." EE to Jay Fox, 4 November 1996, CE-C.

40. "Paul" to "Gloria," 12 January 1990, CE-C.

41. EE to Royal Skousen, draft, 21 February 1991. The final version, same date, includes a handwritten reply from Skousen, EE-P 169.1.

42. Barbara Ehrenreich, "Teach Diversity—with a Smile," *Time*, 8 April 1991.

43. Annotated copy of "Teach Diversity," EE-P 168.1.

44. J. A. Waterstradt to EE, 2 April 1982, EE-P 169.3.

45. EE to Professional Development Committee, 22 March 1982, EE-P 26.8.

46. J. A. Waterstradt to EE, 21 March 1989, EE-P 169.3.

47. John S. Harris to All Members of the English Department, memo, n.d., EE-P 23.5.

48. D[on] Norton to "Gene," n.d., CE-C.

49. EEJ, 24 January 1994.

50. Cecilia Konchar Farr, "Dancing through the Doctrine: Observations on Mormonism and Feminism," in *Religion, Feminism, and Freedom of Conscience: A Mormon/Humanist Dialogue*, edited by George D. Smith, 151 (Salt Lake City: Signature, 1994).

51. "I Am a Mormon, and I Am for Choice," unpublished ms, reproduced in Joanna Brooks, Rachel Hunt Steenblik, and Hannah Wheelwright, *Mormon Feminism: Essential Writings*, 174 (New York: Oxford University Press, 2016).

52. "Thou shalt not murder a child by abortion nor kill that which is begotten," directs the *Teaching of the Twelve Apostles*, a first-century Christian text. *The Ante-Nicene Fathers*, edited by Alexander Roberts and James Donaldson (Grand Rapids, Mich.: Eerdmans, 1975), 7:377.

53. Erastus Snow referred to "destructive medicines" to effect "abortion, infanticide, child murder." Snow, "Conspicuous Position of the Saints," *JD* 25:111; Brigham Young, *CDBY* 4:2476; George Q. Cannon and John Taylor, "Horrifying Statements of Crime in the Eastern States," *JD* 25:315–16.

54. Quoted in Waterman and Kagel, *The Lord's University*, 208.

55. Quoted in Waterman and Kagel, *The Lord's University*, 208.

56. Oaks makes the point that safeguarding choice is no more valid as a defense of abortion than as a defense of other crimes where a second party suffers, naming child abuse, animal cruelty, and fraud as examples. "Weightier Matters," *Ensign*, January 2001, 13–15.

57. A church video affirms Oaks's view: "If we choose to use that [procreative] power

we have to deal with the consequences of that choice." Church of Jesus Christ of Latter-day Saints, "The Plan of Salvation," https://www.churchofjesuschrist.org /media/video/2010-07-002-the-plan-of-salvation.

58. Cecilia Konchar Farr, "Fighting Invisibility and Keeping the Faith," *Student Review*, 10 April 1998.

59. EEJ, 9 February 1999.

60. Russell M. Nelson, "Abortion: An Assault on the Defenseless," *Ensign*, October 2008, 35.

61. EEJ, 14 August 1975.

62. EEJ, 28 October 1975.

63. "Tribute," Kathleen S. Thomas, *Student Review*, 10 April 1998, 5.

64. ME-I 120, pt. 1.

65. "When did you learn to articulate it?" asked her son Mark. "About a year ago," replied the sixty-year-old Charlotte. ME-I 120, pt. 1.

66. Untitled reminiscence, CE-C.

67. Charles Petty, interview with author, 12 June 2017.

68. "Tribute," Gail Houston, *Student Review*, 10 April 1998, 7.

69. Bryan Watterman, "Three Encounters with Gene England," *Student Review*, 10 April 1998.

70. William A. Wilson, "Response to Departmental, College, and University Reviews of Professor Cecilia Farr's Three-Year Continuing Status Application," 26 August 1993, 34; Grant Boswell to Bert Wilson, 18 August 1993. Both cited in Bryan Watterman and Brian Kagel, *The Lord's University: Freedom and Authority at BYU* (Salt Lake City: Signature, 1998), 240. Wilson also pointed out that Farr's comments that day were cited by colleagues as their reason for opposing her tenure.

71. Cecilia Konchar Farr, http://ceciliakoncharfarr.net/new-page-1.

72. Waterman and Kagel, *The Lord's University*, 222.

73. Memo, EE to Neal Lambert, 13 April 1993, EE-P 169.4.

74. Bruce Hafen letter to Neal Lambert, 23 February 1993, EE-P 22.8. Farr would insist that the prohibition on publication was not clearly issued to her.

75. EE to the Editor, *Deseret News*, 18 December 1993; cited in Waterman and Kagel, *The Lord's University*, 231.

76. "BYU Continues," 65.

77. Boyd K. Packer to EE, 21 March 1991, EE-P 171.21.

78. William A. Wilson, "I Came to Where I Was Supposed to Be," in *Proving Contraries: A Collection of Writings in Honor of Eugene England*, edited by Robert Rees, 14 (Salt Lake City: Signature, 2005).

79. Wilson, "I Came to Where I Was Supposed to Be," 15.

80. Waterman and Kagel, *The Lord's University*, 244.

81. D. Michael Quinn, "LDS Church Authority and New Plural Marriages, 1890–1904," *Dialogue: A Journal of Mormon Thought* 18, no. 1 (Spring 1985): 9–105.

82. "The Mormons," interview with D. Michael Quinn, 30 April 2007, https://www
.pbs.org/mormons/interviews/quinn.html.

83. Peggy Fletcher Stack, "Noted Historian Still Believes in Mormonism, but Now as
an Outsider," *Salt Lake Tribune*, 1 October 2013, https://archive.sltrib.com/article
.php?id=56899817&itype=cmsid.

84. "Ex-BYU Professor Claims Beliefs Led to Dismissal," *Salt Lake Tribune*, 30 July
1988.

85. Maxine Hanks, ed., *Women and Authority: Re-emerging Mormon Feminism* (Salt
Lake City: Signature, 1992).

86. Boyd K. Packer, "Devotional Address," address presented to the All-Church
Coordinating Council, 18 May 1993, https://www.lightplanet.com/mormons
/priesthood/prophets/packer_coordinating.html.

87. EE, "On Spectral Evidence," *Dialogue: A Journal of Mormon Thought* 26, no. 1
(Spring 1993): 135–52.

88. EE to Gordon B. Hinckley, 3 December 1980, EE-P 171.11.

89. EE, "Support of Contras Unjustified," *Deseret News*, 3 March 1998.

90. EE, "My View: Was Chamberlain Right?," *Deseret News*, 29 September 1988.

91. EE, "On Trusting God, or Why We Should Not Fight Iraq," *Sunstone*, October
1980, 11–12.

92. EEJ, 16 March 1992.

93. EEJ, 16 March 1992.

94. Russell Arben Fox, "Protest Days," *Times and Seasons*, 25 April 2007, http://www
.timesandseasons.org/harchive/2007/04/protest-days/. See also Lawrence Young,
"Journeying into the Desert: The Faith-Based Witness against Nuclear Weapons,"
Sunstone, March 1993, 11–13, https://sunstonemagazine.com/wp-content/uploads
/sbi/articles/090-11-13.pdf.

95. EE to Henry E. Eyring, 2 March 1993, EE-P 171.5.

96. Leonard Arrington, *Confessions of a Mormon Historian: The Diaries of Leonard Arrington, 1971–1997*, edited by Gary James Bergera (Salt Lake City: Signature, 2018),
3:318–19.

97. Arrington, *Confessions*, 318.

98. EEJ, 13 June 1992.

99. EEJ, 21 June 1992.

100. Tim Slover, "'In Joy and Bliss to Be Me By': How Gene Was in London," *Sunstone*,
January 2002, 52.

101. EEJ, 21 June 1992.

102. Lorraine Bradford, ME-I 113.

103. EEJ, 13 June 1992.

104. EEJ, 21 June 1992.

105. EEJ, 25 June 1992.

106. Mary Bradford, "Reminiscence," CE-C.

107. EEJ 22, June 1994.

108. Mary Bradford, "Reminiscence," CE-C.

109. [Katherine England], "Life with Daddy," remarks at memorial service, CE-C.
110. ME-I 103.
111. [Katherine England], "Life with Daddy," 22.

CHAPTER 12

1. "1990s," BYU English Department, http://english.byu.edu/1990s/.
2. Jay Fox, interview with author, 12 June 2017.
3. EEJ, 1 January 1994.
4. Gene A. Sessions and Craig J. Oberg, eds., *The Search for Harmony: Essays on Science and Mormonism* (Salt Lake City: Signature, 1993).
5. EEJ, 1 January 1994.
6. EEJ, 24 January 1994.
7. EEJ, 24 January 1994.
8. EE to Neal A. Maxwell, 18 January 2000, EE-P 171.18. The letter does not appear to have been sent.
9. EE to Rex Lee, 28 August 1989; Rex Lee to EE, 4 October 1989, EE-P 171.16.
10. EE to Elder Jeffrey R. Holland, 20 August 1997, EE-P 171.12.
11. EE to Rex Lee, 29 December 1994, EE-P 171.16.
12. ME-I 108. The interview took place on 20 December 2000.
13. EE to Jeffrey R. Holland, 20 August 1997, EE-P 171.12.
14. EE to Jeffrey R. Holland, 20 August 1997.
15. EE to Mark England, 20 December 2000, CE-C .
16. EE to Jeffrey R. Holland, 20 August 1997, EE-P 171.12.
17. EE to R. W. Rasband, 13 July 1996, EE-P 169.7.
18. EE to Robert Rees, 12 May 1995. Included as an insert in his unsent letter to Maxwell, 18 January 2000, EE-P 171.18.
19. EEJ, 12 July 1997.
20. Bert Wilson wrote, consoling Gene for "being denied the opportunity to teach in the Honors Program" on 4 February 1997. See "Bert" to "Gene," EE-P 151.2–4.
21. "Bert" to "Eugene," 4 February 199[7]. Personal card, CE-C. The card is dated 1996 but postmarked 1997.
22. EE, "'No Respecter of Persons': A Mormon Ethics of Diversity," *Dialogue: A Journal of Mormon Thought* 27, no. 4 (Winter 1994): 79–100.
23. EEJ, 12 July 1997.
24. Quoted in Thomas More, *A Thomas More Source Book*, edited by Gerard B. Wegemer and Stephen W. Smith (Washington, D.C.: Catholic University of America Press, 2004), 345–46.
25. EEJ, 12 July 1997.
26. ME-I 108.
27. EE to the editor, *Deseret News*, 5 November 1997; cited in the Waterman and Kagel, *The Lord's University*, 434.
28. EE to Jay Fox, memo, n.d., CE-C.
29. EE to Marion D. Hanks, 21 September 1998, EE-P 171.9.

30. Jeffrey Holland to EE, 12 September 1997, EE-P 171.12.

31. EEJ, 12 July 1997.

32. EE to Jeffrey R. Holland, 18 January 2000, EE-P 171.12.

33. EE to Marion D. Hanks, 21 September 1998, EE-P 171.9.

34. EE, "'No Cause, No Cause': An Essay toward Reconciliation," *Sunstone*, January 2002, 35.

35. Translation by Suau'u Pe'a, CE-C.

36. EE to President Dallin Oaks, 20 February 1975, EE-P 172.12.

37. ME-I 115, pt. 1.

38. Geoff Pingree, "A Tribute to Gene," *Student Review*, 10 April 1998.

39. EE to Marion D. Hanks, 21 September 1998, EE-P 171.9.

40. EE, "On Living the Gospel," delivered 6 September 1998. The remarks are available from the Eugene England Foundation website, eugeneengland.org.

41. EE to Jeffrey R. Holland, 4 December 1998, EE-P 171.12.

42. Elaine Eliason Englehardt, "My Memories of Eugene England," CE-C.

43. Brian Birch, "Between Scylla and Charybdis: Eugene England at Utah Valley State College," *Sunstone*, January 2001, 48–49.

44. EE, "Mormon Literature: The State of the Art," *Student Review*, June 1987, 14.

45. EE, "Calculated Risk: Freedom for Mormons in Utah Higher Education," Academic Freedom Symposium, Utah Valley State College, March 2000. Cited in Birch, "Between Scylla and Charybdis," 48.

46. Don Wotherspoon, Brian Birch, Elaine Englehardt, Eugene England, Mary Ellen Robertson, and Scott Kenney, "The Academic Study of Religion: Prospects and Perils," *Sunstone*, 1 January 2000, https://www.sunstonemagazine.com/the -academic-study-of-religion-prospects-and-perils/.

47. Elaine Englehardt, interview with author, 3 May 2016.

48. Elaine Englehardt, "My Memories of Eugene England," CE-C.

49. Email, Wayne Booth to Gene and Charlotte [England], 1 March 2001, CE-C.

50. Dennis Lythgoe, "England Brilliant, Thoughtful, Sensitive," *Deseret News*, 26 August 2001.

51. Steve Carter, interview with author, 3 May 2016.

52. EE to Neal A. Maxwell, unsent letter, 18 January 2000, EE-P 117–18.

53. EEJ, 24 November 2000.

54. EEJ, 28 November 2000.

55. EE to Neal A. Maxwell, 30 November 2000, EE-P 117.18.

56. EEJ, 4 December 2000.

57. EEJ, 20 December 2000.

58. EEJ, 15 January 2001.

59. EEJ, 15 January 2001.

60. Tim Slover, "'In Joy and Bliss to Be Me By': How Gene Was in London," *Sunstone*, January 2002, 52.

61. EE to Neal A. Maxwell, 16 January 2001, EE-P 171.18.

62. EEJ, 16 January 2001.

63. Neal A. Maxwell to EE, 25 January 2001, EE-P 171.18.

64. Levi Peterson, ME-I 109.

65. D. Michael Quinn, ME-I 103.

66. Toby Pingree, ME-I 109.

67. "Your comfort close by," April 2001, CE-C.

68. Email from "England Children," 21 February 2001, CE-C.

69. Sharon Nelson's account, conveyed via email by Don Nelson to Dennis Lythgoe, 27 August 2001, CE-C.

70. Email, Lavina Fielding Anderson to EE, 27 February 2001, CE-C.

71. Quoted in Joan Odd, "Memorial Service for Eugene England," CE-C.

72. Email, Bert to Charlotte and Eugene, 12 March 2001, CE-C.

73. Bert Wilson, "For Eugene," unsigned reminiscence, EE-P 76.52.

74. Email, Mary Bradford to Gene and Charlotte [England], 4 March 2001, CE-C.

75. Katherine England, from memorial scrapbook, CE-C.

CHAPTER 13

1. The words are quoted secondhand in a number of sources, such as Kenneth W. Godfrey, "Review of *The Life and Thought of Orson Pratt* by England Breck," *Western Historical Quarterly* 17, no. 3 (July 1986): 350.

2. EE, "George Eugene England Jr.," CE-C.

3. "Testimony of Eugene England, Fast & Testimony Meeting—February 4, 2001, Pleasant View First Ward," CE-C.

4. Quoted in Dian Saderup Monson, "Eugene England—Master Teacher: The BYU Years," *Sunstone*, January 2002, 26.

5. Karl Rahner, *Dialogue: Conversations and Interviews, 1965–82*, edited by Paul Imhof and Hubert Biallowons (New York: Crossroad, 1986), 207.

6. Charlotte Haven, "A Girl's Letters from Nauvoo," 26 March 1843, *Overland Monthly* 16, no. 96 (December 1890): 626, http://www.olivercowdery.com/smithhome /1880s-1890s/havn1890.htm.

7. Andrew F. Ehat and Lyndon W. Cook, eds., *The Words of Joseph Smith* (Orem, Utah: Grandin, 1991), 346–47.

8. Joseph Smith's brother Hyrum said persons "advance to the Celestial or recede to the Telestial or else the moon would not be a type, [because] it 'waxes & wanes.'" Franklin D. Richards, "Words of the Prophets," in Church History Library; cited in Terryl L. Givens, *Wrestling the Angel: The Foundations of Mormon Thought—Cosmos, God, Humanity* (New York: Oxford University Press, 2015), 313.

9. *CDBY* 2:997.

10. "You that are mourning about your children straying away will . . . get all your sons and daughters in the path of exaltation and glory. This is just as sure as that the sun rose this morning over yonder mountains." Lorenzo Snow, "Preaching the Gospel in the Spirit World," *Collected Discourses*, edited by Brian Stuy (n.p.: BHS, 1989), 3:364.

11. Brigham Henry Roberts, *Outlines of Ecclesiastical History: A Textbook* (Salt Lake City: Cannon & Sons, 1893), 427.

12. James E. Talmage, *Articles of Faith* (Salt Lake City: Deseret, 1899), 421.

13. Bruce R. McConkie to Mrs. Vida H. Lind, 14 March 1973, DW-C.

14. Neal A. Maxwell to Reed C. Durham Jr., 17 August 1970, DW-C.

15. EE, "Becoming a World Religion: Blacks, the Poor—All of Us," *Sunstone*, June–July 1998, 54.

16. EE, "Becoming a World Religion," 53.

17. EE, "Becoming a World Religion," 53–54.

18. EE, "Becoming a World Religion," 52.

19. EE, "'No Respecter of Persons': A Mormon Ethics of Diversity," *Dialogue: A Journal of Mormon Thought* 27, no. 4 (Winter 1994): 99.

20. This was England's paraphrase ("Becoming a World Religion," 51) of 2 Nephi 29:12—"I shall also speak unto all nations of the earth and they shall write it."

21. EE, "'No Respecter of Persons,'" 99.

22. The text is corrupt, but the sense is plain: "Presbyterians any truth. embrace that. Baptist. Methodist &c. get all the good in the world. come out a pure Mormon." Ehat and Cook, *The Words of Joseph Smith*, 234.

23. No transcript exists for this talk, but a recording is found at sunstonemagazine .com (https://sunstonemagazine.com/calculated-risk-the-quest-for-freedom -and-diversity-in-utah-higher-education/). I have borrowed from the excerpted transcript in Charlotte Hansen, "Eugene England's Calculated Risk: The Struggle for Academic Freedom and Religious Dialogue," *Sunstone*, December 2010, 41.

24. While attributing "homosexual feelings" to "genetic, developmental, or environmental influences," and therefore not morally culpable, he also felt that "*all* homosexuals in this life must change, either through repentance or removal of moral accidents." Dean of Religion Robert Matthews made unspecified criticisms referred to in EE to Robert J. Matthews, 5 February 1987, CE-C.

25. "An Interview with Eugene England," *Student Review*, 10 April 1998, 10.

26. Philip L. Barlow, forward to *Leonard J. Arrington: Faith and Intellect: The Lives and Contributions of Latter-day Saint Thinkers*, edited by Gary James Bergera (Salt Lake City: Signature, 2019), viii–ix.

27. One witness to such a fireside recounts the unsettling but transformative experience in Boyd Petersen, "Eugene England and the Future of Mormonism," *Dead Wood and Rushing Water*, https://boydpetersen.com/2016/01/28/eugene-england -and-the-future-of-mormonism/.

28. Ronald W. Walker, Richard E. Turley Jr., and Glen M. Leonard, *Massacre at Mountain Meadows* (New York: Oxford University Press, 2011).

29. *Saints: The Story of the Church of Jesus Christ in the Latter Days* (Salt Lake City: Church of Jesus Christ of Latter-day Saints, 2018–).

30. Monson, "Eugene England—Master Teacher," 26.

31. Monson, "Eugene England—Master Teacher," 27.

32. Lavina Fielding Anderson to Presidents Ezra Taft Benson, Gordon B. Hinckley, and Thomas S. Monson (1 October 1993). The letter is recorded in Anderson's personal diary and was shared with the author.

33. EE, "Enduring," *Dialogue: A Journal of Mormon Thought* 16, no. 4 (Winter 1983): 109.

34. EE, "Enduring," 112–14.
35. EEJ, 2 January 1994.
36. Reported by Bob Rees, ME-I 103.
37. Bob Rees, ME-I 103.
38. Cited in Monson, "Eugene England—Master Teacher," 26.
39. Monson, "Eugene England—Master Teacher," 26.
40. Douglas Thayer, "Memorial Service Talk for Eugene England," 25 August 1981, CE-C.

INDEX

Abélard, Pierre, 125

abortion: political parties' support of, 57; church teachings on, 237–38; England's views of, 239; Farr's views of, 238–39, 242

academic freedom: Historical Department and, 156; at BYU, 221, 222, 224, 232, 243

African Americans, justifications for treatment of, 25, 58–59, 210–13. *See also* racism

agency, 124, 126, 171–73, 238

Air Force, 40–42

Albrecht, Stan, 228

All-Church Coordinating Council, 68–69, 71, 244

Allen, James, 113

Alma (Book of Mormon prophet), 126

"Alternate Voices" (Oaks), 222–23

Anderson, Lavina Fielding, 227–28; "A Dialogue toward Forgiveness," 227–28

Anderson, Vern, 228

Anselm, 124

anthologies, literary, 144, 148

antiwar rallies, 82, 95, 247

"Apostles vs. Historians" (Tanner and Tanner), 169

Aquinas, Thomas, 173

"Are All Alike unto God?" (England), 210–15

"Are Mormons Christian?" (England), 96–97

Arrington, Leonard, 109, 110, 111, 140, 141, 156, 247

"Arts and the Spirit of the Lord" (Packer), 135

Association for Mormon Letters (AML), 146, 148

Astin, Floyd, 20

atonement: as theological concept, 123–29, 191–92; England's views on, 126–32, 255–56

Augustine, 117

authority in the Church of Jesus Christ, 151, 154, 155, 172

Ballard, M. Russell, 216–17

Barber, David, 157

Barlow, Philip, 280

Bateman, Merrill, 130, 254–55, 267

Bearmont, 92–93

Beecher, Maureen Ursenbach, 146

Believing People, A (Cracroft and Lambert), 144, 145

Bennett, James Gordon, 185

Bennion, Adam S., 49

Bennion, Lowell, 223, 259; conflict with authority, 53, 56–57; influence of, 25, 52; private dissension of, 87

Benson, Ezra Taft, 43, 141, 205

Berrett, William E., 56, 69, 81

Bitton, Davis, 141

blacklisting of Mormon intellectuals, 140

"Blessing the Chevrolet" (England), 184–87

Book of Mormon, 205

Booth, Wayne, 265

Bradford, Mary, 183, 273

Brigham Young Academy, 205

Brigham Young University: academic freedom statement of, 222, 232; 1911 intellectual conflict at, 48; religiosity

Brigham Young University (*continued*)
surveys of students and alumni of, 51;
Sunstone symposia and employees of,
222–24. *See also* academic freedom;
English departments: politics of; En-
gland, Eugene: in the BYU English
department
Britsch, Todd, 201
Brown, Hugh B., 54, 70–71, 85–86, 105
Brown, Robert McAffee, 278
Buchanan family, 5
Burton, Alma, 69
Bush, Lester, 85; "Mormonism's Negro
Doctrine," 85–87
Bushman, Richard, 141, 150, 228–29
BYU Studies, 64

California State, Hayward, 95–96
Carlicci, Christine, 100
Carter, Steve, 264–65, 266
Catholicism, 53, 71, 121, 155, 156, 172–73
censorship of art, 201, 258
certainty vs. doubt, 74–75
"Charted Course of the Church in Edu-
cation, The" (Clark), 50–51, 70
Chase, Daryl, 49
choice. *See* agency
Christensen, Gary (Chris), 20
Christensen, Joe, 110, 133
Christianity, compared with the Church
of Jesus Christ, 96–97, 118–22, 123–26,
151, 154–55, 156, 171–74
Clark, Bruce, 106
Clark, J. Reuben, 49, 50–51; "The
Charted Course of the Church in Edu-
cation," 50–51, 70
Collins, Carvel, 41
Coming of Age in Samoa (Mead), 27, 30
congregation, choice of, 196–97
conscience vs. submission, 171–75
consensus, in church councils, 54–55
consequences of choice, in Latter-day
Saint theology, 124, 126
Contributor, 143–44

Correlation Program, Priesthood. *See*
All-Church Coordinating Council
Cracroft, Richard, 144, 146, 148, 219–21;
A Believing People, 144, 219
curse of Lamanites, 34

Danforth Fellowship, 42
Darwinism, 47, 48
Davis, Mitch, 178
DD Daggers, 12
Democratic Party, 57–58, 60
Dialogue: failure of, 136; feminist issue
of, 90–91; first issue of, 68, 72, 75–
76; liberal image of, 78, 91; need for,
63–66; *New York Times* article on, 66–
67; objectives of, 65–68, 74; opposition
to/prejudice against, 69–75, 134–35;
prospectus of, 65; race discussed in,
85–89; second issue of, 78–79; third
issue of, 79–80
"Dialogue toward Forgiveness, A" (Anderson), 227–28
Dick, Thomas, 45–46
discipleship, England's pursuit of, 60,
72–73, 97, 267–71, 276, 281–83
doctrine, dispensed by apostles, 53, 154,
167
doctrine vs. theology, 114–16
doubt vs. certainty, 74–75
Downey, Idaho, 12
Duncan, Adam Mickey, 20, 59
Dunn, Paul H., 182

Eager, Brent, 29
*Early Mormonism and the Magic World
View* (Quinn), 244
earth, creation of, 47–48
"Easter Weekend" (England), 190–92
Eden narrative, as basis for theology, 2–3,
88, 234
education, philosophy of: history of
LDS, 45–46, 48, 49, 50–51, 216–18;
England's, 165, 204, 262–63
Ego, 175

Ehrenreich, Barbara, 225
Emerson, Ralph Waldo, 142
Encyclopedia of Mormonism, 209–10
"Enduring" (England), 187–90
England, Ann Christine, 11
England, Charlotte Hawkins: courtship of, 22–24; emerging feminism of, 239–40; England's adoration of, 158–59; as hostess, 158; and meeting with Wilkins, 258; as Relief Society president, 98; during study abroad, 248; wedding of, 26
England, Dora Rose Hartvigsen, 8–9, 11, 14–15, 138
England, Eugene: on absolutism, 32; academic controversies of, 180, 201–4, 207–9, 219–22, 236, 242, 243; activism of, 61, 82, 95–96, 177–79, 246–47; ancestors of, 5–6; antiwar views of, 43–44, 58, 82, 95, 221, 246–47; awards, 42, 182; baby blessing of, 10; birth of, 9; as bishop, 139, 181–82; on blessings for healing, 184–87; brain cancer of, 271–73; as branch president, 98–100; in the BYU English department, 236–37, 241; in car accident, 112–13; celebrity of, 151; childhood of, 10–13; on community, 150; conflicts with church leaders, 61, 67–68, 70, 81–84, 87, 129–31, 134–35, 162–68, 175, 199–200, 206, 210–11, 215–16, 218–19, 228–31; consecrations of, 19; on courage, 153, 154; courtship of Charlotte, 22–24; as dean of academic affairs, 96–98, 102–3; death of, 271–73; dissertation of, 101–2; early religious experiences of, 14–17; as editor of poetry anthology, 219; empathy of, 36–37, 59; family life of, 9–19, 92–93, 137–38, 159–60; on fear, 187–88; feelings of failure, 136–38, 267–68, 270; and fishing, 193, 283–84; foster children of, 41; funeral of, 275; in graduate school, 42; health issues of, 253, 267, 271, 273; high

school graduation of, 22; home and hospitality of, 157–60; influence and legacy of, 1–2, 60, 148, 179, 261, 262–63, 266, 279–82; on integrity, 170–71, 200, 282; job seeking of, 44–45, 81–82, 102–7, 109–10, 112, 139–40, 254–56; on language, 196; loss of leadership opportunities for, 91, 138; loyalty of, 136, 242; at the Massachusetts Institute of Technology, 40–41; on miracles, 186; mission of, 28–36; on monoculturalism, 225; and Mormon literary history, 139; personal essays of, 183–98; poems by, 16–17, 160, 271; on public prayer, 231; relationship with parents, 14–17, 137–39; relief efforts of, 176–79; on repentance, 128; resignation from BYU, 255–60; resignation from *Dialogue*, 136; and study abroad, 248–52, 262; on suffering, 188–90; as teacher at BYU, 149, 201–5, 258; as teacher at institute, 60, 64, 81–84; as teacher in Samoa, 30, 32–33; as teacher at St. Olaf, 103; as teacher at Utah Valley State College, 204; testimony of, 275–76; views on homosexuality, 261–62, 279; views on war, turning point in, 43; as weatherman, 41; wedding of, 26; youth of, 17–18, 19–22. *See also* England, Eugene, correspondence of; England, Eugene, works of
England, Eugene, correspondence of: with Boyd K. Packer, 135, 180, 218–19; with Bruce R. McConkie, 165–67; about complaints to leaders instead of direct confrontation, 82–83, 201–4, 245; with Dallin H. Oaks, 102, 106; with Marion D. Hanks, 34–35, 61–62, 82–84; with Neal A. Maxwell, 100–101, 129, 209–10, 216, 217–18, 229–30, 266–70; public apologies in, 230–31; with Robert J. Matthews, 208–9; with S. Dillworth Young, 70; about teaching position at St. Olaf, 103–4; about Udall's letter, 81

England, Eugene, works of: "Are All
Alike unto God?," 210–15; "Are
Mormons Christian?," 96–97; "Bless-
ing the Chevrolet," 184–87; "Easter
Weekend," 190–92; "Enduring,"
187–90; "Great Books or True Reli-
gion?," 133–34, 152–53; "Monte Cristo,"
193–94; "The Mormon Cross," 87–89;
"'No Respecter of Persons,'" 257;
"On Fidelity, Polygamy, and Celestial
Marriage," 206, 213; "On Spectral
Evidence," 245–46; "Perfection and
Progress," 163–64; "The Quest for Au-
thentic Faculty Power," 96; "Sweet Are
the Uses of Fidelity," 206–8; "Weeping
God of Mormonism," 121–23; "Why
the Church Is as True as the Gospel,"
194–98; "Why the Church Is More
True than the Gospel," 199–200
England, George Eugene, Sr.: in car acci-
dent, 112–13; consecrations of, 9, 15, 17,
18–19, 112; employment of, 8, 9, 10; as
farmer, 13–14, 15, 19; relationship with
President Kimball, 168; relationship
with England, 137–39; vision of, 8–9;
youth of, 6–8
England, George William, 6–7
England, Jennifer, 42
England, Jody, 40
England, Katherine, 36, 251, 252
England, Martha Jane Hatch, 6
England, Thomas, 6
Englehardt, Elaine, 154, 263
English departments: politics of, 232–34;
at BYU, 236–37, 241
Enoch, 122
Ensign, 153
Equal Rights Amendment, 235–36
Eyring, Henry, 72

Faribault branch, 98–100, 110
farming, 7, 14
Farr, Cecilia Konchar, 237, 240–42
Faust, James E., 229

feminism: and abortion, 237; and BYU,
236–37; Charlotte's expression of,
239–40; and Church of Jesus Christ,
234–36, 279; England's adoption of,
239, 240–41. *See also* women
Fiji, 28
Fitisemanu, 30, 31
flour anecdote, as literary example, 144
Food for Poland, 176–79. *See also* England, Eugene: relief efforts of
Fox, Jay, 253
Francine (England's foster child), 41

Geary, Ed, 13, 144–45, 151
George Air Force Base, Victorville, Cali-
fornia, 41
Geremek, Bronislaw, 177
God: becoming like, 117–18; inefficiency
of, 248, 276, 283; infinite love of, 278;
passibility of, 121–22; progression of,
162–66, 277–78
Godfrey, Kenneth, 69
grace, 118, 120–21
Graduate Student Coordinating Council,
43–44
Graham-Russell, Janan, 212
Gray, Darius, 212
"Great Books or True Religion?" (En-
gland), 133–34, 152–53
Great Depression, 9
Gulf War, 221, 247

Hafen, Bruce, 230–31
Haight, David B., 136
Hales, Robert D., 134, 139
Hancock, Mosiah, 46
Hanks, Marion D.: blessing of Charlotte, 36; as confidant of England, 84;
correspondence with England about
remarks in class, 82–84; counsel about
"abysses," 61; on objections to hiring
England, 107; rebuke of England for
being judgmental, 34–35. *See also* England, Eugene, correspondence of

Hanks, Maxine, 244; *Women and Author-ity*, 244

Hansen, Andy, 112

Hansen, Reese, 210

Harnack, Adolph, 194

Harris, John, 117; "Risk and Terror," 117

Hartvigsen, Jacob Larson (J. L.), 10, 14

Harvest: Contemporary Mormon Poems (England and Clark), 219

Hawaii, 28

Hawkins, George and LaRue, 28

Haycock, Arthur, 81, 182

Hinckley, Bryant S., 10–11

Hinckley, Gordon B., 232

historians, and expansion of primary sources, 77–78

Historical Department of the Church of Jesus Christ, 109–12, 156

historiography, critiques of in *Dialogue*, 76, 79–80

Hoadly, Benjamin, 194

Holland, Jeffrey R., 130, 140, 180, 225, 259

infallibility, prophetic, 195–96

"I Say unto You, Be One" (Packer), 218

John Paul II, 176, 177

Johnson, Lyndon B., 60

Johnson, Sonia, 235–36

Jolley, Clifton, 13

journal entries as literature, 144, 145

Keller, Karl, 79

Kimball, Heber C., 214

Kimball, J. Golden, 272

Kimball, Spencer W., 18, 26, 145–46, 168

kingdoms, progress between, 277

King Lear (Shakespeare), 131–32

Kirn, Walter, 202; "Planetarium," 202–3

Kovalenko, Gene, 64–65

Lambert, Neal, 144; *A Believing People*, 144, 219

Lee, Harold B., 14–15, 28, 36

Lee, Rex, 254

Lincoln, Abraham, 195

literacy rates in Utah, 47

literature: first-person accounts as, 144, 145; Latter-day Saints, history of, 139, 142–47; Latter-day Saint, journal of, 148; "Mormon," disagreements about what constitutes, 219–21; schools of study of, 232–34; selections of, objections to by students, 201–4

Luther, Martin, 118, 121

Malik, Charles H., 146

mantic vs. sophic, 220

"Mantle Is Far, Far Greater than the Intellect, The" (Packer), 168

marriage as metaphor for church congregations, 196–97

Marshall, Richard S., 141

Marty, Martin, 156

Matthews, Robert J., 207–9

Maxwell, John Gary (Max), 20

Maxwell, Neal A.: on England's essay on atonement, 129; on eternal progression, 277; meeting with England in 1990, 215; and advice from England, 100–101; response to England's apology, 229–30; response to England's last letters, 270. *See also* England, Eugene, correspondence of

McConkie, Bruce R., 115, 163–68, 211, 212, 216, 277; *Mormon Doctrine*, 55, 115; "Seven Deadly Heresies," 164–65, 199–200. *See also* England, Eugene, correspondence of

McConkie, Joseph, 162–63

McKay, David O., 53

McMurrin, Sterling, 78–79, 122, 169

Mead, Margaret, 30; *Coming of Age in Samoa*, 27, 30

Meilaender, Gilbert, 175

Menlove, Frances, 76

Millett, Joseph, 144

Millett, Robert L., 120
modernist crisis in the Church of Jesus Christ, 154–56
"Monte Cristo" (England), 193–94
More, Thomas, 257–58
"Mormon Cross, The" (England), 87–89
Mormon Doctrine (McConkie), 55, 115
Mormon History Association (MHA), 66
"Mormonism's Negro Doctrine" (Bush), 85–87
Mormonism's Negro Policy (Taggart), 85
Mormon studies, 262–66
Mother in Heaven, 234
Mysteries, The (drama), 268–69

National Endowment for the Humanities (NEH) grant, 262–64
Negro Doctrine. *See* racism
Nelson, Russell M., 126, 223, 229, 239
New Criticism, 232–33
"New Light on Mormon Origins from the Palmyra Revival" (Walters), 77
Newman, John Henry, 173
New Mormon History, 141, 156, 168–69
Nietzsche, Friedrich, 125
"'No Respecter of Persons'" (England), 257
Novak, Michael, 196

Oahu, Hawaii, 28
Oaks, Dallin H., 102, 105, 205, 215, 238; "Alternate Voices," 222–23. *See also* England, Eugene, correspondence of
Odd, Frank and Jean, 100, 272
Ogden, Kelly, 221
"On Fidelity, Polygamy, and Celestial Marriage" (England), 206, 213
"On Spectral Evidence" (England), 245–46
organizational structure of the Church of Jesus Christ, 53–55

Packer, Boyd K.: on academic freedom, 232; on areas of unrest, 244; on arts and building the kingdom, 135; "Arts and the Spirit of the Lord," 135; on atonement and justice, 126; on *Dialogue*, 134; as dominant figure for pronouncing doctrine, 115–16; "I Say unto You, Be One," 218; on leadership of BYU, 218; "The Mantle Is Far, Far Greater than the Intellect," 168; on patriotism, 43; on "pro-choice" argument, 238; on scholars and revelation, 71, 154, 245; on temptation to tell everything, 168. *See also* England, Eugene, correspondence of
papyri, Egyptian, 70, 77
paradoxes: in *Dialogue*'s combination of inquiry and faith, 72–73; in the Church of Jesus Christ's core beliefs of agency and prophetic authority, 171–73; as ways to truth, 197–98; in the Church of Jesus Christ's views on feminism, 234–35
patriotism, 42–45
Peck, Elbert, 262
"Perfection and Progress" (England), 163–64
Perlman, Itzhak, 251
Peterson, Levi, 220
Petty, Charles, 44
"Planetarium" (Kirn), 202–3
polygamy, 206–8, 213–15, 243–44
Pratt, Orson, 46, 275
Pratt, Parley, 114–15
priesthood ban, 58–59, 80, 85–89
progression, eternal, 162–66, 277–78
Protestantism, 118–121, 154–55, 171, 174, 194–95

"Quest for Authentic Faculty Power, The" (England), 96
Quinn, D. Michael, 168–69, 243–44; *Early Mormonism and the Magic World View*, 244

racism: addressed in *Dialogue*, 80–81, 85–89; based in tradition, 25, 58–59, 210–13; movement away from, 280; in Samoa, 32, 34; in Utah, 20

Rahner, Karl, 257, 276

Rand, Sidney, 103–4

Rees, Robert, 86, 151, 218, 252, 283

Reformation, 172, 194–95

Relief Society, autonomy of, 68–69

Relief Society Magazine, 68

religiosity: of BYU students, 51; of LDS teenagers, 51–52; of Americans, 195

Republican Party, 57–58

Reserve Officers Training Corps (ROTC), 39–40, 97

Restoration, as process, 160–62

revelation: in the Church of Jesus Christ, 172; found in other traditions and religions, 257, 279; language of, 186

revivalism during Joseph Smith's time, 77

righteousness, 120–21

"Risk and Terror" (Harris), 117

Roberts, B. H.: on atonement, 125, 128; on eternal progression, 277; on opportunity to develop doctrine, 116; *The Truth, the Way, the Life*, 49, 115; and lesson manuals, 50; and synthesis of LDS theology, 49, 115

Robinson, Stephen, 120, 221

Rodin, 201, 258

salvation, vicarious, 278

Samoa, 29–37

San Francisco, California, 28

Savage, Levi, 54

science education in the Church of Jesus Christ, 46, 47–48, 50, 53

scripture: historicity of, 155; sufficiency of, 195; universality of, 257

sealings, 161

secret files on dissident members, 228–29

secularism, 49–51, 280

September Six, 245

"Seven Deadly Heresies" (McConkie), 164–65, 199–200

Seventh East Press, 169–70

sexuality in the Church of Jesus Christ, 200–201, 202–3. *See also* England, Eugene: views on homosexuality; censorship of art

Shakespeare, William, 131–32; *King Lear*, 131–32

Silva, Erin, 157

sin, as theological concept, 124

Slover, Tim, 269

Smith, Joseph: on becoming Gods, 117; on Christ as prototype of salvation, 118; on eternal progression, 277; on freedom of belief, 45, 222; on getting truth, 279; on imperfect language, 196; on importance of atonement, 123; on inquiry, 73; on intelligence and education, 45; on progression of God, 162; shared authority with apostles, 54–55; on theology, 114

Smith, Joseph F., 168

Smith, Joseph Fielding, 49, 53, 88–89, 115, 156, 211

Smith, Richard, 253

Solidarity (Polish workers movement), 176–77. *See also* Food for Poland; England, Eugene: relief efforts of

Sperry, Sidney, 49

Spirit, living by the, 118–19

Stegner, Wallace, 42

St. Olaf College, 96, 97

Stone, Howard, 30

Strengthening Church Members Committee, 228–29

Student Review, 222, 261

substitution, in atonement theology, 124–29

suffering, of Christ during atonement, 126–28

Sunstone, 136

Sunstone symposia, 199, 222–24, 227–28, 263

"Sweet Are the Uses of Fidelity" (England), 206–8
Swensen, Russel B., 49
symposia statement, 222–24. *See also* Sunstone symposia

Taggart, Stephen, 85; *Mormonism's Negro Policy*, 85
Talmage, James E., 48, 115, 121, 277
Tanner, George S., 49
Tanner, Jerald, 169; "Apostles vs. Historians," 169
Tanner, N. Eldon, 81
Tanner, Obert Clark, 10
Tanner, Sandra, 169; "Apostles vs. Historians," 169
teaching manuals of the Church of Jesus Christ, 49–50
testimony in the Church of Jesus Christ, 73, 183–84
theology vs. doctrine, 114–16
theosis in the Church of Jesus Christ, 117–18
Truth, the Way, the Life, The (Roberts), 49, 115

Udall, Steward, 80
Ulrich, Laurel Thatcher, 90–91, 231
universities: as best place for exchange of ideas, 95–96; as place for Christ to return to, 146
University of Chicago Divinity School, 49
University of Deseret, 46
Utah Valley State College, 260, 263–64

Vietnam War, 43–44, 58, 80, 82

Walters, Wesley P., 77; "New Light on Mormon Origins from the Palmyra Revival," 77

Wannenwetsch, Bernd, 172
wards, 196–197
Webb, Stephen, 172
"Weeping God of Mormonism" (England), 121–23
West, Franklin, 52
Whitney, Orson, 142–43, 220
"Why the Church Is as True as the Gospel" (England), 194–98
"Why the Church Is More True than the Gospel" (England), 199–200
Widtsoe, John A., 19, 48, 50
Wilkins, Alan, 258
Wilkinson, Ernest, 52–53, 56–57
Wille, Milton, 130–131
Wilson, Bert, 12–13, 234, 243, 257, 272–73
Wimbledon, 250
women: education of, 46–47; literary outlets for, 144; and polygamy, 208–9; and priesthood, 235. *See also* feminism
Women and Authority (Hanks), 244
Woodruff, Wilford, 115, 161
Wordsworth, William, 15
works/experience, theology of, 116–19

Yordan, Philip, 110–11, 112
Young, Brigham: on abortion, 237; on angels and chemistry, 46; on conscience, 174; on eternal progression, 277; on independence, 117; on Joseph bringing together things of earth and things of God, 185; on language of God, 196; movie and biography about, 111–12; on race, 211
Young, Mary Ann, 214
Young, S. Dilworth, 70
Young Men's Club of Centerville, Utah, 47